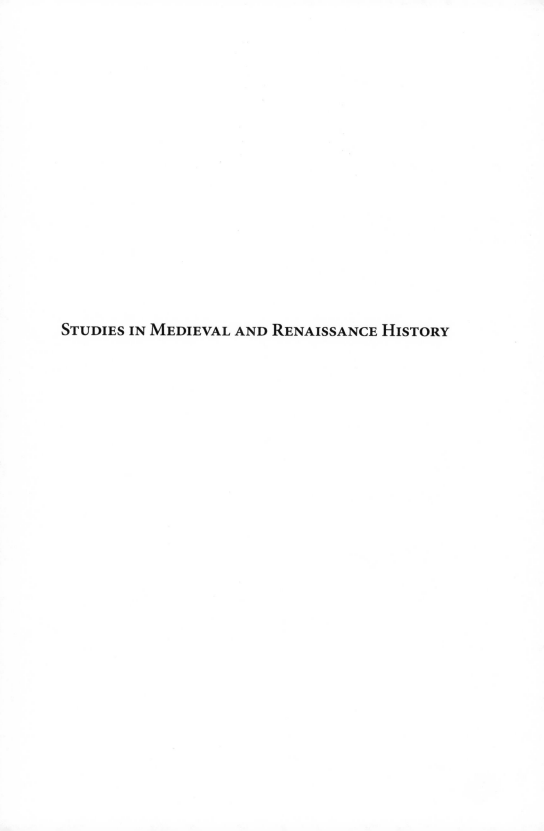

STUDIES IN MEDIEVAL AND RENAISSANCE HISTORY

STUDIES IN MEDIEVAL AND RENAISSANCE HISTORY

Edited by Roger Dahood and Peter E. Medine

THIRD SERIES, VOLUME V
(Old Series, Volume XXX; New Series, Volume XX)

AMS Press, Inc.

New York

Studies in Medieval and Renaissance History
ISSN 0081-8224

Copyright © 2008 by AMS Press, Inc.

Studies in Medieval and Renaissance History is published under the
auspices of the Arizona Center for Medieval and Renaissance Studies.

International Standard Book Numbers

ISBN-13: 978-0-404-64550-2 (Set)
ISBN-10: 0-404-64550-x (Set)

ISBN-13: 978-0-404-64555-7 (Series III.5)
ISBN-10: 0-404-64555-0 (Series III.5)

Library of Congress Catalog Number 63-22098

All AMS books are printed on acid-free paper that meets the guidelines for
performance and durability of the Committee on Production Guidelines
for Book Longevity of the Council on Library Resources.

Manufactured in the United States of America

TABLE OF CONTENTS

Abstracts

Judgment Day: Hopes, Joys, and Sorrows in Medieval England
Eric Gerald Stanley

DOOMSDAY IS CENTRAL to both woe and hope in medieval religious thinking, and for the earliest period we have little record in English of secular thought. In Old English the inherited word for hope was *hyht, hyhtan*, which embraced the joy of indulging in the present the expectation of some good in the future, perhaps too timeless a view for *Spes*, the Theological Virtue. A new word, wholly of the future, was found, the ancestor of our word *hope*. English medieval writings are preponderantly religious, and therefore hope now commonly looks forward to joy to come in a better world, for sorrow is our lot here; and the Old English writers are good on sorrow. Some Middle English writers are still much imbued with sorrow, while others increasingly admit present joys, even rejoicing in joy in this world. What emerges from a wide range of Old and Middle English writings, exemplified in brief quotations, is that hope, joy, and sorrow are not constants, that is, were not always experienced as they are felt now: change is the only constant as the centuries pass before us in earlier writings, even as the words themselves change in form and meaning.

Beauvais Romanesque and Suger's Workshop at Saint-Denis: Creative Appropriation and Regional Identity
Elaine M. Beretz

AFTER C. 1140, artisans working in the northern French city of Beauvais appropriated innovative architectural and sculptural elements either invented in Suger's workshop at Saint-Denis, or used there in a striking manner. This artistic exchange with Saint-Denis locates the Beauvais workshop within larger artistic developments of its time and place. At Beauvais, however, the imported elements were transformed in ways that fall into a clear pattern and afford one of the best insights into the formal characteristics of the local style. The style itself provides a glimpse into the wider urban culture of Beauvais, now almost completely lost, which shaped both the patrons of the art and the artisans they hired. The conscious archaism of the Beauvais Romanesque style in the face of imports from Paris challenges traditional notions of influence, periodization, and regionalism, which are often inappropriately used to classify the culture of this period.

Lambeth Palace Library, MS 260, and the Problem of English Vernacularity
Ralph Hanna

IN THE RECENT spate of "English vernacular studies," many discussions presuppose that "the vernacular," English, is a readily identifiable separate option. In this essay, I challenge such a characterization (well nigh inevitable given our disciplinary formation), particularly for the period 1150–1400. I draw attention to widespread traditions of multilingual writing in medieval England. At the center of the argument is a single book communicating Northern poetry, Lambeth Palace Library, MS 260; this volume offers extensive examples of bilingual relations, constantly renegotiated. In the conclusion, I further qualify traditional arguments about English usage, whether emancipatory and triumphalist or abject, and argue the necessity of detailed studies of multilingual relations during this period.

Game in the Medieval English Diet
Robin S. Oggins

THIS ARTICLE ADDRESSES the questions of who ate game in medieval England, when they ate it, and what kinds of game they ate. The article further investigates such related topics as discrepancies between game ordered by the kings and game actually received, royal gifts of game (to whom and on what occasions), and game as provided for in household dietary ordinances. Available evidence indicates that game served two functions. High-status game, such as deer, boar, crane, and swan, tended to be served on holidays and other important occasions. Other game, such as rabbit, pigeon, or woodcock, might be served on a seasonal basis and provided variety in diet.

Talking with the Taxman about Poetry: England's Economy in "Against the King's Taxes" and *Wynnere and Wastoure*
Brantley L. Bryant

DRAWING ON PARLIAMENTARY history and the evidence of two poems, this essay examines contrasting attitudes toward national economics in mid-fourteenth-century England. The Anglo-Norman and Latin "Against the King's Taxes" (c. 1340), identified by J. R. Maddicott as a poem of "Social Protest," criticizes tax-granting with the language of Christian eschatology. The Middle English *Wynnere and Wastoure* (c. 1352–1370), on the other hand, embraces parliamentary representative ideology by imagining the collective economic good of the realm, seamlessly integrating moral and economic principles in a defense of the political status quo.

Propaganda, Self-Interest, and Brotherly Love: Poverty and Wealth in the Pamphlets of an Early-Reformation Preacher
Jennifer Smyth

JACOB STRAUSS WAS an evangelical preacher and pamphleteer active during the early years of the sixteenth-century German Reformation, a time of intense debate and change not only in the religious sphere but also in relation to the problem of poverty. The theme of the poor and needy neighbor appears frequently in Strauss's pamphlets; this essay addresses his treatment of that subject and its potential reception, and asks what this reveals about the form and extent of the reformation envisaged by one of the proponents of what was at this stage a relatively diverse movement. It also explores the degree to which the association of economic concerns with a reforming message may have served a propagandistic purpose, ultimately concluding, however, that this element of Strauss's writings represented much more than a calculated device to gain support for his teachings.

"The Double Variacioun of Wordly Blisse and Transmutacioun": Shakespeare's Return to Ovid in *Troilus and Cressida*
Bradley Greenburg

THIS ESSAY ARGUES that the Cressida of Shakespeare's *Troilus and Cressida* is a character who is sympathetically portrayed and a victim of a system of male honor, shown to be reified by the literary tradition that insists on her faithlessness. Troilus, a participant in that system of honor, divides his sense of Cressida in two ("This is and is not Cressid") as a form of self-protection but also signals her existence as a woman caught "in a discursive economy of war" that puts her into a game out of her control and yet judges her as faithless. Such a structural position is, I suggest, analogous to the Ariadne of Ovid's *Heroides* as well as the Arachne of *The Metamorphoses*. Shakespeare's deployment of Ovid here is much more than that of source: it is an active transformation of literary character.

Judgment Day: Hopes, Joys, and Sorrows in Medieval England

Eric Gerald Stanley
Pembroke College, Oxford

Judgment Day

PROFESSORS OF ANGLO-SAXON in the University of Oxford receive inquiries that might easily have been resolved by consulting standard works of reference. A clergyman wrote to me a few years ago: "Wasn't it sad," he suggested in his ignorant charity, "that Doomsday should be so called, full of doom and gloom?" I forbore to let him have the whole of my edifying thoughts on the Day of Judgment and sent him away with the knowledge that *doom* just means "judgment," without informing him that at the anticipated judgment, on the day the last trump (of 1 Corinthians 15:52) shall sound, the divine Judge may not in his mercy overlook our sins, and that fear of eternal damnation shall lead to a doom without hope.

Over the centuries not only language changes, but also the thinking expressed in that language; more than the thinking, even the emotions, the passions felt by a speaker of that language, change. We are confined by the limits of that nutshell, confined by a belief that our language of today is and always has been fully expressive and curtailed by Time itself, forgetting that everything has changed, if at all capable of change.

Studies in Medieval and Renaissance History, 3rd Series, Vol. 5 (2008)

A fuller statement for the poor clergyman—*O sancta simplicitas*—
might have begun with the superficially merry (because misunderstood)
tinkle of the burden of the carol from British Library Sloane MS 2593,
the first line of which is *Euery day thou myght lere*; the third stanza and
burden run:[1]

> Thynk, man, on thi synnys seuene,
> Think how merie it is in heuene.
> Prey to God with mylde stefne:
> He be thin help on domysday.
> Gay, gay, gay, gay,
> Think on drydful domisday.

> Consider, man, your seven sins, consider how joyful it is in heaven.
> Pray to God with quiet voice: may he be your help on Judgment
> Day. Woe, woe, woe, woe, consider terrifying Judgment Day.

"Gay, gay, gay, gay" is neither homophile nor homophobe, a sense of *gay*
not recorded before the 1930s, nor even an invitation, ironic or otherwise, to be merry; nor is it, as its editor suggests unconvincingly (with
a reference to an article that has convinced him),[2] the quadruple nam-
ing of "an unrepentant malefactor named Gay (Gayus), whose damnation
is attested by a dance of demons around his death-bed." It is the Old French
interjection *guai*, from Frankish **wai*, the etymon of Modern English *woe*.[3]
We could therefore modernize the burden, if we wish, as "Woe, woe, woe,
woe" or medievalize that as *wei la wei, wei la wei*. There is no joy to be got

---

The poetry and translations presented in this essay appear not aligned side-by-
side, as the author wished, but in vertical alignment as the compositing software and
space on the page permit.—Ed.

[1] Richard Leighton Greene, ed., *The Early English Carols*, 2nd ed. (Oxford,
1977), pp. 199–200, no. 329; notes p. 430. Editorial details, including punctuation,
have not always been followed in quoting texts. Unless otherwise stated, translations
are mine.

[2] Siegfried Wenzel, "The 'gay' Carol and Exemplum," *Neuphilologische Mitteilungen* 77 (1976), 85–91. He has nothing on Old French *gai*, but quotes a use of *heu*
in an identical position.

[3] See Adolf Tobler and Erhard Lommatzsch, eds., *Altfranzösisches Wörterbuch*, 11 vols. (various places of publication, 1925–2002), 4, cols. 720–21, s.v. *guai*;
Walter von Wartburg, ed., *Französisches Etymologisches Wörterbuch* (Basel, 1966),
17:457–58, s.v. *wai*.

out of this burden, though the thought *how merie it is in heuene* may give us hope, if only we had borne ourselves without sin. The period and historical dictionaries of English have let us down, but the dictionaries of French have provided the solution, and I was led to it by some relevant uses of *gay* (interjection) given in Greene's notes on the carol.[4]

Old English Poetic Compounds, *Domdæg* and *Domgeorn*.

If only we had borne ourselves without sin: a regretful, not a hopeful reflection, as one thinks of Doomsday and the joy of the chosen when they sit in glory with God. In the Old English poem *Christ III* (lines 1634–38), that joy is expressed well:[5]

> Þonne þa gecorenan   fore Crist berað
> beorhte frætwe,   hyra blæd leofað
> æt domdæge,   agan dream mid Gode
> liþes lifes,   þæs þe alyfed biþ
> haligra gehwam   on heofonrice

> When the chosen shall carry into Christ's presence gleaming treasures, their prosperity shall live at Judgment Day, to have with God the joy of serene life which will be vouchsafed to each of the holy ones in the kingdom of heaven

The matter is more complicated. Old English *dom* can mean not just "judgment" but also "glory," largely confined to verse, so that *domdæg* instead of the more usual *domesdæg* might mean "day of glory." For the chosen it is a day of glory, for sinners it is a day of damnation, unless saved. The dissatisfaction with the doom and gloom of that day was formed too precipitately by the charitable clergyman, but if he was expecting to be one of the chosen he had a point, a point that scholars of Old English literature attach to the adjective *domgeorn*, as it occurs five times in verse,

---

[4] Another carol (no. 363), to which Greene refers, is not relevant; it uses the adjective "gay," not the interjection. It is possible, however, that its burden, *Gay, gay, to be gay | I holde it but a vanite*, may have arisen through a misunderstanding of *Gay, gay, gay, gay, | Think on drydful domisday.*

[5] George Philip Krapp and Elliott Van Kirk Dobbie, eds., *The Exeter Book*, Anglo-Saxon Poetic Records 3 (New York, 1936), p. 48.

three times in the collocation *duguð domgeorn* "the host [of experienced warriors] eager for glory." No military historian would think it a reasonable supposition that warriors might be eager for judgment, even in times of yore. Though the poems are on sacred subjects—lives of the apostle Andrew and of St. Helena, the mother of Constantine—when writing of military men, the poets, even if monastic, must have shared in the worldly eagerness for glory or renown, of those fighting in a good cause.

In our post-Christian age it is often wise, when trying to understand the thoughts of faithful Christians of earlier times, to go back at least to the sermon-writers of the seventeenth century, probably the greatest period of English sermons after the age of Ælfric, around the year 1000. Archbishop Tillotson is good on hope of posthumous renown, concisely summed in the one word *domgeorn*:

> To the natural Hopes of men. Whence is it that men are so desirous to purchase a lasting Fame, and to perpetuate their Memory to posterity, but that they hope that there's something belonging to them, which shall survive the fate of the body, and when that lies in the silent Grave, shall be sensible of the honour which is done to their memory, and shall enjoy the pleasure of the just and impartial Fame which shall speak of them to Posterity without envy or flattery? And this is a thing incident to the greatest and most generous Spirits; none so apt as they to feed themselves with these hopes of Immortality.[6]

The hopes that renown will live for ever are considered by Tillotson "the natural Hopes of men," and if the word *domgeorn* is correctly interpreted in context, these were natural hopes of the Anglo-Saxons too. But one wonders: are such hopes not of this world, and therefore, in a stricter view, a vanity?

Another occurrence of *domgeorn* used absolutely (that is, without qualifying a noun) comes in *The Wanderer* (lines 11b–18):[7]

---

[6] *Arch-Bishop [John] Tillotson['s Sermons and Discourses]*, 14 vols. (London, 1700–1704), 9, Sermon II, "Of the Immortality of the Soul," pp. 37–72, at p. 59.

[7] Krapp and Dobbie, eds., *Exeter Book*; *The Wanderer*, pp. 134–37.

Ic to soþe wat
þæt biþ in eorle   indryhten þeaw
þæt he his ferðlocan   fæste binde,
healde his hordcofan,   hycge swa he wille.
Ne mæg werig mod   wyrde wiðstondan,
ne se hreo hyge   helpe gefremman,
forðon domgeorne   dreorigne oft
in hyra breostcofan   bindað fæste.

I know for a truth that it is in a man a noble practice that he bind fast his mind's enclosure, keeps locked his treasure-store, let him think as he will. The weary mind cannot resist what is allotted to him, nor can that wrathful thought give help, and so those eager for judgment at all times bind fast a sorrowful (thought) in the enclosure of the breast.

As often in Old English, many details are doubtful in this translation. Here I am concerned only with how *domgeorn* is to be understood. The beginning of the poem is of God's mercy: *Oft him anhaga are gebideð | Metodes miltse* (lines 1–2a). The Toronto *Dictionary of Old English* glosses *gebideð* here as sense 4, "to experience, live to see."[8] But I wonder if it is not rather sense 3, "to expect, look forward to with hope, place one's hope in" and at the same time—who can be certain of God's mercy?—"to await with fear": "Often (or always) the solitary one places hopes and fears in grace, the Lord's mercy." Which of these expectations is justified, hope or fear, will be revealed on the Day of Judgment. The beginning of the poem is recalled at its end: *wel bið þam þe him are seceð | frofre to Fæder on heofonum þær us eal seo fæstnung stondeð* (lines 114b–15), "It is well with him who looks for grace, solace from the Father in heaven where for us all our assurance rests." With that hopeful expression at the end of the poem, assuredly in mind, the solitary one of the beginning—perhaps to be identified with the wise man, *snottor on mode*, of the end (line 111)—has every reason to be *domgeorn* ("eager for Judgment)."

---

8 Angus Cameron, Ashley C. Amos, and Antonette diP. Healey, eds., *Dictionary of Old English* (*DOE*), (Toronto, 1986–), s.v.

Old English Words of Hope: *Hyht, Hycgan,* and *Hopa, Hopian*

If only we had borne ourselves without sin: that is a regretful, not a hope-ful, reflection—a reflection in tune with the thoughts of more firmly Christian times. What is *hope,* verb and noun? What is its etymology? There are cognates in Old Frisian, in Middle Low German, and in Middle High German; the word does not go far back in time, and it forms no compounds or derivatives other than by prefixation of the Old English verb *hopian* and its noun *hopa,* namely *to-hopa* and *to-hopian.* Some-times people, other than linguists, think that etymology reveals the true, the underlying meaning of a word, and the only etymological dictionary of Old English, of 1934 and now rather out of date, by its very wording in some entries encourages that misguided view;[9] thus for the verb that is in Modern English *to bless,* we have in his entry *blædsian, blētsian*: "'segnen, weihen' (eig[en]tl[ich] 'mit Opferblut besprengen'), n[eu]e[nglisch] *bless*" ["to bless, to dedicate or consecrate" (originally "to sprinkle with sacrificial blood"), MnE *to bless*]. All that is involved is that the likely etymology of the verb is from *blod* "blood"; that verb has an etymology: *hopian* has none.

It has, however, an interesting distribution and a very interesting his-tory of scholarship. More than 150 years ago, Franz Dietrich produced an important article, the first by nearly a hundred years of what was to become a flourishing line of lexicological study, on two Old English verbs, *hycgan* and *hopian,* in which he showed, in an analysis of the occurrences, that *hopian* did not occur in verse other than in the West-Saxon *Metres of Boethius,* which I persist in believing to have been written by King Alfred, and in the poem *Judith,* which, *pace* Franz Wenisch, I persist in believing to be West-Saxon.[10] Dietrich knew that the prefixed noun *tohopa* occurs in verse only

---

[9] Ferdinand Holthausen, ed., *Altenglisches etymologisches Wörterbuch* (Heidel-berg, 1934; reprinted 1963), p. 27.

[10] Franz Dietrich, "Hycgan und Hopian," *Zeitschrift für deutsches Alterthum* 9 (1853), 214–22. The *Metres of Boethius* had been published in full as early as 1698 by Edward Thwaites, and again in 1835 by Samuel Fox. *Judith* had been published in full by Edward Thwaites in 1698, by Benjamin Thorpe in 1834 (and further editions), by Heinrich Leo in 1838, most of the poem by Louis F. Klipstein in 1849, and in full by Ludwig Ettmüller in 1850. Franz Wenisch, "*Judith*—eine westsächsische Dichtung?" *Anglia* 100 (1982), 273–300, denies that the poem was composed by a West Saxon, but I am not persuaded.

in *The Metres of Boethius*.[11] If Dietrich had known, as he could not, that the noun *hopa* occurs in two late Old English poems, it would merely have confirmed his findings. Old English dialectology, and especially the distribution of the words in verse and prose, engaged him. He was less concerned to discuss in detail the sense of the words, though what he wrote on the sense was succinct and sufficient for his purpose.

Meanings of the Old English Words of "Hope"

The words *hopa, hopian,* the prefixed words, the noun *tohopa,* and the verbs (occurring in prose only) *ahopian, gehopian, tohopian* have only one sense, "hope." In the noun *hyht,* the verb *hyht(i)an* and its verbal noun *hyhting,* the adjectives *hyhtful, hyhtleas, hyhtlic,* the adverb *hyhtlice,* the prefixed words *gehyht, tohyht, behyhtan, gehyhtan, gehyhtendlic, gehyhtlice,* and the poetic compounds *woruld-hyht, hyht-gifa, hyht-gifu, hyht-plega, hyht-willa, hyht-wynn,* there is more than just "hope." It would be of historical interest to know why words have some particular sense or senses and why some words change their meaning wholly or in part. That knowledge is not available for Old English; however, when knowledge is lacking, speculation is tempting. The lexical wealth of these *hyht*-words is great: their use can be a poetic triumph.

Unlike rare *hopian* and its noun, the *hyht*-words are common in poetry, and not rare in prose. Some of them go on into Middle English, where their sense is weakened. In meaning they embrace in Old English "hope," of course, but also many other aspects of "joy" and "joyous thought." These words have an etymology, unlike the bastardly *hopian*; the etymology of *hyht* and *hyht(i)an* makes them kin to *hygd, hyge* "mind, sense, thought," and *hycgan* "to think, hope." In their many contexts many more shades of meaning are used in translation, and there are many compounds and prefixed forms. Here is an inherited wealth of

---

[11] In Corpus Christi College Cambridge MS 201, *An Exhortation to Christian Living* (line 10) and *The Judgement Day II* (line 222), both published in full by J. Rawson Lumby, ed., *Be Domes Dæge*, EETS, original series 66 (1876). The noun (spelled *hope*) occurs in the late *Instructions for Christians* (line 253), first published by James L. Rosier, ed., "'Instructions for Christians,' a Poem in Old English," *Anglia* 82 (1964), 4–22.

thought, and the traditionality of Old English poetry makes the Anglo-Saxon poets exploit these riches.

The ideas expressed by the words are important, and it would be good to know how or whether the West Saxons distinguished their new words, *hopian* and *hopa*, from the inherited words *hyht, hyht(i)an,* and *hycgan* (and derivatives and compounds). In the *Boethius*, King Alfred uses *hopian* several times for "to hope," but *hycgan* only in the sense "to think"; he uses *hyhtlic*, however, in his free poetic rendering, Meter 21 line 11, with a vivid sense of hoped-for expectation:[12]

> Se ðe ðonne nu sie   nearwe gehefted
> mid þisses mæran   middangeardes
> unnyttre lufe,   sece him eft hræðe
> fulne friodom,   þæt he forðcume
> to þæm gesælðum   saula rædes,
> forþæm þæt is sio an rest   eallra geswinca,
> hyhtlicu hyð   heaum ceolum
> modes usses,   meresmylta wic.

He who is now held in close captivity by the iniquitous love of this vainglorious world, let him quickly look for his perfect freedom again, that he may emerge into the blessings of the soul's salvation, because that is the only resting-place from all travails, the hoped-for haven for the lofty ships of our soul, a calm landing-place.

---

[12] Cf. Walter John Sedgefield, ed., *King Alfred's Old English Version of Boethius De Consolatione Philosophiae* (Oxford, 1899), glossary s.vv.; for the text of the Meter, see p. 186, and the more recent edition by George Philip Krapp, *The Paris Psalter and the Meters of Boethius* (New York, 1932), p. 185. The corresponding prose rendering (Sedgefield, *King Alfred's Old English Version,* p. 89, lines 9–10) has no corresponding adjective: *sio an hyð bið simle smyltu æfter eallum þam ystum & þam yðum urra geswinca* (that one haven is at all times calm after all the tempests and waves of our travails). The Latin, well translated by *smylt*, has the adjective *placidus*; Claudius Moreschini, ed., *Boethius*, Bibliotheca Teubneriana (Munich and Leipzig, 2000), p. 86, III, m. x line 5, *hic portus placida manens quiete* (here a calm port abiding quietly).

Defining "Hope"

There are English words for "hope" from Old English onwards, during that early period words in rivalry with each other. The concept is hard to define. In medieval use, it is not purely the Theological Virtue, and though that too is difficult to define, and complicated by close relation to its sister Virtues, Faith and Charity, the verb "to hope" is in Middle English reduced in semantic weight, meaning no more than such modern uses as "I suppose." Abstracts are brilliantly and succinctly defined by Dr. Johnson in his dictionary of 1755: "HOPE. Expectation of some good; an expectation indulged with pleasure."[13] Johnson's second quotation is from John Locke's *An Essay Concerning Human Understanding*: "*Hope* is that pleasure in the Mind, which every one finds in himself, upon the thought of a probable future enjoyment of a thing, which is apt to delight him."[14] Hope in that definition rests on thought in the present, of pleasure, enjoyment, and delight, which lie wholly in the future.

In Looking-Glass Land, where everything is back to front and left and right are reversed, the discussion between the White Queen and Alice turns on the idea of living backwards:[15]

"That's the effect of living backwards," the Queen said kindly: "it always makes one a little giddy at first—"

"Living backwards!" Alice repeated in great astonishment. "I never heard of such a thing!"

"—but there's one great advantage in it, that one's memory works both ways."

"I'm sure *mine* only works one way," Alice remarked. "I can't remember things before they happen."

---

[13] Samuel Johnson, ed., *A Dictionary of the English Language*, 2 vols. (London, 1755).

[14] Quoted from the edition by Peter H. Nidditch: John Locke, *An Essay Concerning Human Understanding* (Oxford, 1975), p. 231, ch. 20, "Of Modes of Pleasure and Pain," § 9.

[15] Lewis Carroll, *Through the Looking-Glass, and What Alice Found There* (London, 1872), p. 95 (ch. 5).

"It's a poor sort of memory that only works backwards," the Queen remarked.

"A poor sort of memory that only works backwards": is it not a poor sort of hope that only works forwards? The Old English words based on *hyht* did better than that, for that word in its range of senses included the present even when it worked forwards from the present, though it does not include the past other than in a general mindfulness. Unlike the bastardly *hopian* without lineage, the ancestry and congeneracy of *hyht* include nouns and verbs of thought and thinking, among them *hycgan*. A good example of being mindful in the present as the basis of hope comes towards the end of *The Seafarer* (lines 117–22a):[16]

Uton we hycgan   hwær *we* ham agen,
ond þonne geþencan   hu we þider cumen,
ond we þonne eac tilien   þæt we to moten
in þa ecan   eadignesse,
þær is lif gelong   in lufan dryhtnes,
hyht in heofonum.

Let us consider where we have a home and then think how we may come there, and may we then also strive that we may proceed there into the eternal bliss, where life rests on the Lord's love, joy and hope in heaven.

Among the many uncertainties in any translation of an Old English poem, my rendering of *hyht* as "joy and hope" is not meant to represent my failure to determine which it is, either "joy" or "hope," but rather to represent the indissolubility of "joy" and "hope." Glossaries and dictionaries have to find a single sense—is it sense 1 or is it sense 2?—of the word that is the subject of each entry, but often it is both. The collocation *hyht in heofonum* (slightly varied) "joy in and hope of heaven," is common in Old English verse and prose, and *hyht on Gode* "joy and hope in God" is also found. Sometimes in such collocations *hyht* translates Latin *spes*, but that does not mean necessarily that the Old English word is single-strandedly "hope": it remains "joy and hope" though *spes* is monosemantically

---

[16] George Philip Krapp and Elliott Van Kirk Dobbie, eds., *The Exeter Book*, The Anglo-Saxon Poetic Records 3 (New York, 1936), pp. 146–47.

"hope," not "joy and hope." When in late Anglo-Saxon England Old English *hopa* and *hopian* were added to the language, the speakers of that language had, for the first time, words that were singly "hope," not "joy and hope" combined. It is no more than a speculation: perhaps the monastic speakers of and writers in the Germanic languages felt the need to detach the present joy from the future hope, because the joy of heaven and in God was not yet part of an experience in the present.

Old English Pairing of Verbs of Joy, Hope, and Thought

It is not always clear in Old English when near-synonymous words or words in semantic proximity are introduced as word-pairs, thus *hycgan & hyhtan* "to think and to hope" or *hopian & hyhtan*. The latter comes in the cries to Christ of the souls freed at the Harrowing of Hell in the Easter Day Blickling Homily: *Þu come to us, middangeardes Alysend, þu come to us, heofonwara hyht & eorþwara & eac ure hyht, forþon us geara ær witgan þe toweardne sægdon, & we to þinum hidercyme hopodan & hyhtan* "Thou didst come to us, Redeemer of the world, thou didst come to us, hope of heaven-dwellers and of earth-dwellers and our hope too, because long ago prophets told of thee as to come, and we hoped for and trusted to thy coming here."[17] Hope and trust are not easily distinguished in Old English, nor in Modern English. Both *hopian to* and *hyhtan to* are primarily of the future; that is, not only (*hopian to*) "to hope for" but also (*hyhtan to*) "to trust to," not, I think, "to hope for" in the future, and "to rejoice in" in the present. Like all hoping and trusting, the thoughts of those captive in Hell were joyful because of the foretold Harrowing of Hell, and so were the thoughts of all in heaven or on earth at the good news of the foretold Incarnation. In the occurrence of *hyhtan to* at the beginning of *Resignation B* (lines 70–73a) in the Exeter Book, there is emphasis on hope, here coupled with taking courage and laughing:[18]

> hwæþre ic me ealles þæs   ellen wylle

---

[17] Richard Morris, ed., *The Blickling Homilies*, EETS, original series 73 (1880), 87.

[18] Krapp and Dobbie, eds., *Exeter Book*, p. 217. The sentence begins fol. 119ro; see Alan J. Bliss and Allen J. Frantzen, "The Integrity of *Resignation*," *Review of English Studies*, n.s. 27 (1976), 385–402.

habban ond hlyhhan   ond me hyhtan to,
frætwian mec on ferðweg,   ond fundian
sylf to þam siþe . . .

however, from all of this will I take courage and laugh and look
forward to with hope, and deck myself for my soul's journey, and
aspire to that journey . . .

At times *hyhtan* goes with *hycgan*; thus at the end of the Vercelli *Homiletic Fragment I*:[19]

Uton to þam beteran,   nu we cunnon
hycgan ond hyhtan   þæt we heofones leoht
uppe mid englum   agan moton
gastum to geoce,   þonne God wile
eorðan lifes   ende gewyrcan.

Let us take that better course, now that we know how to rejoice in
and look forward to in hope and joy that we may attain to the light
of heaven above with the angels to the comfort of (our) souls, whenever God will bring about the end of life on earth.

Alcuin on the Virtues was translated into Old English, we do not know
when; the only manuscript that has Alcuin on *spes* in English is British
Library MS Cotton Vespasian D.xiv, written about a hundred years after
the Conquest.[20] It uses *hyht* for the Theological Virtue, and has the verb
gehyhtan; thus, *we sculen ure yfele þeawes forlæten & us on God symle
gehyhten* "we must abandon our wicked practices and always set our hope
in God"; and at the end of the chapter, *On Gode is min hæle & min wul-
dor: God is min fultumend & min hyht is on Gode* "In God is my salvation
and my glory: God is my helper and my hope is in God." It would be possible to say that not only hope or trust is in God, but that joy, too, is in
God. That idea is derived from the psalms, as versified in the Paris Psalter

---

[19] George Philip Krapp, ed., *The Vercelli Book*, The Anglo-Saxon Poetic Records
2 (New York, 1932), p. 60. My interpretation is independent of that edition.

[20] Rubie D.-N. Warner, ed., EETS, original series 152 (1917), 93.

(113:20)—though there is no reason for thinking that the translator knew that version:[21]

> Þa ðe a wegen   egsan dryhtnes
> hio hyht heora   habban on drihten.
> He him fultum   fæste gestandeð
> and him scyldend byð   symble æt þearfe.

Those who ever ponder the terror of the Lord they set their hope in the Lord. He firmly proves himself to be their help and is at all times their protector at need.

The Doway translation of Psalm 113:19 reads, "They that feare our Lord, haue hoped in our Lord: he is their helper and their protector." [22] That sentiment is echoed in a Blickling Homily, in which St. Paul's teaching is reported:[23] *ic lærde wlance men & heahgeþungene þæt hie ne astigan on ofermedu, ne upgengra welena to wel ne truwodon, ah þæt hie on God ænne heora hyht gesetton* "I taught those proud and wellborn that they should not exalt themselves in pride nor trust too much in transitory riches, but that they should set their hope in God alone."

In Modern English we perhaps keep the present pleasure separate from, though the basis of, the expectation of a good that lies in the future. The Anglo-Saxons did not. Unlike some other European languages, dead or modern, English distinctions of tense are curiously imprecise. In a devout Christian view, the bliss of heaven that on Doomsday comes to those saved is a certainty in the future, and English expresses that often by a present tense.

---

[21] Krapp, ed., *Paris Psalter*, pp. 98–99.

[22] *The Holie Bible Faithfully Translated into English . . . By the English College of Doway*, 2 vols. (Doway, 1609, 1610), 2:208. The Gallicanum, underlying the versified psalms, reads *qui timent Dominum speraverunt in Domino | adiutor eorum et protector eorum est*; *Biblia Sacra iuxta Latinam Vulgatam Versionem*, 18 vols. (Rome, 1926–1995), 10 Liber Psalmorum, p. 248.

[23] *Blickling Homilies*, p. 185. I have emended, perhaps unnecessarily, *upgendra* to *upgengra*.

Middle English *Hyht*-Words

Hyht-words survive into the fourteenth century. The prefixed and suffixed *unhuhtlic* may have been coined—it occurs nowhere else—by the backward-looking historiographer Laȝamon in the thirteenth century, *Brut* lines 2539–45:[24]

> Þa spec þe moder   milde mid muðe:
> "Ȝit buð mine leoue sunen,   liðeð tosomne
> & iwurðeð sæhte   and euer on blisse,
> Cusse[ð] and cluppe[ð],   cuðie meies;
> Cnihtes ȝit beoð boðe kene   while ich wes quene.
> Nis hit noht unhuhtlic   incker moder inc hateð."
> Þer heo hom custen   þe weren kinges bearn.

Then the mother spoke orally with gentle words: "The two of you are my beloved sons, proceed together and become reconciled and at all times in happiness, kiss and embrace, and show (that you are) kinsmen; the two of you are both bold knights ever since I was queen. It is not unjoyful what your mother commands you." There they kissed each other, who were the king's sons.

That is the text of the British Library MS Cotton Caligula A.ix, which preserves an antiquated language that is thought to go back to the author. The treble negation of *noht unhuhtlic* presumably means "marginally joyful," and that is a subtle characterization of a royal mother's command. Henry Bradley, a brilliant lexicographer on the staff of *Oxford English Dictionary*, defined *unhuhtlic* in his revision of Stratmann's Middle English dictionary as "without joy": that seems right to me, because Laȝamon is a poet who turns away from his linguistic present to a recollected past.[25]

A part of *Sir Gawain and the Green Knight* that may not be much to modern taste, the unlacing of the boar, uses *hiȝtly*. The adverbs in that poem

---

[24] G. L. Brook and R. F. Leslie, eds., *Laȝamon: Brut*, vol. 1, EETS, original series 250 (1963), 132–33.

[25] Francis Henry Stratmann, ed., *A Middle-English Dictionary*, revised by Henry Bradley (Oxford, 1891), s.v.; William A. Craigie's definition in *OED*, s.v. *un-* prefix[1], 3, "unpleasant," published in 1921, seems mistaken.

are often tricky; thus, in the lines quoted below (lines 1605–14), *lufly, on hiȝe, roghe, stoutly:*[26]

> Þenne a wyȝe þat watz wys vpon wodcraftez
> To vnlace þis bor lufly bigynnez.
> Fyrst he hewes of his hed and on hiȝe settez,
> And syþen rendez him al roghe by þe rygge after,
> Braydez out þe boweles, brennez hom on glede,
> With bred blent þerwith his braches rewardez.
> Syþen he britnez out þe brawen in bryȝt brode cheldez,
> and hatz out þe hastlettez as hiȝtly bisemez;
> And ȝet hem halchez al hole þe haluez togeder,
> And syþen on a stif stange stoutly hem henges

Then a man skilled in the arts of hunting willingly begins to unlace this boar. First he cuts off its head and puts it high up, and then tears it quite fiercely along its back, draws out the guts, burns them on red-hot charcoal, rewards his hounds with bread mingled with them. Then he cuts out the flesh in shiny, broad slabs, and gets out the tasty entrails as is beautifully fitting, and further fastens together the sides left quite whole, and then on a strong pole hangs them up firmly.

My translating *hiȝtly* by "beautifully" will seem feeble, and it does not use any of the glosses in *MED*, s.v. *hightlī(che:*[27] adjective, "joyous, pleasant"; adverb, "gladly, joyfully, pleasantly." Where has the sense "hopeful(ly)" gone? The *OED*, s.v. *hightly*, had drawn attention to that loss, "in OE., also 'hopeful',," and *OED* renders the word, "pleasantly, becomingly." I suspect that the no longer new word *hopian*, etc., has driven out the sense "hopeful," because *hyht* was less exact, since it included "joy" too strongly for theological comfort.

---

[26] J. R. R. Tolkien and E. V. Gordon, eds., *Sir Gawain and the Green Knight*, 2nd ed., revised by Norman Davis (Oxford, 1967), pp. 44–45.

[27] Hans Kurath, Sherman M. Kuhn, John Reidy, and Robert E. Lewis, eds., *Middle English Dictionary* (Ann Arbor, 1952–2002), 4:774. Tolkien and Gordon, and Israel Gollancz, ed., *Sir Gawain and the Green Knight*, EETS, original series 210 (1940), in the glossaries to the two editions had given "fitly."

Middle English *Hope*-Words

The early Middle English text *Vices and Virtues* uses *hope* and *hopien* only.[28] That could be because in the author's dialect, Essex,[29] *hyht* and *hyhtan* do not survive, not even for "happiness, joy," though there are many occurrences of *blisse*, *bliðe* (and *bliðeliche*), and *merhþe* "happiness": bliss and hope are kept apart in this text, as they were not in Old English. For example (pp. 29–30):

> Ðies ilke haliӡe mihte, ðar ðe hie cumeð and bieð mid ðe manne, hie makeð him unwurð alle ðo faire þinges ðe on ðare swikele woreld faire þencheð, ne telþ hie na more ðarof ðanne of horewe aӡeanes ðare michele merhþe ðe hie hopeð te habbene on heuene riche.

> This aforementioned holy Virtue, wherever it comes and is with man, it makes for him worthless all those excellent things which seem excellent in our false world, nor does he value it any more highly than muck in contrast to that great joy to which he hopes to attain in the kingdom of heaven.

Academics prize clarity of exposition as one of the highest of intellectual virtues, and when *Vices and Virtues* is judged at all, other than as a valuable philological specimen, it is praised for its clarity and also for continuing, so it has been alleged, in thought and words the great vernacular homiletic tradition of Anglo-Saxon England. It may not be quite as simple as that: the words have changed in usage and meaning: *hope* in late Old English was "hope" only, not "hope and joy"; and the noun *hopa* was used by neither Ælfric nor Wulfstan, the greatest of Anglo-Saxon homilists; the verb *hopian* often by Ælfric but never by Wulfstan.

---

[28] Ferdinand Holthausen, ed., *Vices and Virtues*, EETS, original series 89 (1888), and 159 (1921); the chapter *Of feste hope*, pp. 29–35.

[29] For the dialect see Margaret Laing, ed., *Catalogue of Sources for a Linguistic Atlas of Early Medieval English* (Cambridge, 1993), p. 106, British Library MS Stowe 34.

A Weakened Sense of the Verb *hope(n* in Middle English

In later Middle English, a new sense is developed for the verb *hopen*, "to think, suppose, infer." In the very passus of *Piers Plowman*, which opens with *Spes* personified, that sense occurs in what is very much a joyless expectation, the lesson that the story of *Dives* teaches:[30]

> Vch a riche, I rede · rewarde at him take,
> And gyueth ȝowre good to that God · that grace of ariseth,
> For thei that ben vnkynde to his · hope I none other,
> But thei dwelle there *Diues* is · dayes withouten ende.

> Let every rich man, I advise, pay attention to his example, and give your wealth to that God from whom grace arises. For those who are niggardly to his creatures, I expect nothing else other than that they shall dwell where Dives is in endless days.

The Fully Joyous Sense of *hope* in Late Middle English

A use of words of hoping, more charged with the full sense of the word, comes in a carol to the Virgin by James Ryman at the very end of the Middle English period:[31]

> O gate of Lyfe, moder and wyfe,
>   O hope and trust of synners alle,
> In angwyshe, woo, trouble, and stryfe
>   For thy comfort we crie and calle,
>   Bothe olde and yonge, both gret and small:
>   Therfore oure help and comfort be
>   Sith oure trust is onely in the.

Ryman is generally neglected or treated with disdain when mentioned at all by historians of late Middle English verse, no doubt because his carols,

---

[30] Walter W. Skeat, ed., *The Vision of William Concerning Piers the Plowman*, parallel text edition, 2 vols. (Oxford, 1886), 1:514, B XVII, lines 265–68.

[31] Greene, *Early English Carols*, p. 134, no. 205, stanza 5.

of which there are many (too many in the eyes of some), make poetry of standard themes. There are worse practitioners in that trade.

A half-century or more earlier than Ryman, *hope* comes in John Audelay's salutation to the body of Christ (poem 8, lines 55–62):[32]

> Hayle, ground ay of my goodness, and my couernowre,
> Hayle, sustenans to my soule, and my Saueour,
> Hayle, cumforder of þe sek, and al here socour
>   In þe Lord hit is.
> Hayle, solans to hom þat beþ sory,
> Hayle, help to hom þat beþ gulte,
> Hayle, hope of grace and of mercy,
>   Þou grawnt vs al þy blys.

> Hail, thou eternal foundation of what is good in me, and my ruler, hail, thou support of my soul, and my Saviour, hail, thou that dost give comfort to the sick; and all their succor is in the Lord. Hail, thou solace to them that are in sorrow, hail, thou help to them that are sinners, hail, thou hope of grace and mercy, grant us all to share in thy happiness.

The only occurrence of the noun *hope* in *Pearl* comes when the maiden continues her instruction of the dreamer. As always it is difficult to translate this poem.[33] The stanza quoted proclaims Hope on that one death, of Christ crucified; to understand that will be achieved completely only in heaven (lines 853–64).[34]

> Lasse of blysse may non vus bryng
> Þat beren þys perle vpon oure bereste,
> For þay of mote couþe neuer mynge
> Of spotleȝ perleȝ þat beren þe creste.
> Alþaȝ oure corses in clotteȝ clynge,

---

[32] Ella Keats Whiting, ed., *The Poems of John Audelay*, EETS, original series 184 (1931), 64.

[33] The verb *hope* with the meaning "to suppose, believe" appears much more frequently in *Pearl*, and in the other poems of the *Pearl* manuscript.

[34] E. V. Gordon, ed., *Pearl* (Oxford, 1953), p. 31. I have also profited from Malcolm Andrew and Ronald Waldron, eds., *The Poems of the Pearl Manuscript* (London, 1978), p. 95.

And ȝe remen for rauþe wythouten reste,
We þurȝoutly hauen cnawyng:
Of on dethe ful oure hope is drest.
Þe Lombe vus gladeȝ, oure care is kest,
He myrþeȝ vus alle at vch a mes.
Vchoneȝ blysse is breme and beste,
And neuer oneȝ honour ȝet neuer þe les.

No one can reduce the happiness of us who wear this pearl on our breast, for they could never think of disputing (the happiness) of those who wear the device of the immaculate pearls. Though our bodies waste away in clods of earth, and though you lament in your grief ceaselessly, we have complete understanding: our hope is based fully on one death. The Lamb gladdens us, our sorrow is cast out, he brings to all of us joy at every mass. The bliss of each one of us is intense and (each one's) is best, and the high rank of each one of us is never any the less.

Strangely, Gower several times collocates *hope* with the verb *weyven* "to drive away," as at *Confessio Amantis*, IV, lines 823–24 (how Phyllis was disappointed in her trust of Demephon), and 3690–92 (the lesson of the tale of Iphis and Araxarethen):[35] *Bot al for noght, sche was deceived,* | *For Venus hath hire hope weyved* "But all in vain, she was deceived, for Venus has driven out her hope"; and *Wherof that thou thiself avise* | *Good is, er that thou be deceived,* | *Wher that the grace of hope is weyved* "It is good that you should beware of that, rather than that you should be deceived, where the gift of hope is removed." This is an enforced abandonment of hope, in other words, it is despair.

Chaucer's Parson Binds Hope to *Wanhope*, "Despair": In *The Knight's Tale*, Hope Presages Palamoun's Success in Love

Hope is one of the Theological Virtues, but in *The Parson's Tale* the Parson seems incapable of thinking of Hope without at the same time speaking

---

[35] G. C. Macaulay, ed., *The English Works of John Gower*, 2 vols., EETS, extra series 81 (1900), and 82 (1902), 1:323, and 400–401.

of *Wanhope*, "Despair." Chaucer does better for Hope, away from theology, when in *The Knight's Tale* the symbolic temple of Venus has Hope, not *Wanhope*, among the painted figures to be seen, highly significant for Palamoun—may Hope, the reader shall think, guide him, the true servant of Venus, to success in Love (I (A) lines 1918–35):[36]

> First / in the temple of Venus / maystow se
> Wroght on the wal / ful pitous to biholde
> The broken slepes / and the sykes colde,
> The sacred teerys / and the waymentynge,
> The firy strokes / of the desirynge
> That Loues seruantz / in this lyf enduren,
> The othes / that hir couenantz assuren;
> Plesance / and Hope / Desir / Foolhardynesse,
> Beaute and Youthe / Baudrye / Richesse,
> Charmes and Force / Lesynges / Flaterye,
> Despense / Bisynesse / and Ialousye
> That wered / of yelowe gooldes a gerland
> And a cokkow / sittyng on hir hand,
> Festes / instrumentz / caroles / daunces,
> Lust and array, / and alle the circumstaunces
> Of Loue / whiche þat I rekned / and rekne shal,
> By ordre / weren peynted on the wal
> And mo than / I kan make of mencion.

First, you can see in the temple of Venus created on the wall, very affecting to contemplate, the broken sleeps and the cold sighs, the sacred tears and the lamentation, the ardent pangs of that longing that Love's servants suffer in life on earth, the oaths that confirm their promised commitments: Delight and Hope, Longing, Rash Adventurousness, Beauty and Youth, Gaiety, Abundance, Blandishments and Violence, Deceptions, Flattery, Free-Spending, Solicitude, and Jealousy wearing a garland of yellow marigolds and with a cuckoo sitting on her [Jealousy's] hand, feastings, musical instruments, round dances, dancing, enjoyment and celebration, and all Love's particularities that I have listed and shall go on to

---

[36] F. J. Furnivall, ed., *A Six-Text Print of Chaucer's Canterbury Tales*, Chaucer Society, 1st series 1 (1868), pp. 55–56. Cf. *The Riverside Chaucer*, p. 51.

list, they all were painted on the wall by order, and still more than I am able to give an account of.

Nowhere else that I know of in Old or Middle English is so rich a picture painted of the *circumstaunces*, "the particularities," of the goddess of Love. In this reckoning of all that attends Venus there is just one pivotal word that is not of past experience, but of the future: that word is *Hope*. Those, who are with Palamoun, Love's servant, and not with Arcite who serves Mars, may, in their reading of *The Knight's Tale*, count with assurance on that Hope that when Venus strives against Mars she has the victory.

From Hope to Sorrow, and What the Passion Sorrow Is

One turns reluctantly from Hope to Sorrow. Sadly, as emotion is indistinguishable from emotionality, as sentiment is indistinguishable from sentimentality, so Sorrow is indistinguishable from Grief, now infected by grieving. James Murray's definition of the medieval and post-medieval concept *passion* is verbosely comprehensive: *OED*, s.v. *Passion*, 6.a., makes no mention of the Middle Ages or of Patristics:

> Any kind of feeling by which the mind is powerfully affected or moved; a vehement, commanding, or overpowering emotion; in psychology and art, any mode in which the mind is affected or acted upon (whether vehemently or not), as ambition, avarice, desire, hope, fear, love, hatred, joy, grief, anger, revenge. Sometimes personified.

I should have preferred Murray to have used "sorrow," not "grief," for in our post-Diana age "grief" is a retrospective affection, often weighed down or buoyed up by contagious sentimentality. A hundred years is a long time in the history of semantic change, and "grief" may not have been so in 1904 when Murray wrote the definition for *OED*, then *NED*, *The New English Dictionary on Historical Principles*.[37]

---

[37] For dating parts of *OED*, cf. Darrell R. Raymond, ed., *Dispatches from the Front: The* Prefaces *to the Oxford English Dictionary* (Waterloo, Ontario, 1987).

Sorrow as Understood in Post-Reformation England

To try and understand sorrow historically we must disentangle ourselves
from Diana's "mortal coil," and go back at least some 450 years to Thomas Cranmer, who may be regarded as one of the founding fathers of
English modernism, or rather as the man of whom it can be said that the
muffled bells rung at his martyrdom (if they were not suppressed) tolled
out the English Middle Ages. His *Book of Common Prayer* places *sorrow*
among afflictions other than *grief*: "And wee moste humbly beseche thee
of thy goodnes (O Lorde) to coumforte and succoure all them, whych in
this transitory lyfe bee in trouble, sorowe, nede, sycknes, or any other
aduersitie."[38] Sorrow then is in the post-medieval world, and in more recent
understanding, an affliction, an adversity, to be distinguished from *melan-*
choly, regarded by physicians and poets as a kind of madness that fills the
pages of Robert Burton's *Anatomy of Melancholy*, and is more succinctly
summed by Dr. John Armstrong, who was both a successful physician and a
not very successful poet:[39]

> Chiefly where Solitude, sad nurse of care,
> To sickly musing gives the pensive mind.
> There madness enters; and the dim-ey'd Fiend,
> Sour Melancholy, night and day provokes
> Her own eternal wound.

Sorrow as the Poet of *Beowulf* Writes of It

Sorrow, care, grief: of course, the Anglo-Saxons knew them; in an
extreme case, of which the poet of *Beowulf* wrote, a solitary father may
have come close to melancholy, to clinical depression, in his grieving. It
used to be alleged that the Anglo-Saxons were congenitally melancholy—
"Die angeborene Schwermut der Angelsachsen"[40]—and the excellence and

---

[38] *The Booke of the Common Prayer* (London: E. Whitchurche, 1549), fol. cxvi[ro]
= sig. P.iiii[ro] [*STC* 16270a].

[39] John Armstrong, *The Art of Preserving Health: A Poem* (London, 1744), pp.
108–9, Book IV, lines 90–94.

[40] Alois Brandl, *Geschichte der altenglischen Literatur*, Pauls Grundriss der ger-
manischen Philologie, 2nd ed., 2 (Strasbourg, 1908), [x], 941–1134, at p. 975 (= 35 of
separate).

variety of those of their poems that were designated "elegies" were thought
to demonstrate that sad characteristic. Here is the *Beowulf*-poet's account
of the father's *sarig sang* as he mourns for his son who has suffered bootless
(that is, "inexpiable") death on the gallows (lines 2444–62a):[41]

> Swa bið geomorlic   gomelum ceorle
> to gebidanne   þæt his byre ride   2445
> giong on galgan.   Þonne he gyd wrece,
> sarigne sang,   þonne his sunu hangað
> hrefne to hroðre,   ond he him helpe ne mæg
> eald ond infrod   ænige gefremman,
> symble bið gemyndgad   morna gehwylce   2450
> eaforan ellorsið: oðres ne gymeð
> to gebidanne   burgum in innan
> yrfeweardas   þonne se an hafað
> þurh deaðes nyd   dæda gefondad.
> Gesyhð sorhcearig   on his suna bure   2455
> winsele westne,   windge reste
> reote berofene.   Ridend swefað,
> hæleð in hoðman.   Nis þær hearpan sweg,
> gomen in geardum   swylce ðær iu wæron.   2460
> Gewiteð þonne on sealma,   sorhleoð gæleð
> an æfter anum.   Þuhte him eall to rum
> wongas ond wicstede.

So it is sad for an old man to live to see that his son must ride young
on the gallows. Then let him utter this tale, a song of sorrow, when
his son hangs a sport for the raven, and he, old and wise, can give
him no help whatever; he never ceases to be reminded each morning of his son's journey far away: he has no thought of living to see
within his halls another heir while that one has experienced the end
of his actions, through death's force. Sorrowful he sees in his son's
dwelling the deserted hall of revelry, now a windy resting-place
made joyless. The riders sleep in death, men now in their graves.

---

[41] Julius Zupitza, ed., *Beowulf . . . in Facsimile*, 2nd ed. by Norman Davis, EETS,
original series 245 (1959), pp. 114 (= fol. 184ʳ) – 115 (= fol. 185ᵛ). Cf. F. Klaeber, ed.,
Beowulf and The Fight at Finnsburg, 3rd ed. (Boston (later issues Lexington, Mass.),
1950), p. 92. The passage is authoritatively explained by Dorothy Whitelock, "*Beowulf*
2444–2471," *Medium Ævum* 8 (1939), 198–204.

> There is no sound of the harp, no joyful sports in those dwellings,
> such as there used to be. Then he goes to his couch, sings a song of
> lamentation, the one after the other. All too spacious seem to him
> those fields and that dwelling-place.

Any translator has to confess that lexical details and sometimes syntac-
tical structures and constructions are far from securely understood in
the ancient text, and therefore far from securely rendered in translation.
With *Beowulf* there is the integral problem of how to translate the poet's
subtle semantic and structural complexities.

The ingredients of grief are manifold in this passage. The father's
solitude is expressed in the last three lines quoted. The double use of *an*
(2462a) is ambiguous. I take the half-line, *an æfter anum*, to mean literally, "one [the old man] after one [the young man dead]," though others
have taken the three words to mean "one song after another."[42] In the last
two and a half lines quoted, he seems clinically depressed, as he takes to his
couch, an impression heightened by the editor's, that is, Klaeber's note (pp.
213–14) in the unlikely answer to his question about lines 2457b–58a: "Why
should a number of dead warriors be referred to? . . . The explanation is that
the old man falls into a reverie, seeing with his mind's eye the scene of deso-
lation, or, in other words, the poet passes from the actual specific situation
to a typical motive of elegiac poetry." The poet in this long passage agglom-
erates elegiac motifs, and neither the poet nor the old man had need to fall
into a reverie to do so. The plural *ridend* and the couch on which the old
man sings, the gallows on which the young man is hanged as a feast for the
raven (2446–48a), and the description of the son's palace empty and wind-
swept (2455–59), now merely reminders of the wine, the harp and its melody,
the sports, pleasures such as used to be the joyful scene formerly inhabited
by the young man. The words expressive of misery include *geomorlic, sarig,
hrefn*—here the bird that feeds on the unburied dead (the bird untouched
by the glory of Woden's divinity, if that was known to the Anglo-Saxons)—
ellorsið, deaðes nyd, sorhcearig, reote berofen, swefan, and *sorhleoð.*

---

[42] Matti Rissanen, "Two Notes on Old English Poetic Texts: 'Beowulf' 2461,
'Ruthwell Cross' III 3," *Neuphilologische Mitteilungen* 68 (1967), 276–88, at pp.
276–83.

Sorrow a Vice

It is unlikely that the poet of *Beowulf* would have seen the father's sorrow in relation to the sin of *Tristitia*. Even if the intended first audience was monastic, as is not unlikely, the poet would probably not have expected them to have understood as sinful the father's lament for his heir and his reluctance to consider another person as his *yrfeweard*, that is, as a possible or suitable guardian of his heritable possessions. For a stern moralist like Ælfric, that might have seemed a possible reading, for, first in his *Catholic Homilies*, in an account of the eight Capital Sins, Sorrow (*Tristitia*), comes as the fifth; and so again in his alliterative *Sermo de Memoria Sanctorum*:[43]

> Se fifta is tristitia . þæt is ðissere worulde unrotnyss | þæt is þonne se man geunrotsoð . ealles to swyðe | for his æhta lyre . þe he lufode to swyðe . and cid þonne wið God . and his synna geeacnað | Twa unrotnyssa synd . an is þeos yfele | and oðer is halwende . þæt is þæt se man | for his synnum geunrotsige.

> The fifth is *Tristitia*, that is, the sorrow of this world, that is when the person is all too sorrowful for loss of his possessions, which he loved too much, and then he rails against God, and increases his sins. There are two sorrows: one is this evil kind, and the other is salutary, which is that a person should feel sorrowful on account of his sins.

Whether *unrotnys* and *geunrotsian* are best translated by "sorrow" and "to feel *or* be sorrowful" or "to sorrow" is questionable. These words are a negation of "joy, joyousness, to rejoice." Ælfric shows how *unrotnyss* is a vice when lamenting the loss of things valued in the world, but it is a good emotion when lamenting one's sins. None of the other Vices are expressed as the negation of the corresponding Virtue. *Gula* is *gyfernyss*

---

[43] First, Malcolm Godden, ed., *Ælfric's Catholic Homilies, The Second Series*, EETS, supplementary series 5 (1979). *Tristitia*, in Old English *unrotnys*, Homily XII, lines 514–19 (pp. 124–25); here described as of two kinds, one harmful, *derigendlic*, the other salutary, *halwendlic*. See the notes on the sources in Godden, ed., *Ælfric's Catholic Homilies: Introduction, Commentary and Glossary*, EETS, supplementary series 18 (2000), pp. 462–65. Secondly, Walter W. Skeat, ed., *Aelfric's Lives of Saints*, EETS, original series 82 (1885), p. 367, XVI lines 289–94.

"greediness" (not "non-abstemiousness"). *Fornicatio* is *forligr* "illicit intercourse, adultery" (not "non-chastity"). *Avaritia* is *yfele gitsung* "evil covetousness" or *unafylledlice grædignyss* "insatiate greediness" (and that is as near to a negative adjective as this list gets, but "greediness" remains utterly negative). *Ira* is *weamodnyss*, impossible to translate idiomatically, but unidiomatically perhaps "malicious intemperateness." *Accidia* is *asolcennyss* "languidness" or *slæwð* "inertness" (not "unenergeticness"). *Iactantia* is *ydel gylp* "purposeless boasting," characterizing a person who is *lofgeorn . . . for gylpe* "eager to be praised for show" (not "lacking modesty"). *Superbia* is *modignyss* "arrogance," but as the entries in Bosworth–Toller show, *modig* and derivatives have both bad senses and good senses, yet, unlike *halwende unrotnyss* "salutary sorrow," the basis for believing that *modignyss*, which is not a rare word, is anything other than Pride, the worst of all sins, rests on only two or three manuscript readings.[44]

---

[44] *An Anglo-Saxon Dictionary Based on the Manuscript Collections of Joseph Bosworth*, edited and enlarged by T. Northcote Toller (Oxford, 1882–1898); T. N. Toller, ed., *Supplement* (Oxford, 1908–1921); Alistair Campbell, ed., *Enlarged Addenda and Corrigenda to the Supplement* (Oxford, 1972). The alleged positive sense of *modignes* rests on the following evidence. Two related psalter glosses have *modignes* for *benignitas* "kindness": A. P. Campbell, ed., *The Tiberius Psalter* (Ottawa, 1974), p. 131, Ps. 51:5, *Dilexisti malitiam super benignitatem* glossed *þu lufodest yfelnesse ofer modignesse*; and so also James L. Rosier, ed., *The Vitellius Psalter*, Cornell Studies in English, 42 (1962), p. 125. It is likely, however, that this use of *modignes* is the result of scribal misreading of *medomnisse* (*medumnysse*) of the shared exemplar (cf. Rosier's *apparatus criticus*), and a single scribal act of copying underlies this use because of the close relationship of the two psalter glosses involved. One manuscript of Wulfstan's *Institutes of Polity* has *modignes* as one of eight pillars that strongly support a just kingdom: the edition by Benjamin Thorpe [*Ancient Laws and Institutes of England*, octavo ed., 2 vols. (London, 1840), 2:304, 305 = folio ed., p. 423] followed by Bosworth–Toller translates *modignes* as "magnanimity," but it is a mistaken rendering of *patientia*. See Karl Jost, ed., *Die «Institutes of Polity, Civil and Ecclesiastical»: Ein Werk Erzbischof Wulfstans von York*, Schweizer anglistische Arbeiten 47 (1959), p. 52, I, 17. Only Corpus Christi College Cambridge MS 201 reads, *Soðfæstnes & modignes & rumheortnes & rædfæstnes & egesfulnes & firðrungnes & lihtengnes & rihtwisnes*. British Library MS Cotton Nero A.i and Oxford Bodleian Library MS Junius 121 have (apart from minor orthographic differences) *modþwærnes*, not *modignes*. All three manuscripts have Latin equivalents for the eight "pillars" (with minor differences), *ueritas, patientia, largitas, persuasibilitas, correctio malorum, exaltatio bonorum, leuitas tributi, equitas iudicii*, "truth, patience, generosity, persuasiveness, amendment of evils, elevation of good, mildness of taxes and imposts, equity of judgements." A single manuscript of *Institutes of Polity* has this positive

The Sorrow of Barren Sarah

The poetic word *geomor* (and its derivatives) always means "sorrow"; and *sar on mode* "sad of mind," together with the rare compound *ferhðcearig*, with the same meaning, point the way to the rare compound *geomorfrod* "sad and old," all in *Genesis A*, leading, with wordplay on Sarah and *sar*, to Sarah's wish that Hagar should be invited by Abra(ha)m to bear in concubinage the son and heir that has been denied to Sarah in wedlock (lines 2216–27):[45]

Þa wæs Sarran   sar on mode
þæt him Abrahame   ænig ne wearð
þurh gebedscipe   bearn gemæne,
freolic to frofre.   Ongann þa ferhðcearig
to were sinum   wordum meðlan: 2220
"Me þæs forwyrnde   Waldend heofona
þæt ic mægburge   moste þinre
rim miclian   roderum under
eaforum þinum,   nu ic eom orwena
þæt unc *se* eðylstæf   æfre weorðe   2225
gifeðe ætgædere: ic eom geomorfrod,
Drihten min,   do swa ic þe bidde."

Then Sarah was sad in mind that none had been born to them, to her and to Abraham, a child of them both, being bedfellows, a noble son as a comfort to them. Then she, sorrowful in spirit, did speak in solemn words to her husband: "The Ruler of the heavens has denied to me that I might increase by way of your offspring the number of your descendants under the firmament, since I am in despair that there will ever be granted to the two of us together that support of the family estates: I am old in my misery. My lord, do as I beg you."

---

sense of *modignes*. The scribal blunders in the two psalters and in *The Institutes of Polity* are not sufficient evidence that the word might have been used positively to mean "highmindedness," as well as negatively, to mean "pride."

    [45] Sir Israel Gollancz, ed., *The Cædmon Manuscript* (London, 1927), pp. 100–101. Cf. A. N. Doane, ed., *Genesis A: A New Edition* (Madison, Wis., 1978), p. 187.

Here *tristitia* weighs heavily on Sarah because she is barren. The biblical account, Genesis 16:1–4, has nothing about Sarah's sorrow, and it is sorrow not only that she has failed to produce offspring, but sorrow, more poignantly, that the descendants will not be increased so that the family estates will have the protection they need when Abraham is dead. Should she not have had Faith that God would do for them what was best, for them and for posterity in founding the dynasty and establishing the Covenant? All this comes later in the Bible and in the poem, when Sarah is shown to be a silly old woman, silly because she lacked Faith. One may wonder if the poet of *Genesis A* saw Sarah's insufficiency in such a sin-laden view. It might appear that the very language prepares the Anglo-Saxon reader or listener for that view, a language in which the very concept of despair was expressed as *orwena*[46]—in Sarah's words, *ic eom orwena*—that is, without the most delight-giving of the Theological Virtues, Hope: *orwena* "lacking Hope." Old English seems to do well in its simple expressiveness for "despair," the saddest of feelings, defined in *OED* (within a longer definition) as "a state of mind in which there is entire want of hope," and for the theological basis of which Dr. Johnson (*Dictionary,* s.v. *despair,* noun, 3) gives the sense, "Loss of confidence in the mercy of God"; here *confidence* has the full sense of "trust, security."[47] It is significant that the mourning father in *Beowulf* (line 2453) laments that he has no heir, no *yrfeweard,* and that Sarah's sorrow emphasizes a similar dynastic discontinuity. The poet of *Genesis A* has added that emphasis to the biblical account, and, without searching for Germanic antiquities in the poem, a modern reader may presume that such dynastic discontinuity would have been felt deeply in Anglo-Saxon society.[48]

---

[46] The word comes most often in collocation with words meaning "life," and "despairing of life."

[47] This sense of *orwenness,* "despair," as understood by the Anglo-Saxons, is well exemplified in the opening of an Old English homiletic fragment, A. S. Napier, ed., "Ein altenglisches Leben des heiligen Chad," *Anglia* 10 (1888), 131–56, "De Cogitatione," at p. 155, *Se swicola deofol, þe syrwð ymbe mancynn, asent yfele geþohtas & þwyrlice ongean God on þæs mannes heortan þæt he mage hine gebringan on orwenesse þæt he ortruwian sceole be Godes mildheortnesse forþam mānfullum geþohtum,* "The deceitful devil, who plots against mankind, sends forth evil and depraved thoughts against God into a person's heart so that he [the devil] may be able to bring him [the person] to despair that he is to lose faith in God's mercy on account of wicked thoughts."

[48] As by C. C. Ferrell, *Teutonic Antiquities in the Anglo-Saxon Genesis* (Halle, 1893), now wholly outmoded.

Synonyms and Near-Synonyms of *sorrow* in Old English

It is easy to see "sorrow" among other passions or emotions, and to understand that it may have been felt sinful at times; it is as important to acknowledge our limited understanding of how the Anglo-Saxons viewed such feelings, how precisely they used synonyms or near-synonyms, mainly poetic, of sorrow. The following words well exemplify our semantic difficulty: *gnorn* with the verbs *gnornian, begnornian*, and *gnornung* (as well as the compound *heah-gnornung*), and the compounds *gnorn-cearig, gnorn-hof, gnorn-scendende* (if to be regarded as a compound), *gnorn-sorg*, and *gnorn-word*; and *gnyrn* and the compound *gnyrn-wracu*.[49]

The verse of the Paris Psalter is a good place to begin; for here the relationship with the Gallican Psalter is some use in establishing what one not very good versifier made of his biblical source. The occurrences are *gnorne* Ps 103:20.2, *gnornendra* Ps 78:11.3, *gnorniað* Ps 58:15.3, *gnorniende* Ps 101:4.6, *gnornige* Ps 54:2.1, and *gnorn-scendende* Ps 89:10.4.[50] In Old English *gnorne* nominative plural is not distinguishable from the adverb, so that at Ps 103:20.1–2 (cf. Vulgate 103:21) we cannot tell if *leon hwelpas . . . grymetigað gnorne* means at once "the *gnorn* whelps of the lion roar" and equally "the whelps of the lion roar *gnorn*-ly." Since *gnorne* is one of the words the versifier has added to the Latin, the Vulgate is no use to us in establishing the sense, whether "sad" or "fierce": in the context—that God has established dark night—we may imagine, if we wish to indulge our sentimentality, that the little whelps are dejected and that they roar sadly, or that being young lions they are savage and that they roar fiercely. The versifier uses the verb more frequently. At Ps 54:2.1 *ic gronige* (cf. Vulgate 54:3, *contristatus sum*, Doway 54:4 "I am made sorrowful"), the meaning is clearer, "to be sorrowful" or "to be made sorrowful," and there is no great difference. Like some of the psalter glosses, at Ps 58:15.3 *fela g-norniað* (cf. Vulgate 58:16 *murmurabunt*, Doway "they wil murmur also"), it looks as if "they are complaining much"

---

[49] Compounds composed of adjective + noun and noun + adjective are not always distinguishable from phrases composed of adjective + noun and noun + adjective.

[50] Cf. J. B. Bessinger, Jr, and Philip H. Smith (ed. and programmer), *A Concordance to the Anglo-Saxon Poetic Records* (Ithaca, 1978); G. P. Krapp, ed., *Paris Psalter and Meters of Boethius*; *Biblia Sacra*, 10 Liber Psalmorum; *Holie Bible*, 2 (Doway, 1609, 1610).

because they are going hungry. Whether in that context the verb means "to lament, grieve" is questionable: all we are told by the Vulgate is that they murmur. The present participle at Ps 78:11.3 *gnornendra care* (cf. Vulgate *gemitus*, Doway "the groning") uses two words close in meaning; we may be content to render them "the sorrows of those lamenting ones," and we may wish to extend "lamenting" to "groaning" to accommodate the Latin. Ps 101:4.6 *Forðon me is swære stefn | hefig gnorniende heortan getenge, | ætfeolen eac min ban flæsce minum* greatly expatiates on the Vulgate 101:6 *a voce gemitus mei adhesit os meum carni meae* (Doway "For the voyce of my groning, my bone hath cleaued to my flesh"). I am not sure that I understand the Psalmist's pathology better than the versifier did, but it looks as if it might mean "For my sad voice, heavy and lamenting, touches my heart, moreover my bone has adhered to my flesh." Later in this Psalm, 101:18.1, the versifier uses the compound *heah-gnornung*, where *heah* facilitates the alliteration (as does *bitere* in the next line): *he þa gehyrde heah-gnornunge | þæra ðe gebundene bitere wæron* "he [God] gave ear to the loud lamentation of those who were cruelly bound" (Vulgate 101:21 *ut audiret gemitum compeditorum*, Doway "That he might heare the gronings of the fettered"). Ps 89:10.4 very freely renders the Latin, *beoð ure geardagas gnorn-scendende* "the years of our life are hastening away in sorrow." It seems that most often the versifier thinks that *gnorn* and related words express an audible sorrow, a groaning, a loud lament.

Sorrow in the Poem *Elene*

It would take too much space to go through all the occurrences of these words in Old English, and I shall confine myself to those in *Elene*.[51] In that poem are to be found not only words based on *gnorn*, but also on *gnyrn*

---

[51] The following works have been consulted, largely to display the variety of translation: Jacob Grimm, ed., *Andreas und Elene* (Cassel, 1840); J. M. Kemble, ed., *The Poetry of the Codex Vercellensis*, Ælfric Society, 6 (London, 1856); Christian W. M. Grein, *Dichtungen der Angelsachsen stabreimend übersetzt*, 2 (Göttingen, 1857, 1859); Julius Zupitza, ed., *Cynewulfs Elene*, 3rd ed. (Berlin, 1888); Richard Simons, ed., *Cynewulfs Wortschatz*, Bonner Beiträge zur Anglistik, 3 (1899); F. Holthausen, ed., *Cynewulfs Elene*, 2nd ed. (Heidelberg, 1910), 4th ed. (Heidelberg, 1936); Albert Stanburrough Cook, ed., *The Old English Elene, Phœnix, and Physiologus* (New Haven, 1919); G. P. Krapp, ed., *Vercelli Book*; Pamela O. E. Gradon, ed., *Cynewulf's Elene* (London, 1958).

(with *i*-mutation). The verb *gnornian* occurs in the runic epilogue, line 1259b, where the name of the *yr*-rune is the subject of *gnornode*. What the rune stands for here is in doubt, and the epilogue "makes a heavy count of [Cynewulf's] sins and miseries."[52] With all this sinful heaviness it is small wonder that in the next line the *nyd*-rune is the first element of a compound the second of which is *gefera*, with *nyd* meaning "need, necessity." The compound *nyd-gefera* perhaps means "inevitable companion" (Gradon) or "companion in need, *Notgefährte*"; in this context it probably means "one who has need as his companion," and who has *nearusorge dreah* "endured oppressive care, crushing sorrow"; so that in these lines, as elsewhere, *gnornian* means "to grieve, feel sorrow." The compound *gnornsorg* occurs twice, at lines 655 and 976; and superficially at least the two elements seem synonymous: Grein, who attempts to translate both elements into a compound, gives *Kummersorge*, but most translators use a single word, "grief, sorrow: *Kummer, Sorge*." The immediate context is unhelpful: Judas, as he was speaking to St. Helena, *gnornsorge wæg* "felt grief-laden sorrow."[53] A few lines earlier,[54] we learn why Judas is so miserable (lines 609b–10): *ne meahte he þa gehðu bebugan, | oncyrran* cyning-*geniðlan, he wæs on þære cwene gewealdum* "he could not avoid that misery, alter [the mind of] his *royal* foe, he was in the power of the queen." At line 976 the compound comes again, and has a more intellectual, less physical implication (lines 976–79a):

ond wæs Iudeum   gnornsorga mæst,
werum wansæligum   wyrda laðost,
þær hie hit for worulde   wendan meahton,
Cristenra gefean.

and it was to the Jews the greatest of grievous sorrows, the most hateful of outcomes to those unblessed men, if only they could change for all the world the joy of the Christians.

---

[52] Kenneth Sisam, *Studies in Old English Literature* (Oxford, 1953), p. 24.

[53] So also *Guthlac B*, line 1335b; Jane Roberts, ed., *The Guthlac Poems of the Exeter Book* (Oxford, 1979), p. 123.

[54] With an emendation, *cyning*, not relevant to the sense of the word under discussion; see F. Holthausen, "Zur altenglischen Literatur. XI," *Anglia Beiblatt* 21 (1910), 174–76, at p. 174.

As always, words are not to be rendered reliably when they enfold passions, emotions, affections, as well as judgments, for on each in every context the translator impresses his or her assessment on what is implied. German *Kummersorge* means little more than "grief" or "sorrow," to which the glossaries of English editions of the poem reduce their rendering of *gnornsorg*. A reading of old English verse has one's ears ringing with audible sorrow, so that *gnornsorg* is more than mere "grief": it is grief or sorrow that manifests itself in groaning, wailing, lamenting. That a profound emotion is involved is shown in the lines just quoted by *wansælig* describing the Jewish men, a word translated traditionally into German as *unselig*, that is, "wretched, unfortunate, ill-starred, disastrous." *Deutsches Wörterbuch*, however, founded by Hermann Paul in 1897, directs us to a triple use by Luther that underlies some current German usage, amounting to "accursed," the sense given for *wansælig* by Pamela Gradon.[55] The Authorized Version has "miserable." The sense of *unselig* in Luther's Bible is, I think, "unblessed," because punished by God's wrath, and that is probably the (now obsolete?) sense of *miserable* in the Authorized Version too.[56] In the biblical

---

[55] Cf. W. Scholze-Stubenrecht and J. B. Sykes, eds., *The Oxford Duden German Dictionary* (Oxford, 1990), s.v. *unselig*. Hermann Paul, ed., *Deutsches Wörterbuch*, 7th ed. (ed. Werner Betz) (Tübingen, 1976), s.v. *unselig*. Martin Luther, *Faksimilierte Ausgabe der Lutherbibel von 1545* (Württemberg, [1968]), II, fol. CCV^ro, Baruch 4:25–32, writing from the Babylonian captivity to the Jews in Jerusalem: [25] IR Kinder / leidet gedültiglich / den zorn der von Gott vber euch komet . . . [27] SEid getrost jr Kinder / vnd schreiet zu Gott / Denn der euch hat wegfüren lassen / wird ewr nicht vergessen . . . [30] IErusalem sey getrost / Denn der wird dich trösten / nach dem du genennet bist. [31] Vnselig müsse sein die dir leid gethan / vnd vber deinem Falle sich gefrewet haben. [32] Vnselig müssen sein die Stedte / welchen deine Kinder gedienet haben / Vnd vnselig müsse sein /die deine Kinder gefangen helt.

Cf. the Authorized Version [quoted from Alfred W. Pollard, ed., *The Holy Bible, an Exact Reprint in Roman Type . . . of the Authorized Version . . . 1611* (London, 1911)]: 25 My children, suffer patiently the wrath that is come vpon you from God . . . 27 Be of good comfort, O my children, and cry vnto God: for you shall be remembred of him that brought these things vpon you . . . 30 Take a good heart, O Ierusalem: for hee that gaue thee that name, will comfort thee. 31 Miserable are they that afflicted thee, and reioyced at the fall. 32 Miserable are the cities which thy children serued: miserable is she that receiued thy sonnes.

[56] Cf. *OED* s.v. sense 1., and the quotation there given, Adam's cry of bitter regret, towards the end of *Paradise Lost* (see *John Milton Paradise Lost 1667* [Menston, 1968], sig. Qq2^vo, Book 10 lines 497–99, = later editions Book 11 lines 500–502): "O miserable Mankind, to what fall | Degraded, to what wretched state reserv'd! | Better end heer unborn."

passage the Jews of Jerusalem are told to be of good cheer, for the cities of their afflictions and captivity are outside the operation of divine favor; that is, they are unblessed, whereas God will remember Jerusalem and his people. The German translation of *wansælig* is not exact, unless the whole semantic history of *unselig* is understood; "unblessed" reflects that sense, and in addition, like the Old English adjective in context, it gives the cause. *Elene*, the poem on the Invention of the Cross, celebrates that event, not to encourage the relic industry, but because in the words divinely spoken to Constantine, and given in Old English (lines 92b–93) *Mid þys beacne ðu . . . feond oferswiðesð*, "with this sign shalt thou overcome the enemy."[57] The sign had not yet exercised its power over Judas, as it was to do later: at line 977 he was still "unblessed."

A long speech (this part not indebted to the source) includes the word, in the dative plural, *gnyrnwræcum* (lines 357b–60, part of a long sentence paragraph):

> & þa weregan neat
> þe man daga gehwam   drifeð & þirsceð
> ongitaþ hira goddend,   nales gnyrnwræcum
> feogað frynd hiera   þe him fodder gifeð

and the wretched cattle that are driven and beaten day after day recognize those who are kind to them, by no means do they with *gyrnwræcum* hate their friends who give them fodder.

Sense, Sounds, and Obscurities of Sense in Old English Words for Wailful Sorrow

With excellent sense for shades of meaning, Heinrich Leo in his dictionary provides German equivalents for both elements of the compound, introducing an auditory sense for *gnyrn-* by translating the compound *gnyrn-wræcum* as *grollende Verfolgung* "growling persecution";[58] but alas, Modern

---

[57] These words come in that opening part of the poem that scholars used to read principally to find Germanic antiquities; for example, Milo B. Price, *Teutonic Antiquities in the Generally Acknowledged Cynewulfian Poetry* (Leipzig doctoral dissertation, 1896), pp. 44–48.

[58] Heinrich Leo, ed., with alphabetic index by Walther Biszegger, *Angelsächsisches Glossar* (Halle, 1872, 1877), col. 80 lines 49–50, s.v. *gnyrn-vräce*, and col.

German has in most uses, except when referring to thunder, lost much of the auditory element, and *grollend* might well be understood as "grudging."

The etymology of *gnorn, gnyrn-* is obscure. It may be that, like Modern English *growl*, it is synaesthetic. It is not confined to English, for Old Saxon has *gnornon* "to mourn, lament"; it also has *gornon* and *grornon*, and Old English has *grornian, begrornian, grorn, grorne*, and compounds include *grorn-hof* at *Juliana* line 324 and *gryn-smið* at *Andreas* line 917, as well as a compound **grorn-torn* created by the lexicographers and editors.[59]

---

353 line 32, s.v. *gnyrn-vrace*. Kemble, p. 22 (his lines 714–20), had translated *gnyrn-wræcum feogað* as "with enmity hate," following Grimm (p. 149), who had translated *gnyrnwræcum feogað* as *odiis prosequuntur* "pursue with enmities." Grein, in his translation (p. 113), introduces the notion of vengeance, *mit Rache . . . verfolgend*"; a few years later, in his *Sprachschatz* s.v. *gnyrn-vracu*, he has *ultio injuriarum*, "revenge for injuries" [*Sprachschatz der angelsächsischen Dichter*, 2 vols., Bibliothek der angelsächsischen Poesie, 3, 4 (Cassel and Göttingen, 1861, 1864), 3:517. Later lexicographers and glossators follow Zupitza's glossary, and his glossary heightens the drama s.v. *gnyrnwrc* by rendering the compound *rache für erlittenes unrecht*, "revenge for wrong suffered." The second element of the compound means "persecution, revenge," but the "wrong suffered" is a figment of Zupitza's imagination, arising presumably from *gyrn-wracu*, which occurs twice in *Beowulf* and once in *Guthlac A*, translated in Grein's *Sprachschatz* as *ultio moeroris vel injuriarum*, "persecution for grief or injuries." In his translation, *Dichtungen der Angelsachsen*, 1:253, he had *Rache des Kummers*, "vengeance for grief" and *Jammers Rache* "Vengeance for misery (or wailing)" (1:279). Cf. John M. Kemble, *A Translation of the Anglo-Saxon Poem of Beowulf* (London, 1837), p. 86, "with vengeance for *her* grief." The occurrence at *Guthlac A*, line 434a, *gyldan gyrn-wræce*, was understood by Benjamin Thorpe, ed., *Codex Exoniensis* (London, 1842), p. 128 line 16, as "pay for *his* voluntary exile" (perhaps taking *gyrn-* as from *georn*); by Israel Gollancz, ed., *The Exeter Book*, I, EETS, original series 104 (1895), p. 130, "requite . . . with vengeance for their misery"; by Jane Roberts, *Guthlac Poems*, glossary s.v. *gyrnwracu*, "vengeance for injury." "Injury" comes into the *gyrn-* element of the compound *gyrn-stæf* at *Juliana* line 245 in Grein's *Sprachschatz*, as *injuria, tribulatio*; and in his translation *gleaw gyrnstafa* is rendered *der Fallstrick-erfahrene* following Thorpe's rendering (p. 257 line 10), "*the* skill'd in snares." Gollancz, *Exeter Book*, p. 257, has "versed in cruel trickery"; Rosemary Woolf, ed., *Juliana* (London, 1955), glossary s.v. *gyrnstæf* gives "affliction."

[59] MS *grom torn* has been generally emended to *grorn torn*, and that was first regarded as a compound in Grein's *Sprachschatz*; see the note on line 66a, in O. D. Macrae-Gibson, ed., *The Old English Riming-Poem* (Cambridge, 1983), p. 53. The second half-line is corrupt. If *grorn-torn* is correctly emended, perhaps the two elements are not synonymous, and the meaning is "wailful grief."

This group of words, beginning with /gn/ or /gr/, well illustrates the insecurity of our understanding of Old English. A consequence of recognizing that insecurity is that it is not wise always to assume that solutions advanced for problems are safe in a subject studied diligently and extensively for more than 160 years, often by excellent scholars. The convenience of accepting the most recent work or the work of the most eminent scholar is to be resisted. We are dealing with a sliding scale of probabilities: my guess is that this group of words expresses an auditory aspect of sorrow, grief, tribulation, or affliction, such as lamentation, wailing, or growling; it is more certain that it does not directly express wrongs or injuries.

Middle English Sorrows, and Tears for Those Who Cannot Weep

Middle English manifests different aspects of sorrow, very moving at their best, especially in lyrics on the subject of Christ Crucified, next to him his mother, weeping, and comforted by St. John; thus one of several versions of a lyric (ultimately derived from a Latin meditation):[60]

> Quanne hic se on rode
> Ihesu mi lemman
> An besiden him stonden
> Marie an Iohan,
> And his rig isuongen
> And his side istungen
> For þe luue of man,
> Wel ou hic to wepen
> And sinnes forleten
> Yif hic of luue kan
> Yif hic of luue kan
> Yif hic of luue kan.

---

[60] Carleton Brown, ed., *English Lyrics of the XIIIth Century* (Oxford, 1932), pp. 62–63 (no. 35B). The meditation is printed in C. Brown, ed., *Religious Lyrics of the XIVth Century*, 2nd ed., revised by G. V. Smithers (Oxford, 1952), p. 242.

> When I see on the cross my beloved Jesus and standing beside him
> Mary and John, and his back is scourged and his side is pierced for
> love of mankind, truly I ought to weep and to give up sins if I know
> what love is if I know what love is if I know what love is.

The repetition at the end makes it likely that the lyric was set to music,
but no music is extant. From seeing Christ Crucified we ought to learn to
weep, as Mary learnt to weep. That is the message of a much later lyric, a
pietà carol of the fifteenth century, the first stanza of which goes:[61]

> With fauoure in hir face / ferr passyng my reason,
> And of hir sore weepyng / this was the enchesone:
> Hir soon in hir lap lay, / she seid, slayne by treason.
> Yif wepyng myght ripe bee / it seemyd þan in season.
>   "Ihesu!" so she sobbid,
>   So hir soone was bobbid
>   and of his lif robbid;
> Saying þies wordis, / as I say þee,
> "Who cannot wepe / come lerne at me."

> With noble beauty in her countenance far beyond my understanding,
> this was the cause of her sad weeping: her son lay in her lap, mur-
> dered, she said, by betrayal. If there ever is a right time for weeping
> it seemed to be then. "Jesu!" so she sobbed, as her son had been
> buffeted and robbed of his life. And she said these words, as I say
> to you, "Let him who knows not how to weep, come and learn from
> me."

---

[61] The carol is extant in two versions. It has been published several times (often
slightly modernized in spelling), first by Sir Samuel Egerton Brydges, ed., *Censura
Literaria* 10 (London, 1809), 186–87 (Number XXXVIII, art. 5); Greene, ed., *Early
English Carols*, no. 161; Carleton Brown, ed., *Religious Lyrics of the XVth Century*
(Oxford, 1939), pp. 17–18 (no. 9); Celia and Kenneth Sisam, eds., *The Oxford Book
of Medieval English Verse* (Oxford, 1970), pp. 486–87 (no. 227); Douglas Gray, ed., *A
Selection of Religious Lyrics* (Oxford, 1975), pp. 21–22 (no. 24). Cf. A. George Rigg, *A
Glastonbury Miscellany of the Fifteenth Century—A Descriptive Index of Trinity Col-
lege, Cambridge, MS. O.9.38* (London, 1968), pp. 86–87.

The last line is repeated at the end of the next two stanzas. The second stanza begins with the lines:[62]

> I said, I cowd not wepe, I was so harde hartid.
> She answerd me *shortly* with wordys þat smarted,
> "Lo, nature shall move þee, þou must be conuerted."

> I said, I could not weep, I was so hard-hearted. She answered briefly with words that hurt, "Behold, your humanity shall move you, you must be brought to it."

Middle English *nature* is a word of many meanings. I translate it "your humanity," though that attaches the general sense of "human kindness" more closely to the speaker than the Middle English word warrants. In the weeping Virgin her humanity is stressed, and it is from her in her humanity that the hard-hearted may learn to weep in his humanity. The words of the poem are echoed in several late Middle English poems, in some of which Christ speaks from the cross to hard-hearted mankind.

The most startling adaptation is perhaps by John Skelton in *Phyllyp Sparowe*, a pseudo-lament, delighting in liturgical and literary redolences, for the favorite pet sparrow belonging to Jane Scrope, whose sorrow recalls the graver woe of the Virgin Mary, as Jane Scrope addresses a female reader or listener:[63]

> I sighed and I sobbed
> For that I was robbed
> Of my sparowes lyfe.
> O mayden, wydow, and wyfe,
> Of what estate ye be
> Of hye or lowe degree,
> Great sorowe than ye myght se,
> And lerne to wepe at me.

---

[62] The text of Trinity College Cambridge MS O.9.38 justifies the emendation of *with wordys shortly* to *shortly with wordys* adopted by Celia and Kenneth Sisam and Douglas Gray.

[63] John Scattergood, ed., *John Skelton: The Complete English Poems* (Harmondsworth, 1983), p. 73, lines 50–57.

It is difficult to recognize the spiritual complexity of men and women of past ages. In our understanding of medieval piety we are perhaps inclined to believe, not without a degree of condescension, in their simple religiousness. Skelton teaches us the art of playful sacrilegiousness, displayed by him without loss of faith.

The *Double Sorwe of Troilus*, and the Joyful Tears of Those Who Attend Griselde Reunited with Her Children

Statistics are a convenient resource when ideas are wanting or are insecure. *Troilus and Criseyde* has (adjusted for length) eleven times the number of occurrences of the words *sore* and *sorrow* compared with *The Clerk's Tale*.[64] The woeful verses themselves weep as Chaucer tells of *the double sorwe of Troilus*, his sorrowful falling in love, and how in sorrow he lost his love. The opening of the poem dwells on the sadness of it all, and we are assured by Chaucer that he himself looks sad when telling this *sorwful tale*. *The Clerk's Tale* of patient Griselda is of infinite sadness. The naïve reader, failing to see in it the ideal of wifely patience and obedience as vowed in holy matrimony, may find it difficult to believe what we are told at the end: *Ful many a yeer / in heigh prosperitee | Lyuen thise two / in concord and in reste*.[65] There are of course other words, such as *grief, greue, agreued*, and for these the incidence in *Troilus* is not disproportionately heavy. The statistics of *tear(s* and *weep(ing* show a similar greater heaviness in *Troilus*. Sorrow is experienced by both Troilus and Criseyde: but the adjective *tery* is reserved for the beblubbered Criseyde in a detailed description of her in tears and ashamed (IV, 813–21), and,

---

[64] Akio Oizumi, ed., *A Complete Concordance to the Works of Geoffrey Chaucer*, 10 vols. (Hildesheim, 1991). The figures for ClT = *Clerk's Tale* and Tr = *Troilus and Criseyde* (ignoring minor spelling differences) are as follows: *sorwe(s* ClT 1, Tr 118; inflected forms of the verb *sorwen* ClT 0, Tr 8; *sorwful* ClT 0, Tr 28; *sorw(e)fulli(ch* ClT 1, Tr 10; *sorwynge* ClT 0, Tr 1; *sory* ClT 0, Tr 12. *The Clerk's Tale* is 1,156 lines long and *The Troilus* is 8,239 lines long, so that for a true comparison the *Troilus* numbers should be divided by a little over 7; that would result in these totals: ClT 2, Tr 177 = 25 adjusted for length.

[65] F. J. Furnivall, ed., *A Six-Text Print of Chaucer's Canterbury Tales in Parallel Columns*, 5, Chaucer Society Publications, first series (1873), p. 439, Canterbury Tales, IV (E) 1128–29; cf. Larry D. Benson (gen. ed.), *The Riverside Chaucer* (Boston, 1987), p. 152.

if the dictionaries are right, the word makes its first appearance in the language for her sorrowful face.

Tears of joy flow freely from many of those who witness the restoration to Griselda of her and Walter's children in the two most joyous stanzas in *The Clerk's Tale*, the stanzas that follow Griselda's double swooning, reunited with the children whom she had thought dead, and she at one with Walter (lines 1100–13):

> And in hire swogh / so sadly holdeth she
> Hir children two / whan she gan hem tembrace
> That with greet sleghte / and greet difficultee
> The children from hir arm / they gonne arace.
> O, many a teer / *on* many a pitous face
> Doun ran / of hem þat stoden hir bisyde:
> Vnnethe aboute hire / myghte they abyde.
>
> Walter hir gladeth / and hir sorwe slaketh:
> She riseth vp abaysed / from hir traunce,
> And euery wight / hir ioye and feste maketh
> Til she / hath caught agayn hir contenaunce.
> Walter hir dooth / so feithfully pleasaunce
> That it was deyntee / for to seen the cheere
> Bitwix hem two / now they been met yfeere.

And in her swoon she holds so firmly her two children when she embraced them that only with great skill and great difficulty did they pull the children away from her arm. Oh, many tears ran down many compassionate faces of those that stood next to her: they could hardly bear to be in attendance upon her. Walter comforts her and abates her sorrow: abashed she gets up from her faint, and everybody brings her joy and festive cheer till she has regained her composure. Walter in such good faith gives her pleasure that it was a sweet thing to see the joyous harmony between the two now that they are at one.

The Joys of the Humble Poor, with a *Hey Nonny, Nonny*

We have arrived at the saddest of joys in Middle English. Unalloyed joy is hard to find in this vale of tears as viewed in the Middle Ages. Before descending into the full negativity of the joys of this world, I want to mention some merry lines on the sweet content of the poor, as sung in the first Act of *The Pleasant Comedie of Patient Grissill*:[66]

> Art thou poore, yet hast thou golden Slumbers:
> Oh sweet content!
> Art thou rich, yet is thy minde perplexed?
> Oh punnishment!
> Dost thou laugh to see how fooles are vexed?
> To ad to golden numbers, golden numbers.
> O sweet content, o sweet, o sweet &c.
> [Burden] Worke apace, apace, apace, apace:
> Honest labour beares a louely face,
> Then hey noney, noney: hey noney, noney.

What might ring true in Chaucer's Griselda, raised in unblissful wedlock from poverty to the rank of marchioness, rings false in *Patient Grissill*; and similarly it rings false in a carol of the very end of the Middle English period, described by one of its editors amazingly as "politics in song," and by another as a "convivial carol." The carol is a "God speed the plough" song, from Oxford Bodleian Library MS Arch. Selden B.26, where it survives with music. The third stanza gives some idea of the honest toil of the husbandman, as seen by the sophisticated non-rustic who composed the poem and perhaps the music. The ploughman with his ploughing, *erynge* in Middle English, has earned a special place in it:[67]

> Aboute barly and whete
> Þat maketh men to swete,
> God spede þe plowe al day!
> The merthe of alle þis londe
> Maketh þe gode husbonde,
> With erynge of his plowe.

---

[66] Fredson T. Bowers, ed., *The Dramatic Works of Dekker*, 4 vols. (Cambridge, 1951–1961), 1:207–90, at p. 218.

[67] Editions include Rossell Hope Robbins, ed., *Historical Poems of the XIVth and XVth Centuries* (New York, 1959), pp. 87–88, no. 37; and R. L. Greene, *The Early English Carols*, pp. 248–49, no. 418.2.

In judging the truth or falseness of tone of earlier periods the reader responds to the arts of the poet, in Goethe's words, *Dichterkünste machen's wahr* (*les arts poétiques* make it true).[68]

The Old English *Riming Poem*

From such scenes of joy I must get back to pre-Conquest England and a grander mirth. There have been studies of the humoristic side of the literary endeavors of the Anglo-Saxons. More than half a century ago an article appeared with the promising title, "*Glæd wæs ic gliwum*—Ungloomy Aspects of Anglo-Saxon Poetry."[69] The Old English quotation in that title is from very near the beginning of *The Riming Poem*, as difficult a piece of verse as the Anglo-Saxons achieved in the vernacular, but, having taken these words for her title, the author did not discuss that poem (lines 1–4):

> Me lifes onlah   se þis leoht onwrah
> ond þæt torhte geteoh,   tillice onwreah:
> glæd wæs ic gliwum,   glenged hiwum
> blissa bleoum,   blostma heowum.

> He granted life to me, who revealed this light,
> brought that forth brightly, displayed it well:
> rejoicing in joys I was, colorfully arrayed
> in colors of joys, in the hues of flowers.

Every line of this translation can be challenged. What is clear, however doubtful the details, is that this is a radiantly colorful world, and God, who made it, granted life to the speaker of the poem, *Me lifes onlah*, "granted life to me"—but only for a while.[70]

Toward the end of the poem the temporariness of that bestowal of life is revealed as the poet adverts to one of the favorite themes of the Anglo-Saxons (lines 70–77):

---

[68] *Goethe's Gedichte*, 2 vols. (Stuttgart and Tübingen, 1815), 1:105.

[69] Jean I. Young, "*Glæd wæs ic gliwum*—Ungloomy Aspects of Anglo-Saxon Poetry," in *The Early Cultures of North-West Europe, H. M. Chadwick Memorial Studies*, ed. Sir Cyril Fox and Bruce Dickins (Cambridge, 1950), pp. 273–87.

[70] Old English *onleon* (past tense *onlah*) "to grant as a loan."

Me þæt wyrd gewæf   ond gewyr*h*t forgeaf
þæt ic grofe græf,   ond þæt grimme *scr*æf
flean flæsce ne mæg.   Þonne flanhred dæg
nydgrapum nimeþ,   þonne seo neah*t* becymeð
seo me eðles *o*fonn   ond mec her *e*ardes onconn,
þonne lichoma ligeð,   lima wyrm friteþ,
ac him w*y*nne gewigeð   ond þa wist geþygeð,
oþ þæt beoþ þa ban—   an.

Destiny allotted that to me and assigned that task that I should dig
my grave, and from that cruel cavern my flesh cannot take flight.
When that arrow-swift day will grip me in coercive clutches, when
that night will come that grudges me my homeland, accusing me
of my home here, then my corpse will lie for the worm to eat my
limbs, for the worm will feel joy as it consumes that feast, until
bones remain—alone.

Again, much is doubtful in the details of that translation, and the very
word *wynn(e* "joy" has had to be emended from *wenne* of the manuscript.
With that emendation, it seems clear that the flower-colored joyousness
of the opening of the poem leads only to the more sombre joy the grave-
worm feels as it feasts on the corpse of the person who had taken this
world to be a place of delight. We may feel sorrow, we may grieve, as the
grave is dug, and the flesh of the buried dead becomes the worm's feast.
There is a better joy to end the poem (lines 80–87):[71]

Ær þæt eadig geþenceð   he hine þe oftor swenceð,
byrgeð him þa bitran synne,   hogaþ to þære betran wynne,
gemon m*e*orþa lisse.   Her sindon miltsa blisse,
hyhtlice in heofona rice.   Uton nu, halgum gelice
scyldum biscyrede   scyndan generede,
wommum biwerede,   wuldre ge*m*erede,   85
þær moncyn mot,   for Meotude rot,
soðne God geseon   ond aa in sibbe gefean.

---

[71] I have emended in line 85 the second occurrence of *generede* "saved" to
gemerede "purified." The emendation of <n> to <m>, *gemerede*, is slight, just one
minim.

The blessed man had considered that, he had penanced himself all the more often, saved himself from bitter sin, trusting to that better joy, he is mindful of the lenity of rewards. Here are the delights of mercy, full of hope in the heavenly kingdom. Let us now, like the saints cut off from sins, hasten saved, defended from evils, gloriously purified, to where mankind, joyous in the presence of the Lord, shall see the true God and for ever rejoice in peace.

Some Old English Words for "Joy"

The following words for "joy" (and related concepts) are found in these three brief extracts of the Old English *Riming Poem*: *bliss, glæd, gliw, rot, wynn*, and perhaps *eadig* and *liss*; in other parts of the poem there are more words expressing the same range of joyful concepts: *blissian, dream, gefeon* "to rejoice," *fægnian, lust*; perhaps *hyhtgiefu* and *hyhtlic(e, symbel* "banquet, feast(ing)" perhaps symbolic of "belly-joy,"[72] perhaps the often emended *wencyn* understood by Macrae-Gibson as "kindred of joy" (with *wen = wynn*), but more probably "kindred of hope" (here "the band of those once united in vain joyous expectation"). This is a long list of probably subtly distinguished variants of joy. Some quite common Old English words are not in this poem, the common adjectives for "happy," *ge)sælig* and *bliþe* for example, though the related noun *bliss < bliþs* and the verb *blissian* are in. It is never possible to account for the absence of a word in a text, nor usually for the choice of a word.

Shades of meaning are involved for these Old English words, corresponding, though not exactly, to such Modern English words as *delight, to exult, glad, joy, happy, pleasure*, and several more, and all their derivatives in different parts of speech. One is conscious of an inability to produce definitions for these Modern English words such as would help someone who is not an English-speaker toward idiomatic usage. Usually the most one can do by way of definition is to enlist collocational habitualness. The concordances may help us now and again to do the same for Old English: *dream* and *wynn* are quite often used in the verse with *worold*, when such ideas as "worldly joys" are expressed, and so is *hyht* "hope, joy," though less frequently. There

---

[72] Murray, writing the *OED* [then *NED*] entry *belly*, 15.b., in 1887 marked *belly-joy* as obsolete, and he gives no quotation for the compound after c. 1530.

is much talk of joy in *The Riming Poem*, and many words are used expressive of joy. But it is hardly the blissful state as we in the twentieth century and after may think of it, nor even, in Shakespearean terms, with reference to post-medieval literature, "all that Poets faine of Blisse and Ioy."[73] The poet of these difficult, rhyming Old English verses encapsulates a gloomy attitude to joy, that true joy is not for this world, but a joy to which those purged of sin may attain eternally in heaven in the presence of God. It will be rightly argued that such a gloomy view of joy is monastic, but then the extant literature of the Anglo-Saxons was probably written and certainly preserved in the monasteries of England. It is likely that outside the religious houses of the country a different view of joy was held; but the sound of Anglo-Saxon secular voices is not much recorded in verse or prose.

Ælfric Rejoices in God amid the Sorrows of This Cruel World

In the homily by Ælfric (edited by Skeat, and quoted above to illustrate the sin of *Tristitia*, the fifth in his list) immediately after the account of the Sins is his account of the Virtues; and Joy, Spiritual Joy, *Spiritualis Laetitia* in English *gastlic bliss*, comes as the fifth:[74]

> Seo fifte miht is spiritualis laetitia, | þæt is seo gastlice blys, þæt is þæt man on God blyssige | betwux unrotnyssum þysre reðan worulde, | swa þæt we on ungelimpum ormode ne beon, | ne eft on gesælðum to swyðe ne blyssian; | and gif we forleosað þas lænan woruld-ðingc, | þonne sceole we witan þæt ure wunung nis na her | ac is on heofonum gif we hopiað to Gode. | Þyder we sceolan efstan of ðyssere earfoðnysse | mid gastlicre blisse. Þonne bið seo unrotnyss | mid ealle oferswyðed mid urum geðylde.

> The fifth virtue is *spiritualis laetitia*, that is that spiritual joy which is that one rejoice in God amid the sorrows of this cruel world, so that we may not be in despair in misfortunes, nor, on the other

---

[73] Charlton Hinman, ed., *The Norton Facsimile: The First Folio of Shakespeare* (New York, 1968), p. 503, *3 Henry VI*, I.ii.31.

[74] W. W. Skeat, ed., *Aelfric's Lives of Saints*, p. 360, XVI, lines 345–55.

hand, exult too much in good fortune; and if we suffer the loss of the transitory things of this world, then we should know that our dwelling is not at all here but is in heaven if we trust in God. Thither we must hasten from this tribulation with spiritual joy. Then will the sorrow be entirely overcome by our patience.

King Alfred's Joy Hardly Other Than a Sorrowlessness

Though this paper is now on joy and no longer on sorrow, this joyful part looks much the same. It could not be other than gloomy when speaking of joy in this vale of tears as described in Anglo-Saxon times largely by monastic authors as transmitted by cenobitic scribes. We know that King Alfred belonged to the literate laity, an author, though he may have been too high socially to wield a quill or reed. In introducing the joyous Psalm 29, *Exaltabo te Domine—Ic fægnige, Drihten, and þe herige* "I rejoice, Lord, and praise thee"—Alfred dwells on the historical situation as he perceives it politically, that the victory celebrated should lead to the exaltation of God, and not to the glorification of David himself (Psalm 29:6–7):[75]

> Þeah we wepon on æfen he gedeð þæt we
> hlihhað on morgen. Ic cwæð on minum
> wlencum and on minum orsorhnesse: "Ne
> wyrð þisses næfre nan wendincg."

> Though we weep in the evening he causes that we laugh in the morning. I said in my pride and in my sorrowlessness: "Never will there be a change from this."

> ad uesperum demorabitur fletus et ad matutinum laetitia./ ego autem dixi in mea abundantia non mouebor in aeternum.

---

[75] Patrick P. O'Neill, ed., *King Alfred's Old English Prose Translation of the First Fifty Psalms* (Cambridge, Mass., 2001), pp. 132, 220; with my translation. Below it, for comparison, the Latin, *Romanum*; see Sherman M. Kuhn, ed., *The Vespasian Psalter* (Ann Arbor, 1965), pp. 24–25; with the Doway translation (of *Gallicanum*, but no significant difference).

At euening shal weeping abide: and in the morning gladnesse. And
I said in my abundance: I wil not be moued for euer.

The editor of Alfred's psalms, Patrick O'Neill, draws attention to the
rendering of *in mea abundantia*, not positively "in my abundance *or*
prosperity": that is in Old English *on minum genyhtsumnesse* "in my suf-
ficiency" in all the other psalter renderings.[76] Alfred, however, as O'Neill
says, "renders Ro[manum] *abundantia* (v. 7) with *orsorhnesse*, a word he
often employs with unfavorable connotations of false security based on
wealth," and moreover he refers to "my pride" as well as to this false security. For Alfred in the governmental reality of late ninth-century England, but not for the Psalmist, abundance or prosperity in this world is no
more than a sorrowless condition leading to pride.

Harmful Worldly Joys, and the Joy of a Coronation
at Whitsuntide

In the late Old English poem *The Judgment Day II* (line 234), *worulde
gefean* occurs, introducing the pleasures of the world by *deriende* in the
preceding line, "the harmful pleasures of the world." Though repetitiously
expressed, it is a powerful passage, translating Bede's powerful Latin
poem.[77] We see what company worldly pleasures keep in the dark imagi-
nations of the Latin poet and his translator. First, we get a picture of Hell

---

[76] With slight spelling differences; see Phillip Pulsiano, *Old English Glossed
Psalters Psalms 1–50*, Toronto Old English Series, 11 (2001), p. 371.

[77] In *Bede the Poet*, The Jarrow Lecture 1993; reprinted in *Bede and His World*,
2 vols. (n.p., 1994), vol. 2, The Jarrow Lectures 1979–1993, pp. 927–56, at pp. 932–33,
Michael Lapidge finds the "expansive verbosity" of Bede's poem not to his taste, and
uncharacteristic of Bede. Variety of style found in the works of some poets may disturb some critics looking for uniformity of poetic performance. I have used elsewhere
the example of *Gertrude of Wyoming* by Thomas Campbell, the poet of "Ye Mariners
of England," to illustrate a case of such variety, and to warn that no conclusion is to
be drawn from it (E. G. Stanley, "The Verse Forms of Jon the Blynde Awdelay," in *The
Long Fifteenth Century Essays for Douglas Gray*, ed. Helen Cooper and Sally Map-
stone [Oxford, 1997], pp. 99–121, at pp. 102–30). Bede's Latin text is conveniently
printed in Hans Löhe, ed., *Be Dōmes Dæge*, Bonner Beiträge zur Anglistik, 22 (1907),
and as an appendix by Graham D. Caie, ed., *The Old English Poem* Judgement Day II
(Cambridge, 2000), pp. 129–33. The standard edition is by J. Fraipont, *Bedae Venera-
bilis Opera*, 4, Corpus Christianorum series latina, CXXII (1955), pp. 439–44.

and its miseries, perhaps thought all too horribly familiar to the damned earthlings, now without peace or hope, consolation or help, but the ceaseless wailing of a weeping multitude: terror, fear, sorrow, depression (if *sari mod*, line 229, means that), gnashing of teeth, sickness, wrath, and weariness, and the Latin has also trembling and groaning, and fierce indignation. Then they contemplate how, after the Last Judgment, the pleasures of the world, evil and perhaps not so evil, have been left behind (lines 233–40):[78]

> Þonne deriende   gedwinað heonone,
> þysse worulde gefean   gewitað mid ealle
> þonne druncennes   gedwineð mid wistum
> and hleahter and plega   hleapað ætsomne
> and wrænnes eac   gewiteð heonone
> and fæsthafolnes   feor gewiteð,
> uncyst onweg   and ælc gælsa
> scyldig scyndan   on sceade þonne

Then those harmful (joys) will disappear from here, the pleasures of this world will depart withal when drunkenness vanishes with feasting and laughter and sport jump away together and lechery too departs hence and niggardliness departs far, lack of liberality and all kinds of lasciviousness hasten guilty into the shades then.

The Latin source has a somewhat different set of worldly pleasures. Here, too, we are made to feel the miseries of Hell, gnashing of teeth and woes without help or solace. The worldly pleasures that are not to be enjoyed in Hell are in the source (lines 118–19):

> Ebrietas, epulae, risus, petulantia, iocus,
> Dira cupido, tenax luxus, scelerata libido.

Drunkenness, carousals, laughter, sauciness, joking, detestable desire, persistent debauchery, polluted wantonness.

---

[78] The edition used is that by Caie, *The Old English Poem* Judgement Day II, whose text, notes, translation, and glossary have been consulted; they have not, however, been followed without modification. See this edition for the emendations here in italics. See especially p. 124, the note on lines 235–40; whether the expansive translator improves on his source, as Caie avers, is a matter of taste.

In both the Old English and the Latin versions there are introductory fears before we come to more worldly joys to be foregone in Hell. The pleasure of avarice, which the Anglo-Saxon translator introduces, is a well-observed worldly joy: the pleasure of gloating over what one has and holds, the delight in not giving anything away. The lists are interesting in themselves, and the place joy has in them is a reminder that joy is a passion.

Before leaving so sorrowful a subject as the joys described in Old English religious writings, a glance at a short poem in the Anglo-Saxon Chronicle versions reveals a somewhat happier strain of joy. The following lines describe the celebration at Edgar's coronation, A.D. 973, when, as the poet relates, a lot of priests and a great crowd of monks were present: *Þær wæs blis micel | on þam eadgan dæge eallum geworden | þone niða bearn nemnað & cigað Pentecostenes dæg* "There great joy came to all on that blessed day which the children of men name and call the Day of Pentecost."[79] Though Edgar's coronation and the people's rejoicing may be thought a mainly secular subject, it is likely that the poem was written by a priest, and the special joy was that the day appointed for the coronation was Whitsun.

John Audelay's Rapturous Salutation of God the Father and the Son, and of the Virgin Mary

Unlike the spirit in which an Old English poet might have said, with Torrismond in Dryden's at one time highly successful tragicomedy *The Spanish Fryar*,[80] "My joys are gloomy, but withall are great," the spirit of Middle English poetry was less gloomy. John Audelay, in his *Salutationes beate Marie Virginis*, addresses to Mary the first nine stanzas, and then he addresses Jesus in the second half. The end of the poem, a prayer unit twice thirteen lines long, is a summation of the hopes and joy of the devout, and it includes six of the joys of the Virgin, and God the Father is not left out:[81]

---

[79] Janet M. Bately, ed., *The Anglo-Saxon Chronicle MS A*, vol. 3 of a collaborative edition (Cambridge, 1986), p. 76, lines 5b–8a. MS *þonne* emended to *þone*.

[80] Vinton A. Dearing and Alan Roper, eds., *The Works of John Dryden*, 14 (Berkeley, 1992), p. 157, *The Spanish Fryar*, III.iii.290.

[81] E. K. Whiting, *Poems of John Audelay*, pp. 154–55; poem 19, lines 150–75. The editor has joined the couplet (giving instructions to the reader) to the end of the

O Ihesus, when I schal ryse vp þe to se,
O Ihesu, at dredful domysday,
O Ihesu, me grawnt perpetualy
Ioy and blys fore euer and ay.
O þou moder of God, quene of heuen, I say,
O þou lady of þe word, of hele empers,
O þou moder of merce, I þe pray,
Þou grawnt me part of paradyse.
Hayle, maydyn! hayle, moder! hayle, vergyn swete!
Hayle! grawnt ham þe grace þat þus con þe grete.
I pray þe, Fadur omnipotent,
Graunt mercy tofore þy iugement,
And alle þat don ȝow here seruyse
O þou graunt hom part of paradyse,
Allmyȝty God euer-lastyngle:
For holy Gabryel salutacion,
And for þy blesful natiuite
And for þy gloryouse resurexcion,
And for þy merueles ascencion,
And for þe assumpcion of oure ladye,
And for þes ioyes and coronacion
Þat Mary, þy modur, heo had of the,
For heere loue to vs graunt ȝe
To haue forȝeuenes of oure syn,
And from alle sorowes delyuered to be
And to haue euerlastyng ioyes, amen.

O Jesus, when I shall rise to see thee, O Jesus, on the fearful Day
of Judgment, O Jesus, grant to me for all time joy and bliss for ever
and ever. O thou mother of God, queen of heaven I call thee, O thou
sovereign lady of the world, empress of salvation, O thou mother
of mercy, to thee I pray, grant that I may share in paradise. Hail
maiden! hail mother! sweet virgin, hail! hail! give grace to them
that know how to salute thee thus. I pray to thee, Father almighty,
give mercy to those before thee at thy judgment, and to all who
here serve you [Jesus, Mary, and God the Father], O thou [Father]
grant them to share in paradise, almighty and eternal God. For

---

poem, but it is not displayed in the manuscript as a unit with the preceding twenty-
six lines: *Wel ys hym þat wil and may | Say þis prayere eueryday.*

St. Gabriel's greeting, and for thy nativity full of bliss, and for thy resurrection in glory, and for thy ascension in wonder, and for the assumption of our lady, and for these her joys and coronation that Mary, thy mother, had from thee, for her love's sake, do you grant to us to have forgiveness of our sins, and to be delivered from all our sorrows and to have eternal joys. Amen.

In the hymnody of England five joys had been the tradition, and that was augmented to seven, keeping the joys in balance with the seven sorrows of the Virgin; but the number is variable.

Gloomy Joys Not Wholly Forgotten in Middle English

Audelay's salutations belong to a different world of joy and sorrow from that of the Anglo-Saxons. In Middle English the gloomy joys of those earlier days are still found, as in the following lyric that survives with its music. Its first stanza gives a sufficient taste; I quote it from the least reprinted of the three extant manuscripts, Oxford, Bodleian Library MS Digby 86:[82]

Uuorldes blisse ne last non þrowe,
Hit wint and went awei anon.
Þe lengore þat hic hit icnowe
Þe lasse ich finde pris þer on;
For al hit is imeind wiþ kare,
Wiþ serewen and wiþ euel fare
And at þe laste poure and bare,
Hit let mon wen hit ginneþ agon.
Al þe blisse þat is her and þere
Biloukeþ an ende wop and mon.

---

[82] Judith Tschann and M. B. Parkes, eds., *Facsimile of Oxford, Bodleian Library, MS Digby 86*, EETS, supplementary series 16 (1996), p. xxviii, article 57, fol. 163vo–164ro. *Biloukeþ* in the last line of the quotation is not passive, but seems to mean "finally engulfs weeping and lamentation"; that does not give good sense, and, in spite of the unusual word order, the lines mean "Weeping and lamentation finally engulf all the happiness that is anywhere," and that is how the lines are interpreted in my translation; but cf. C. Brown, ed., *English Lyrics of the XIIIth Century*, nos. 46 A and B, line 10, pp. 78 and 80, and glossary s.v. *bi-louken*: there is nowhere in that edition a hint that the word order is unusual.

Worldly joy lasts not a moment; it moves forth and soon goes away. The longer that I have known it the less excellence I find in it, for it is entirely mingled with grief, with sorrows and with wicked behavior, and in the end, [when we are] poor and naked, it abandons us as it begins to leave. Weeping and lamentation finally engulf all the happiness that is anywhere.

Gower's View of Married Bliss, and What the Wife of Bath Thinks of Such Matters

Worldly joy for Florent and his wife is the reward at the end of Gower's "Tale of Florent," when the woman's sovereignty (that is, the inverse of her vow of obedience given to the man in holy matrimony) is the answer to the question, "What do all women desire most?" It is a tale of a beautiful eighteen-year-old princess bewitched into ragged, aged loathliness, a tale grander in rank and moral than that of Papagena, though it lacks the music (*Confessio Amantis*, I, lines 1844–55):[83]

> "... my Stepmoder for an hate,
> Which toward me sche hath begonne,
> Forschop me, til I hadde wonne
> The love and sovereinete
> Of what knight that in his degre
> Alle othre passeth of good name:
> And, as men sein, ye ben the same,
> The dede proeveth it is so;
> Thus am I youres evermo."
> Tho was plesance and joye ynowh,
> Echon with other pleide and lowh:
> Thei live longe and wel thei ferde.

"... my stepmother for hatred, which she entertained toward me, transformed me, till such a time as I might win the love of and sovereignty over whatever knight might in rank and high repute surpass all others: and, as all the world tells me, you are that one. The

---

[83] *English Works of John Gower*, 1:87–88.

very fact [of my restoration] proves it to be true; thus I am yours, and ever shall be." There was delight and joy in plenty, each of the two had laughing dalliance with the other: they lived long, and in prosperity

With whatever innocence we may read this tale in Gower, we may be sure that in the Wife of Bath's telling of much the same tale its innocence and ours soon evaporate in the very fact of the restoration of the loathly hag immediately after Arthur's knight has put himself into her wise governance (*Canterbury Tales*, III (D) 1250–64):[84]

And whan the knyght saw verraily al this,
That she so fair was, / and so yong therto,
For ioye he hente hire / in his armes two,
His herte bathed / in a bath of blisse.
A thousand tyme arewe / he gan hir kisse,
And she obeyed hym / in euery thyng
That myghte do hym plesance / or likyng.
And thus they lyue / vnto hir lyues ende
In parfit ioye:/ and Ihesu Crist vs sende
Housbondes meke, / yonge, / and fressh a bedde,
And grace / t'ouerbyde hem that we wedde;
And eek / I praye Ihesu shorte hir lyues
That noght wol be gouerned / by hir wyues;
And olde / and angry nygardes of dispence
God sende hem soone / verray pestilence!

And when the knight saw all this in truth, that she was so beautiful and moreover so young, he took her in delight into his arms, his heart bathed in a bath of happiness. Again and again, a thousand times he kissed her, and she obeyed him in whatever might give him delight or pleasure. And so they live to the end of their lives in perfect joy. And may Jesus Christ grant us to have compliant and youthful husbands, vigorous in bed, and may he give us grace to outlive those whom we marry; and further I pray that Jesus cut

---

84 F. J. Furnivall, ed., *A Six-Text Print of Chaucer's Canterbury Tales in Parallel Columns*, 4, Chaucer Society Publications, first series (1872), p. 370; cf. *The Riverside Chaucer*, pp. 121–22.

short the lives of those that will not be ruled by their wives; and as for the old—cross, feeble performers—may God quickly send them the very plague.

Conclusion

That pious thought of the Wife of Bath may be a good place to leave the Middle Ages, but not without a backward glance. Piety is in sorrow, but too much sorrow, or sorrow misdirected, is a vice; piety is in joy, though there is not much joy in this world, and what there is may be misdirected. We may think, as in sorrowful mood I do, that the Wife's Prologue and Tale enshrine, wittily told, the tragedy of the aging woman. Regardless of whether we take that or a more joyful view of Alisoun, Wife of Bath, the post-medieval world of English literary sensitivity may seem to begin with her and her Tale in Chaucer's telling. Even tears piteously wept are not all they should be when she sheds them, as explained in the marginal gloss:[85] *Fallere flere, nere statuit deus in mulier,* and in her words, *Deceite, / wepyng, spynnyng God hath yeue | To wommon kyndely,* "Deceiving, weeping, spinning, God has granted to womankind." Piety, and the affections, the emotions, the passions all change their meanings and associations as the centuries go by, in regretful retrospection and in hopeful forward looking: for most writers in the Middle Ages, clerkly or lay, who bear the unbearable sins since the Fall of Man, that sustaining hope of joy is not for this world of sorrows.[86]

---

[85] Cf. the note on *Canterbury Tales,* III (D) 401, in *The Riverside Chaucer,* p. 868; and see the *Six-Text Print,* 4:345, Corpus Christi College, Oxford MS 198, for the Latin.

[86] I am very grateful to professors Roger Dahood and Antonette diP. Healy (Toronto) for reading a draft of this paper and making suggestions for substantial improvements, and for correcting inconsistencies and mistypings. They are of course not responsible for such faults as remain.

Beauvais Romanesque and Suger's Workshop at Saint-Denis: Creative Appropriation and Regional Identity

Elaine M. Beretz
Bryn Mawr College

IN ITS HEYDAY of the eleventh and twelfth centuries, the northern French city of Beauvais saw the construction or renovation of at least twenty-seven sizeable stone structures.[1] That impressive number, comparable to the volume of building in other leading centers of the time such as Paris and Canterbury,[2] attests to Beauvais's economic prosperity and

A grant from the Getty Foundation funded the earliest stages of this project. The rich resources of Bryn Mawr College were instrumental in completing it. The conference "Saint-Denis Revisited: Suger, Art, and Architecture," 24–25 October 2003, sponsored by the Index of Christian Art at Princeton, inspired me to frame the topic as I have. Many generous scholars provided help and encouragement along the way. All those years ago, Pamela Blum allowed me to look over her shoulder while she edited Sumner Crosby's last book for publication. John James sent offprints of some of his works not readily available in the United States. R. Emmet McLaughlin read many drafts of this study. Lindy Grant, Brunhilde Sismondo Ridgway, Thomas Waldman, and the anonymous readers for this journal made invaluable suggestions. I thank them all.

[1] My accounting differs markedly from Murray's estimate of about a dozen or so: Stephen Murray, *Beauvais Cathedral: Architecture of Transcendence* (Princeton, N.J., 1989), p. 8.

[2] Gardner counted thirty-five churches built or renovated in Paris between c. 1125 and c. 1150: Stephen Gardner, "Theory of Centripetal Implosion and the Birth

cultural vitality.[3] Designating the products of this building boom "Beauvais Romanesque" acknowledges an artistic tradition that predates the thirteenth-century choir of the city's more famous cathedral, often cited as the epitome of the Gothic style.

To date, discussions of Beauvais Romanesque have focused mainly on details: individual buildings, components of structure, and ornamental motifs.[4] Any further analysis is hampered by the wholesale destruction of

---

of Gothic Architecture," in *World Art: Themes of Unity in Diversity*, ed. Irving Lavin, Acts of the 26th International Congress of the History of Art (University Park, Penn., 1989), p. 111. Tatton-Brown counted twenty-six churches built or rebuilt in Canterbury from 1066 to the mid-twelfth century: Tim Tatton-Brown, "Medieval Parishes and Parish Churches in Canterbury," in *Church in the Medieval Town*, ed. Terence R. Slater and Gervase Rosser (Aldershot, 1998), pp. 236–71.

[3] Antiquarian scholarship about Beauvais is still fundamental to any study of the city's history: Charles Delettre, *Histoire du diocèse de Beauvais depuis son établissement au 3me siècle, jusqu'au 2 septembre 1792* (Beauvais, 1842–43); Léon-Honoré Labande, *Histoire de Beauvais et ses institutions communales jusqu'au commencement du XVe siècle* (Paris, 1892); Antoine L'Oisel, *Mémoires de pays, villes, comté et comtes, evesché et evesques de renom de Beauvais et Beauvaisis* (Paris, 1617); Pierre Louvet, *Histoire et antiquitez du pais Beauvaisis* (Beauvais, 1631–32); Denis Simon, *Supplément aux mémoires de l'histoire civile et ecclesiastique du Beauvaisis* (Paris, 1704).

Among the more detailed recent works: Charles Fauqueux, *Beauvais, son histoire* (Beauvais, 1935–38; repr. Paris, 1996); Olivier Guyotjeannin, *Episcopus et comes: Affirmation et déclin de la seigneurie épiscopale au nord du royaume de France (Beauvais-Noyon, Xe-début XIIIe siècle)* (Geneva, 1987); Robert Lemaire, *Histoire du département de l'Oise et des pays qui l'ont constitué des origines à nos jours*, vol. 1 (Beauvais, 1993); Michel Roblin, *Terroir de l'Oise aux époques gallo-romain et franque: Peuplement, défrichement, environment* (Paris, 1978); Fernand Vercauteren, *Étude sur les civitates de la Belgique seconde: Contribution à l'histoire urbaine du nord de la France de la fin du IIIe à la fin du XIe siècle* (Brussels, 1934).

[4] I am particularly indebted to two general works about Saint-Étienne: Annie Henwood-Reverdot, *Église Saint-Étienne de Beauvais: Histoire et architecture* (Beauvais, 1982); J. David McGee, "The Romanesque and Early Gothic Church of Saint-Étienne (Saint-Vaast) at Beauvais," (PhD diss., Indiana University, 1983). Although Henwood-Reverdot gave only a cursory discussion of the building boom in the city during the eleventh and twelfth centuries, hers was the first attempt to make order out of the diffuse evidence: *Saint-Étienne*, p. 89. She also discussed many of the remaining scraps of sculpture from the city in comparison to Saint-Étienne's decoration: *Saint-Étienne*, esp. pp. 135–54. McGee accomplished much the same thing for the extant architecture.

For brief surveys of Beauvais's architecture: Maryse Bideault and Claudine Lautier, *Ile-de-France gothique*, vol. 1, *Églises de la vallée de l'Oise et du Beauvaisis* (Paris,

the city's built environment and its once rich archives (see Appendix I). As the plates to this study show only too clearly, what little architecture and sculpture remains is badly damaged, even fragmentary. Air pollution, eroding the regional chalk stone, has effaced many decorative details, and these losses are accelerating. Undertaking a composite analysis of Beauvais Romanesque is in part an act of preservation, which involves photographing and describing what is rapidly deteriorating. Even more importantly, it is an act of reclamation, which required mining antiquarian scholarship, archaeological discoveries, and the few extant written documents for evidence of structures that have left no other traces.[5] The resulting inventory (Appendix II keyed to fig. 20) contains much raw data that merits further study. Here it serves simply as a larger background against which to sort surviving scraps of sculpture and architecture into

---

1987), pp. 70–104; Anne Prache, *Ile-de-France romane* (Paris, 1983), pp. 179–90. For brief surveys of its sculpture: Pierrette Bonnet-Laborderie, *Pierres et bois sculptés du Musée départmental de l'Oise du XIIe au XVIe siècles* (Beauvais, 1975); Margund Claussen, "Romanische Tympana und Türstürze in der Normandie," *Mainzer Zeitschrift* 75 (1980), 1–61; André Lapeyre, *Des façades occidentales de Saint-Denis et de Chartres aux portails de Laon: Études sur la sculpture monumentale dans l'Ile-de-France et les régions voisines au XIIe siècle* (Mâcon, 1960), esp. pp. 21–25 and 201–18; Geneviève L. Micheli, *Décor géometrique dans la sculpture de l'Aisne et de l'Oise au XIe siècle: Recherches sur Morienval et son groupe* (Paris, 1939).

[5] The best sources for archeological activity in Beauvais are the periodic reports in *Gallia: Fouilles et monuments archéologiques en France métropolitaines*. For excavations at Beauvais's cathedral: Émile Chami, "Chronique des fouilles médiévales en France: Oise, Beauvais, Notre-Dame-de-la-Basse-Oeuvre," *Archéologie médiévale* 1 (1971), 277–80; Chami, "Chronique," *Archéologie médiévale* 3–4 (1973–74), 403–4; Chami, "Chronique," *Archéologie médiévale* 6 (1976), 339–42; Chami, "Chronique," *Archéologie médiévale* 7 (1977), 259–61; Chami, "Chronique," *Archéologie médiévale* 11 (1981), 275. For excavations at Saint-Étienne: Jean-Pierre Paquet, "Rapport sur les fouilles de Saint-Étienne," unpublished material, *Médiathèque centrale*, Beauvais. Henwood-Reverdot edited a portion of Paquet's report (*Saint-Étienne*, pp. 228–31). For excavations at Saint-Lucien: Claire Fons, "Abbaye Saint-Lucien de Beauvais: Étude historique et archéologique," *Positions des thèses: École nationale des chartes* (1975), 77; Jacques Henriet, "Saint-Lucien de Beauvais, mythe ou réalité?" *Bulletin monumental* 141 (1983), esp. p. 292 n. 7; Jean Hubert, "Fouilles de Saint-Lucien de Beauvais et les origines du plan tréflé," in his collected essays *Arts et vie sociale de la fin du monde antique au moyen âge: Études d'archéologie et d'histoire. Receuil offert à l'auteur par ses élèves et ses amis* (Geneva, 1977), pp. 537–44; Pierre Leman, "Fouilles de l'abbaye de Saint-Lucien de Beauvais (campagne 1966)," *Cahiers archéologiques de Picardie* 4 (1977), 277–88.

meaningful categories and to locate them within cycles of construction in the city. Both tasks are preliminary to the larger process of analyzing those scraps as a product of their larger urban milieu.

How might we characterize a local style when so much of its art and built environment is destroyed? How might artistic style speak for its historical context when the context itself is now lost?[6] Three patterns within the remnants of Beauvais Romanesque provide some answers to these questions. The first pattern points to a single workshop, generations old, that was centered in Beauvais itself. Buildings constructed in the same period employed identical elements of architecture and decoration, and a good number of those elements were in use from the mid-eleventh century through the late twelfth century. Many of the same elements also appeared in projects scattered throughout this wide diocese (such as those at Trie-Chateau, Bury, and Saint-Germer-de-Fly). This artistic evidence reinforces written sources, discussed below, that point to Beauvais's bishop-counts as the workshop's foremost patrons. Their economic hegemony within the city allowed them to dictate artisan employment and to exercise a measure of control over the workshop's output.

When explored in conjunction with the first, a second pattern permits a more detailed appreciation of the relationship between patrons

---

[6] My assumptions about the interconnections between artistic style and society draw primarily from Schapiro's seminal definition of style as "a motive or pattern, or . . . some directly grasped quality of the work of art, which helps . . . to localize and date the work and to establish connections between groups of works or between cultures. Style here is a symptomatic trait, like the non-aesthetic features of an artifact." Meyer Schapiro, "Style," in *Anthropology Today: An Encyclopedic Inventory*, ed. Alfred L. Kroeber (Chicago, 1953), p. 287. Schapiro's legacy is most evident in the field of archaeology, where his definition of style, and his approach to analyzing it, are essential tools: see esp. the review essay by Michelle Hegmon, "Archaeological Research on Style," *Annual Review of Anthropology* 21 (1992), 517–36. Other studies that have built on Schapiro's theoretical stance include James T. Lang, "Continuity and Innovation in Anglo-Scandinavian Sculpture: A Study of the Metropolitan School at York," in *Anglo-Saxon and Viking Sculpture and its Context*, ed. James T. Lang (Oxford, 1978), pp. 145–72; Steven Lubar and W. David Kingery, eds., *History from Things: Essays on Material Culture* (Washington, D.C., 1993); Jules Prown, "Mind in Matter: An Introduction to Material Culture Theory and Method," *Winterthur Portfolio* 17 (Spring 1982), 1–15; Jules Prown, "Style as Evidence," *Winterthur Portfolio* 15 (Autumn 1980), 197–210; Kendall L. Walton, "Style and the Products and Processes of Art," in *The Concept of Style*, ed. Berel Lang (Ithaca, N.Y., 1987), pp. 45–66.

and artisans. In the second half of the twelfth century, Beauvais's workshop appropriated some innovative architectural and sculptural elements shared with, or borrowed from, the workshop that Abbot Suger (1122–51) had gathered at Saint-Denis. This appropriation is one facet of an alliance between Suger and two of Beauvais's bishop-counts, and it had an immediate effect on the working habits of the Beauvais workshop. Formal similarities to the work done at Saint-Denis show that Beauvais's artisans were open to novelty and participated in the larger artistic developments of their time. At Beauvais, however, the shared elements were transformed in ways that continued the older and distinctive local style. Differences thus assume an importance equal to, if not greater than, similarities. The ways in which the Beauvais elements contrast with their counterparts at Saint-Denis constitute a third pattern that affords the best insight into the formal characteristics of Beauvais Romanesque.

That Beauvais's artisans continued to create variants on the local style throughout the twelfth century challenges conventional ideas about evolution in artistic style, as well as some common assumptions about the mechanics of influence. The response of Beauvais's workshop to innovative elements was rooted in cultural context and historical circumstances, which shaped both the patrons' motives and the working habits of the artisans they employed. Using the cultural exchange with Saint-Denis to explore the interaction between patrons and artisans at Beauvais thus opens a window into the proud regional culture of this once thriving city, now mostly destroyed.[7]

---

[7] Other explorations of artistic style and building practices as functions of social and cultural history include Peter V. Addyman and Richard Morris, eds., *Archaeological Study of Churches* (London, 1976); Sauro Gelichi, ed., "Archeologia dell'architettura," in *Congresso nazionale di archeologia medievale*, Pisa, 29–31 maggio 1997 (Florence, 1997), pp. 437–69; Sheila Bonde and Clarke Maines, "Archaeology of Monasticism: A Survey of Recent Work in France," *Speculum* 63 (1988), 794–825; Stephen Chaplin, "Towards a History of Medieval Architecture," *Art History* 9 (1986), 388–95; Helen Clarke, *Archaeology of Medieval England* (Oxford, 1984), pp. 63–80; Maureen C. Miller, *Bishop's Palace: Architecture and Authority in Medieval Italy* (Ithaca, N.Y., 2000); Richard Morris, "Parish Churches," in *Urban Archaeology in Britain*, ed. John Schofield and Roger Leech (London, 1987), pp. 177–91; André Mussat, "Cathédrales dans leur cités," *Revue de l'art* 55 (1982), 9–22; Charles M. Radding and William W. Clark, *Medieval Architecture, Medieval Learning: Builders and Masters in the Age of Romanesque and Gothic* (New Haven, 1992); Warwick Rodwell, *Archaeology of Religious Places: Churches and Cemeteries in*

Shared Elements, Previous Interpretations, Working Definitions

Two architectonic elements, the rose window and the statue column, are the most striking manifestations of the cultural exchange between Beauvais and Saint-Denis. The same techniques of construction were used to install the north rose of Saint-Étienne, Beauvais (fig. 1), and the west rose of Saint-Denis (fig. 2).[8] The same craft of sculpting produced the statue columns from the cloisters of Saint-Quentin, Beauvais (fig. 3)

Britain (Philadelphia, 1989); Brigitte Bedos-Rezak, "Towards a Cultural Biography of the Gothic Cathedral," in *Artistic Integration in Gothic Buildings*, ed. Virginia C. Raguin et al. (Toronto, 1995), pp. 262–74; B. Sudnér, "Archaeology of the Medieval Churches," in *Study of Medieval Archaeology*, ed. Hans Andersson and Jes Weinberg (Stockholm, 1993), pp. 199–210; Marvin Trachtenberg, "Some Observations on Recent Architectural History," *Art Bulletin* 70 (1988), esp. 220–22.

[8] For the direct influence of Saint-Denis's rose on that at Saint-Étienne: Lindy Grant, *Abbot Suger of Saint-Denis: Church and State in Early Twelfth-Century France* (London, 1998), p. 271; Lapeyre, *Façades*, pp. 21 and 204–8. For the direct influence of Saint-Denis's cloister statues on those from Saint-Quentin: Kathleen D. Nolan, "The Early Gothic Portal of Notre-Dame in Etampes," (PhD diss., Columbia University, 1985), p. 376.

Both roses have undergone extensive restorations. At Saint-Denis, symbols of the evangelists were added in the spandrels and some of the decorated moldings were replaced after 1837 when François Debret restored the façade: Sumner McK. Crosby, *The Royal Abbey of Saint-Denis from its Beginnings to the Death of Suger, 475–1151*, ed. Pamela Z. Blum (New Haven, Conn., 1987), p. 170. Lapeyre expressed skepticism that any of Debret's work reflected the twelfth-century structure or ornament: *Façades*, p. 21. While there is no evidence that the evangelist symbols around the rose were part of the original façade design, the ornament presently in the outer molding of the rose closely followed what survived from the Middle Ages.

The program around Saint-Étienne's rose was never restored, although the figures were grouted in the nineteenth century: Dossier 1 [Saint-Étienne, Beauvais], *Archives des monuments historiques*, Paris (partial edition in Henwood-Reverdot, *Saint-Étienne*, pp. 73–74). The ornament underwent successive restorations in the nineteenth century: Dossiers 1–4 [Saint-Étienne, Beauvais], *Archives des monuments historiques*, Paris (partial edition in Henwood-Reverdot, *Saint-Étienne*, pp. 217–27). Henri LeSecq took a photograph in 1851 of the Beauvais rose [now #76–CTN–87 of the *Caisse nationale des Monuments historiques et des sites*, Paris] before the restorations started. Comparing the LeSecq photograph with the recent one by James Austin (fig. 1) proves that the restoration precisely duplicated the original decoration.

and Saint-Denis (see fig. 4 for the one surviving).[9] Both elements were rare in this period and region. Suger's workshop at Saint-Denis quite possibly invented the rose window.[10] The statue column had been introduced into northern France only recently.[11] More significantly, both elements required extraordinary expertise. Even today, building a rose window into a wall is among a mason's greatest challenges.[12] For all intents and purposes, the statue column was a free-standing sculpture, a medium

---

[9] Saint-Quentin's statue columns are now in the Musée départemental de l'Oise, Beauvais. Badly damaged when the English destroyed the abbey in 1472, the statues lay hidden in a cave under Saint-Quentin until workmen discovered them in 1824. For more detailed analyses and photographs: Pierre Durvin, *Histoire de la Préfecture de l'Oise: Ancienne abbaye Saint-Quentin de Beauvais* (Beauvais, 1978), pp. 105–6 and pls. 2–5; Bernhard Kerber, *Burgund und die Entwicklung des französischen Kathedralskulptur im zwölften Jahrhundert* (Recklinghausen, 1966), pp. 36 and 91 n. 141; Bernhard Kerber, "Vier Skulpturen der Sammlung Ludwig: Zur Entstehung des Säulenfigur," *Aachen Kunstblätter* 39 (1969), 85–88; Lapeyre, *Façades*, pp. 212–13; McGee, "Saint-Étienne," pp. 151–52; Nolan, "Notre-Dame," pp. 373–76 and 386; Bonnet-Laborderie, *Pierres*, pp. 4 and 7.

Although the statue columns from Saint-Quentin are broken off below the knees, their full height was c. 1.15m: Bonnet-Laborderie, *Pierres*, p. 7. This is commensurate with the 1.17m of the statue column surviving from Saint-Denis's cloister: Crosby, *Royal Abbey*, p. 196. Saint-Denis's statue column is now in the Metropolitan Museum of Art, New York. For more detailed analyses: C. Edson Armi, *The "Headmaster" of Chartres and the Origins of "Gothic" Sculpture* (University Park, Penn., 1994), pp. 92–98; Pamela Z. Blum, "The Statue-Column of a Queen from St.-Thibaut, Provins, in the Glencairn Museum," *Gesta* 29 (1990), 227–28 (with discussion of its restoration, p. 232 n. 41); Heinrich G. Franz, *Roman tardif et le premier gothique*, trans. Adelheid Gascuel (Paris, 1973), p. 104; Vera K. Ostoia, "A Statue from Saint-Denis," *Metropolitan Museum of Art Bulletin* 13, no. 10 (June 1955), 298–304; Léon Pressouyre, "Did Suger Build the Cloister?" in *Abbot Suger and Saint-Denis: A Symposium*, ed. Paula L. Gerson (New York, 1986), pp. 236–38.

[10] Crosby, *Royal Abbey*, p. 122. Among those who followed Crosby: Henwood-Reverdot, *Saint-Étienne*, p. 131; Prache, *Ile-de-France*, pp. 75–76; Conrad Rudolph, *Artistic Change at Saint-Denis: Abbot Suger's Program and the Early Twelfth-Century Controversy over Art* (Princeton, N.J., 1990), p. 100 n. 19. In another place, however, Crosby qualified this by asserting that the rose at Saint-Denis was the first in a *western* façade: *Royal Abbey*, p. 282.

[11] Most recently: Willibald Sauerländer, "Die gestörte Ordnung oder 'le chapiteau historié,'" in *Studien zur Geschichte der europäischen Skulptur im 12. und 13. Jahrhunderts*, ed. Herbert Beck and Kerstin Hengevoss-Dürkop (Frankfurt am Main, 1994), esp. pp. 432–36, with a summary of previous debates.

[12] John James, *Contractors of Chartres* (Dooralong, 1979), esp. p. 495.

virtually unknown in the Early Middle Ages.[13] Beauvais's artisans fully mastered both techniques. In fact, Saint-Étienne's rose window exceeded the diameter of Saint-Denis's by half a meter and consequently was the more difficult to assemble.[14]

There is also evidence of shared ornamental motifs, especially a naturalistic palmette. An updated version of the venerable acanthus foliage, palmette ornament consists primarily of fleshy leaves arranged in a fan shape. The basic form is amenable to an almost infinite number of variations: single leaves with lobes closed or open; a spare geometric symmetry or a lush curling of the lobes; two or more leaves linked with thick tendrils; bunches of leaves or leaves in profile spreading out across a surface; fruit and animals intertwined in the foliage, etc. All these variants were deeply drilled and carved in high relief, often exhibiting a complex layering of ornament. Carving palmette ornament, as did constructing the rose window and sculpting the statue columns, demanded a high degree of skill.[15]

At Beauvais, Saint-Étienne's rose window (figs. 1, 5, and 6) displays three variants of palmette along its "rims," three more in its "spokes," and yet another along the molding uniting the two smaller windows beneath the rose. Saint-Étienne's north door (figs. 7 and 8) is richer still. A variety of figures inhabit palmette scrollwork in all three recesses of the archivolt. Two other variants of palmette appear in the tympanum

---

[13] One larger slab of stone was worked into two attached volumes. The figure itself was carved almost in the round and backed by a column designed to slot into a portal jamb or a cloister arcade: see esp. Leslie Brubaker, "Column Figure," in *Dictionary of the Middle Ages*, ed. Joseph Strayer et al., vol. 3 (New York, 1983), p. 487. Also Jean Bony, introduction to *Studies in Western* Art, vol. 1, *Romanesque and Gothic Art*, ed. Millard Meiss, Acts of the 20th International Congress of the History of Art (Princeton, N.J., 1963), p. 84; Franz, *Roman tardif*, pp. 105 and 112; Louis Grodecki, "La 'première sculpture gothique': Wilhelm Vöge et l'état actuel des problèmes," *Bulletin monumental* 117 (1959), 271–72.

[14] For the dimensions of the Beauvais rose: Bideault and Lautier, *Ile-de-France*, 1:98; Jean Bony, *French Gothic Architecture of the Twelfth and Thirteenth Centuries* (Berkeley, 1983), p. 498 n. 28. For the challenges of constructing the rose: Elaine M. Beretz, "Adjustments for the Innovative: Installing the Rose-Window into the North Façade of Saint-Étienne, Beauvais," *AVISTA Forum Journal* 14 (2004), 17–24.

[15] Ann S. Zielinski, "Variations of the Acanthus and Other Foliate Designs at St.-Martin-des-Champs, Paris," in *Acanthe dans la sculpture monumentale de l'antiquité à la Renaissance* (Paris, 1993), pp. 327–44.

and its frame; yet another, in the lintel and framing the archivolt; six different (but equally intricate) tendrils, in the capitals that support the archivolt. The campaign responsible for Saint-Étienne's rose window and north door, begun after 1140, marked the first known appearance of palmette in Beauvais.[16] As I will show below, that ornament differs markedly in refinement and depth from earlier decoration in the church and the city as a whole.

The ornament had appeared in Paris at least a decade earlier. Palmette decorates capitals in the choir of Saint-Martin-des-Champs, dated c. 1130–40.[17] More significant for this argument, palmette covers the inner recesses of Saint-Denis's rose window (fig. 2), where it is inhabited by masks. Palmette also inlays the shafts and capitals of Saint-Denis's western portal (see the lower half of fig. 9). Both the rose and the portal are dated c. 1135–40.[18] A *bas-relief* made at Saint-Denis between 1140 and 1150 (fig. 10) exhibits an even wider variety of palmette: a thick band of one species frames the whole; variants decorate the capitals and shafts of the arcade columns; other forms run along each arch; still others are nestled in the spaces between the arches.[19] Ambulatory capitals carved at Saint-Germain-des-Prés in those same years combine palmette foliage with animals and human figures.[20] The *bas-relief* from Saint-Denis and

---

[16] This is a revised dating for Saint-Étienne's rose window and door. See below, note 26.

[17] For the connections of Saint-Martin's ornament with that at Beauvais: Zielinski, "Variations," esp. p. 340, figs. 3–11 and fig. 20. For connections of Beauvais's architecture with that at Saint-Martin: Jacques Henriet, "Édifice de la première génération gothique: L'abbatiale de Saint-Germer-de-Fly," *Bulletin monumental* 143 (1985), 125; McGee, "Saint-Étienne," p. 142 n. 54.

[18] Calculated, that is, between the presumed opening of Suger's workshop in c. 1135 and the consecration of the narthex in 1140: Crosby, *Royal Abbey*, pp. 123–24; Grant, *Abbot Suger*, p. 245; Radding and Clark, *Medieval Architecture*, p. 64.

[19] Crosby had dated the *bas-relief* to the early 1140s: Sumner McK. Crosby, *The Apostle Bas-Relief at Saint-Denis* (New Haven, Conn., 1972), pp. 24 and 72. Blum dated it to the mid-1140s: "Statue Column," p. 232 n. 43. Sauerländer preferred c. 1150: Willibald Sauerländer, Review of *The Apostle Bas-Relief*, by Sumner McK. Crosby, *Art Bulletin* 56 (1974), 439.

[20] For the connections between Saint-Germain and Saint-Denis: Philippe Plagnieux, "Abbatiale de Saint-Germain-des-Prés et les débuts de l'architecture gothique," *Bulletin monumental* 158 (2000), esp. pp. 18–24. The choir of Saint-Germain was begun in 1140 and consecrated in 1163. The most recent dating of the capitals sets them close to 1150: Plagnieux, "Saint-Germain," 7–8 and 63. This

the capitals at Saint-Germain testify to the ornament's continued (and varied) use in Paris through the mid-twelfth century.

The elaborate ornament along the outer circumference of Saint-Étienne's rose (figs. 1, 5, and 6) approaches the depth and crispness of work done in Paris, but the overall design of the rose façade strikingly distinguishes it from the corresponding work at Saint-Denis. Saint-Denis's rose (fig. 2) was fully integrated into the structure of the wall. Its purpose was to provide light to the upper chapel of the narthex. The rose's decoration was spare, confined to the recesses or tucked into the corners of its frame. By contrast, Beauvais's rose intrudes into the façade structure. Its rims spill out onto the surrounding masonry; the sculpted program at its periphery is tacked onto the wall. While it also provides light to the transept interior, its purpose was to mark off the space on the exterior. The statue columns from Saint-Quentin (fig. 3) and Saint-Denis (fig. 4) were worked in equally contrasting styles. The Saint-Denis statue has an elongated, slender line. Its proportions are balanced. Thin, carefully incised folds emphasize the fall of drapery. Restrained gestures articulate a calm demeanor. The Saint-Quentin statues are bulkier, with broader gestures. Thick bands, formed of double incisions, rim deeply cushioned folds across the torsos. The hands and heads are disproportionately large.

---

chronology assumes that Saint-Germain's choir derived its design from that of Saint-Denis. On that basis alone, Héliot had specified a span of dates for Saint-Germain's choir between 1150 and 1155: Pierre Héliot, "Remarques sur l'abbatiale de Saint-Germer et sur les blocs de façade du XIIe siècle," *Bulletin monumental* 114 (1956), 111. Bideault and Lautier followed Héliot when they (as did Plagnieux) dated the choir and the capitals, after c. 1150: *Ile-de-France*, 1:250.

This dating is by no means certain and is caught up in wider controversies about the place of Saint-Germain's choir in the evolution of the Gothic style in Paris. Clark favored a dating for the choir in the 1130s and 1140s, seeing it as one venue for experiments that led to the more polished construction of Saint-Denis's choir between 1140 and 1144: William W. Clark, "Spatial Innovations in the Chevet of Saint-Germain-des-Prés," *Journal of the Society of Architectural Historians* 38 (1979), 355 n. 21. McGee cautiously followed Clark, dating the choir and its capitals before 1150: McGee, "Saint-Étienne," p. 178. Bony was more explicit. He considered Saint-Germain a typical Parisian structure of the 1120s and early 1130s and identified Saint-Germain as the direct inspiration for the design of Saint-Denis's choir: Jean Bony, "What Possible Sources for the Chevet of Saint-Denis?" in *Abbot Suger*, ed. Gerson, pp. 134–35.

Saint-Étienne's north façade and Saint-Quentin's cloister statues, in short, present what can only be termed an archaic appearance, since they exhibit characteristics usually associated with the great Romanesque façades of previous decades.[21] This convinced Arthur Kingsley Porter that the Beauvais works predated those at Saint-Denis. In this regard, Porter relied on Eugene Lefèvre-Pontalis, who suggested that the Beauvais rose had been the model for that of Saint-Denis.[22] Until recently, this hypothetical relationship with Saint-Denis has been the primary criterion for dating Beauvais's sculpture and architecture. It had even wider implications, making Beauvais an important field of investigation for the still mysterious origins of the Gothic style.[23]

---

[21] For archaizing décor in other monuments of this period: Willibald Sauerländer, "Romanesque Sculpture in its Architectural Context," in *The Romanesque Frieze and Its Spectator*, ed. Deborah Kahn (London, 1992), p. 32; George Zarnecki, "English Twelfth-Century Sculpture and Its Resistance to St. Denis," in his collected essays *Studies in Romanesque Sculpture* (London, 1979).

[22] Arthur K. Porter, *Romanesque Sculpture of the Pilgrimage Roads,* vol. 1 (Boston, 1923), p. 221. He had also asserted this in his earlier architectural survey, *Medieval Architecture*, vol. 2 (New York, 1909), p. 105. Among those who followed him: Durvin, *Saint-Quentin*, p. 106; Henwood-Reverdot, *Saint-Étienne*, pp. 131–32; Kerber, *Burgund und die Entwicklung*, p. 91 n. 141; McGee, "Saint-Étienne," esp. pp. 150–52.

Eugène Lefèvre-Pontalis, *Architecture religieuse dans l'ancien diocèse de Soissons au XIe et XIIe siècle*, vol. 1 (Paris, 1894), p. 134. Among those who followed him: Helen J. Dow, "The Rose-Window," *Journal of the Warburg and Courtauld Institutes* 20 (1957), 248–97, 256, and 269; Franz, *Roman tardif*, p. 24; Walter Wulf, *Die Kapitellplastik des Sugerbaus von Saint-Denis* (Frankfurt am Main, 1979), pp. 93–94.

[23] Literature exploring the origin and spread of the Gothic style is vast and contentious. Most helpful for clarifying the issues at hand: Jean Bony, "Genèse de l'architecture gothique: Accident ou nécessité?" *Revue de l'art* 58–59 (1982–83), 9–20; Franz, *Roman tardif*; Gardner, "Centripetal Implosion," pp. 111–16; Grant, *Abbot Suger*, esp. pp. 239–58 and 304–7; Grodecki, "Première," pp. 265–89; Pierre Héliot, "Oeuvres capitales du gothique français primitif et l'influence de l'architecture anglaise," *Wallraf-Richartz Jahrbuch* 20 (1958), 85–114; Pierre Héliot, "Diversité de l'architecture gothique à ses débuts en France," *Gazette des beaux-arts*, 6th ser., 69 (1967), 269–306; Pierre Héliot, "Du roman au gothique: Échecs et réussites," *Wallraf-Richartz Jahrbuch* 35 (1973), 109–48; Plagnieux, "Saint-Germain," pp. 6–86; Radding and Clark, *Medieval Architecture*, esp. pp. 100–142; Willibald Sauerländer, "Sculpture on Early Gothic Churches: State of Research and Open Questions," *Gesta* 9 (1970), 32–48; Willibald Sauerländer, "Style or Transition? Fallacies of Classification Discussed in the Light of German Architecture, 1190–1260," *Architectural History* 30 (1987), 1–29; the essays "Transition from Romanesque to Gothic," in *Studies in Western Art*, ed. Meiss, 1:81–158.

The opinions of Porter and Lefèvre-Pontalis have conditioned most subsequent assessments of Beauvais's artistic heritage. Recent archaeology at Saint-Denis, teamed with new information about Beauvais, makes it necessary to rethink their connection.[24] Most important, it is now possible to date the products of the two workshops with greater precision than before and to date them independently of each other. Saint-Denis's rose, one of the last elements completed in the narthex, dates immediately before the consecration ceremony of 1140.[25] A new chronology of c. 1140–50 for the Beauvais rose dates it after Saint-Denis's rose was completed.[26] Saint-Denis's cloister was built sometime between 1140 and

---

[24] For the continuing excavations at Saint-Denis: Michaël Wyss and Nicole Meyer-Rodrigues, eds., *Atlas historique de Saint-Denis: Des origines au XVIIIe siècle* (Paris, 1996); Pamela Z. Blum, *Early Gothic Saint-Denis: Restorations and Survivals* (Berkeley, 1992). For the Parisian context of Suger's building campaign: Bony, "What Possible Sources?" in *Abbot Suger*, ed. Gerson, esp. pp. 131–42; William W. Clark, "Merovingian Revival Acanthus Capitals at Saint-Denis," in *Acanthe*, pp. 345–56; William W. Clark, "'The Recollection of the Past Is the Promise of the Future': Continuity and Contextuality: Saint-Denis, Merovingians, Capetians, and Paris," in *Artistic Integration*, ed. Raguin et al., pp. 92–113; Stephen Gardner, "Église Saint-Julien de Marolles-en-Brie et ses rapports avec l'architecture parisienne de la génération de Saint-Denis," *Bulletin monumental* 144 (1986), 7 and 27 n. 2; Gardner, "Centripetal Implosion," pp. 111–16; Grant, *Abbot Suger*, pp. 71–72, 260–63, and 300; Henriet, "Saint-Lucien," p. 290; Nolan, "Notre-Dame," pp. 307–8, 339–41, and 348; Prache, *Ile-de-France*, pp. 31–82.

Here, too, there are crucial gaps in evidence, since so much of the art and a good part of the archives are lost: Blum, *Early Gothic*; Crosby, *Royal Abbey*, pp. 192–201; Fabienne Joubert, "Recent Acquisitions, Musée de Cluny, Paris: Tête de Moïse provenant du portail droite de Saint-Denis," *Gesta* 28 (1989), 107; Charles T. Little, "Monumental Sculpture at Saint-Denis under the Patronage of Abbot Suger," in *The Royal Abbey of Saint-Denis in the Time of Abbot Suger (1122–1151)*, ed. Sumner McK. Crosby et al. (New York, 1981), pp. 25–31; Léon Pressouyre, "Tête de reine du portail central de Saint-Denis," *Gesta* 15 (1976), 151–60; Nolan, "Notre-Dame," pp. 245–48; Stephen K. Scher, ed., *Renaissance of the Twelfth Century: An Exhibition* (Providence, R.I., 1969), pp. 149–55.

[25] See especially Stephen Gardner, "Two Campaigns in Suger's Western Block at St.-Denis," *Art Bulletin* 66 (1984), 574–87. Among those who followed him: Crosby, *Royal Abbey*, pp. 159–61; Radding and Clark, *Medieval Architecture*, pp. 64–69; Rudolph, *Artistic Change*, p. 107 n. 12. In an argument to the contrary, Grant asserted a break in construction between the eastern and the western bays of the narthex: *Abbot Suger*, pp. 253–55.

[26] The traditional dating of the Beauvais rose at c. 1120–40 remains stubbornly entrenched in the scholarly literature. The author traces the long chain of scholarship

1170.[27] The Saint-Quentin statue columns recently have been dated c. 1160–70, making them contemporary with those at Saint-Denis, or a bit later.[28]

The seemingly older style of the Beauvais works does not date them before their counterparts at Saint-Denis. On the surface, this runs counter to deeply ingrained notions of periodization in medieval art. According to the strictest of these notions, the consecration of Saint-Denis's narthex was the critical moment in the artistic history of the twelfth century. It drew a clear line between the beginning of the Gothic period and the end of the Romanesque. Traces of that notion still linger. They result in a tendency, even now and even in the most careful scholarship, to value all

---

derived from that dating and explores its implications for the historiography of Gothic origins in *A Question of Chronology: Dating the North Rose of Saint-Étienne, Beauvais,* forthcoming in the monograph series of the American Philosophical Society. Close analysis of the façade structure, undertaken in light of archaeological discovery at Beauvais, instead dates Saint-Étienne's rose and its decoration between c. 1140 and c. 1150. In the *Question of Chronology,* the author also explores this evidence in detail, confirms the new dating for the rose window, and revises the chronology for the rest of the building. Her findings are summarized below and in #17 in Appendix II. For much shorter assertions of this new dating for the Beauvais rose: Bony, *French Gothic,* p. 494 n. 28; Chantal Hardy, "Rose de Notre-Dame de Noyon et sa place dans la technique du troisième chantier de la cathédale," *RACAR: Revue d'art canadian* 13, no. 1 (1986), 7 and 20; Henwood-Reverdot, *Saint-Étienne,* p. 132: McGee, "Saint-Étienne," esp. pp. 150–52, 188, 214, 226, and 251.

[27] Dates for Saint-Denis's cloister have not been established with any precision. Blum argued for the 1150s: "Statue-Column," pp. 232 n. 41 and 233 n. 43. Pressouyre preferred the 1160s, perhaps as late as 1170: "Cloister," pp. 242 and 244 n. 29. Most recently, Grant dated the cloister between c. 1145 and c. 1155, but felt that it was most likely begun in the late 1140s: *Abbot Suger,* pp. 251–52.

[28] Dates for Saint-Quentin's cloister are no more precise than those for the cloister at Saint-Denis. This is largely because the two had long been dated relative to one another, with the Saint-Quentin statue columns assumed to have been earlier than the one surviving from Saint-Denis. In the 1960s, Kerber, the first scholar to date the Saint-Quentin figures independently of Saint-Denis, proposed a dating in the mid-twelfth century: *Burgund und die Entwicklung,* p. 91 n. 141; "Vier Skulpturen," pp. 84–88. Nolan followed Kerber: "Notre-Dame," pp. 373 and 376. Comparison with the more securely dated figures at Gercy, Angers, and Chartres, however, has indicated that the Saint-Quentin statue columns were more likely carved between 1160 and 1170: Walter Cahn, "Portail à statues-colonnes oublié," *Bulletin monumental* 130 (1972), 45–50; Alain Erlande-Brandenburg, preface to Bonnet-Laborderie, *Pierres,* p. 4.

art and architecture after Saint-Denis only insofar as each work anticipates the characteristics of the mature Gothic style.[29] The corresponding
tendency is to judge the persistence of older styles negatively: as a lack of
skill, unwillingness to try a new way of working, failure to understand
innovation, or stubborn resistance to change.[30] The traditional bent of
Beauvais's workshop has been characterized at different times in all these
ways.[31] These negative evaluations stem from a larger assumption that
regional artistic traditions were and are "provincial," that their style is out

---

[29] For a recent critique of this tendency: Lawrence R. Hoey, "A Critical Account
of Suger's Architecture at Saint-Denis," *AVISTA Forum Journal* 12 (1999), 12–19. See
also Bony, "Genèse," pp. 9–20; Dorothy M. Gillerman, "Cosmopolitanism and *Cam-
panilismo:* Gothic and Romanesque in the Siena Duomo Façade," *Art Bulletin* 81
(1999), 437–55; Stephen Murray, Review of *French Gothic Architecture of the Twelfth
and Thirteenth Centuries*, by Jean Bony, *Art Bulletin* 69 (1987), 300; Sauerländer,
"Sculpture," esp. pp. 40–41; Sauerländer, "Style or Transition?" pp. 1–29.

[30] For the idea that traditional artisans lacked skill, see Stoddard's discussion
of the sculptors of the portal at Toulouse: Whitney S. Stoddard, *Sculptors of the
West Portals of Chartres Cathedral: Their Origins in Romanesque and Their Role in
Chartrain Sculpture* (New York, 1987), p. 46. For the idea that traditional artisans
lacked the will to change, see Héliot's discussion of the sculptor of Saint-Germer:
"Saint-Germer," p. 112; and Brouillette's discussion of the sculptor of Notre-Dame-
en-Vaux: Diane C. Brouillette, "Early Gothic Sculpture of Senlis Cathedral," (PhD
diss., University of California, Berkeley, 1981), p. 364. For the idea that traditional
artisans failed to understand the innovative: Rudolph, *Artistic Change*, p. 47; George
Zarnecki, "Transition from Romanesque to Gothic in English Sculpture," in *Studies in Western Art*, ed. Meiss, 1:155. For the idea that traditional artisans stubbornly resisted change: Jean Bony, "Resistance to Chartres in the Early Thirteenth-
Century Architecture," *Journal of the British Archaeological Association*, 3rd ser.,
20–21 (1957–58), 35–52; Robert Branner, *Burgundian Gothic Architecture* (London,
1960), esp. pp. 50 and 83; Brouillette, "Senlis," p. 48; Héliot, "Oeuvres," pp. 109–10;
Zarnecki, "English Twelfth-Century Sculpture," pp. 83–92. Closely related to this is
Franz's characterization of the Gothic style as progressive: *Roman tardif,* esp. pp. 5,
18, and 99.

[31] To name but a few examples: Branner discussed in some detail what he saw as
Beauvais's resistance to change: Robert Branner, "Gothic Architecture 1160–80 and
its Romanesque Sources," in *Studies in Western Art*, ed. Meiss, 1:92–104. Greenhill
called the Saint-Quentin statue columns "primitive": Eleanor S. Greenhill, "Eleanor, Abbot Suger, and Saint-Denis," in *Eleanor of Aquitaine: Patron and Politician*,
ed. William W. Kibler (Austin, 1976), p. 109 n. 91. Lapeyre felt that the clientele of
Beauvais, like other people north of the Seine, would be shocked by innovations:
Façades, p. 29.

of step with the major trends of its time, maladroit, and creatively rigid.[32] The remnants of Beauvais Romanesque on their own argue against such judgments. The lively style is far from unskilled. Since they were open to imports, Beauvais's artisans were anything but isolated.

The negative connotations of "provincial" are a distant echo of a nine-teenth-century French political outlook that associated regionalism in art and in politics with the clericalism and feudalism the Revolution claimed it had abolished. In such a view, all expressions of regional character were properly subordinated to a French nation with Paris at the center. This complicates study of the past, since throughout the Middle Ages the ter-ritory that would become France was polycentric rather than national, regional rather than centralized. In that period, "France" was nothing more (or less) than a jumbled collection of separate units of ecclesiasti-cal or secular feudalism. On the elite level, regional self-definition was a powerful combination of military command and economic privilege. Beauvais's bishop-counts could add the binding force of religion to the mix. Beneath the feudal hierarchy, there was a local culture of longstand-ing and particular depth that predated the feudal age and was often inde-pendent of noble culture.[33]

A French nation with Paris at its center and Gothic as its signature style was by no means a foregone conclusion in the twelfth century. Appreci-

---

[32] For example, Branner contrasted rural churches in the Romanesque style with the "modern" churches built by larger workshops in courts or cities, which he saw as more open to new influences: *Burgundian Gothic*, p. 81. Franz considered the possibility that Romanesque survivals in central Germany were due to a lack of communication with the Ile-de-France: *Roman tardif*, p. 99. Micheli defined art as provincial when it is based on traditional forms, and characterizes it as "popular" rather than professional: *Décor*, pp. 77 and 84.

[33] Older, but still valuable, surveys of the question include Pierre Francastel, *Humanisme roman: Critique des théories sur l'art du XIe siècle en France* (Paris, 1942); Josiah C. Russell, *Medieval Regions and Their Cities* (Bloomington, Ind., 1972), esp. pp. 15–30. More recent discussions include Brigitte Bedos-Rezak, "French Medieval Regions," *Historical Reflections/ Reflexions historiques* 19 (1993), 151–66; Bony, "Introduction," p. 83; Tina Waldeier Bizzarro, *Romanesque Architectural Crit-icism: A Pre-History* (Cambridge, 1992), esp. pp. 13 and 153–57; Wayne Dynes, "Art, Language and the Romanesque," *Gesta* 28 (1989), 6–7; Elizabeth M. Hallam and Judith Everard, *Capetian France, 987–1328*, 2nd ed. (London, 2001), esp. pp. 27–63; Elizabeth Liskar, ed., *Probleme und Methoden der Klassifizierung*, Acts of the 25th International Congress of the History of Art, vol. 3 (Vienna, 1985); Radding and Clark, *Medieval Architecture*, esp. pp. 96–142.

ating the vestiges of a regional and pre-Gothic artistic style at Beauvais in their own right requires redefining "provincial" as one expression of a proud regional culture. This was the normal state of affairs. It seems unreasonable to expect it to change with every passing fashion. As I will argue below, the ways in which the Beauvais Romanesque style transformed Parisian imports were deliberately archaic and were intended to express a carefully cultivated independence.[34]

Given the loss of so much other evidence about medieval Beauvais, exploring its cultural exchange with Saint-Denis has proven a most effective hook on which to hang many of the scattered remnants, documentary as well as artistic, of Beauvais's regional culture. Like all other sharp instruments, this hook requires careful handling. At every stage, it is necessary to pay equal attention to the new elements Beauvais imported from Paris and to the established practices that transformed those elements. In particular, it is crucial to avoid designating the Saint-Denis elements as the models and the Beauvais elements as their copies; that is, valuing the Beauvais work only to the extent that it reproduced Saint-Denis's version of the same element. Doing so, as Eric Fernie has pointed out, would make "influence the dynamic agent and the person influenced into a passive recipient." In reality, responding to influence is a much more subtle process by which (again to quote Fernie) "the person influenced . . . does all the work in choosing, altering and reusing in order to produce something new."[35] Thinking of influence in this way focuses on the

---

[34] For this sort of artistic independence in other regions: Héliot, "Diversité," esp. pp. 273–74 and 292–94; Plagnieux, "Saint-Germain," pp. 6–87.

[35] Both quotations, and indeed much of this paragraph, draw from Eric C. Fernie, *Art History and Its Methods: A Critical Anthology /Selection and Commentary* (London, 1995), p. 361.

The question of influence is a popular topic in recent critical literature. Most helpful for the subject at hand are Michael Baxandall, *Patterns of Intention: On the Historical Explanation of Pictures* (New Haven, Conn., 1985), pp. 58–62; Hans J. Böker, "The Bishop's Chapel of Hereford Cathedral and the Question of Architectural Copies in the Middle Ages," *Gesta* 37 (1998), 44–54; Robert Deshman, "Anglo-Saxon Art after Alfred," *Art Bulletin* 56 (1974), 176–200; Thomas W. Gaehtgens, ed., *Künstlerisher Austauch/ Artistic Exchange*, Acts of the 28th International Congress of the History of Art, 3 vols. (Berlin, 1993); Suzanne Lewis, "Henry III and the Gothic Rebuilding of Westminster Abbey: The Problematics of Context," *Traditio* 50 (1995), 129–72; Robert S. Nelson and Richard Shiff, eds., *Critical Terms for Art History* (Chicago, 1996), s.v. "Originality" and "Appropriation," pp. 103–28; Plagnieux,

conscious strategies that shape artistic style, rather than the unconscious impulses usually discussed under the rubric of "inspiration" or audience response.[36] In the case of Beauvais Romanesque, the person influenced was not an individual, but two parties in the city working in close cooperation: the bishop-counts and the artisans they employed.

Written documents and patterns of patronage in other places, discussed below, make clear what motivated Beauvais's bishop-counts to sponsor art. The decisions of the artisans are less readily apparent, although what we know about the crafts of building and sculpting in this period provides some essential clues. At Beauvais as elsewhere, artistic style resulted from a carefully organized method of production, rather than one individual's self-expression. As a consequence, style was slow to change. Sculptors and masons worked as their masters had and passed the methods they had learned on to their apprentices. The use of templates for ornament, also handed down from generation to generation,

---

"Saint-Germain," esp. pp. 75–76; Corine Schleif, "Hands that Appoint, Anoint, and Ally: Late Medieval Donor Strategies for Appropriating Approbation through Painting," *Art History* 16 (1993), 1–32; Anat Tcherikover, "Concerning Angoulême, Riders, and the Art of the Gregorian Reform," *Art History* 13 (1990), 425–57.

[36] For conscious strategies in artistic production: esp. Xavier Barral i Altet, ed., *Artistes, artisans et production artistique au moyen âge*, 3 vols. (Paris, 1986–90); Lynn T. Courtenay, ed., *Engineering of Medieval Cathedrals* (Aldershot, 1997); Roland Recht and Jacques Le Goff, eds., *Batisseurs des cathédrales gothiques* (Strasbourg, 1989). More general surveys: Günther Binding, *Baubetrieb im Mittelalter* (Darmstadt, 1993); Jean Gimpel, *Cathedral Builders*, trans. Carl F. Barnes, Jr., (New York, 1961); Pierre Du Colombier, *Chantiers des cathédrales: Ouvriers, architectes, sculpteurs*, rev. ed. (Paris, 1973); Georges Duby, *Age of the Cathedrals: Art and Society, 980–1420*, trans. Barbara Thompson (Chicago, 1981), pp. 30–135; Karl A. Nauratil, "Labor, Patronage and Social Structure," (PhD diss., University of Toronto, 1986). Also of importance: Walter Cahn, "Artist as Outlaw and *Apparatchik*: Freedom and Constraint in the Interpretation of Medieval Art," in *Renaissance*, ed. Scher, pp. 10–14; Nicola Coldstream, *Masons and Sculptors* (Toronto, 1991); Alain Erlande-Brandenburg, *Du pierre, d'or et de feu: Création artistique au moyen âge, IVe–XIIe siècle* (Paris, 1999), esp. pp. 121–237; John H. Harvey, *Mediaeval Craftsmen* (New York, 1975); Douglas Knoop and Grace P. Jones, *Mediaeval Mason: An Economic History of English Stone Building in the Later Middle Ages and Early Modern Times* (Manchester, 1949); Andrew Martindale, *Rise of the Artist in the Middle Ages and Early Renaissance* (New York, 1972); Wolgang Schöller, *Die rechtliche Organisation des Kirchenbaues im Mittelalter vornehmlich des Kathedralbaues: Baulast-Bauherrenschaft-Baufinanzierung* (Cologne, 1989).

ensured consistency over time and from location to location.[37] Recent studies have demonstrated the remarkable uniformity with which sculptors rendered small details, even when they were experimenting with new techniques or shaping their work to new tastes.[38] Architectural style and building practice were quite idiosyncratic, since in this period plans were carried in a designer's head, not committed to paper.[39]

The highly localized character of medieval style points to a particular group of artisans and the place(s) they trained. By the same token, changes in a local style most often indicate that new artisans, and the techniques they brought along with them, were incorporated into established ways of working. The introduction of the statue column and the rose window after 1140 expanded the repertoire of the Beauvais workshop, without changing its basic stylistic character. Achieving such a balance between old and new was a profoundly creative act that involved negotiation within the

---

[37] For the conservative nature of medieval style: esp. Herbert L. Kessler, "On the State of Medieval Art History," *Art Bulletin* 70 (1988), 181–83; Elizabeth B. Smith, " 'Ars mechanica': Gothic Structure in Italy," in *Engineering*, ed. Courtenay, pp. 231–32; Lon R. Shelby, "Geometrical Knowledge of Mediaeval Master Masons," in *Engineering*, ed. Courtenay, pp. 32–33. For the use of templates: esp. John James, *Template Makers of the Paris Basin: Toichological Techniques for Identifying the Pioneers of the Gothic Movement* (Leura, 1989). Also: Janet Adams, "Use of Templates in Gothic Architecture: A Key to Design and Execution," *Bulletin of Research in the Humanities* 83 (1980), 280–91; Alain Erlande-Brandenberg, *Cathedral: Social and Architectural Dynamics of Construction*, trans. Martin Thom (Cambridge, 1994), pp. 256–60; John H. Harvey, "The Tracing Floor of York Minster," in *Engineering*, ed. Courtenay, p. 82; Lon R. Shelby, "Mediaeval Mason's Templates," *Journal of the Society of Architectural Historians* 30 (1971), 140–54.

[38] For example: Armi, *Headmaster*; Millard F. Hearn, *Romanesque Sculpture: Revival of Monumental Stone Sculpture in the Eleventh and Twelfth Centuries* (Ithaca, N.Y., 1981); Nauratil, "Labor," pp. 211–12; Stoddard, *Sculptors*, esp. pp. 178–235; Anat Tcherikover, *High Romanesque Sculpture in the Duchy of Aquitaine, c. 1090–1140* (Oxford, 1997), esp. pp. 95–134.

[39] There is some evidence for architectural drawing in the Early Middle Ages, but its interpretation remains controversial: Erlande-Brandenberg, *Cathedral*, pp. 257–59. The earliest drawings date from the late twelfth century: Wolfgang Schöller, "Dessin d'architecture à l'époque gothique," in *Batisseurs*, ed. Recht and LeGoff, pp. 227–35. Architectural plans became standard practice only in the late thirteenth century: François Bucher, "Medieval Architectural Design Methods, 800–1560," *Gesta* 11 (1972), 37–51; Lynn T. Courtenay, introduction to *Engineering*, ed. Courtenay, xvi–xviii; Werner Müller, "Dessin technique à l'époque gothique," in *Batisseurs*, ed. Recht and LeGoff, pp. 236–54.

expanded workshop. It also involved negotiation of the workshop with the patrons at whose instigation the new elements, and new workers, came to Beauvais. The result was a revitalized Beauvais Romanesque style, which had a decisive effect on the city's art for the rest of the century.

This study will first outline the long history of cultural exchange between Beauvais and Saint-Denis to highlight its shifting balance after the mid-twelfth century. It will then explore the larger implications of Beauvais's borrowing from Saint-Denis from two perspectives: the motives of the patrons and the working habits of the artisans. These two facets of artistic production in Beauvais, taken together, identify some of the cultural forces that fostered a vibrant local artistic tradition.

Tracing the Connection before the Mid-Twelfth Century

The cultural exchange between Beauvais and Saint-Denis in the mid-twelfth century built on a long history of connections between the larger Oise valley and Paris. Thirty altars to Saint-Denis in the diocese of Beauvais attest to the abbey's promotion of its patron saint there. The abbey encouraged other saints' cults in Beauvais as well, such as those of Hilaire and Clair.[40] Saint-Denis's possessions in the city of Beauvais and the Oise dated from at least the seventh century and were carefully maintained throughout Suger's abbacy.[41]

The Beauvaisis had many ties, also primarily ecclesiastical, with the city of Paris as a whole. In 1107 the lay owners of Saint-Pantaléon, Beauvais (#5 in Appendix II), gave the church to the Parisian abbey of Saint-Martin-des-Champs.[42] Walo, once abbot of Saint-Quentin and then bishop of Beauvais (1101–4), moved to the see of Paris (1104–16). Walo's old abbey of

---

[40] For the cult of Saint Denis, Roblin, *Terroir*, pp. 197–98; for that of Saint Hilaire, *Terroir*, p. 190; for that of Saint Clair, *Terroir*, p. 191.

[41] Roblin edited a series of twenty-five charters ranging from the years 627 to 899: *Terroir*, pp. 299–309. In 1183, Philippe de Dreux, bishop of Beauvais, confirmed all of Saint-Denis's holdings in the diocese: *Gallia christiana*, 9:732.

[42] Earlier historians of Beauvais had claimed that Saint-Pantaléon was donated to Saint-Denis: *Gallia christiana*, 9:718–19; Delettre, *Histoire*, 2:39. This was a misreading of Pope Pascal's confirmation, which was issued at Saint-Denis but on behalf of Saint-Martin: René Largillière, "Église Saint-Pantaléon de Beauvais," *Mémoires de la Société academique d'archéologie, science et arts du département de l'Oise* 25 (1925), 125 n. 6.

Saint-Quentin had institutional connections with a number of Augustinian foundations in Paris, notably Saint-Victor.[43] These examples could be multiplied, but the essential point in listing them is to establish that links between Beauvais and Saint-Denis (or Paris in general) are not isolated accidents within a diminished base of evidence.

Documented ecclesiastical ties between the two centers lend significance to more diffuse indications of their artistic connection at least from the early twelfth century. Jean Bony credited the Beauvaisis with the invention of the ogive vault, one of the major components of the first Gothic architecture in Paris. He also argued that the Beauvais vaults were based on Norman structural technology.[44] Recent archaeology has supported Bony on both scores, lending credence to Lindy Grant's suggestion that architects from the Oise built Saint-Denis's narthex (c. 1135–40).[45] If this was the case, the regional prestige of Beauvais Romanesque during the early years of the twelfth century matched, if it did not surpass, that of Paris.

The direction of this cultural exchange shifted after 1140 when Beauvais's artisans adopted the elements of statue column and rose window that also inspired Suger's workers. This was also the period that saw the first uses of palmette ornament to decorate Beauvais's buildings. The technical skill necessary to successfully execute all these imports could only have come from experience. It is most unlikely that implementing drawings, designs, or simple description would have produced the same results. This further evidence that the two workshops shared personnel raises specific questions about patterns of employment. Did the Beauvais

---

[43] For the career of Walo: *Gallia christiana*, 9:717–18. For the ties between Saint-Quentin and Saint-Victor: *Gallia christiana*, 9:818–22.

[44] Especially Bony "Genèse," pp. 12-13; Bony, *French Gothic*, pp. 26–43; Bony, "Sources," p. 137. Here Bony explored a pattern suggested by Eugène Lefèvre-Pontalis in "Influences normandes au XIe et XIIe siècles dans le nord de la France," *Bulletin monumental* 70 (1906), 7–8. Lefèvre-Pontalis also influenced Marcel Anfray, *Architecture normande, son influence dans le nord de la France aux XIe et XIIe siècles* (Paris, 1939), pp. 64, 164–65, 263–64, and 321; Marcel Aubert, "A propos de l'église abbatiale de Saint-Lucien de Beauvais," in *Gedenkschrift Ernst Gall*, ed. Margarete Kühn and Louis Grodecki (Berlin, 1965), pp. 53–54; Héliot, "Oeuvres," pp. 110–12; Héliot, "Diversité," pp. 290–91.

[45] Grant, *Abbot Suger*, p. 254. For Bony's legacy: Claussen, "Tympana," pp. 1–61; Gardner, "Saint-Julien," pp. 11–26; Millard F. Hearn, "The Rectangular Ambulatory in English Medieval Architecture," *Journal of the Society of Architectural Historians* 30 (1971), esp. 195; Henriet, "Saint-Lucien," p. 289.

builders, lured by Suger to work at Saint-Denis, then return home after the narthex was complete? Did the group expand to include artisans, not originally from Beauvais, who then joined the Beauvais workshop when their employment at Saint-Denis ended? Did some of them, who built the rose into Saint-Denis's west façade, then turn that skill to installing the rose at Saint-Étienne, Beauvais? Did the expanded group of artisans also include experts in carving palmette ornament and figural sculpture?

Any, or all, of this was indeed possible, since appropriation of the innovative elements from Saint-Denis occurred under the tenure of two of Beauvais's bishop-counts with especially close ties to Suger. Bishop Eudes II (1133–44) perhaps helped consecrate Saint-Denis's narthex. More definite evidence proves a close friendship between Eudes and Suger.[46] As a Capetian prince, Bishop Henry of France (1149–62) had a long familial connection with Saint-Denis, which became stronger under Suger's abbacy. Suger showed a paternal oversight of Henry, an indication of a well-established personal relationship.[47] Eudes and Henry also

---

[46] For Eudes's career: Bideault and Lautier, *Ile-de-France*, 1:293–94; Delettre, *Histoire*, 2:85–96; Guyotjeannin, *Episcopus*, pp. 123–25; Henriet, "Saint-Germer," esp. pp. 99, 109–10, and 136. For Eudes's role in consecrating Saint-Denis: Suger, *De consecratione*, sec. 4, in *Abbot Suger on the Abbey Church of Saint-Denis and its Art Treasures*, ed. and trans. Erwin Panofsky (Princeton, N.J., 1979), p. 96; *Gallia christiana*, 9:721. See also the discussions of this passage in Sumner McK. Crosby, *Abbaye royale* (Paris, 1953), p. 51; Delettre, *Histoire*, 2:92; Grant, *Abbot Suger*, p. 245. As Grant rightly points out, however, Suger lists Manasses of Meaux, rather than Eudes, in *De administratione*, sec. 26, in *Abbot Suger*, ed. Panofsky, p. 44.

For Suger's friendship with Eudes: Delettre, *Histoire*, 2:85; Grant, *Abbot Suger*, pp. 161 and 198. Eudes witnessed Suger's will in 1137: Suger, *Testamentum*, in *Oeuvres complètes de Suger*, ed. Albert Lecoy de la Marche (Paris, 1867), p. 341; *Gallia christiana*, 9:721. Eudes witnessed another charter for Suger in 1140: *Oeuvres complètes*, ed. Lecoy de la Marche, p. 360.

[47] Henry was the brother of King Louis VII. For Henry's career: esp. Thomas R. Green, "Henry of Rheims, 1122–1165: A Study in Ecclesiastical-Royal Relations," (PhD diss., New York University, 1967). Shorter treatments: Delettre, *Histoire*, 2:110–42; Anselme Dimier, "Henri de France, frère du roi Louis VII, moine de Clairvaux, évêque de Beauvais, archévêque de Reims," *Cîteaux commentarii cistercienses* 26 (1975), 106–8; Guyotjeannin, *Episcopus*, pp. 126–31; McGee, "Saint-Étienne," esp. pp. 33–35.

In 1149, the clergy of Beauvais asked Suger to urge Henry to accept his election as bishop: *Oeuvres complètes*, ed. Lecoy de la Marche, p. 307. For discussions of this letter: Delettre, *Histoire*, 2:111–16; L'Oisel, *Mémoires*, p. 100; Louvet, *Histoire*, 1:23. For other instances in which Suger exercised influence over Henry: Grant, *Abbot Suger*, pp. 17, 133–34, 176, and 282–83.

shared Suger's enthusiasm for art and showed an interest in the products of the Saint-Denis workshop long before their tenures as bishops of Beauvais. This is especially clear in the sculpture carved for the south portal of Notre-Dame d'Etampes under Henry's abbacy (c. 1137–47).[48] Eudes had hoped to rebuild the church of Saint-Germer-de-Fly when he was abbot there (1126–33) and realized his ambition after he moved to the see of Beauvais in 1133. A vault key in Saint-Germer's nave displays palmette ornament identical to that of the rose window and the north door of Saint-Étienne, Beauvais, discussed above. The ornament in both locations shares motifs with Saint-Denis and also approaches the quality of the Parisian carving.[49] Perhaps even more interesting, the structure and ornament of Saint-Germer exhibits many similarities to the structure and ornament of Saint-Denis, which neither shares with buildings in Beauvais.[50]

---

[48] Dimier, "Henri," p. 106; Kerber, *Burgund und die Entwicklung*, p. 38; Stoddard, *Sculptors*, p. 28. Nolan was of the opinion that Henry was not the patron, even though he was abbot: "Notre-Dame," pp. 87–88. But her reason, that Henry was not a known patron of the arts, is not borne out by his later career in Beauvais and Reims. Although Etampes's sculpture is most strikingly related to that of Chartres' west portals, it also exhibits clear debts to Saint-Denis: Nolan, "Notre-Dame," abstract, pp. 17, 31–32, 117–19, 124–30, and esp. 244–54; Stoddard, *Sculptors*, pp. 21–22, 29–31, and 177.

[49] For Eudes's abbacy: Henriet, "Saint-Germer," p. 98. For general discussions of the connections between the architecture and sculpture of Saint-Germer and Saint-Étienne, Beauvais: Bideault and Lautier, *Ile-de-France*, 1:98–99 and 300; Henriet, "Saint-Germer," pp. 125–26; McGee, "Saint-Étienne," p. 237. To name some specific similarities between the two buildings: 1) Atlas figures with the same facial characteristics and drapery style: McGee, "Saint-Étienne," pp. 236–37; Nolan, "Notre-Dame," p. 372 and fig. 190; 2) Many of the same motifs decorate the ambulatory capitals in Saint-Germer and the nave capitals in Saint-Étienne: Brouillette, "Senlis," p. 68. Mark Pessin argued that the many similarities between Saint-Étienne and Saint-Germer were due to the common influence of Saint-Lucien, Beauvais: "The Twelfth Century Abbey of Saint-Germer-de-Fly and Its Position in the Development of the First Gothic," *Gesta* 17 (1978), 71.

[50] To name a few similarities between the architecture and sculpture of Saint-Denis and Saint-Germer: 1) Choir elevations and vaults: Bideault and Lautier, *Ile-de-France*, 1:301–2; Héliot, "Saint-Germer," pp. 82 and 111; Henriet, "Saint-Germer," pp. 110–14; Radding and Clark, *Medieval Architecture*, pp. 100–102; 2) Choir capitals: Henriet, "Saint-Germer," p. 123. It is interesting to note that, like their close analogies in the Beauvais workshop, Saint-Germer's sculpture and architecture "archaized" the elements it shared with Saint-Denis: Bideault and Lautier, *Ile-de-France*, 1:298; Henriet, "Saint-Germer," esp. p. 120; McGee, "Saint-Étienne," p. 238.

Eudes and Henry participated in what Lindy Grant has termed a "network of artistic patronage" centered on Suger. Such patronage played a key role in the dissemination of the earliest Gothic style, accounting for the rapid spread of innovative sculptural motifs and structural technology.[51] Participants in Suger's network engaged in competitive building, paying top money to attract the best artisans. A desire to display wealth, prestige, or connections motivated that competition, of course, but appropriating artistic elements from Saint-Denis at the same time had clear political overtones.[52] This is precisely the period in which Paris was consolidating its position as the Capetian capital. Suger, as chief political advisor and especially as regent (1147–49), worked to make his

---

[51] For brief, but compelling, mentions of Suger's "network:" Grant, *Abbot Suger*, pp. 146, 185, 251–55, 272–74, and 300. For the spread of particular motifs from Saint-Denis to other buildings in northern France (and beyond): esp. Maylis Baylé, "Première sculpture gothique à La Trinité de Fécamp," in *Pierre, lumière, couleur: Études d'histoire de l'art du moyen âge en l'honneur d'Anne Prache*, ed. Fabienne Joubert and Dany Sandron (Paris, 1999), pp. 89–101; Bony, "Genèse," pp. 9–20; Bony, "Introduction," pp. 81–84; Franz, *Roman tardif*; Gardner, "Centripetal Implosion," pp. 111–16; Grodecki, "Première," pp. 265–89; Héliot, "Oeuvres," p. 104; Héliot, "Diversité," pp. 269–306; Héliot, "Roman au gothique," pp. 109–48; Plagnieux, "Saint-Germain," p. 29; Radding and Clark, *Medieval Architecture*, esp. pp. 100–22; Sauerländer, "Sculpture," pp. 32–48; Sauerländer, "Style or Transition?" pp. 1–29.

[52] On the wider question of politics and artistic style: esp. Barral i Altet, ed., "Conception de l'oeuvre," in *Artistes*, 2:9–182. Among the many, more focused explorations of this question: Böker, "Bishop's Chapel," esp. pp. 51–53; Mathias Delcor, "Prieures augustins en Roussillon et la statuaire romane," *Cahiers de Saint-Michel de Cuxa* 2 (1971), 57–66; Mirjam Gelfer-Jørgesen, *Medieval Islamic Symbolism and the Paintings in the Cefalù Cathedral* (Leiden, 1986), esp. pp. 151–75; James T. Lang, "Survival and Revival in Insular Art: Some Principles," in *Insular Tradition*, ed. Catherine E. Karkov, Michael Ryan and Robert T. Farrell (Albany, N.Y., 1997), pp. 63–77; Raghnall Ó Floinn, "Innovation and Conservatism in Irish Metalwork of the Romanesque Period," in *Insular Tradition*, pp. 259–81; Hélène Toubert, "Renouveau paléochrétien à Rome au début du XIIe siècle," *Cahiers archéologiques* 20 (1970), 153–55; Bryan Ward-Perkins, "Constantinople: A City and its Ideological Territory," in *Towns and Their Territories between Late Antiquity and the Early Middle Ages*, ed. Gian Pietro Brogiolo, Nancy Gauthier, and Neil Christie (Leiden, 2000), pp. 325–45; John Mitchell, "Artistic Patronage and Cultural Strategies in Lombard Italy," in *Towns and Their Territories*, pp. 347–70; Otto K. Werckmeister, "The Political Ideology of the Bayeux Tapestry," *Studi medievali* 3rd ser., 17 (1976), 525–95.

abbey the capital's spiritual heart and to put its prestige at the service of the monarchy's campaign to centralize power.[53]

Suger's policies had a particular impact on Beauvais. The city's position at the frontier of the Vexin gave it strategic importance in this time of heightened tensions between the Capetian and Anglo-Norman monarchs. As a consequence, Suger took every opportunity to reconcile Beauvais's interests with those of the French kings. This prompted Suger to step into Beauvais's troubled politics on a number of occasions:[54] for example, during the Stephen Garland affair, as an arbiter between the commune and Galeran of Lèvemont in 1148–49, and later between the commune and Bishop Henry in 1149–50.[55] Given the nature of these alliances, Eudes and Henry were expressing more than friendship or admiration when they appropriated elements from Suger's building at Saint-Denis. Further

---

[53] For the process by which Paris became the Capetian capital: esp. Robert-Henri Bautier, "Quand et comment Paris devint capitale," in his collected essays *Recherches sur l'histoire de la France médiévale: Des Mérovingiens aux prémiers Capétiens* (Hampshire, 1991), essay 1; Colette Beaune, *Naissance de la nation France* (Paris, 1988), esp. pp. 83–90; Russell, *Medieval Regions*, pp. 146–54; Willibald Sauerländer, "Medieval Paris, Center of European Taste: Fame and Realities," in *Paris Center of Artistic Enlightenment,* ed. George Mauner et al. (University Park, Penn., 1988), pp. 12–25. For the ways in which the abbey of Saint-Denis supported Capetian ambitions: esp. Jean Dunbabin, *France in the Making, 843–1180,* 2nd ed. (Oxford, 2000), esp. pp. 256–68 and 295–99, with comprehensive bibliography and excellent short reviews of previous scholarship; Grant, *Abbot Suger,* esp. pp. 299–300.

[54] Suger recounted his interest in Beauvais's politics in a letter of 1150, which he addressed to Henry of France, the clergy, and the people of Beauvais: Suger of Saint-Denis, *Epistola 23: Ad Henricum Belvacensem episcopum, clerum, et populum Belvacensem,* in *Oeuvres complètes,* ed. Lecoy de la Marche, p. 277. In addition to the occasions mentioned below, Suger intervened in the case of Peter de Milly and in a boundary dispute in the diocese of Beauvais between the counts of Vermandois and Clermont: Delettre, *Histoire,* 2:99–100.

[55] The appointment of Stephen Garland, a royal favorite, as bishop of Beauvais occasioned great controversy. Bernard of Clairvaux wrote to Suger about the affair: *Epistola 78: Ad Sugerium Abbatem Sancti Dionysii,* secs. 11–13, in *S. Bernardi Opera,* vol. 7, *Epistolae,* ed. Jean Leclercq and Henri Rochais (Rome, 1974), pp. 208–10. For discussions of this letter: Grant, *Abbot Suger,* pp. 55–57 and 100–129; Rudolph, *Artistic Change,* p. 82 n. 14. For the effects of the controversy on the internal politics of Beauvais: *Gallia christiana,* 9:715–20; McGee, "Saint-Étienne," pp. 30–31. For the conflict between Galeran of Lèvemont and Beauvais's commune: *Oeuvres complètes,* ed. Lecoy de la Marche, p. 299. For discussions of Henry's dispute with the commune: Dimier, "Henri," p. 107; Delettre, *Histoire,* 2:125–27; Labande, *Histoire,* pp. 62–64; L'Oisel, *Mémoires,* p. 100; McGee, "Saint-Étienne," pp. 33–35.

research will likely establish Suger's network of patronage as a key index of the shifting political landscape in the regions north of Paris during this crucial period of the Capetian monarchy's centralizing ambitions.

The Dynamics of Artistic Difference

The alliances among Eudes, Suger, and Henry intensified the earlier cultural exchange between Saint-Denis and Beauvais and, as we have seen, tipped the balance toward Saint-Denis after 1140. At the same time, Beauvais showed interest in only one innovation of Saint-Denis's workshop (the rose) and in only a few developments in sculpture (the statue column and palmette ornament). It is impossible to know precisely why these elements were selected over all the others displayed so strikingly at Saint-Denis. Perhaps the patrons were fascinated with the aesthetic possibilities of the palmette or with the technological bravado of the rose window and the statue column. Perhaps the choice simply reflects the particular skills of the artisans available to relocate or come home to Beauvais. Perhaps, too, other examples of this kind of borrowing are now lost. What is clear is that the imported elements we can now identify were transformed into a style more consonant with the traditions of Beauvais Romanesque. If politics inspired Beauvais's bishops to adopt artistic elements from or shared with Saint-Denis, did politics also motivate them to specify that the adopted elements be transformed into the local style?

In this regard, too, scarcity of evidence allows only speculation. Certainly, the monarchy's growing power and centralizing strategies threatened ancient regional character and political autonomy, especially of the strong independent counties like Beauvais. As often as not, Beauvais's bishop-counts resisted royal incursions, whether from the Anglo-Norman or Capetian monarchs. During the twelfth century, most of Beauvais's bishops played the monarchs off against each other in an attempt to divert them from this rich and strategic city on the frontier between the two realms. The bishops' alliance with Paris and Suger in the mid-twelfth century, therefore, was not a move to join a "nation." Instead, it was a strategic calculation of one feudal lord to support a peer, or the decision of a bishop to back a duly consecrated king. Probably it was a bit of both. Seen in this light, the connections between Beauvais Romanesque and Suger's workshop at Saint-Denis speak with subtle elegance of independence as well as alliance.

While it is unlikely that they were the only patrons for art and architecture in the diocese, Beauvais's bishop-counts took a commanding role in artistic production, as they did in all other aspects of economic and cultural life in the city.[56] By custom (and as it eventually would be enshrined in canon law), bishops were ultimately responsible for constructing and maintaining all the churches under their control.[57] As counts, Beauvais's bishops were also charged with the upkeep of public buildings and defensive works.[58] To fulfill these obligations, Beauvais's bishop-counts had great wealth at their disposal. Their income from the taxes and tariffs they levied on the city's trade and industry on its own was substantial, since Beauvais's position at the confluence of three wide rivers and two Roman roads made it a powerful player in interregional trade.[59] The bishop's income from the city was supplemented by rich

---

[56] Thierry Crépin-LeBlond, "Demeure épiscopale du XIIe siècle, l'exemple de Beauvais (actuel Musée départemental de l'Oise)," *Bulletin archéologique* 20–21 (1988 for 1984–85), 45 and 49; Henwood-Reverdot, *Saint-Étienne*, esp. p. 89; McGee, "Saint-Étienne," pp. 18 and 22; Micheli, *Décor*, p. 30; Murray, *Beauvais Cathedral*, pp. xiv, 27, and 31–41.

[57] For Beauvais in particular: Murray, *Beauvais Cathedral*, pp. 4, 27, and 49; Vercauteren, *Civitates*, p. 373. For evidence that most medieval bishops tried to meet that ideal, see (among many excellent discussions) Erlande-Brandenberg, *Cathedral*, pp. 29–30 and 233–34; Nauratil, "Labor"; Schöller, *Rechtliche Organisation*, esp. pp. 215–32; Wilhelmus-Hermanus Vroom, *De Financiering van de Kathedraalbouw in de Middeleeuwen: In het bijzonder van de Dom van Utrecht* (Maarssen, 1981), esp. pp. 30–57 and 63–67.

[58] Bishop Phillippe de Dreux (1185–1217), for example, reinforced the walls of the *cité* and built walls around the suburbs: Delettre, *Histoire*, 2:174–75; McGee, "Saint-Étienne," pp. 36–37; Marie-Joséphe Salmon, *Palais-musée à Beauvais: Tours et détours de l'ancienne demeure épiscopale* (Beauvais, 1984), p. 10. The bishop-counts built bridges and storehouses as well: Vercauteren, *Civitates*, p. 387. For this obligation in other cities: Philippe Bernardi, "Construction et politique en Provence: Approvisement en matériaux, une affaire publique?" in *La ville au moyen âge*, vol. 2, *Sociétés et pouvoirs dans la ville* (Aix-en-Provence, 1998), pp. 9–20

[59] For the rivers and canals through Beauvais: Bideault and Lautier, *Ile-de-France*, 1:10–12; Labande, *Histoire*, p. 82; Murray, *Beauvais Cathedral*, p. 30; Roblin, *Terroir*, pp. 214–15; Vercauteren, *Civitates*, p. 462. For the Roman roads through Beauvais: Anfray, *Architecture normande*, pp. 9–10; Pierre C. Barraud, "Beauvais et ses monuments pendant l'ère Gallo-Romaine et sous la domination Franque," *Bulletin monumental* 27 (1861), 42 and 217–26; Hubert, "Fouilles," p. 537; Roblin, *Terroir*, p. 214; Vercauteren, *Civitates*, pp. 376–77. For a broader context: Robert-Henri Bautier, *Histoire économique de la France médiévale: La route, le fleuve, la*

holdings in the countryside, which had the abundant natural resources of fertile soil, thick forests, and excellent native stone.[60] A canny harvesting of these riches sustained the city's prosperity even in times when trade was difficult.[61]

Beauvais's bishop-counts channeled some of the city's wealth into artistic patronage and had a stake in shaping the built environment in a way that reflected their position. The vibrant and self-confident style of Beauvais Romanesque, as well as the high volume of building in the city, owed much to their generosity. Alliances with Suger explain how artistic innovations migrated north from Saint-Denis to Beauvais and provide one explanation for why those innovations were worked in the way they were. Preservation of the regional artistic tradition, especially in the face of striking imports from Paris, asserted the combined political and cultural independence of this powerful county.

Issues of lordship, economics, and interregional politics interacted in the artistic patronage of Beauvais's bishop-counts, and this interaction places Beauvais in the center of the culture and politics of northern France in this period. But to leave the discussion at this point would equate Beauvais's culture solely with its elite level and would privilege the structures of comital and ecclesiastical administration, often imposed from outside.

---

foire (Aldershot, 1991); André Guillerme, *The Age of Water: The Urban Environment in the North of France, AD 300–1800* (College Station, Tex., 1988), esp. pp. 51–117; Richard C. Hoffmann, "Economic Development and Aquatic Ecosystems in Medieval Europe," *American Historical Review* 101 (1996), 631–69; Congrès national des sociétés savants, *Recherches sur l'économie de la France médiévale: Les voies fluviales—la draperie*, Actes du 112e Congrès, Lyon 1987 (Paris, 1989), pp. 7–92.

[60] For a detailed survey of Beauvais's natural resources: Lemaire, *Histoire*, 1:362–88. Among the shorter treatments: Bideault and Lautier, *Ile-de-France*, 1:10–12; Guyotjeanin, *Episcopus*, p. 71; Henwood-Reverdot, *Saint-Étienne*, p. 19; John James, "An Investigation into the Uneven Distribution of Early Gothic Churches in the Paris Basin, 1140–1240," *Art Bulletin* (1984), 22 and 32; Labande, *Histoire*, pp. 57–58 and 100–101; Lapeyre, *Façades*, p. 14 n. 8; McGee, "Saint-Étienne," pp. 13–16; Murray, *Beauvais Cathedral*, pp. 30–31 and 46; Roblin, *Terroir*, pp. 214–15; Vercauteren, *Civitates*, pp. 286 and 462–66. For a broader context: Bautier, *Histoire économique*, esp. essays 1–6; Raymond Dion, *Histoire de la vigne et du vin en France des origines au XIXe siècle* (Paris, 1959), esp. pp. 197–243; Congrès national des sociétés savants, *Recherches sur l'économie*, pp. 95–272.

[61] Guyotjeanin, *Episcopus*, esp. pp. 157–69; Labande, *Histoire*, esp. pp. 201–3; Lemaire, *Histoire*, 1:362–88; Murray, *Beauvais Cathedral*, pp. 46–49; Roblin, *Terroir*, pp. 214–15; Vercauteren, *Civitates*, pp. 376–77 and 462–66.

The survivals of Beauvais Romanesque provide an even more tantalizing glimpse into a "native" culture that is much older than the feudal age and much deeper than the patronage of its bishop-counts. The bishops doubtless availed themselves of Beauvais's distinct culture to make political statements and to consolidate their authority. Since most of them came to the office from outside the region, however, they were never really a part of that culture. It was already there for them to exploit.

Beauvais had an ancient and glorious past. Once the tribal home of the Bellovaci, it became a Roman outpost after Caesar's conquest. Archaeology has confirmed legends of a Christian presence in the city since at least the third century. Beauvais emerged as a key center in the Carolingian heartland of Neustria and became an important stronghold against the Vikings during the ninth and tenth centuries. The city was ideally situated in the eleventh century to forge ties with the duchy of Normandy (and eventually with Norman England) that continued throughout the twelfth century.[62] Beauvais's bishop-counts used those ties with Normandy, as they used those with Paris, to their political advantage. The deeper connections among the three regions, however, came from trade. Since at least the mid-eleventh century, Beauvais's merchants had worked the lucrative markets of Paris and Normandy where they traded mostly in the city's own products of cloth and wine. Beauvais's lords benefited from the city's natural advantages, and they exercised hegemony over its economy. But the economy itself was driven by a strong industrial base, intrepid merchants, and the skilled trades.

Building was preeminent among those trades. The twenty-seven stone structures underway in Beauvais during the eleventh and twelfth centuries meant enough work for a large group of artisans to sustain itself in the city for generations.[63] Unlike the bishop-counts, artisans trained

---

[62] For excellent brief surveys: Lemaire, *Histoire*, vol. 1; Roblin, *Terroir*; Vercauteren, *Civitates*. For more detailed studies of Neustria: Hartmut Atsma, ed., *Neustrie, les pays au nord de la Loire de 650 à 850: Colloque historique international* (Sigmaringen, 1989).

[63] For patterns of employment in Beauvais during the Early Middle Ages: Bideault and Lautier, *Ile-de-France*, 1:16–38; Henwood-Reverdot, *Saint-Étienne*, pp. 118 and 150; McGee, "Saint-Étienne," esp. pp. 226–38; John Ottaway, "Traditions architecturales dans le nord de la France pendant le premier millénaire," *Cahiers de civilisation médiévale* 13 (1980), 230. As is the case for most of Europe, written evidence about Beauvais's artisans and its guild structure survives only from the Later Middle Ages: Pierre Goubert, *Cent mille provinciaux au XVIIe siècle: Beauvais et les*

at Beauvais were truly part of the city's culture. Looking at artistic production simply from the perspective of the patron too often suggests a one-to-one correspondence between the patron's desires and the finished building or decorative program. This effectively writes the artisans out of the equation, or at best casts them as the passive instruments of their employers. By doing this, historians miss an opportunity to explore the most reliable evidence about the skilled trades before the thirteenth century. Encoded in the remnants of Beauvais Romanesque is proof that the artisans took an active role in expressing and perpetuating the city's distinct culture.[64] The response of the Beauvais atelier to imports from Paris is best measured in their creative updating of the traditional style, which reveals both a creative openness toward experimenting within their traditional repertoire and judiciousness in expanding it. To return to Fernie's definition of influence, quoted above, the artisans—not the patrons—did most of "the work of choosing, altering and reusing to create something new."

Beauvaisis de 1600–1730 (Paris, 1968), pp. 283–361; Labande, *Histoire*, pp. 201–23; Victor LeBlond, *L'art et les artistes en Ile-de-France au XVIe siècle (Beauvais et Beauvaisis) d'après les minutes notariales* (Paris and Beauvais, 1921).

[64] For sculptors and architects who played this role in other cities and regions: André Chédeville, *Chartres et ses campagnes (XIe–XIIe siècles)* (Paris, 1973), esp. pp. 446–60; Christopher Dyer, "Trade, Towns, and the Church: Ecclesiastical Consumers and the Urban Economy of the West Midlands, 1290–1540," in *The Church in the Medieval Town*, ed. Slater and Rosser, p. 63; Eric Husson, "Métiers de bâtiment à Dijon sous le 'mécénat' de Philippe le Hardi, duc de Bourgogne," in *Métiers au moyen âge: Aspects économiques et sociaux*, ed. Paschale Lambrechts and Jean-Pierre Sosson (Louvain, 1994), pp. 129–42; David Jacoby, "Migration of Merchants and Craftsmen: A Mediterranean Perspective (Twelfth–Fifteenth Centuries)," in his collected essays, *Trade, Commodities and Shipping in the Medieval Mediterranean* (Aldershot, 1997), essay 1; Derek Keene, "Continuity and Development in the Urban Trades: Problems of Concepts and the Evidence," in *Work in Towns, 850–1850*, ed. Penelope J. Corfield and Derek Keene (Leicester, 1990), pp. 1–16; Nauratil, "Labor," pp. ii, 49–50, and 89–90. For workers in other artistic media who played the same role: Robert Branner, *Manuscript Painting in Paris during the Reign of Saint-Louis: A Study of Styles* (Berkeley, 1977); Sophie Cassagnes-Brouquet, "Au coeur de la société urbaine: Milieu professionel, les peintres, verriers, et enlumineurs dans la Bourgogne des ducs Valois," *Le Moyen Âge* 104, no. 2 (1998), 273–90; Michael W. Cothren, "Suger's Stained Glass Masters and their Workshop at Saint-Denis," in *Paris*, ed. Mauner et al., pp. 51–54; Jane W. Williams, *Bread, Wine and Money: Windows of the Trades at Chartres Cathedral* (Chicago, 1993), esp. pp. 8–11.

Seeing the Artisans in the Artistic Style

An intense building boom in Beauvais during the mid-twelfth century provided many opportunities for artisans to experiment with new forms. Documents indicate that Bishop Henry of France (1149–62) himself oversaw the construction or renovation of the *Basse-Oeuvre* [#2 in Appendix II], Notre-Dame-du-Châtel [#1], Saint-Barthélemy [#4], Saint-Laurent [# 12], and Saint-Michel [#6].[65] All of this activity was in addition to the work at Saint-Étienne and Saint-Quentin central to the argument here. Artisans in Beauvais would not have been idle. Those trained in Beauvais, but not working there, had an incentive to return home. The increased volume of building likely required even more workers. The alliance of Eudes and Henry with Suger gave them access to artisans who had worked in Paris. Those artisans would have found the wealthy city of Beauvais an attractive venue. The new workers brought to Beauvais the architectural elements and decorative forms they had mastered at Saint-Denis. The expanded workshop had a significant influence on the working habits of the local artisans and revived the Beauvais Romanesque style. Artisans new to Beauvais shared motifs and techniques with their colleagues. Those trained in Beauvais's workshop sized up the stylistic imports and new building techniques critically and did so with an eye to what would work with the city's established tastes. They chose only a few of the innovations and even then transformed them to match the traditional aesthetic.

The rose window at Saint-Étienne and the statue columns from Saint-Quentin retain three traces of this creative appropriation: 1) the style of standing structures in and around the city played a decisive role in design; 2) the artisans consciously mixed old and new motifs to decorate Saint-Étienne's rose window and north door; and 3) they refined Beauvais's figural style for Saint-Étienne and Saint-Quentin's cloister. Looking at each of these in turn gives three closely-related perspectives on the way new elements enhanced the local style, without substantially altering it.

---

[65] Delettre, *Histoire*, 2:100 and 141–42.

Aesthetics of Environment

The southern nave exterior of Saint-Étienne, dated c. 1110–30 (fig. 11), and its south façade, dated c. 1130 (fig. 13), attest to the traditionally austere character of Beauvais Romanesque architecture. Other structures surviving from the mid- to late-eleventh century (such as the *Basse-Oeuvre* [#2], Saint-Lazare [#22], and the old choir of Saint-Quentin [#18]) exhibit the same characteristics, as do other structures now known only from engravings. In them all, small rounded windows alone break blank expanses of walls built from the regional chalk stone. For the most part, the hood moldings are unornamented; the buttresses, heavy. The distinctive *corniche beauvaisine* (see esp. fig. 11) runs under the eaves of the roofs. These characteristics remained consistent from the early eleventh century well into the thirteenth. The structures of the High Middle Ages likely continued many elements of a much older architectural tradition, although nothing much at all survives from before the eleventh century.[66]

Even if they were not trained in Beauvais, artisans working there in the mid-twelfth century had close at hand ample evidence of this preferred architecture style. Archaeological discovery indicates that two churches had remained unchanged since the eleventh century: the small church recently discovered alongside the cathedral [#3] and Sainte-Véronique [#7]. Written documents attest to two other churches in the suburbs before the end of the eleventh century: Saint-Hippolyte [#27] and Saint-Sauveur [#13]. Although there is no indication of when they were built, Saint-Hippolyte stood until 1479, and Saint-Sauveur, which was

---

[66] For Beauvais's traditional wall structure: McGee, "Saint-Étienne," p. 114. For Beauvais's traditional architectural plans: Hearn, "Rectangular Ambulatory," pp. 193–95; McGee, "Saint-Étienne," pp. 51–68 and 260–61. For the regional stone and how its properties shaped structure and carving: Bideault and Lautier, *Ile-de-France*, 1:12; Henwood-Reverdot, *Saint-Étienne*, p. 96; John James, "Funding the Early Gothic Churches of the Paris Basin," *Parergon*, n.s., 15 (1997): 41–42; James, "Investigation," pp. 26 and 30–32; McGee, "Saint-Étienne," pp. 74–75; Murray, *Beauvais Cathedral*, pp. 13 and 30–31; Paquet, "Rapport," p. 7. For the customary form of Beauvais's hood moldings: Durvin, *Saint-Quentin*, pp. 104–5; McGee, "Saint-Étienne," esp. pp. 147–48. For the customary form of Beauvais's buttressing: Henwood-Reverdot, *Saint-Étienne*, pp. 119–22. For the distinctive Beauvais cornice: Jean Vergnet-Ruiz, "Corniche beauvaisine," *Bulletin monumental* 127 (1969), 307–22.

not renovated until after the fire(s) of 1180/88,[67] stood until 1799. The *Basse-Oeuvre* [#2], the pre-Gothic cathedral of Beauvais, was originally built in the late tenth century. The standing structure reveals that renovations in the mid-eleventh and the mid-twelfth centuries were done with care to preserve the original design.

Other churches first built in the ninth or tenth centuries were transformed gradually during the eleventh and twelfth. The ninth-century structures of Saint-Étienne [#17], Saint-Lazare [#22], and Saint-Lucien [#19] retained their original plans and decoration until they were rebuilt starting in the late eleventh century, as did the tenth-century churches of Saint-Gilles [#26] and Saint-Laurent [#12]. Saint-Symphorien, dating from the mid-tenth century, was not reconstructed until the early twelfth. Saint-Michel [#6], first built in the mid-tenth century, was not renovated until the mid-twelfth. Notre-Dame-du-Thil [#20] stood by 1030 and was not remodeled until sometime in the twelfth century. Saint-Nicholas [#8], rebuilt in stone after 1052, was renovated later in the century. The eleventh-century churches of Saint-Barthélemy [#4] and Saint-Pantaléon [#5] were virtually unchanged until the mid-twelfth century. Before their renovation or rebuilding, these structures stood as testament to a well-established architectural style, which was a material expression of Beauvais's distinguished history and its unique culture.[68]

A combined sense of place and history guided Beauvais's artisans when they transformed the element of the rose window for Saint-Étienne's north façade and the element of statue column for Saint-Quentin's cloister. These new elements, inserted into structures already partially built, were carved to match the style of the standing fabric. The statue columns are the only surviving parts of Saint-Quentin's cloister, although the abbey church [#18 in Appendix II] provides a larger context. Construction of the church began in 1067, and the choir was dedicated in 1069. Work continued into the second half of the twelfth century, since a capital (discussed below) from the transept or nave owed much to motifs in Saint-Étienne's rose and north door. The Saint-Quentin figures, carved between 1160 and 1170, indicate that the cloister was begun (or renovated) after the church

---

[67] It is not clear in the sources whether there was one fire (making one or the other date a scribal error) or two fires eight years apart. Here and in Appendix II, "the fire(s) of 1180/88" is shorthand for "the fire of 1180, the fire of 1188, or both."

[68] For the influence of buildings still standing on architectural design: Ottaway, "Traditions," esp. pp. 141 and 239.

was completed. The new (or renewed) cloister occupied an abbey precinct dominated by a church whose choir dated from a hundred years earlier and whose transept and nave were built some thirty years before. The sculptor(s) of the cloister figures took this into account, carving them in a style consonant with the abbey church's traditional appearance.

The same holds true for Saint-Étienne's rose window. The walls under the rose date from a larger campaign that also built Saint-Étienne's choir and first nave bay. This campaign was completed by c. 1110 [#17 in Appendix II]. The rose was inserted into the partially built north façade only after the rest of the nave was finished up to the clerestory level by c. 1140 (fig. 12). The north door (figs. 7, 8, and 12) dates from the same phase of construction as the rose. Both were finished by c. 1150. The north façade was designed to match the overall character of the standing structure, whose austere architectural style looked back to the early twelfth century (compare fig. 11 with fig. 12; fig. 13 with fig. 14). The façade itself echoes the elevation of its earlier counterpart to the south (fig. 13). The lower registers of the north façade retain the traditional characteristics of blank masonry and simple rounded windows. The builders of the Beauvais rose departed from tradition when they borrowed the architectonics from Saint-Denis. The dense application of ornament on Saint-Étienne's north transept façade and its north door (figs. 7, 8, and 12) was an equally radical change from the simplicity of the rest of the church. At the same time, the builders attached the ornament and figures to the rose façade in a way that deliberately presented an archaic appearance.

Ornament

The conscious mixing of old and new that characterized the overall appearance of Saint-Étienne's north exterior is even more evident in the decorative details of its rose window and north door. A sequence of masks in foliage once decorated the outer recess of the north door (now mostly effaced, see fig. 8). Old photographs show that the masks were arranged radially in a way that echoed the ornament along the outer recess of Saint-Denis's rose (fig. 2). The arrangement at Saint-Étienne updated the more scattershot placement of masks on earlier buildings in the Oise.[69]

---

[69] For the tradition of mask decoration in the Oise: Micheli, *Décor*, pp. 54–57. That the masks at Saint-Denis inspired an updating of Beauvais's traditional motifs

Saint-Étienne's rose façade gives an even better insight into this skillful blending of old and new motifs. Some "spokes" of the rose (figs. 1, 5, and 6), sculpted with the newly imported palmette foliage, alternate with capitals whose water-leaf decoration continues the most common ornament found in the city's earlier buildings. The best collection of the traditional water-leaf is preserved in Saint-Étienne's nave interior (fig. 15).[70] The ornament consists of four broad leaves hugging the cushion and curving outward toward the abacus. It has only two major variants: the tips of the leaves either curl inward toward the cushion or outward; the crease outlining the upper part of each leaf and demarcating one leaf from another is either deep or shallow. In contrast to the lush variety and deep carving of palmette ornament, water-leaf is simple in the extreme. Interweaving the old forms of water-leaf with new forms of palmette in the spokes of the rose window preserved the old ornament while using it in an arresting new way.

Combination with palmette also updated a much older tradition of geometric ornament. Saint-Étienne's palmette-encrusted rose opens under a large gable (fig. 14) overlaid with squared lozenges in a latticework pattern. Saint-Étienne's gable was modeled on that of the west façade of Saint-Lucien, Beauvais (c. 1130) [#19 in Appendix II].[71] A network of small hexagons fitted around terra-cotta diamonds inlays the massing of Saint-Étienne's north door (figs. 7 and 12), providing a geometric frame

---

for Saint-Étienne: Henwood-Reverdot, *Saint-Étienne*, p. 147; Kerber, *Burgund und die Entwicklung*, p. 91 n. 141; Lapeyre, *Façades*, p. 21 and 208 n. 2.

[70] Wulf, *Kapitellplastik*, pp. 92–93. Water-leaf was also the most common ornament in the region as a whole during the eleventh and twelfth centuries: Micheli, *Décor*, esp. pp. 29, 37, 52–53, and 78.

[71] The only remaining evidence for the façade's design is an engraving commissioned in 1673 by Jacques Bénigne Bossuet, commendatory abbot of Saint-Lucien: Anfray, *Architecture normande*, fig. 39; Louis-Eudore Deladreue and Jean-Baptiste Mathon, "Histoire de l'abbaye royale de Saint-Lucien (Ordre de Saint-Benoît)," *Mémoires de la Société academique d'archéologie, science et arts du département de l'Oise* 8 (1871), pl. 1; Stephen Gardner, "Sources for the Façade of Saint-Lucien in Beauvais," *Gesta* 25 (1986), 93 and 95. For similar ornament throughout the region: Anfray, *Architecture normande*, p. 264; Claussen, "Tympana," p. 11; Lapeyre, *Façades*, p. 206 n. 3; Lefèvre-Pontalis, "Influences," pp. 23–25; Victor Lhuillier, *Paroisse et l'église Saint-Étienne de Beauvais* (Beauvais, 1896), p. 138.

for the elaborate palmette forms in the recesses and tympanum.[72] Arch stones in the eleventh-century *Basse-Oeuvre* [#2] display a related pattern of geometric ornament.[73]

These geometric motifs continued centuries-old traditions. Geneviève Micheli argued that there had already been two successive waves of geometrism in Beauvais before the twelfth century. The first was Gallic and thus very old. The second, at the end of the eleventh century, drew on the first, but wove in forms borrowed from Normandy. She linked the second wave to the interest Beauvais's masons showed in Norman vaulting technology.[74] The mixing of palmette with the geometric forms in the mid-twelfth century began a third wave of geometrism, which owed much to the two earlier waves. The result was a variety of blended geometric forms so popular that they predominated in the decorative repertoire of Beauvais for the rest of the twelfth century and much longer.[75]

Figural Style

An analogous blending of old and new shaped Beauvais's figural style after the mid-twelfth century. The figures around Saint-Étienne's rose (figs. 1, 5, and 6) exhibit the same stylistic characteristics as Saint-Quentin's statue columns (fig. 3) carved some twenty years later. The Saint-Quentin figures are badly damaged, but the fleshiness of the cheeks and the molding of the jaws are very close to the faces of the Saint-Étienne rose figures,

---

[72] Claussen, "Tympana," p. 12; Eugène Lefèvre-Pontalis et al., "Guide archéologique du Congrès de Beauvais," *Congrès archéologique de France* 72 (Beauvais, 1905), 16; McGee, "Saint-Étienne," pp. 172–73.

[73] Philippe Bonnet-Laborderie, *Cathédrale Saint-Pierre: Histoire et architecture* (Beauvais, 1978), p. 35.

[74] *Décor*, esp. pp. 5–6, 54–62, 73–77, and 83–86. Micheli built on Lefèvre-Pontalis, "Influences," pp. 3–37, as did Anfray, *Architecture normande*, pp. 337–79; Claussen, "Tympana," esp. pp. 1–26; Gardner, "Sources," esp. p. 96. By contrast, McGee suggested that the gable at Saint-Étienne, Beauvais, was based directly on Carolingian ornament: "Saint-Étienne," pp. 156 and 226.

[75] According to a photo of 1936, a Renaissance house boasted a wall plate decorated with a motif identical to the massing of Saint-Étienne's north door: Fernand Watteeuw, *Beauvais et les Beauvaisis des années 40: Ville française sous l'occupation allemande* (Beauvais, 1980), p. 15. The house, destroyed in the bombing of 1940, once stood at 17, rue Jean-Baptiste Oudry.

those in the tympanum of the north door, and those in its outer recess. Each of these figures also exhibits goffered sleeves and deeply cushioned folds across the chests that are rimmed by double incisions. All in addition display an exaggerated proportion of heads and hands to bodies, as well as agitated gestures and postures.

J. David McGee and Geneviève Micheli have argued that Saint-Étienne's rose figures continued a local style from (at least) the early twelfth century.[76] Loss of evidence makes it hard to confirm this, although the atlas in the southeastern corner of Saint-Étienne's transept (fig. 16), dating from c. 1130, provides an instructive comparison.[77] The atlas's face is crudely formed. Bulging eyes in an elongated almond shape give a misshapen breadth to the upper part of the face. The rose figures (c. 1140–50) retain many of the characteristics of the atlas figure, especially the working of the sleeves and the necklines, and the heavy folds that form the drapery. Compared to the atlas, however, the rose figures are much more polished and exhibit a more supple grace in the gestures. The features of the rose figures are regular: precisely delineated eyes, deeply drilled, and prominent noses. The refinement of the rose figures, which approaches that of work done in Paris (compare to fig. 10),[78] anticipates the technical mastery of the statue column form for Saint-Quentin.

These and other creative combinations of old and new would prove decisive for later products of Beauvais's workshop. There were many chances to devise new variations within this expanded vocabulary of forms, since a high volume of building continued in the city throughout the twelfth century. Between c. 1140 and c. 1180, construction or renovation took place at Notre-Dame-de-Thil [#20], Sainte-Marie-Madeleine [#15], and Saint-Nicholas [#8]. Written evidence testifies to a number of other churches standing by the end of the twelfth century, although it is unclear when they were built: Notre-Dame-de-Marissel [#21], Saint-André [#14], Saint-Jacques de Voisinlieu [#23], Saint-Jean [#25], and Saint-Martin [#11].

---

[76] McGee, "Saint-Étienne," p. 97 n. 18; Micheli, *Décor*, pp. 54–57.

[77] For a more detailed analysis of the atlas's style: Henwood-Reverdot, *Saint-Étienne*, pp. 92 and 115–17; McGee,"Saint-Étienne," pp. 81–82.

[78] See also McGee, "Saint-Étienne," esp. pp. 124 and 142 n. 55.

Figures decorating a cloister that once stood on the rue Saint-Pierre [#9] date from this period,[79] as do the atlas figures at Saint-Lazare [#22] and Saint-Symphorien [#24].[80] In all three projects, the artisans continued the more refined style of Saint-Étienne's rose figures and their matching characteristics in the Saint-Quentin statue columns. Saint-Gilles [#26], Saint-Lucien [#19], and the episcopal palace [#10] were also expanded, decorated, or both during the second half of the twelfth century. Here, too, the artisans drew on motifs in Saint-Étienne's rose and north door and shaped them in yet more creative combinations.[81] Among the more striking reproductions of the motifs in the recesses and tympanum frame of Saint-Étienne's north door (figs. 7 and 8) are a capital (fig. 17) from Saint-Quentin [#18] in which lions swallow palmette leaves held by a beaded band; a capital (fig. 18) from Saint-Lucien [#19] in which beast heads swallow palmette scrolls; and a capital from the episcopal palace [#10] in which birds drink from a common cup.[82] The bodies and postures of dragons in a tympanum (fig. 19) from Saint-Gilles [#26] are very close to those of the winged lions in a capital from Saint-Quentin (fig. 17), which themselves allude to the lions in the middle recess of Saint-

---

[79] In the mid-nineteenth century, when Alexandre Lenoir imagined details for the cloister, he sketched figures at the springing of the arches with the same posture and drapery as the figure enthroned at the top of Saint-Étienne's rose (fig. 1). Lenoir's accuracy, however, is impossible to assess. Lenoir's engraving was published by Henwood-Reverdot (*Saint-Étienne*, fig. 103). There is also an old photograph of the cloister, but it shows the figures mostly effaced: published in *Saint-Étienne*, fig. 102; Watteeuw, *Beauvais*, p. 12.

[80] Saint-Symphorien's atlases are now incorporated into a farmhouse on the outskirts of the city. McGee provides a photograph and discusses their close parallels to the atlases at Saint-Étienne: "Saint-Étienne," pp. 82–83 and pl. 36. For a discussion of Saint-Lazare's atlas and an excellent plate: Pierre Durvin, *Maladrerie Saint-Lazare de Beauvais* (Amiens, 1975), p. 57 and fig. 13; McGee, "Saint-Étienne," p. 82. Saint-Lazare's tympanum also matches the massing of Saint-Étienne's north door: Claussen, "Tympana," pp. 12–14, Durvin, *Saint-Lazare*, p. 53, pl. 7a, and p. 57; McGee, "Saint-Étienne," pp. 172–73.

[81] Barraud, "Beauvais," pp. 297–98; Claussen, "Tympana," p. 38; Lapeyre, *Façades*, pp. 29 and 201.

[82] This capital (Inv. # 86–1, Musée départmental) was uncovered during recent excavations in the twelfth-century palace. A second capital (Inv. # 86–2), found in the same precinct of the palace, exhibits palmette interlace identical to that of Saint-Étienne's rose and door. Zielinski published plates of these capitals: "Variations," figs. 18 and 19.

Étienne's north door (fig. 8).[83] But none of them are precisely the same. All are energetic recombinations of the revitalized Beauvais Romanesque style that since the mid-twelfth century had balanced imported elements of style with old favorites.

To the extent that it is the surviving document of production techniques within the workshop, artistic style offers valuable evidence for the tastes, traditions, and cultural forces at work in periods and regions (such as medieval Beauvais) where most other forms of evidence are lost. Deeper analysis of Beauvais Romanesque and the fruits of on-going archeological excavations in the city will establish this large workshop as an urban institution and provide insight into the self-consciousness of the skilled trades that contributed to the city's economic power. Perhaps it will also link that self-consciousness to the political aggression of Beauvais's commune.[84]

Historical circumstances conditioned the style of the Beauvais workshop, but they did not determine it completely. The artisans had an influence on their culture, too, both in their own right and in collaboration with their most important patrons, the bishop-counts of Beauvais. The design and decoration of the buildings encoded their decisions to shape their built environment in a particular way and hints at the reasons for those choices. The act of building in and of itself made visible the ambitions of patrons and artisans. Patterns of building within the city of Beauvais and its region, therefore, give a larger context in which to assess Beauvais Romanesque, while the style itself enhances our knowledge of

---

[83] Also Claussen, "Tympana," pp. 37–39; Fons, "Saint-Lucien," p. 82; Henwood-Reverdot, *Saint-Étienne*, pp. 145–50; Lapeyre, *Façades*, p. 209.

[84] Most studies of the building crafts within medieval urban society focus on later centuries. They lay the foundations, though, for making sense out of the less abundant evidence about Beauvais and elsewhere from the eleventh and twelfth centuries. There are excellent bibliographical essays: Geoffrey Crossick, "Past Masters: In Search of the Artisan in European History," in *The Artisan and the European Town, 1500–1900*, ed. Geoffrey Crossick (Aldershot, 1997), pp. 1–40; Wilfried Reininghaus, "Stadt und Handwerk: Ein Einführung in Forschungsprobleme und Forschungsfragen," in *Stadt und Handwerk in Mittelalter und früher Neuzeit*, ed. Karl H. Kaufhold and Wilfried Reininghaus (Cologne, 2000), pp. 1–19. More detailed studies include James R. Farr, *Artisans in Europe 1300–1914* (Cambridge, 2000); Jacqueline Hamesse and Colette Muraille-Samaran, eds., *Les métiers au moyen âge: Le travail au moyen âge. Une approche interdisciplinaire* (Louvain, 1990); and Heather Swanson, *Medieval Artisans: An Urban Class in Late Medieval England* (Oxford, 1989).

the society that produced it. The connection between the Beauvais workshop and that at Saint-Denis touches on all of these various aspects of artistic production in Beauvais and gives what is perhaps the clearest insight into their interaction.

Conclusion

Jean Gimpel personalized the stylistic importance of Suger's new abbey church at Saint-Denis by observing that each prelate who attended its consecration returned home eager to match, if not outdo, the abbot's achievement.[85] That observation has become axiomatic in the literature, and like all axioms, it contains a large measure of truth. Two of Beauvais's bishop-counts, with firsthand knowledge of the products of Suger's workshop, were instrumental in introducing the rose window and the column statue into Beauvais's artistic repertoire. It is likely that Beauvais's bishops hired artisans who had once worked for Suger. Those artisans brought with them new ways of carving and innovative building techniques.

Gimpel's observation is far from the whole story, however. At Beauvais (and I suspect almost everywhere else), new workers and new forms were introduced into an already established workshop. While receptive to stylistic imports from Paris, Beauvais's artisans adopted only a few of them and even then transformed them in ways that consciously matched Beauvais's traditional tastes. This selective appropriation of imported elements confounds conventional notions of influence, periodization, and "evolution" in artistic style. At the same time, it redefines assumptions every bit as ingrained about "regional schools" in French Romanesque art.

Such a self-confident response to innovation attests to a strong artistic tradition centered at Beauvais. For reconstructing that tradition and defining its formal characteristics, contrasts with the products of Saint-Denis are much more important than any similarities among the shared motifs or architectonics. These contrasts fall into a clear pattern, affording one of the best insights into Beauvais's once large and influential workshop. The design decisions and habits of working encoded in the Beauvais Romanesque style, in turn, provide glimpses, fleeting and imperfect as they might be, into a once vibrant urban culture.

---

[85] Gimpel, *Cathedral Builders*, trans. Barnes, p. 31.

FIGURE 1
North rose. Transept façade, Saint-Étienne, Beauvais.
© James Austin. Courtesy James Austin.

FIGURE 2
West rose, Saint-Denis.
Photo: Elaine M. Beretz.

Figure 3
Statue columns from Cloister of Saint-Quentin, Beauvais.
Beauvais, *Musée départemental de l'Oise.*
Photo: Elaine M. Beretz.

FIGURE 4
Statue column from Cloister of Saint-Denis.
New York, Metropolitan Museum.
Photo: The Metropolitan Museum of Art, Purchase Joseph Pulitzer Bequest,
1920 (20.157). Image © The Metropolitan Museum of Art.

Figure 5
Figure to lower right. North rose. Saint-Étienne, Beauvais.
Photo: Elaine M. Beretz.

FIGURE 6
Figure to lower left. North rose. Saint-Étienne, Beauvais.
Photo: Elaine M. Beretz.

Figure 7
North door. Saint-Étienne, Beauvais.
Photo: Elaine M. Beretz.

FIGURE 8
Detail. Recesses of north door. Saint-Étienne, Beauvais.
Photo: Elaine M. Beretz.

FIGURE 9
Central portal. Western doors. Saint-Denis.
Photo: Elaine M. Beretz.

FIGURE 10
Apostle bas-relief. Ambulatory chapel. Saint-Denis.
Photo: Elaine M. Beretz.

Figure 11
Nave exterior from the south. Saint-Étienne, Beauvais.
Photo: Elaine M. Beretz.

FIGURE 12
Nave exterior from the north. Saint-Étienne, Beauvais.
Photo: Elaine M. Beretz.

FIGURE 13
South façade. Saint-Étienne, Beauvais.
Photo: Elaine M. Beretz.

FIGURE 14
North façade. Saint-Étienne, Beauvais.
Photo: Elaine M. Beretz.

Figure 15
Water-leaf capitals. North nave interior. Saint-Étienne, Beauvais.
Photo: Elaine M. Beretz.

FIGURE 16
Atlas. Southeastern corner of transept. Saint-Étienne, Beauvais.
Photo: Elaine M. Beretz.

FIGURE 17
Detail of a capital from Saint-Quentin, Beauvais.
Beauvais, *Musée départemental de l'Oise.*
Photo: Elaine M. Beretz.

FIGURE 18
Capital from Saint-Lucien, Beauvais.
Beauvais, *Musée départemental de l'Oise.*
Photo: Elaine M. Beretz.

Figure 19
Tympanum from Saint-Gilles, Beauvais.
Beauvais, *Musée départemental de l'Oise.*
Photo: Bildarchiv Preussicher Kulturbesitz/ Art Resource, NY.

Church Building in Beauvais, 1000–1200
(for demonstration only; not drawn to scale)

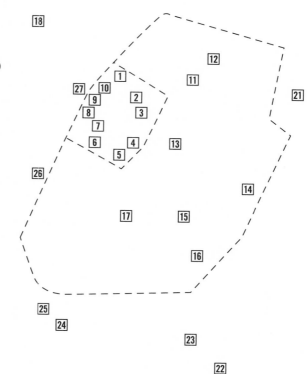

1. Notre-Dame du Châtel
2. Cathedral (St-Pierre)
3. Small church (vocable unknown)
4. St-Barthélemy
5. St-Pantaléon
6. St-Michel
7. Ste-Véronique
8. St-Nicholas
9. Cloister on Rue St-Pierre
10. Episcopal Palace
11. St-Martin
12. St-Laurent
13. St-Sauveur
14. St-André
15. Ste-Marie Madeleine
16. St-Thomas
17. St-Étienne
18. St-Quentin
19. St-Lucien
20. Notre-Dame du Thil
21. Notre-Dame de Marissel
22. St-Lazare
23. St-Jacques
24. St-Symphorien
25. St-Jean
26. St-Gilles
27. St. Hippolyte

Outline of city walls redrawn after M. Roblin, *Le Terroir de l'Oise* (Paris, 1978), fig. 30.
© 2000 Elaine M. Beretz

FIGURE 20
Church building in Beauvais, 1000–1200.
Graphic: Elaine M. Beretz.

Appendix I

Loss of Beauvais Romanesque

Most of Beauvais's artistic heritage has disappeared. Some of it was lost centuries ago to age, to war, or to the conscious destruction of renovation: three churches before the late eighteenth century; eight, in revolutionary fervor; and three more sometime before the mid-nineteenth century.[1] Most of the remaining structures were destroyed in 1940, when German bombardment leveled more than 80 percent of the city.[2]

Today only Saint-Étienne [#17 in Appendix II] retains any significant portion of its twelfth-century structure, although a new choir in the sixteenth century altered its original appearance, as did the bell tower that replaced the two northwestern bays of the Romanesque nave. The pre-Gothic cathedral [#2], the *Basse Oeuvre*, was brutally truncated in the early thirteenth century to make way for new construction. Saint-Quentin [#8], which now serves as the *Préfecture* of the Oise, was extensively rebuilt in the early eighteenth century. A single chapel from the late eleventh century survives. Saint-Lazare [#22] is a shell after years as

---

[1] Structures lost before the late eighteenth century include 1) Saint-Hippolyte [#27 in Appendix II], destroyed after 1479; 2) Saint-Gilles [#26], destroyed in 1674; and 3) Saint-Nicholas [#8], destroyed in 1788. For the effects of the Revolution on Beauvais's architecture: G. J. Humbert, *Histoire religieuse de l'église et de la paroisse Saint-Étienne pendant la Révolution* (Beauvais, 1892). Those churches in the city that succumbed to secularization include 1) Saint-André [#14]; 2) Notre-Dame-du-Châtel [#1]; 3) Saint-Laurent [#12]; 4) Saint-Lucien [#19]; 5) Saint-Michel [#6]; and 6) Saint-Sauveur [#13]. Sainte-Marie-Madeleine [#15] and Saint-Pantaléon [#5] were partially dismantled. The churches of Saint-Jean [#25], Saint-Martin [#11], Saint-Thomas [#17], and Sainte-Véronique [#7] were no longer standing when Barraud compiled his catalogue in the mid-nineteenth century. No evidence, written or material, survives to indicate when they were destroyed.

[2] The destruction was appalling. Of 4,250 houses in the city, 1,778 were totally destroyed and 721 others were seriously damaged. Of the 82 structures registered as historical monuments, 60 disappeared entirely, as did the medieval *châtel* and the *Hôtel de Ville*. The cathedral alone was hit by eight bombs: Watteeuw, *Beauvais*, esp. pp. 11 and 67. Bonnet-Laborderie discusses the destruction of medieval canons' houses that once stood in the precinct around the cathedral: *Cathédrale*, p. 41.

a grange. Fragments of Saint-Symphorien [#24] are incorporated into a farmhouse on the outskirts of the city. A single unornamented wall from Notre-Dame-du-Châtel [#1] remains. Notre-Dame-du-Thil [#20] retains vestiges of its twelfth-century plan, although its exterior was redone later in the Middle Ages. Its interior was modernized only a few years ago. Saint-Jacques de Voisinlieu [#23] has been thoroughly modernized.

Beauvais's eleventh- and twelfth-century churches were decorated with a vast body of sculpture. Capitals and hood moldings alone must have numbered in the hundreds. Sadly, that sculpture has met the same fate as the city's architecture. Only the tiniest percentage survived the Revolution, and most of that was lost when the bombing of 1940 also destroyed the old Musée archéologique de Beauvais.[3] The ornament of Saint-Étienne's rose (figs. 1, 5, and 6) and that of its north door (figs. 7 and 8) are the largest extant ensembles of decorative sculpture from twelfth-century Beauvais. Some tympana from other buildings survive (see, for example, fig. 19), as do a few capitals (see, for example, figs. 17 and 18). Saint-Étienne also contains the largest sampling of figural sculpture. In the interior, two atlases remain in the transept (see fig. 16 for one of them) and four capitals in the south nave tribune include figures. On the exterior, Saint-Étienne displays twelve figures around its north rose (fig. 1) and others in the tympanum and recesses in its north door (figs. 7 and 8). Three statue columns are left from Saint-Quentin's cloister (fig. 3) and two atlas figures remain from Saint-Lazare and Saint-Symphorien.

Written sources supplement this spotty evidence. Here, too, there are severe limitations, since Beauvais's libraries were also a casualty of the bombardment in 1940. Only a small number of manuscripts survived the burning of the *Bibliothèque municipale*, which once held the libraries gathered from monasteries and collegial houses of the city and the surrounding area. The communal archives were lost when the Hôtel de

---

[3] Henwood-Reverdot, *Saint-Étienne*, p. 151 n. 219; Bonnet-Laborderie, *Pierres*, p. 5; Watteeuw, *Beauvais*, p. 67. Most of the remaining sculpture is preserved in the current Musée départemental de l'Oise, Beauvais: Bonnet-Laborderie, *Pierres*. For the last complete accounting of the sculpture before World War II: Jean-Baptiste Mathon, "Catalogue du Musée archéologique de Beauvais," *Mémoires de la Société académique d'archéologie, science et arts du département de l'Oise* 5 (1862–64), 103–56 and 595–614.

Ville burned.[4] The library of the Société académique, arts, sciences du département de l'Oise is now lost, as are the most important private librar-ies that held materials related to the history of Beauvais.[5] Current holdings in the Archives départementales de l'Oise are fragmentary at best for the High Middle Ages and almost completely lacking for architectural his-tory. Although many manuscripts from the various medieval libraries of the city were scattered before the twentieth century, the work of locating and cataloguing them is far from complete. The work done thus far has only highlighted how much has been lost.[6] All too often it is necessary to rely on a partial edition, or a short snippet, of medieval sources in the antiquarian histories of the city, but those materials are usually quoted out of context, giving no indication of provenance or date.[7]

---

[4] Watteeuw reproduced a letter by the historian Charles Fauqueux describing the losses: *Beauvais*, pp. 30–31, 67, and 91. For a catalogue of manuscripts held in the *Bibliothèque municipale* [now the *Médiathèque centrale*] before World War II: Henri A. Omont, "Manuscrits de la bibliothèque de Beauvais," *Catalogue générale des man-uscrits des bibliothèques publiques de France: Départements* (Paris, 1885), 3:315–32. For an accounting of manuscripts now lost: France, Direction des bibliothèques de France, *Catalogue générale: Manuscrits des bibliothèques sinistrées de 1940 à 1944*, vol. 53 (Paris, 1962), esp. pp. 1 and 11; and France, Direction des bibliothèques de France, *Catalogue générale: Suppléments*, vol. 57 (Paris, 1971), pp. 77–92. For gaps in the communal archives: Henwood-Reverdot, *Saint-Étienne*, pp. 24 and 240–41.

[5] Especially that of the LeMareschal family: Henwood-Reverdot, *Saint-Étienne*, p. 23; Victor LeBlond, "Église et la paroisse Saint-Étienne de Beauvais au XVe siècle d'après les comptes des marguilliers et des chanoines," *Bulletin philologique et histo-rique du Comité des travaux historiques* (1913), 152. Copies of some of the materials in the LeMareschal collection, once held in the library of the *Société academique*, are now lost, too.

[6] For a thorough catalogue of the Archives départementales: Marie-Joséphe Gut, *Guide des archives de l'Oise* (Beauvais, 1990). For a recent accounting of extant manuscripts: Guyotjeannin, *Episcopus*, pp. xix–li; Dietrich Lohrmann, *Papsturkun-den in Frankreich*, n.s., vol. 7, *Nördliche Ile-de-France und Vermandois* (Göttingen, 1976), pp. 17–68. For the scattering of volumes once in the cathedral library: Henri A. Omont, *Recherches sur la bibliothèque de l'église cathédrale de Beauvais* (Beau-vais, 1914), pp. 6–15. The manuscripts once held in the *chateau* of Troussures were sold in 1909: *Manuscrits du VIIe au XVe provenant de la bibliothèque du chateau de Troussures* (Paris, 1909).

[7] The most important antiquarian histories of the city: Delettre, *Histoire*; Labande, *Histoire*; L'Oisel, *Mémoires*; Louvet, *Histoire*; Simon, *Supplément*. The 93 volumes of the *Collection Bucquet-aux-Cousteaux* (now held at the *Médiathèque cen-trale*, Beauvais) are the largest compilation of documents for the history of Beauvais.

Even within these limitations, combing the surviving documents and archaeological reports, in tandem with a survey of extant architecture and sculpture, has produced much raw data about a once thriving workshop, which was much larger than scholars had previously realized.

A team of scholars, mostly the members of two local families, worked throughout the eighteenth and nineteenth centuries to gather notes for a comprehensive narrative of Beauvais's history. The resulting collection is very difficult to use, however, since the materials were arranged by subject, rather than by date. For a history of the collection and an inventory of its contents: Victor LeBlond, *Inventaire sommaire de la Collection Bucquet-Aux-Cousteaux* (Beauvais and Paris, 1907). Many of the volumes were lost or damaged in World War II.

Appendix II

Church Building in Beauvais, 1000–1200
(Fig. 20)

Pierre C. Barraud's survey, published in 1861, remains indispensable for any study of Beauvais's artistic heritage, since he described so many structures lost since the mid-nineteenth century.[1] This catalogue supplements Barraud, using material from recent excavations and adding the mentions of buildings from Beauvais's antiquarian scholarship. I have also expanded Barraud's chronological scope to the beginning of the thirteenth century. The scattered nature of the evidence makes it impossible to verify that I have included everything even of immediate interest, however, and the information I have collected is uneven. Some structures merited only one passing reference in a single document. Others have received monographic treatments. Still others, such as Saint-Lucien and Saint-Étienne, have been the subjects of long controversy.

The selected bibliography included with each entry is divided into three categories: 1) primary sources, which include written documents, engravings, and photographs of structures now lost; 2) monographic treatments; and 3) significant discussions of the buildings themselves or of the institutions housed there. Numbers assigned to the buildings in the catalogue and in fig. 20 follow the tripartite division of medieval Beauvais into the city proper, which stands on the old Roman settlement and was surrounded by Gallo-Roman walls; the suburbs, which hugged the circumference of the old city walls and which were themselves enclosed with walls in 1182;[2] and the directly outlying rural precincts whose monastic complexes exhibit so many significant parallels in structure and ornament with churches in the city and suburbs.

---

[1] "Beauvais et ses monuments pendant l'ère Gallo-Romaine et sous la domination Franque," *Bulletin monumental* 27 (1861), 29–64, 217–36, and 294–316.

[2] Delettre, *Histoire*, 2:174–75; McGee, "Saint-Étienne," pp. 36–37.

Churches Inside the Gallo-Roman Walls
(Numbers 1–10, in Fig. 20)

1) Notre-Dame-du-Châtel

Its foundations were laid in 1136. The choir was completed under Bishop Barthélemy de Montcourt (1162–75). Construction was still underway in 1217 when Bishop Philippe de Dreux (1175–1217) left money to its building fund. The building was destroyed in 1793.

Bibliography. **Primary sources**: *Gallia christiana*, 9:740; Dietrich Lohrmann, *Papsturkunden in Frankreich*, n.s., vol. 7, *Nördliche Ile-de-France und Vermandois* (Göttingen, 1976), p. 39. **Discussions**: Barraud, "Beauvais," p. 236; Philippe Bonnet-Laborderie, *Cathédrale Saint-Pierre: Histoire et architecture* (Beauvais, 1978), p. 41; Charles Delettre, *Histoire du diocèse de Beauvais depuis son établissement au 3me siècle, jusqu'au 2 septembre 1792*, vol. 2 (Beauvais, 1843), pp. 141 and 158; Stephen Murray, *Beauvais Cathedral: Architecture of Transcendence* (Princeton, 1989), pp. 32 and 154.

2) Cathedral Saint-Pierre [Pre-Gothic cathedral, called the "Basse-Oeuvre"]

The first documented construction began under Bishop Hervé (987–97). Work continued under Bishops Roger of Champagne (998–1022) and Warin (1022–30). The façade of the tenth-century building was restored after a fire in the mid-eleventh century. According to the obituary (now lost) of Beauvais's cathedral chapter, Bishop Henry of France (1149–62) repaired it at great expense. The *Basse-Oeuvre* was truncated during construction of the new cathedral after 1225.

Bibliography. **Primary sources**: *Gallia christiana*, 9:704–705 and 730–31; Pierre Louvet, *Histoire et antiquitez du pais Beauvaisis*, vol. 2 (Beauvais, 1632), p. 292. **Monographs**: Maryse Bideault and Claudine Lautier, *Ile-de-France gothique*, vol. 1, *Églises de la vallée de l'Oise et du Beauvaisis* (Paris, 1987), pp. 70–93; Bonnet-Laborderie, *Cathédrale*; Eugène Lefèvre-Pontalis et al., "Guide archéologique du Congrès de Beauvais," *Congrès archéologique de France* 72 (Beauvais, 1905), 3–15; Murray, *Beauvais Cathedral*. **Discussions**: Barraud, "Beauvais," pp. 302–303; Émile Chami, "Chronique des fouilles médiévales en France: Oise, Beauvais, Notre-Dame-de-la-Basse-Oeuvre," *Archéologie médiévale* 1 (1971),

277 and 279; Chami, "Chronique," *Archéologie médiévale* 11 (1981), 275; Delettre, *Histoire,* 2:141–42; Denis Simon, *Supplément aux mémoires de l'histoire civile et écclesiastique du Beauvaisis* (Paris, 1704), p. 53; Anne Prache, *Ile-de-France romane* (Paris, 1983), pp. 181–82.

3) Small church (vocable unknown)

This small sanctuary was discovered in excavations alongside the cathedral. It has been dated c. 1035–58, to coincide with the episcopate of Bishop Druon (or Drogo).

  Bibliography. **Discussions**: Bonnet-Laborderie, *Cathédrale,* p. 37; Chami, "Chronique," *Archéologie médiévale* 3–4 (1973–74); Chami, "Chronique," *Archéologie médiévale* 6 (1976), 341.

4) Saint-Barthélemy

Bishop Druon (or Drogo, 1035–58) funded a building at this site after 1037 when he founded a college of canons to serve there. The church was rebuilt under Bishop Henry of France (1149–62).

  Bibliography. **Primary sources**: *Gallia christiana,* 9:708; Lohrmann, *Papsturkunden,* p. 38; Louvet, *Histoire,* 1:684. **Monograph**: Pierre C. Barraud, "Description de l'ancienne église collégiale de Saint-Barthélemy," *Mémoires de la Société académique d'archéologie, science et arts du département de l'Oise* 4 (1859), 734–74. **Discussions**: Barraud, "Beauvais," p. 236; Delettre, *Histoire,* 2:141; Pierre Durvin, *Histoire de la Préfecture de l'Oise: Ancienne abbaye Saint-Quentin de Beauvais* (Beauvais, 1978), p. 3; Lefèvre-Pontalis et al., "Guide," p. 20; Murray, *Beauvais Cathedral,* p. 32; Michel Roblin, *Terroir de l'Oise aux époques gallo-romain et franque: Peuplement, défrichement, environment* (Paris, 1978), pp. 185 and 186 n. 77; Fernand Vercauteren, *Étude sur les civitates de la Belgique seconde: Contribution à l'histoire urbaine du nord de la France de la fin du IIIe à la fin du XIe siècle* (Brussels, 1934), p. 284 n. 3.

5) Saint-Pantaléon

A sanctuary stood on this site by the mid-tenth century. An early twentieth-century photograph, analyzed in conjunction with nineteenth-century descriptions of the standing structure, indicates that a new church was built in the late eleventh century. The structure was repaired in the mid-twelfth century. Its façade was radically reworked in the early fourteenth century. The building was sold during the Revolution and partially dismantled. Portions of the structure survived up to the bombing of 1940.

Bibliography. **Primary sources**: Pope Calixtus II, *Epistolae et privilegia* 53, *Patrologia latina* 163:1142–43; Louvet, *Histoire*, 2:171–2; *Gallia christiana*, 9:718–19; a photograph of the early twentieth century held in the Conway Library, Courtauld Institute, London. **Monograph**: René Largillière, "Église Saint-Pantaléon de Beauvais," *Mémoires de la Société académique d'archéologie, science et arts du département de l'Oise* 25 (1925), 121–49. **Discussions**: Barraud, "Beauvais," p. 236; *Gallia: Fouilles et monuments archéologique en France métropolitaine* 21 (1963), 367; Annie Henwood-Reverdot, *Église Saint-Étienne de Beauvais: Histoire et architecture* (Beauvais, 1982), p. 61; Lefèvre-Pontalis et al., "Guide," p. 21; Delettre, *Histoire*, 2:39.

6) Saint-Michel

The earliest documented structure was begun under Bishop Hervé (987–97) and completed under Bishop Roger (998–1022). The community was reformed in 1146, prompting the rebuilding of the church. The parish was suppressed during the Revolution. The building was destroyed in 1810.

Bibliography. **Primary sources**: *Gallia christiana*, 9:723 and 777; Lohrmann, *Papsturkunden*, pp. 37–38; Victor LeBlond and Albert Marie Pierre de Luppé, eds., "Obituaire de l'église Saint-Michel," in *Obituaires des églises Saint-Nicholas et Saint-Michel de Beauvais* (Paris, 1923), pp. 113–223. **Discussions**: Barraud, "Beauvais," pp. 234–35; Bonnet-Laborderie, *Cathédrale*, p. 41; Delettre, *Histoire*, 2:100 and 141; Victor Lhuillier, *Paroisse et l'église Saint-Étienne_de Beauvais* (Beauvais, 1896), pp. 18 and 113; Vercauteren, *Civitates*, p. 284 n. 2.

7) Sainte-Véronique

This chapel once stood on the rue Philippe-de-Beaumanoir (also rue-Saint-Veronique). A document (now destroyed) dates its rebuilding to the tenth century, after Pierre de Gerberoy gave a prebend there to Beauvais's cathedral chapter. Excavations in the 1950s uncovered a sizable building with extensive ornament, all impossible to date precisely. The structure was dismantled before the mid-nineteenth century.

Bibliography. **Monograph**: L. N. Barré, "Chapelle de Sainte-Véronique et l'hôtel des Vidames de Gerberoy," *Mémoires de la Société académique d'archéologie, science et arts du département de l'Oise* 11 (1882),

636–42. **Discussions:** Barraud, "Beauvais," pp. 306–307; *Gallia* 12 (1956), 144; J. David McGee, "The Romanesque and Early Gothic Church of Saint-Étienne (Saint-Vaast) at Beauvais," (PhD diss., Indiana University, 1983), p. 43 n. 40.

8) Saint-Nicholas

A wooden church stood on this site before c. 1052. It was rebuilt in stone at the end of the eleventh century after Raoul L'Enfant, seneschal of France, gave a sizeable gift. The establishment of a college of canons (1078) to serve the church prompted another rebuilding after the late eleventh century. The building was torn down in 1788.

    Bibliography. **Primary sources:** *Gallia christiana*, 9:710; Lohrmann, *Papsturkunden*, p. 38; Louvet, *Histoire*, 1:689–92; LeBlond et Luppé, eds., *Obituaires*, pp. 1–112. **Discussions:** Barraud, "Beauvais," p. 227; Bonnet-Laborderie, *Cathédrale*, p. 41; Delettre, *Histoire*, 1:508; Durvin, *Saint-Quentin*, p. 3; Victor LeBlond, *Une curé de Saint-Étienne au XVIIe siècle* (Beauvais, n.d.), p. 30; Louvet, *Histoire*, 1:688–89; McGee, "Saint-Étienne," p. 41 n. 30; Pierre-César Renet, *Saint-Lucien et les autres saints du Beauvaisis: Études historiques, liturgiques, chronologiques* (Beauvais, 1892), p. 184; Roblin, *Terroir*, pp. 205 and 218 n. 27; Vercauteren, *Civitates*, pp. 279–80 and 284 n. 3.

9) Cloister on Rue Saint-Pierre

The cloister once stood on the rue Saint-Pierre across from the cathedral. Sometime before the twentieth century, the cloister was filled in and became the outer walls of a house. The house and all traces of the cloister were destroyed in the bombing of 1940.

    Bibliography. **Primary sources:** a photograph and an engraving in Henwood-Reverdot, *Saint-Étienne*, figs. 102 and 103; the photograph alone in Fernand Watteeuw, *Beauvais et les Beauvaisis des années 40: Ville française sous l'occupation allemande* (Beauvais, 1980), p. 12. **Discussions:** Margund Claussen, "Romanische Tympana und Türstürze in der Normandie," *Mainzer Zeitschrift* 75 (1980), 2; Henwood-Reverdot, *Saint-Étienne*, pp. 150–51; Watteeuw, *Beauvais*, p. 31.

10) Episcopal Palace

The palace was built in the twelfth century on the foundations of the Gallo-Roman walls. Its great hall was uncovered in recent excavations under the present sixteenth-century structure.

Bibliography. **Monographs:** Thierry Crépin-LeBlond, "Demeure épiscopale du XIIe siècle, l'exemple de Beauvais (actuel Musée départe-mental de l'Oise)," *Bulletin archéologique* 20–21 (1988 for 1984–85), 7–58; Francis Salet, "Palais épiscopal de Beauvais," *Bulletin monumental* 149 (1991), 240–41; Marie-Joséphe Salmon, *Palais-musée à Beauvais: Tours et détours de l'ancienne demeure épiscopale* (Beauvais, 1984). **Discussions:** Lefèvre-Pontalis et al., "Guide," p. 28; Aymar Verdier, *Architecture civile et domestique au moyen âge et à la Renaissance* (Paris, 1855–57), 1:123 and 2:199.

Churches in the Suburbs (Numbers 11–17, in Fig. 20)

11) Saint-Martin

A church stood on the site by the late twelfth century, as it was damaged in the fire(s) of 1180/88. The rebuilt structure was dismantled before the mid-nineteenth century.

Bibliography. **Primary sources:** Louvet, *Histoire,* 2:308. **Discussions:** Barraud, "Beauvais," p. 301; Delettre, *Histoire,* 2:174; Lhuillier, *Saint-Étienne,* p. 23; Murray, *Beauvais Cathedral,* pp. 152–53; Roblin, *Terroir,* p. 188.

12) Saint-Laurent

The first documented building on this site was begun under Bishop Hervé (987–97). It was expanded under Bishop Druon (or Drogo, 1035–58) and then rebuilt under Bishop Henry of France (1149–62). The building was destroyed in 1798.

Bibliography. **Primary sources:** *Gallia christiana,* 9:705 and 708. **Mono-graph:** Louis-Eudore Deladreue, "Notice sur l'église collégiale de Saint-Laurent de Beauvais," *Mémoires de la Société académique d'archéologie, science et arts du département de l'Oise* 9 (1876), 123–46. **Discussions:** Barraud, "Beauvais," pp. 298–99; Delettre, *Histoire,* 2:141; Henwood-Reverdot, *Saint-Étienne,* p. 8 n. 54 and 89; Jacques Henriet, "Édifice de la première génération gothique: L'abbatiale de Saint-Germer-de-Fly,"

Bulletin monumental 143 (1985), 138 n. 3; McGee, "Saint-Étienne," p. 18; Murray, *Beauvais Cathedral*, p. 32.

13) Saint-Sauveur

The earliest evidence of a church on this site is a charter (1072) of Bishop Guy, giving the curate to the canons of Saint-Vaast. The building burned in the fire(s) of 1180/88. The rebuilt structure was dismantled between 1799 and 1808.

 Bibliography. **Primary source:** Louvet, Histoire, 1:694. **Discussions:** Barraud, "Beauvais," p. 301; Delettre, Histoire, 2:174; Henwood-Reverdot, Saint-Étienne, p. 27; Lhuillier, Saint-Étienne, pp. 23 and 29; Louvet, Histoire, 1:56 and 2:308; Simon, Supplément, p. 98.

14) Saint-André

A church stood on this site by the late twelfth century, as it burned in the fire(s) of 1180/88. It was rebuilt under Bishop Milo of Nanteuil (1217–34). The building was sold during the Revolution and torn down in 1831.

 Bibliography. **Discussions:** Barraud, "Beauvais," pp. 301–302; Delettre, *Histoire,* 2:174; Louvet, *Histoire,* 1:59 and 2:308.

15) Sainte-Marie Madeleine

Ruins of the church, photographed in 1946, point to a date in the mid-twelfth century. The form of its buttresses and the decoration of its hood moldings match those of Saint-Étienne. It was damaged in the fire(s) of 1180/88. The parish was suppressed during the Revolution and the building was partially dismantled then.

 Bibliography. **Primary source:** a photograph made in 1946, in Watteeuw, *Beauvais,* p. 90. **Discussions:** Barraud, "Beauvais," p. 302; Delettre, *Histoire,* 2:174; Lefèvre-Pontalis et al., "Guide," p. 20; Henwood-Reverdot, *Saint-Étienne,* pp. 59 and 122; Lhuillier, *Saint-Étienne,* pp. 23 and 113; Louvet, *Histoire,* 2:308; Murray, *Beauvais Cathedral,* pp. 152–53.

16) Saint-Thomas

A church stood on this site by the late twelfth century, since it was badly damaged in the fire(s) of 1180/88. By 1225, a group of Franciscans used the ruins as their base of operations and rebuilt the church. That structure was dismantled before the mid-nineteenth century.

Bibliography. **Primary source:** Louvet, *Histoire*, 1:737–38. **Discussions:** Barraud, "Beauvais," p. 302; Delettre, *Histoire*, 2:174; Louvet, *Histoire*, 1:58 and 2:308; Lhuillier, *Saint-Étienne*, p. 23; Murray, *Beauvais Cathedral*, pp. 152–53.

17) Saint-Étienne

Legend claims that the first church was built in the third century over Saint Firmin's prison, but its dedication to Saint Stephen suggests instead a foundation in the fifth century. A building certainly stood at this site by 881, when the body of Saint Vaast was translated there from Arras during the Viking invasions. That structure was rebuilt under Bishop Hervé (987–97). It was expanded and completely redesigned after c. 1090 to accommodate the college of canons Bishop Guy (1062–85) established there in 1072.

The author revises the chronology of the new building in *A Question of Chronology: Dating the North Rose of Saint-Étienne, Beauvais,* forthcoming in the monograph series of the American Philosophical Society. A summary: the choir and the first nave bay were complete by c. 1110; nave bays 2–4 up to the clerestory level, by c. 1140; the rose and the north door, by c. 1150. The nave was vaulted in the 1180s; the west door was decorated between c. 1180 and 1220.

Bibliography. **Primary sources:** Lohrmann, *Papsturkunden,* p. 36; Henwood-Reverdot, *Saint-Étienne,* pp. 190–237; *Translatio S. Vedasti Bellovacum et relatio Atrebatum,* in *Acta sanctorum,* February, vol. 4, 799; *Vita S. Firmini,* in Roblin, *Terroir,* p. 320. **Monographs:** Bideault and Lautier, *Ile-de-France,* 1:94–109; Lefèvre-Pontalis et al., "Guide," pp. 15–20; Henwood-Reverdot, *Saint-Étienne*; J. David McGee, "Early Vaults of Saint-Étienne at Beauvais," *Journal of the Society of Architectural Historians* 45 (1986), 20–31; McGee, "Saint-Étienne;" Victor LeBlond and Jean Lafond, *Église Saint-Étienne de Beauvais* (Paris, 1929); Jean-Pierre Paquet, "Rapport sur les fouilles de Saint-Étienne," unpublished material, Médiathèque centrale, Beauvais; Prache, *Ile-de-France,* pp. 183–88. **Discussion:** Barraud, "Beauvais," p. 297.

Churches outside the Suburban Walls (18–27 in Fig. 20)

18) Saint-Quentin

The church was begun in 1067; its choir was dedicated in 1069. An engraving (1733) indicates that construction continued through the third quarter of twelfth century. A capital discussed above (fig. 17), probably from the transept or the nave, dates to around or after the mid-twelfth century.

Bibliography. **Primary sources:** *Gallia christiana,* 9:709; Helinand de Froidmont, *Chronicon,* in *Patrologia latina,* 212:959; Léon-Honoré Labande, ed., "Cartulaire de Saint-Quentin de Beauvais," *Mémoires de la Société académique d'archéologie, science et arts du département de l'Oise* 14 (1891), 665–66; Lohrmann, *Papsturkunden,* p. 36; Ludo Milis, "Coutumier de Saint-Quentin de Beauvais," *Sacris erudiri* 21 (1972–73), 435–81; Sigebert of Gembloux, *Auctarium Belvacense,* in *Monumenta germaniae historica, Scriptores,* 4:462; *Vita S. Romanae virginis martyris, II: S. Romanae reliquiarum translatio,* in *Acta sanctorum,* October, 2:135–36; an engraving of 1733 in Durvin, *Saint-Quentin,* p. 104. **Monographs:** Céline Dumont, "Abbaye de Saint-Quentin de Beauvais (XIe –XIIIe siècles)," *Positions des thèses. École nationale des chartes* (1991), 55–61; Durvin, *Saint-Quentin;* Henri A. Omont, "Donations d'Yves de Chartres et de l'évêque Gui à l'abbaye de Saint-Quentin de Beauvais," *Bibliothèque de l'École des chartes* 64 (1905), 631–32. **Discussions:** Delettre, *Histoire,* 1:485–86; Durvin, *Saint-Quentin,* pp. 7 and 104–105; Edouard de La Fontaine, *Histoire politique, morale et religieuse de Beauvais* (Beauvais, 1840), 2:115; McGee, "Saint-Étienne," pp. 114, 141 n. 42, and 205.

19) Saint-Lucien

Foundations dating from late antiquity, discovered in the 1960s, support the legend that a church was built over Lucien's tomb as early as the third century. The Vikings burned a later structure in 845. The church was rebuilt under Bishop Eudes I (862–81), but it was burned again by the Normans in 1075. The new choir, begun c. 1090, was dedicated in 1109. Vault keys from the transept or nave, found during recent excavations, date to c. 1110–30; the west façade, to c. 1130; the lantern tower, before the mid-twelfth century. A capital (fig. 18), discussed above, dates to around or after the mid-twelfth century. The building was destroyed in 1812.

Bibliography. Primary sources: *Historia translationis S. Vedasti*, in *Acta sanctorum*, February, vol. 4, 819; *Gallia christiana*, 9:694 and 778; Lohrmann, *Papsturkunden*, pp. 45–48; "Chilpéric I fonde l'abbaye de Saint-Lucien," in Roblin, *Terroir*, p. 322. Engraving of 1673 in Marcel Anfray, *Architecture normande, son influence dans le nord de la France aux XIe et XIIe siècles* (Paris, 1939), fig. 39; Louis-Eudore Deladreue and Jean-Baptiste Mathon, "Histoire de l'abbaye royale de Saint-Lucien (Ordre de Saint-Benoît)," *Mémoires de la Société été académique d'archéologie, science et arts du département de l'Oise* 8 (1871), pl. 1; Stephen Gardner, "Sources for the Façade of Saint-Lucien in Beauvais," *Gesta* 25 (1986), 93. **Monographs:** Marcel Aubert, "A propos de l'église abbatiale de Saint-Lucien de Beauvais," in *Gedenkschrift Ernst Gall*, ed. Margarete Kühn and Louis Grodecki (Berlin, 1965), pp. 51–58; Deladreue and Mathon, "Saint-Lucien," pp. 257–385 and 541–701; Claire Fons, "Abbaye Saint-Lucien de Beauvais: Étude historique et archéologique," *Positions des thèses: École nationale des chartes* (1975), 75–84; Ernst Gall, "Die Abteikirche St. Lucien bei Beauvais. Ein Rekonstruktionsversuch," *Wiener Jahrbuch für Kunstgeschichte* 4 (1926), 59–71; Stephen Gardner, "Notes on a View of St. Lucien at Beauvais," *Gazette des beaux-arts*, 6th ser., 96 (1980), 149–56; Gardner, "Sources," pp. 93–100; Jacques Henriet, "Saint-Lucien de Beauvais, mythe ou réalité?" *Bulletin monumental* 141 (1983), 273–94; Jean Hubert, "Fouilles de Saint-Lucien de Beauvais et les origines du plan tréflé," in his collected essays *Arts et vie sociale de la fin du monde antique au moyen âge: Études d'archéologie et d'histoire. Receuil offert à l'auteur par ses élèves et ses amis* (Geneva, 1977), pp. 537–44; Pierre Leman, "Fouilles de l'abbaye de Saint-Lucien de Beauvais (campagne 1966)," *Cahiers archéologiques de Picardie* 4 (1977), 277–88. **Discussions:** Anfray, *Architecture normande*, p. 64; Barraud, "Beauvais," pp. 307–10; *Gallia* 22 (1967), 196–97; Pierre Héliot, "Oeuvres capitales du gothique français primitif et l'influence de l'architecture anglaise," *Wallraf-Richartz Jahrbuch* 20 (1958), 101 and 104; Henwood-Reverdot, *Saint-Étienne*, pp. 7, 89–90, 102, 123, and 151; McGee, "Saint-Étienne," pp. 92 and 206–207; Murray, *Beauvais Cathedral*, p. 31; Renet, *Saint-Lucien*, pp. 112–13 and 122–25; Roblin, *Terroir*, pp. 199 n. 116 and 322.

20) Notre-Dame-du-Thil

This was the site of the original cemetery for the monks of Saint-Lucien and their lay dependents. The earliest mention of a church structure is a document dated 1030. Today, the church retains vestiges of a twelfth-century plan and structure, particularly in the nave.

Bibliography. **Primary sources**: "Abbaye de Saint-Lucien, Beauvais," *Médiathèque centrale*, Beauvais, ms. 141, fols. 145–46; Louvet, *Histoire*, 1:388. **Discussions**: Durvin, *Saint-Quentin*, p. 3; John James, "An Investigation into the Uneven Distribution of Early Gothic Churches in the Paris Basin, 1140–1240," *Art Bulletin* 66 (1984), 39; Renet, *Saint-Lucien*, pp. 107 and 140–41.

21) Notre-Dame de Marissel

A church stood on this site by the end of twelfth century, although no evidence indicates when the church was built.

Bibliography. **Monograph**: Lefèvre-Pontalis et al., "Guide," pp. 32–34. **Discussion**: Watteeuw, *Beauvais*, pp. 8–9.

22) Saint-Lazare

A sanctuary stood on this site as early as the ninth century. Bishop Guy (1062–85) organized a lepers' hospital with the old chapel at its center and then sponsored a larger church building around the chapel. Construction continued there well into the mid-twelfth century, since the ornament and hood moldings date to c. 1120–40 and an atlas to after the mid-twelfth century. Parts of the twelfth-century structure still stand.

Bibliography. **Primary sources:** Victor LeBlond, ed., *Cartulaire de la maladrerie de Saint-Lazare de Beauvais* (Beauvais, 1922); Lohrmann, *Papsturkunden*, p. 68. **Monographs**: Pierre Durvin, *Maladrerie Saint-Lazare de Beauvais* (Amiens, 1975); Lefèvre-Pontalis et al., "Guide," pp. 36–38. **Discussions**: Barraud, "Beauvais," pp. 313–14; Durvin, *Saint-Quentin*, p. 3; McGee, "Saint-Étienne," p. 143 n. 58; Prache, *Ile-de-France*, pp. 36–38.

23) Saint-Jacques de Voisinlieu

There is no evidence to date the construction of this church. A bull of Pope Lucius III (1182) confirmed it as a holding of the abbey of Saint-Symphorien.

Bibliography. **Primary sources**: Louvet, *Histoire*, 1:560; "Le pape Lucius III confirme les biens de Saint-Symphorien de Beauvais (1182)," in Roblin, *Terroir*, p. 313. **Discussion**: Lefèvre-Pontalis et al., "Guide," p. 20.

24) Saint-Symphorien

There was a sanctuary on this site by the mid-tenth century. A new building was dedicated in 1121. Atlases, now embedded in the walls of a farmhouse, date close to the mid-twelfth century. The church burned in the fire(s) of 1180/88.

Bibliography. **Primary sources:** *Gallia christiana*, 9:807; Lohrmann, *Papsturkunden*, p. 48; Louvet, 2:171–72. **Discussions:** Barraud, "Beauvais," p. 312; Delettre, *Histoire*, 2:174; Durvin, *Saint-Quentin*, p. 3; Lefèvre-Pontalis et al., "Guide," pp. 20–21.

25) Saint-Jean

A church stood at this site by the late twelfth century, since a bull of Pope Lucius III (1182) confirmed it as a holding of the abbey of Saint-Symphorien. The building burned in the fire(s) of 1180/88.

Bibliography. **Primary sources:** Louvet, *Histoire,* 2:560; "Le pape Lucius III confirme les biens de Saint-Symphorien de Beauvais (1182)," in Roblin, *Terroir,* p. 313. **Discussions:** Barraud, "Beauvais," pp. 303–304; Delettre, *Histoire*, 2:174; Louvet, *Histoire*, 2:308; Murray, *Beauvais Cathedral*, pp. 152–53.

26) Saint-Gilles

A structure at this site was damaged in the fire of 886. It was rebuilt under Bishop Hervé (987–97) and perhaps again under Bishop Guy (1063–85). A tympanum (fig. 19) dates to the middle or late twelfth century. The building was dismantled in 1674.

Bibliography. **Monograph:** Pierre C. Barraud, "Notice sur l'église et la paroisse de Saint-Gilles à Beauvais," *Mémoires de la Société académique d'archéologie, science et arts du département de l'Oise* 5 (1862), 44–99. **Discussions:** Barraud, "Beauvais," p. 300; Claussen, "Tympana," p. 38; Lhuillier, *Saint-Étienne*, p. 66; Henwood-Reverdot, *Saint-Étienne*, p. 8 n. 54; McGee, "Saint-Étienne,"p. 18; Bonnet-Laborderie, *Cathédrale*, p. 6.

27) Saint-Hippolyte

A church stood at this site by the third quarter of the eleventh century, since a bull of Pope Gregory VII (1083) confirmed it as a holding of the canons of Saint-Quentin, Beauvais. Pope Clement III confirmed the holding again in 1189. Worship ceased there in 1479. The building was torn down sometime soon after.

Bibliography. **Primary sources:** *Gallia christiana,* 9:711; "Le pape Clément III confirme les biens de Saint-Quentin de Beauvais (1189)," in Roblin, *Terroir,* p. 314. **Discussion:** Durvin, *Saint-Quentin,* pp. 14 and 30.

Lambeth Palace Library, MS 260, and the Problem of English Vernacularity

Ralph Hanna
Keble College, Oxford

ELSEWHERE I HAVE offered paleographic and provenance notes on Lambeth Palace Library, MS 260, a large miscellany, mostly copied in the second decade of the fifteenth century. The main scribe, who signs the book as "Wilfrid," writes in the dialect of Beverley, East Yorkshire, and some of his texts are strongly suggestive of a mendicant context. The book was certainly in mendicant hands sometime near the Dissolution, when it belonged to Peter Tollar, a brother of the Dominican house located between Micklegate and North Street, York.

Lambeth 260 is mostly given over to extremely good copies of two very lengthy and regionally canonical verse texts of instruction, *The Northern Homily Cycle* and *The Prick of Conscience*. Neither text *qua* text has any visibility in contemporary English studies; indeed, neither has ever been properly edited. Yet both are well known simply on the basis of their prologues, selections reprinted to demonstrate the growth of an English vernacular literary consciousness.[1] Such a narrative the Lambeth

---

[1] See "Lambeth Palace Library, MS 260, and Some Aspects of Northern Book History," *Journal of the Early Book Society* 9 (2006), 131–40. The only edition of the original version of the *Homilies* (the form of the text in this MS) is from a fragmentary manuscript, John Small, *English Metrical Homilies from Manuscripts of the*

MS quite definitively rebuffs, and this essay will investigate the qualifications it may offer to ideas about an English vernacular.

Certainly Lambeth 260 represents a substantial English book, of which the two poems absorb something like 60 percent (the *Homilies* fols. 1–63; *The Prick* fols. 101–36ᵛ). But the remainder of the volume, all of it in Wilfrid's hand with the exception of an intruded late fifteenth-century quire with John de Sacro Bosco's *De sphaera*, is nearly totally Latin: two sets of abbreviated or outline sermons (one for the "commune sanctorum," one "de tempore," fols. 63–66ᵛ and 84–90ᵛ, respectively), Robert Holcot's "Convertimini" (an exemplum book, fols. 67–79), a further Latin exemplum book with English verse, to be published in the Appendix and discussed here, amid the narratives (fols. 79–83ᵛ), and a very detailed (more than six hundred head entries, one for about every fifteen verse lines) Latin "tabula" to *The Prick*. As the final two items I cite will indicate, the volume may be situated along a particularly fluid and perturbed linguistic frontier, one commonplace in the English Middle Ages but largely invisible, both to those who concern themselves only with metropolitan canonical poetic texts (read "Chaucer") and to those who investigate only texts in carefully edited printed versions.

There are excellent reasons, largely matters of professional history, that this invisibility should persist. All English medievalists are hugely in the debt of the Victorian Early English Text Society (EETS), which produced the first (and in many cases, still only) editions of Middle English literary monuments. But the EETS editors, as any cursory survey of prefaces to their editions will copiously demonstrate, engaged in the project out of an interest in national glory and devotion to English culture. Caught between, on the one hand, a belief in the retarding effects on "English" nationhood exerted by the Norman Yoke and, on the other, a considerable anxiety about the glorious national past unearthed by German philological scholarship, they saw Englishness (or English-only) projectively, as the foundation upon which coming Elizabethan glory would rest.[2]

Fourteenth Century (Edinburgh, 1862); *The Prick* was edited from a very good (but not the best) copy by Richard Morris (Berlin, 1863). But cf. Jocelyn Wogan-Browne et al., *The Idea of the Vernacular: An Anthology of Middle English Literary Theory, 1280–1520* (University Park, Penn., 1999), pp. 125–30, 241–44, for selections from the two prologues.

    [2] For a quick introduction, see Anthony Singleton, "The Early English Text Society in the Nineteenth Century: An Organizational History," *Review of English Studies* 56 (2005), 90–118, esp. the quotations at 94–95.

Such overt jingoism might well be submerged. However, it entirely programs the conventional privileging of metropolitan culture within Middle English studies—in whatever historically variable combination, Chaucer, Gower, Hoccleve, Lydgate would be the tradition that endured. And the nationalist narrative that privileges these authors (along with such corollaries as "the triumph of English") persists, in part because of its implicit invocation in Carleton Brown and Rossell H. Robbins's *Index of Middle English Verse*, and is central to conceptions of a medieval English archive (if not canon).[3] Rather than seek to describe literary manuscripts (although Brown's original *Register* awkwardly straddles reports on single manuscripts and on verse), the editors of the *Index* sought to prioritize verse (as a uniquely evocative literary form, à la the Romantics?), and verse in English only. One would not want to diminish Brown and Robbins's immense contribution to a modern conception of the archive, but one does need to realize that theirs was an immensely selective contribution.[4]

Of course, Brown and Robbins failed in their quest to identify every single possibly poetic scrap of Middle English. The customary recognition of this failure does not, as I wish to do, query the assumptions and procedures the editors followed but rather assumes that careful archival checking will remedy their oversights and provide a complete account of *verse in English* for the period. The standard approach has been the brief note offering a new item Brown and Robbins missed, these oddments eventually grouped into larger volumes, essentially cloned from the original *Index*.[5]

---

[3] (New York, 1943), the successor to Brown, *A Register of Middle English Religious and Didactic Verse*, 2 vols. (Oxford, 1916–20).

[4] It has taken a very long time to achieve comparable coverage of what is equally medieval and "English"; cf. Richard Sharpe, *A Handlist of Latin Writers of Great Britain and Ireland before 1540*, Publications of the Journal of Medieval Latin 1 (Turnholt, 1997) (although avowedly a continuation of a project begun by Leland and Bale in the 1530s and 1540s); and Ruth J. Dean, *Anglo-Norman Literature: A Guide to Texts and Manuscripts*, ANTS occasional publications series 3 (London, 1999).

[5] One example of a legion: Curt F. Bühler, "A Middle English Versified Prayer to the Trinity," *Modern Language Notes* 66 (1951), 312–14 (a third copy of *Index* 246, from Princeton University Library, MS Kane 21, fol. 112ᵛ). Cf. Robbins and John L. Cutler, *Supplement to the Index of Middle English Verse* (Lexington, Ky., 1966); and the *New Index* (another supplement) of A. S. G. Edwards and Julia Boffey (London, 2005).

But if one knows and looks at manuscript books, one immediately becomes aware of the futility of this procedure. Quite simply, if one is interested, probably more "items" of Middle English verse remain out there waiting to be found in manuscript than there are "items" included in the published *Index* and its supplements. All these volumes overlook substantial amounts of English verse usage, materials that resist discovery or ready identification as English because they do not appear in contexts one would consider securely "English" but, like Lambeth 260, are situated along a hazy linguistic frontier.[6]

I offer a somewhat brief example (although like many things about medieval books, it is probably a great deal too complicated). Brown and Robbins surveyed with considerable care Oxford, Balliol College, MS 149, a collection of Latin sermons. They found there (or offered clues to Robbins and Cutler to add in) twenty items listed in the *Index* and its supplement, eleven from a single verse-laden sermon at fols. 31^v–36.[7] But elsewhere the indexers' search procedures went awry. Balliol 149 (fols. 1–15^v, 77–86^v) contains three sermons ascribed to a minor literary figure,

---

6 The great master of this field is Siegfried Wenzel, to whom I am indebted for many kindnesses over the years. See his three monumental studies, *Preachers, Poets, and the Early English Lyric* (Princeton, 1986); *Macaronic Sermons: Bilingualism and Preaching in Late Medieval England* (Ann Arbor, 1994); and *Latin Sermon Collections from Later Medieval England: Orthodox Preaching in the Age of Wycliffe* (Cambridge, 2005). Although, like Wenzel, I concentrate here upon sermons, the reader should recognize that this is a reasonably arbitrary decision, driven by the manuscript that forms the center of my interest. As I go on to argue, such bi- or polylingualism is endemic in about any site of writing one chooses to examine in the later Middle Ages; cf. the work of Laura Wright on business English, for example, *Sources of London English: Medieval Thames Vocabulary* (Oxford, 1996); "Bills, Accounts, Inventories: Everyday Trilingual Activities in the Business World of Later Medieval England," in *Multilingualism in Later Medieval Britain*, ed. D. A. Trotter (Cambridge, 2000), pp. 149–56 (with a full bibliography at pp. 151–52 n. 5); and of Tony Hunt on grammatical and medical texts, for example, *Popular Medicine in Thirteenth-Century England: Introduction and Texts* (Cambridge, 1990, 1994); *Teaching and Learning Latin in Thirteenth-Century England*, 3 vols. (Cambridge, 1991); *Three Receptaria from Medieval England: The Language of Medicine in the Fourteenth Century*, Medium Ævum Monographs ns 21 (Oxford, 2001).

7 See Richard Hamer, *A Manuscript Index to the Index of Middle English Verse* (London, 1995), p. 41; Wenzel describes the collection at *Macaronic*, pp. 177–80 (and edits the heavily versified sermon, pp. 212–67). For Henry Champernon, the subject of the next paragraphs, see further Wenzel, *Latin Collections*, pp. 125–31.

Henry Chambron or Champernon, from the name a South Devon man, educated at Exeter College, Oxford (*c.* 1382), and eventually a Franciscan. From these, Brown and Robbins reported one set of verses (*Index* 14, fol. 11ᵛ), and the *Supplement* found two further examples (*Index Sup.* 161.5 and 427.5, fols. 79ᵛ and 11, respectively). The first and third of these are "poems" in the sense that they extend over several couplets. But the second is a three-line monorhymed "sermon division," a mnemonic listing in English of the points developed by the preacher, both to direct his audience as they listen and for them to take away from the church as remembered instruction. "Divisions" are thoroughly ubiquitous in late medieval Anglo-Latin sermons (and there are literally thousands of examples), and Brown and Robbins deliberately tried to avoid listing them, because they perceived them as essentially punctuating Latinity (and thus not really "English" at all).[8]

One could consider the appearance of *Index Sup.* 161.5 just a glitch, a place where Robbins and Cutler forgot to follow their own rules (and thereby accidentally made English in a Latin context visible). But overinclusiveness is not the real indexing problem here. If one reads through Champernon's sermons in Balliol 149, one finds substantial omissions in the reportage. If one should be listing "sermon divisions," then Robbins and Cutler missed an example on fol. 80ᵛ, as well as its slightly variant repetition at fol. 85. Worse still, if one desires completeness of the English archival record, they overlooked two six-line stanzas (one rhyming ababcc, the second axbaxb) on fol. 82ᵛ and a loose English couplet on fol. 84ᵛ.

I don't offer these gleanings as scholarly one-upmanship or notes toward an "improved" *Index*. Rather, I consider the indexers' troubles here indicative of ill-focused (untheorized, if you will) effort. The vicissitudes of indexing demonstrate how difficult it is to find the English archive, because it is entirely unclear, even to careful researchers, that there is one. In some sense, Brown and Robbins were done in by the form of presentation in Balliol 149, clearly for them most confusing. Unlike the usual vernacular verse anthology, with poems introduced by subject-title

---

[8] Neither *Index* nor *Register* mentions this exclusion, although Robbins, in conversation, was always clear that this had been *Index* policy; cf. *Supplement*, p. xix. Such English oddments are deeply derivative of Latinate practice, a "translation" of a stylistic device, since the same technique of division by rhyming triplets is endemic in purely Latin contexts; cf. the Lambeth 260 intrusion into the Northern Homily for 1 Lent ("Triplex est ieiunium"), cited at p. 347 below.

headings, concluded with *Explicits*, and carefully laid out in verse lines, the Balliol scribe offered them no recognition procedures. Like most such persons, he wrote his verse in the same manner as the rest of the sermon, as prose within large blocks of prose, and he offered no signal either of linguistic (Latin to English to Latin) or stylistic (prose to verse to prose) variation. In such a situation, Brown and Robbins were routed; they were faced with reading large tracts of manuscript Latin on the chance hope that there might be some English in there somewhere.[9]

When Brown, Robbins, and Cutler looked at Balliol 149, the verses receded into their Latin surround and, in a substantial set of cases, were literally invisible as English. But that is precisely the point. One cannot be sure from the record whether Champernon delivered his sermons in English, in Latin (perhaps with English insertions), or as some combination of the two languages. But only pieces of them have a recorded English manuscript form, and that is one that is, on the evidence, tremendously difficult to disentangle from its Latinate surround. In essence, the English archive the indexers sought to unveil becomes a Latin one; for whatever reason (and several hypotheses are possible), Champernon's sermons are recorded primarily in Latin, and thus English exists here in a bilingual suspension, one in which the Latin overwhelmingly enshrouds it.

Moreover, it is clear that when Brown came to print one of these poems (*Index* 14), he substantially misrepresented it (as he did many others). He removed virtually the entire Latin surround as extraneous (although that represents the possibly English context in which the poem was supposed to have been meaningful to Champernon's congregation) and presented the work not as prose but in consecutive English lines and stanzas, about as if it were a piece of John Donne or George Herbert.[10] However, in whatever form the archive was found, Brown thought it necessary to report it

---

[9] Matters are really not so dire as this; to a competent paleographer, the English in such contexts (always assuming one were reading only to extract it) "jumps off the page." Because different languages have differing frequencies of letter use and differing frequently repeated letter sequences, the same scribe's hand never looks quite the same when he switches from one language to another. Hence patches of odd *usus scribendi* stand out, like reset passages in a pair of print books viewed in a "Hinman collator."

[10] See *Religious Lyrics of the XIVth Century* (Oxford, 1924), no. 128 at p. 228, with "context" provided by single sentence quotations from the Latin surround.

to readers (and literary historians) as if essentially similar to what was recognizably "the English national literary tradition."

Yet this analysis fails to exhaust problems associated with Champernon's English. One of the Balliol sermons (in two versions, fols. 77–86ᵛ) exists in five other copies (one a fragment), all in collections probably for use as models, and these further challenge one's security about how to fit the sermon into an English archive. At the opening, in the protheme, where Balliol 149 reads straight on in Latin, two other copies—Cambridge University Library, MS Ee.vi.27 (fol. 73ʳᵛ) and Arras, Bibliothèque de la ville, MS 184 (fol. 61ᵛᵇ)—present six lines of English verse not in Balliol (nor included in *Index*). At this point, at least vis à vis Balliol, the English archive has truly disappeared altogether, presumptively as a decision inherent in the scribal transmission of the text.

This kind of problem may be more acutely illustrated in the sermon that opens Balliol 149. There the text begins, in best bilingual fashion: "Crist in hys passion reliquit vobis quomodo schil don etc." At least three other copies of this sermon here read something along the lines of "Cryst yn hys passion exempel hath yeue how ye schold don" (Oxford, Christ Church, MS 91, fol. 122ʳᵃ; cf. Arras, fol. 51ᵛᵇ; British Library, MS Harley 331, fol. 80). Obviously, Balliol has chosen to report partially as Latin what may, in that scribe's exemplar, have been less linguistically varied than what shows in his copy, and perhaps completely English (although the other scribes show various mixtures; for instance, "exemplum" for "exempel").

But there is a further problem here. From Brown's perspective, this passage might simply be ignored, since it is not verse (and it is then thoroughly lost to scrutiny as part of an English archive, since no comparable index of prose in manuscript exists).[11] But that bit of suppression would be completely factitious positivism; the remainder of the sermon discusses Christ as an "exemplum vite," and the English here is certainly metrical verse. No scribe has bothered to write out the pretty obvious remainder of a couplet's second line, "and how ye schold lyue." Hence in book-producer and scribal terms, the English verse becomes "Latinized"

---

[11] One makes do with R. E. Lewis et al., *Index of Printed Middle English Prose* (New York, 1985), supplemented, for selected individual collections, by an ongoing series of fascicles, *The Index of Middle English Prose* (Cambridge, 1984–). For the treatment of Balliol 149, see S. J. Ogilvie-Thomson, *Handlist VIII: . . . Oxford College Libraries* (Cambridge, 1991), pp. 127–28.

in the scribal procedure of its suppression (and variously so across the copies); the truncated English accords with the convention that, in sermon manuscripts (as well as various kinds of more sophisticated theological writing), scribes rarely report full Vulgate biblical citations. The assumption seems to be, "If you can use this book, then you know your Bible well enough for me not to worry about writing it out." The partial record of English verse here (which makes it not verse, not recognizable from the perspective of traditional archivism) rests on the scribes' similar confidence about the intelligence of Champernon's readers. They are to perceive their English according to the conventions they adopt for the Latin with which it is intermixed.

Actually, variations in reporting English as such are endemic through this particular sermon, in all its copies. Bilingual text keeps slipping back into the language of Latin record. For example, Balliol 149, fol. 11 reports: "Cristus in sua passione reliquit nobis exemplum amoris quem ille precepit he badde et erat tercium principale" (similarly Harley, fol. 94; Christ Church fol. 128ra reads "hadde," and Arras fol. 58va is fully Latin, lacking the English phrase). Similarly, Arras states, near the end of the "first principal" part of the sermon (fol. 55rb): "Cristus in passione huius vite ostendit exemplum vite þat he ladde"; he opens the "second principal": "dixi quod Cristus in passione sua reliquit nobis exemplum pene quam habuit." In the first case, Harley, fol. 87 reads "had" instead of "ladde," but the remaining copies report only Latin; all copies agree in providing Latin in the second case, although "quam habuit" has plainly been written for "þat he hadde." Only Christ Church 91, and then as later hand interlineations, actually reproduces what was clearly Champernon's English:

> Intelligitis pro processu sermonis quod Cristus in passione sua
> inter alia reliquit homini exemplum /quadruplex sequendum/:
> Exemplum vite quam duxit /he ladde/
> Amoris quem precipit /he badde/
> Pene quam habuit /he hadde/
> Doctrine quam legit /he radde/ (fol. 122vb).

For this scribe a text written in Latin was recuperable, at least where it needed to be, in English. The languages might be taken, by a canny or accustomed user, as functionally interchangeable and English rhymes intuited, even from Latin forms that didn't rhyme so exactly. I would imagine this later interlineating hand actually belonged to the slow guy among the scribes who record this sermon (in addition to the English equivalents, he needs to add a Latin bridge with reminder that Christ's example is fourfold—not the expected triple division of a *sermo modernus*); he required a visual English reminder to get things right. The other copyists appear all to have known intuitively, to have been more competent bilingualists who needed no graphic English clues to reproduce appropriate English out of Latin.

Examples like these, and one can proliferate them pretty much ad lib out of manuscript, should substantially query the notion that there is a definable and discrete Middle English vernacular archive that one might prioritize. A further example, which at a certain level involves no English record at all (and no contentious problems about what verse or the language of record are) may serve to advance the argument somewhat further. Cambridge, Jesus College, MS Q.A.13 includes a sermon for the inclaustration of a holy woman, one Alice Huntingfield, inferentially delivered *c.* 1386 by an anonymous west Norfolk Franciscan preacher. At fol. 81[rv], by way of commending Alice and her holy vocation, the preacher runs through a series of allegorizations of her name. In quick succession, he tells his audience (the record is in Latin) that

(a) Alice's name directs attention to the four things that support "ciuitas anime" (a phrase from his sermon theme): amor dei, laus dei, ymago dei, and sapiencia;

(b) her name might be construed as "al ys"; that is, she is complete;

(c) her name might be etymologized as "alliciens"; that is, attracting [God's good will].

Like Henry Champernon's text, this example shows the instability of an acknowledged bilingualism in the record (with Champernon no two of the manuscripts agree in where or if English is recorded). Here, in six or seven manuscript lines, one can watch the language expressed (but not necessarily written) negotiated at every point in the Latin text. Option (b) (Alice/"all is") is fully English; the pun doesn't work as "omnis est." In contrast, option (c) (Alicia/"alliciens") must be fully Latin. And option (a) is completely bilingual: the name must be in its English form (not Latin Alicia), but the identifications proposed for its elements require the Latin and not the English terms (love, praise, ymage, wisdom would make nonsense of the point).[12] This example will prove especially generative in a later stage of the argument, when I move to examine the English verses in Lambeth 260.

Before proceeding, however, I want to disrupt the boundaries a little further, since, as Wright and Hunt have demonstrated, presenting the problem of English vernacularism as one of bilingualism distorts and simplifies the record.[13] So I turn to an anonymous monk of St. Augustine's Abbey, Canterbury. At some point early in the fourteenth century, he scribbled a note on the rear flyleaf of a Priscian, now Oxford, St. John's College, MS 152, fol. 112: "Alauda cyrrita, gallice coppede laueroc; hic cirris idem est quod cop." Of course, both "cop(pen)" and "lark" are anything but French, yet glosses like these, with "mistaken" linguistic identifications, are legion, and thus neither ignorant nor accidental.[14] At one noninquisitive level, one could read this as Latinate snobbery; both "gallice" and "anglice" could refer, from this vantage point, to languages one could imagine as "vernacular," or perhaps better "informal" (since in England at the time of this record, Anglo-Norman was every bit as much a learned language as Latin). But the scribe can only have written the record because he cared enough to record a vernacular equivalent for a

---

12 I discuss other aspects of this manuscript at "Verses in Sermons Again: The Case of Cambridge, Jesus College, MS Q.A.13," forthcoming in *Studies in Bibliography*.

13 Although I present the Jesus College sermon in the preceding paragraph as if bilingual, that is a deliberate reduction of possibility. "Alys" is an English spelling, but, after all, interchangeable with French "Alice." Thus option (b) could represent bilingual English-French and option (a) either bilingual Latin-French (in perhaps indeterminate relations, since the French derivatives would produce the acrostic every bit so well as the Latin), or a fully trilingual utterance. Matters are yet further complicated here: the scribe, from his hand and his behavior, was not an Englishman or English speaker (probably Dutch or south German) and copied any English segments in his stint *literatim*.

14 See Hunt, *Teaching*, 1:13 and the surrounding discussion. In my own experience, trilingual medical glosses (esp. the type called "Alphita," lists of herb simples and their properties) provide a rich haul of such oddments; see *Alphita: A Medico-Botanical Glossary*, ed. J. L. G. Mowat, Anecdota oxoniensa . . . Medieval and Modern Series 1, ii (Oxford, 1887), pp. 1–199. The texts themselves are significant since they presuppose that users might have found an herb named in any of the three languages (and thus could use them all).

reasonably erudite phrase,[15] perhaps as the mnemonic that would keep it in mind. It thus indicates that he in fact "thought through" some Latin at least in one other language, and, I would suggest from the linguistic identification (as well as two French glosses he wrote in on this leaf), probably two others, on some ad lib basis, a procedure to which the conclusion of this essay will direct attention. Obviously enough, the bilingualism I have been outlining has to be reformulated as at least optional polylingualism, involving individuals variously and simultaneously gifted in English, Anglo-Norman, and Latin.[16]

Lambeth Palace MS 260 demonstrates the variety of ways in which English and Latin interweave in the presentation of "vernacular" texts. Generally, the book shows English poetry mined for vernacular (or "commune") consumption, yet this procedure is not "lewed" but an at least putatively appropriative gesture. Where the English texts of the Lambeth MS speak of addressing "lewed" or "commune" readers, they distinguish these users from an undifferentiated (and here, it is claimed, unaddressed) clerical readership. Such people, the prologues to *The Northern Homily Cycle* and *The Prick of Conscience* argue, don't need books like

---

[15] So far as I can tell, the phrase is neither biblical, classical, nor patristic. Although perhaps simply a bit of accurate natural observation (the "tufted lark"), it might be an attempted gloss on Alain of Lille's two references to "alauda cithar(ist)a," *De planctu naturae*, p1 and m3.

[16] Had I the competence, I should discuss here a fourth, regionally delimited (the marches, the western edges of south Wales, Anglo-Ireland) element complicating this mixture, Celtic languages. For some early examples of multilingual Welsh texts, see Daniel Huws, *Medieval Welsh Manuscripts* (Aberystwyth, 2000), pp. 9 and 67; for another salient example, see Ieuan ap Hywel Swrdwal's "hymn to the virgin," in English, but in a traditional Welsh meter and recorded in the spelling conventions of Welsh, in *Transactions of the Honourable Society of Cymmrodorion*, n.v.n., ed. E. J. Dobson (1954), pp. 70–124. Such behavior might throw up a different view of John Trevisa's famous claim about the transformation of grammar school Latin learning from French to English; both Trevisa's named grammarmasters (like himself, a little local pride here) have Cornish surnames and may have been quadrilingual, and thus especially aware of the difficulties of imposed polylingualism at an early age. See Kenneth Sisam, ed., *Fourteenth Century Verse and Prose* (Oxford, 1921), pp. 148–49.

this, for they know their contents already—and implicitly, on the basis of the prologues' linguistic comments, know them as clerical Latin.[17]

But Lambeth 260 effectively defies this distinction, since the book itself in construction, ownership, and use shows clear signs of clerical provenance. In the grossest terms, its contents, in their juxtaposition, imply its usefulness to east Yorkshire mendicants in their public evangelical mission. In the first of the two parts in which the scribe Wilfrid constructed the volume, *The Northern Homilies*, composed of a series of English verse homilies for each Sunday of the year with at least one added exemplum for each occasion, abuts a set Dominican exemplum book, a collection of further exempla, and a partial series of *sermones de tempore*, all in Latin. The English and Latin replicate one another (and as I will show shortly, are occasionally even more interpenetrative).

Lambeth 260 is written in the dialect of Beverley, and at least its last medieval owner was certainly a Dominican of the York convent. Situating the book in either locale might offer some qualifications to the notion that it reflects a "clericism" either unific or totalizable. Both cities, *c.* 1420, house a range of sites (and thus differing, potentially competitive clerical interests) from which an interested Christian might obtain religious instruction. York was, of course, England's second metropolis, and many of its institutions (for example, Minster canons, parish and craft guilds) were very well known. But even in a smaller place (about one-third the size, yet still in medieval terms a large city) like Beverley, one should have had these instructional options: the Minster with its canons (likely nonresident), chapels, and a college of parochial vicars; a rather splendid parish church, St. Mary, almost adversarily situated at the opposite end of town at the North Bar; and two mendicant houses, Dominican and Franciscan, not to mention other possible outlets (a hospital with chapel, for example).[18] One might well imagine that each venue would have offered

---

17 Cf. Wogan-Browne et al., *The Idea of the Vernacular*, p. 127, lines 33–44, 65–80; pp. 242–43, lines 9–12 (and cf. n. 30). To some extent, of course, clerical appropriation of such texts simply represents a return to origins: the poets who composed the poems obviously utilized this very clerical mode and will have considered themselves benign mediators of "learnedness."

18 For the medieval provenance, see "Lambeth 260" (n. 1 above), pp. 134–36. For the relative sizes of Beverley and York, see D. M. Palliser, ed., *The Cambridge Urban History of Britain*, vol. 1, *600–1540* (Cambridge, 2000), p. 758 (more distantly, pp. 755, 766). Clerical competitiveness is rarely discussed outside the context of

users unique services: differing statutory functions, differing optimal clienteles (and thus opportunities for fellowship), differing degrees of access, differing degrees of allowed intimacy. Rather than the monolithic clericism the poems identify, even in the absence of specifically localized texts, the devout could choose from a veritable smorgasbord. For this reason, Lambeth 260 should be considered a book produced to meet an ecclesiastical situation involving various parties, competitively and interestedly engaged.

Besides the attention to clerically directed benefits (alms, death benefits, etc.), professionalism and honest devotion to the *cura animarum* might also encourage the improved or facilitated efforts at clerical practice this book bespeaks. But the clerical demographics of places like York or Beverley equally imply that what might have been on offer could not be totalized as Latinate, clerical, or whatever—the book testifies that practice itself had to adapt, differentiate, address niche markets, and take on graduated dimensions in a search for particular appeal to an audience. (Even the identifiable Latinate Beverley books analogous to Lambeth 260 take implicitly different stances on what might appeal—a set Dominican exemplum book and an ad lib one in Oxford, University College, MS 67, but with a different set text and with negligible attention to English; and a set Latin sermon series with added exempla in a lost book given the Franciscans in 1508.)[19] Among the local differentiations one might consider is that of language: however the texts are graphically communicated, they were potentially capable of further dispersal, both oral and written, over a range of linguistic possibility, and were geared to the audience at hand.

Imagining this book as situated within a multiform clerisy only mirrors the shifting and polyvalent interchanges between Latin and English inscribed within it. Even if the book might be localized within a situation of diverse ecclesiastical offerings, the linguistic processes inscribed there are far from single. In this section of the essay, I will try to indicate their diversity (moving from simple and commonplace to more complicated examples) and some of their implications, both for conceptions of "the clerical" and for language use in general.

---

antimendicancy, but see Wendy Scase, *"Piers Plowman" and the New Anticlericalism*, Cambridge Studies in Medieval Literature 4 (Cambridge, 1989).

[19] For these, see "Lambeth 260," p. 134.

At the grossest, Lambeth 260 neither looks like an English book, nor has it been treated as one on the page. Wilfrid's page format allows an especially dense textual block, one that might be seen as normal for his Latin materials, but not his English. There he routinely writes a highly compressed script, rarely more than three or four millimeters high, of a sort considered legible in a Latinate context but scarcely a style frequent in English poetic manuscripts. Such script habits may have seemed natural enough for Wilfrid, who might have made the book for private consultation, or his patron (another mendicant brother?), but any other reader is apt to feel desperately short of guidance among a series of lengthy, complex, and not always clearly subdivided English texts. The book needs an imposed "ordinatio" to make it readily consultable, and it received several layerings of such guidance, some (a bit fitfully) from Wilfrid himself—but virtually all of it in Latin. Much (but far from all) of the remainder was imposed (in the 1520s or 1530s?) in the hand of the book's last medieval owner, Peter Tollar or Towlar, Dominican of York.[20]

I'll discuss Wilfrid's most provocative annotations later. But one addition will illustrate the interpenetrative effects of the Latin surround to the English verse. Below the colophon concluding *The Prick* (fol. 136[vb]), Wilfrid wrote, "In septem partes huius libri diuiditur, videlicet prima pars . . ." (the anacoluthon is his own), with one-line Latin summaries of the content of each part. But the note merely doubles the text, in a different language, for Wilfrid has been guided by the author's own English verse summaries (348–65, 9533–44).

Peter's annotation, visible throughout the two-part volume, is more rigorous and consistent. Throughout English portions of the volume (but interestingly, never in the Latin, which inferentially he found perfectly readable in its impenetrable state), he provided Latin running titles. One always knows which Sunday's homily is at hand, or which part of *The Prick* one is looking at.

In addition, Peter took up what Wilfrid had left imperfectly done and provided extensive directive marginalia. He double-marked the incipits of every portion of *The Northern Homilies*, extending Wilfrid's flourished

---

20 For "ordinatio," see Malcolm B. Parkes, "The Influence of the Concepts of *Ordinatio* and *Compilatio* on the Development of the Book," *Scribes, Scripts, and Readers: Studies in the Communication, Presentation, and Dissemination of Medieval Texts* (London, 1991), pp. 35–70.

lombard and four-millimeter Latin text-ink heading by a large marginal notation of the sermon occasion. He similarly marked the subsidiary exempla, often with a designation of subject, "De X" or "Contra Y," for example. In addition, he regularly noted statements ascribed to *auctoritates* (Augustine, Gregory, Bernard, etc.), and also provided varyingly full biblical references, sometimes (like Wilfrid more sporadically) quoting the relevant bit of the Vulgate. Without exception, such materials are in Latin, not English.

This is a clerical book, and as Parkes shows (see n. 20), both Wilfrid and Peter are following a procedure established in clerical academic environments. But it will not do to say that Lambeth 260 shows these features "naturally," as it were—because they are clerical behaviors and because its users are such. For the procedures Wilfrid and Peter follow here appear widely, if not nearly ubiquitously, in English literary manuscripts. Medieval vernacular readers were entirely dependent upon nonvernacular, Latinate means of textual access, especially for close textual consultation. The obverse to the disappearing vernacular archive as I have described it above, the procedures they followed have simply been rendered invisible to modern readers of the works.

This situation follows from the conventions of modern textual presentation of medieval texts, never intended for reading in the form now customary. Following good EETS ideology (at least as an originary gesture), medieval authors should, the argument goes, be presented like the rest of the (postmedieval) canon, in a format consonant with that of their more recent fellows. The author's text—what fits in the ruled text column of the manuscript—is important, and the remainder of the manuscript record, because often variable from copy to copy, must largely represent vicissitudes of textual transmission, and should be ignored. As a result, the textual surround in which the author was made intelligible for a contemporary reader simply does not and cannot appear in a modern printed text.[21]

---

[21] The (bitterly contested) modern locus classicus has been the passus-headings of *Piers Plowman*, suppressed totally in the standard edition, gen. ed. George Kane, 3 vols. (London, 1960–97); cf. Robert Adams, "The Reliability of the Rubrics in the B-Text of *Piers Plowman*," *Medium Ævum* 54 (1985), 208–31; "Langland's *Ordinatio*: The *Visio* and the *Vita* Once More," *Yearbook of Langland Studies* 8 (1994), 51–84; and Laurence M. Clopper, "Langland's Markings for the Structure of *Piers Plowman*," *Modern Philology* 85 (1988), 245–55; "A Response to Robert Adams, 'Langland's

Thus, the marginal materials of Lambeth 260, while "clerical," are not peculiar. Medieval English texts always are rendered access-easy through Latin of varying degrees of sophistication, each instance individually describable. Readers of Middle English could process the texts in a sophisticated fashion only insofar as they were readers of Latin. This technique is, of course, explicit in some texts, often considered exceptional, where the Latin isn't a marginal aid but integral—*Confessio Amantis* and *Piers Plowman*, for example. But one might notice, in a survey of Gower or Langland manuscripts, a certain scribal hesitation, and sometimes confusion, as to whether one is copying directive Latinate annotation or legitimate text; Latin frequently tends to get written in the margin, to be recognized as "ordinatio," whatever one might think of authorial intent.

But other examples more nearly resemble the handling of Lambeth 260. Chaucer appears to modern readers, consonant with directions inscribed in various texts, as fully English. But this is an accident of modern Chaucer consumption, largely predicated upon the Hengwrt and Ellesmere *Canterbury Tales*, both of which use fully English headings. Elsewhere matters are scarcely so clear; a sequence of early copies, generally perceived as integral to the textual tradition, provide such materials (and sometimes indexes) in Latin, for example, Oxford, Corpus Christi College, MS 198; Cambridge, University Library, MS Dd.iv.24; and British Library, MS Egerton 2726. Indeed, the emphatically "English Chaucer" historically has encouraged editors to remove from the text anything that fails to accord with triumphant vernacular monolingualism, for example, a traditional Latin verse prologue to Statius's *Thebaid* which occurs in-column at *Troilus* 5.1498. In this process, many and sometimes lengthy marginal glosses, most prominent in Ellesmere and secondarily Hengwrt, involving Latin of some difficulty and including patristic and classical citation, have simply been suppressed altogether in editions. For

---

Ordinatio,'" *Yearbook of Langland Studies* 9 (1995), 141–46. Quite ironically, Bodleian Library, MS Laud misc. 581 simultaneously confirms and rebuffs one's worst suspicions. On the one hand, the scribe carefully, in light marginal references, copied the rubrics of his exemplar; then, when he returned to rubricate the places, he ignored what he had copied and supplied what he wanted. But a case could be mounted that the exemplar from which this scribe copied the ignored guides for headings was actually Langland's fair copy and what he ignored thoroughly authoritative.

all his vernacular claims, Chaucer was most emphatically like everyone else and expected Latinity of his readers.[22]

Perhaps the most persuasive example of the procedure comes from a text, like those of Lambeth 260, of Yorkshire spiritual instruction, the unpublished *Speculum Vitae*. Like Lambeth 260 texts, it is very, very long and emphatic in its address to the "lewed." At 16,100 lines, the poem is not in any sense one that might be considered "readable"; instead it is a complete compendium of religious knowledge, to be dipped into for consultation of specific points, yet intricate (and non-obvious) in its construction. For example, *Speculum Vitae* contains a complete penitential handbook; but this appears attached to the fourth member of a *distinctio* on spiritual warfare, this *distinctio* a subordinate portion of a discussion of the virtue fortitude, and this discussion presented within a more extensive treatment of the fourth petition of the "Pater noster."

In such a situation, the "lewed" reader to be instructed needs a great deal of guidance. This was provided, authorially or archetypally (the whole or substantial portions of the apparatus appear across the forty-odd surviving extensive copies), through an elaborate "ordinatio" and "compilatio." In the most careful copies, each page has a running title, often presenting three different points of entré into the text; this has been carefully coordinated with marginal sidenotes, identifying subjects discussed, authorities, and occasionally proverbs and Vulgate verses. All of these, in all copies, are in Latin, and not always obvious material. The "lewed" reader who wants to find out about cowardice, for example, does have to be able to handle "pusillanimitas." The relative popularity of

---

[22] Everyone, I assume, reads Larry D. Benson et al., *The Riverside Chaucer* (Boston, 1987) and recognizes from it comments like *Troilus* 5.1793–98. For the supratextual headings, see William McCormick, *The Manuscripts of the Canterbury Tales: A Critical Description of Their Contents* (Oxford, 1933), pp. 85–93, 95–100, 119–26 (and cf. such later, fully Latinate examples as British Library, MS Additional 5140; and Bibliothèque nationale, MS fonds anglais 39, at pp. 1–8, 379–86). In *Riverside*, the Statius prologue appears as a text-page note at p. 580. But the glosses appear in this edition only sporadically in the notes, at junctures when the taste of various annotators has found them relevant to explaining the English, for example, pp. 865 and 868, n. 278. Similarly, John M. Manly and Edith Rickert reported them only "selectively" and in an obscure spot safely removed from the text, *The Text of the Canterbury Tales*, 8 vols. (Chicago, 1940), 3:483–527. Steven B. Partridge has, for years, promised a full edition, a development of his 1992 Harvard PhD dissertation; at this time, such glosses are only visible from facsimiles.

this text across the northern half of England indicates that it was widely read—that it was successful in finding the target audience, since very few copies are overtly "clerical"—and that the "lewed" audience could cope with such a monster, through the medium of Latin.[23] The poem exemplifies the major point I hope my description of Lambeth 260 will illustrate more variously: so late as the fifteenth century, Latin clerical techniques, typically in Latin form, routinely provide a reading matrix in interplay with English, and English across a variety of genres.

Whereas Latinate marginalia may indicate the bilingualism of Middle English and its seeking to invest itself with the trappings of Latin, other forms of reception in Lambeth 260 illustrate different procedures. All these reflect not the later work of Peter Tollar but that of the original scribe Wilfrid, working in the 1410s. These gestures, in the main associated with copying the book, place English in a shifting series of juxtapositions, both generic and physical, with Latin. Various in their form—and thus yet further illustration that Latin/vernacular does not represent a smooth binary opposition—these negotiations indicate that certain kinds of consumption, not those imagined and inscribed by the authors of the English works here reproduced, required some form of Latinate treatment.

The most striking of these behaviors is Wilfrid's unparalleled "tabula" or index to *The Prick*, one that I imagine he composed himself. Indexing is entirely foreign to this text—and indeed to English writing at large before print. The most flagrant examples (the "tabula" to *Polychronicon* and table of chapters to *De Proprietatibus Rerum*) John Trevisa provided simply as part of his translations of the works, on the basis of their Latin

---

[23] Only 370 lines have ever been printed; see F. Ullman, "Studien zu Richard Rolle de Hampole," *Englische Studien* 7 (1884), 415–72 at 468–72 (lines 61–88 include the address to "lewed men"). For an illustration of a typical copy and discussion, see Vincent Gillespie, "Vernacular Books of Religion," in *Book-Production and Publishing in Britain, 1375–1475*, ed. Jeremy Griffiths and Derek Pearsall (Cambridge, 1989), pp. 317–44 at 318, 322–25; and the only extended critical discussion the poem has received, in Gillespie's "The Literary Form of the Middle English Pastoral Manual . . .," 2 vols. (unpub. Oxford University D.Phil. thesis, 1981), 1:132–40. For a mapping of many surviving copies, see Richard Beadle, "Middle English Texts and Their Transmission, 1350–1500: Some Geographical Criteria," in *Speaking in Our Tongues*, ed. Margaret Laing and Keith Williamson (Cambridge, 1994), pp. 69–91 at 83–85.

transmission.[24] As Trevisa's work shows, indexing represents a Latinate literary behavior, in Lambeth 260 imposed on a text usually understood to be consumptible without such an aid. Given that each part of *The Prick* averages something like 1,200–1,500 lines, it can be managed segment by segment, one at a sitting or oral reading, and largely on that broad topical basis (death, judgment, purgatory) carefully announced at the head of each part.

In the Latinate culture in which indexes are normal, the most commonplace examples occur at the ends of sermon cycles, especially annual *de tempore* collections created for consultation as models (for example, John Waldeby's *Novum opus dominicale* or, contemporary with Wilfrid's work, John Felton's *Sermones Mawdeleyn*). Hard-pressed preachers can construct their own Sunday sermons from these volumes either by going to the occasion they are faced with and extracting exemplary materials from a model for the occasion, or, if they have determined a thematic focus for their sermon, by using the index to find the treatment of their topic elsewhere in the collection. Indexes always function as a supplement to straightforward "ordinatio"-driven consultation that seeks the obvious, the most relevant locus in the book; thus they need never be searching or complete.[25]

Indeed, given that most indexes to sermon manuscripts are fragmentary and far from comprehensive search tools, Wilfrid's represents an extraordinary effort to order a vernacular poem, through the medium of a Latinate consultative device *composed in Latin*. This "tabula" is hugely extensive—more than six hundred head-entries (that is, one for about every dozen or so lines of *The Prick*), all of them easily retrieved through references to the numbered openings Wilfrid imposed on the text sheets while copying. This unprecedented aid to a vernacular text exists as a remarkably clean fair-copy at fols. 137–38ᵛ, a folded sheet separate from

---

[24] Neither Latin nor English "tabula" is printed in *Polychronicon Ranulphi Higden . . .*, ed. Churchill Babington and J. Rawson Lumby, Rolls Series 41, 9 vols. (London, 1865–86), but see M. C. Seymour et al., *On the Properties of Things . . .*, 3 vols. (Oxford, 1975–87), 1:1–38.

[25] Cf., for example, Richard H. and Mary A. Rouse's description of the massive Franciscan exegetical index, *Tabula Septem Custodiarum*, at *Registrum Anglie de Libris Doctorum et Auctorum Veterum*, Corpus of British Medieval Library Catalogues 2 (London, 1991), pp. ci–iii.

the actual text; Wilfrid must have made draft notes for it elsewhere and recopied the results here. The "tabula" itself shows only that Wilfrid went about the job sequentially, but not when; he might have constructed his tool either while copying, or later, while rereading the leaves he had written. But, as "tabula," this is rough and a bit *retardetaire*; it is alphabetically ordered, but only for the first letter of each entry, ordering within each letter being that of the first noted attestation of each indexed item.[26]

Such a detailed tool almost rebuffs analysis; on the other hand, one can only discuss a manuscript "tabula" by attempting to use it, a procedure in which I have engaged selectively.[27] Obviously enough, the index offers, given its meticulousness, often concordance-like access to *The Prick*; many items include multiple references, allowing access to a fair conspectus of usages. The most heavily referenced entries—"omnes" 11x, "qui" 11x, "luxuria" 10x, "non" 10x, "dies" 7x, "quod" 7x—will indicate the absence of any single overt emphasis in Wilfrid's activity and the broad use to which he imagined subjecting *The Prick*.

In the main, but far from entirely, the "tabula" appears to have been keyed to *The Prick*'s many Latin citations (sometimes, as in 1324–25, where both "continuus" and "dampnacio" are indexed, more than one

---

[26] Cf. the opening of "P," for example: Populus 2, 23; paruulus 3, 24, 73; puluis 3, 5; peccatum 3, 11, 14 (dupliciter dicitur), 23; per 4, 17, 23; producere 4, 7; pediculus 4; permanere 4; potestatibus 4, 33; paucitas 4; post 5; prospera 6, etc. On the development of fully alphabetical indexing (not simply alphabetizing the first, or first two or three letters) during the thirteenth century, see Richard H. Rouse and Siegfried Wenzel's review of E. J. Dobson, *Moralities on the Gospels*, *Speculum* 52 (1977), 649–50.

[27] I have examined all references given for the first fifteen entries under "P" and all those for one three-opening (that is, the verso+recto combination to which Wilfrid's numeration refers) tranche of the text (openings 5–7, roughly lines 850–1620), another seventy-five entries. One should notice that Wilfrid began the index in a considerably more expansive (and Latinate) mode than he continued it, a tendency elsewhere apparent in the Latin-English relations of the manuscript (see pp. 348 below). Early entries, through "D," direct the user not just to the opening but include a letter as well; following a system developed to divide chapters in preversified Vulgates (there seven sections, a through g), Wilfrid appears to have contemplated dividing each opening into sixteen lettered sections a through q (that is, four for each column). But not only did he not persist in these more exact references, Wilfrid never provided marginal indexing signs in the text.

key term in the citation).[28] Through this activity, Wilfrid converted the Middle English text into a genre rather different from the original; a discussion of "the four last things" became a searchable encyclopedia of devotional and instructional material. As a result of his labors, Wilfrid could "concord" the English text with any particular Latinate scriptural *locus* that might have interested him and mined it for the kinds of exemplary material in which the text delights. "Foresta," for example, mentioned in n. 28, appears in the poem as one member of four linked comparisons, "the world is like . . ." (1211–56); the index also includes entries for "mundus" and "suavitas," both of which also refer to this locus and its surround.

Given the mendicant provenance of Lambeth 260, this device should have been useful for producing public vernacular sermons. These typically will have taken a "theme" from the assigned gospel for the day, offered a threefold division of a phrase from this locus, and practiced traditional rhetorical "amplificatio" to develop a protracted and detailed sermon argument.[29] Moreover, the Latin quotations may have appeared a convenient way to accomplish these goals, since Wilfrid may have found the Latin lines in the poem easier to spot on the page than an English reference (cf. n. 9, a skill I can't imagine, but which worked routinely, when required, for medieval readers).

One might pause a moment to consider what these "tabula" procedures mean. On the assumption that Wilfrid imagined constructing vernacular sermons, both his input and product were thoroughly English, although they differed in mode: a received and very widely known vernacular poem (one that probably itself could have been cited as "authoritative")[30] and an original "translation" of its information into a different rhetorical situation, oral homiletic instruction. But for Wilfrid

---

28 English references include "diuisio 5" (to either 948–79 or 986–1005, the latter with "In twa partes deuised"), "foresta 6" (to 1235–44), "fortuna 6" (to 1273–86, but also in Latin at 1312), "hic 7" (to "here" 1372 but relevant to the more general discussion of "hic mundus" that follows), and "ire de mundo 7" (to "til we sal hethen turne" 1375 and the subsequent discussion of being "aliens" or "pilgryms," for example, 1394–95).

29 Cf. Th. M. Charland, *Artes praedicandi: Contribution à l'histoire de la rhétorique en moyen âge* (Paris, 1936); and see n. 8 above.

30 In his sermon, however, Wilfrid is more apt to have cited the authorities the poem itself cites (as if he knew the full texts thoroughly) and to have elided altogether his mode of access to them.

to negotiate between these two analogous, yet differently emphatic, acts of vernacular instruction, he found it necessary to construct a mediating tool entirely Latinate, not only in its history as a tool but in the language that it uses and the language to which it normally refers in *The Prick*.

Wilfrid's indexing challenges a number of conventional assumptions about both "clericism" and language relations in medieval England. Through indexing, the scribe converts *The Prick* into something like a kit for producing a book differing from the received text in both emphasis and use. Moreover, this "book" is entirely "virtual," and is not present for our scrutiny. Its form was the oral, and very likely unfixed, situational and improvisational, instruction Wilfrid might offer his congregation. Lambeth 260 does not occupy a simple language boundary, but one that confounds categories of "clerical" and "vernacular," "written" and "oral," in ways often unnoticed. In essence, a Latinate clerical activity, indexing, allows Wilfrid to use a vernacular text as if it were a (Latinate) "authority" while he proceeds in an oral, uninscribed vernacular mode (and whether homiletic or confessional, at some remove programmed by Latinate manuals). This reversal typifies other features of Lambeth 260.

The volume includes among its other materials a Latin exemplum book with interspersed English lyrics (to which I will turn in greater detail in a moment). This item is particularly striking because portions of its materials can be paralleled elsewhere, and their transmission and presentation again involve some variety of clerical orality. For example, the Latin surround to what is presented in the Appendix as verses **b** also appears in British Library, MS Harley 7322 but in a significantly more attenuated form than in Lambeth 260.

Such variable transmission is, in some sense, in the nature of the Latinate genre. Literarily conceived "exemplum books," such as Holcot's *Convertimini* in Lambeth 260, typically have texts about as fixed as any other medieval Latin work circulating in manuscript, but the personally tailored collections of Harley or Lambeth, like (for example) modern adolescents' books of jokes, frequently display only a notional sense of "the text." As a rule, such collections appear to consist of items the compiler has read or heard (perhaps in another sermon, perhaps in its oral delivery; perhaps in a refectory reading—or just as refectory conversation) and found interesting, potentially useful, and worthy of record. The status of exempla as "texts," however, is entirely freeform, each version some approximative recounting, including whatever detail will serve as mnemonic to stimulate the compiler, when he goes to appropriate the text to illustrate a point in an oral sermon.

A particularly telling example occurs in one of the texts edited in my Appendix. At the end of verses **d**, following an attenuated account of a British king killed by means of a poisoned fountain, the exemplum introduces a moralization that involves covering the fountain with a "cumulus terre." The reader might well wonder where this pile of earth has come from, since it is unsignaled at any earlier point in the anecdote. Actually, the narrative portion of the exemplum has been communicated in truncated form, and, in the source account, Geoffrey of Monmouth's learned Latin *Historia*, the "cumulus" in fact occurs. Wilfrid's text here deliberately suppresses a portion of the Latin source nonetheless integral to his account. The form of record thus resembles whatever English instruction Wilfrid generated from indexing *The Prick*; once again, mnemonic stimulus has superseded textual fidelity. And the accuracy one might expect from a Latin text with a learned basis has again dissolved into a doubly oral virtuality—in reception, perhaps clerical gossip, and potentially in any of three languages; in final transmission, an episode within a sermon about mercy, perhaps, but not necessarily, in English.

Indeed, although they frequently show considerable variation, the English verses recorded in these contexts tend to be relatively stable. That is, they more closely resemble a customary intuitive view of authoritative Latin textuality than does the Latinate exemplary surround in which they appear. Just as Wilfrid might invoke *The Northern Homilies* or *The Prick* as a perhaps silenced authority underlying an oral exchange of spiritual information, the verses show an authoritative fidelity not usually associated with vernacular texts.

One might ascribe a further wavery kind of "authority" to the Latin exempla as well. They frequently assert their reliance upon preexisting texts (ones in Latin), and the power of their rhetorical appeal rests, to some degree, upon the assurance of Latinate scholarly fidelity to dignified and august sources—vehicles of emphatic truthfulness. But ascriptions of authority in the Lambeth 260 exempla often turn out to be somewhat less "authoritative" than they seem. The Geoffrey anecdote I discuss above is ascribed generically, and not authorially, "in gestis Anglorum," although it concerns the *British* king Uther.

Or again, one might well be perplexed by the ascription of appendix verses **e** to "Romulus in annalibus Iudeorum," with further elaboration claiming for him an Æsop translation as well, all "mis[si] Tiberio filio suo." While "Romulus" was certainly well known in the Middle Ages as a pseudonymous late Latin fabulist whose prologue addresses his son Tiberinus, he is not a historian. Given that the information here appears to be from Josephus's *Antiquitates* (4.223–24), perhaps fleshed out from its source in Deut. 17, the bibliographic reference to Æsop may well have started life as a misreading of a comparable Josephus bibliography. The historian, after all, wrote a *Contra Apion*, and this title, misconstrued, may have generated further prolific misinformation. The ascription, designed to confer authority on an account ultimately biblical, at the end of the day nearly parodies learned Latinity.[31]

I return briefly to Wilfrid's "tabula" and its reliance on the inset Latin quotations in *The Prick of Conscience*. Wilfrid may have wished to attend to the poem's Latin for reasons other than simple convenience of reference. For unlike texts like *Confessio Amantis* and *Piers Plowman*, *The Prick*, while riddled with grammatically integrated Latin citations, also accommodates a potentially "lewed" target audience, and it translates everything. Thus, through the Latin, Wilfrid could be directed to useful and usable English verses, conversion of a brief Bernardine *sententia* into English couplets, for example. He would be spared the trouble of "inventio." For *The Prick*'s roughly four-stress couplets entirely accord with the kind of "poetry," those brief mnemonics, that typically appears recorded within Latin homiletic contexts.

A pretty substantial amount of such verse appears in Lambeth 260, but accessing it requires behaviors rather different from Wilfrid's other

---

[31] For the Geoffrey anecdote, from *Historia regum Britanniae* 8.24, see *The Historia Regum . . . I: Bern, Burgerbibliothek, MS. 568*, ed. Neil Wright (Cambridge, 1985), ¶ 142 at 100 (with the sentence, not in Lambeth 260, "Succubuerunt etiam centum homines post illum, donec comperta fraude cumulum terre superapposuerunt." [And a hundred men also died as he had, until, having discovered this treason, they covered the fountain with a mound of earth.]). Cf. Appendix verses **b**, ascribed as "Secundum commentatorem Macrobii . . . in tres voluminibus," probably only a reference to Macrobius's commentary on "Somnium Scipionis" itself (see 1.4.58–60, 62–75); the three volumes are simply the Ciceronian text and the two books of commentary on it. See further the amusing scribalism at the head of verses **i**, but also notice an apparently accurate reference to Josephus *in propria persona*, at the head of an exemplum on fol. 80[va].

encounters with English verse in Lambeth 260. I print as an appendix ten English snatches, nine unknown to Brown-Robbins-Cutler.[32] One of these is relatively freestanding and follows the conclusion to Wilfrid's first sequence of sermons; the remainder, like the disappearing English archive I have earlier described, is embedded within Latin (but eight items certainly presented as verse, set off as short lines with line-brackets). In this instance, the verse is transmitted within a sequence of thirty exempla, about a quarter of them with verses. If one could imagine Wilfrid's Latinate access to *The Prick* as relatively straightforward, these English bits raise the prospect of constantly negotiated interlingual relations of a type I have earlier described in the sermon for Alice Huntingfield's inclaustration.

Such embedded verse initially might lead one to ask whether it is English at all. This question means something more than simply a linguistic identification (it is surely English). Can such verses, as Carleton Brown wished, be recuperated independently of the recorded context, the Latin surround in which they have been placed and rendered bilingual? Wilfrid's poem (Appendix verses a) stands apart as a careful direct translation of a preexisting Latin lyric. But the remaining verses, at least insofar as they have transmissional histories, appear only in a "bound" bilingual form. They are not known outside the context of Latin records of exempla, the same guise in which they appear here.[33]

Within this transmission, a relevant criterion to consider might be called "degree of boundedness." To what extent do these verse bits form clearly independent English "lyrics"? How well might each stand on its own, detached altogether from the Latinate surround in which it is

---

[32] M. R. James and Claude Jenkins, in *A Descriptive Catalogue of the Manuscripts in the Library of Lambeth Palace*, 2 vols. (Cambridge, 1930–32), 1:406–9, noticed the presence of English in these folios.

[33] Wilfrid's lyric is a version of Hans Walther, *Initia carminum ac versuum Medii Aevi posterioris Latinorum*, 2nd ed. (Göttingen, 1969), no. 12993. Five sets of the verses within the exempla here are unique. Four of those paralleled elsewhere have been derived from the same sources as those available to compilers of a pair of manuscripts, National Library of Scotland, MS Advocates 18.7.21 and British Library, MS Harley 7322. Both are preacher's notebooks, both certainly from the western edge of Norfolk, and both inferentially (Advocates certainly) Franciscan in origin. For full particulars, see the head notes to each section of the Appendix; for discussion, including some notice of other residual South Yorkshire use, see "Jesus College" (see n. 12 above); "Lambeth 260," p. 134.

found? Answers to such questions are quite various; the verses resist any totalizing generalization.[34]

Perhaps the most clearly embedded English bit of all appears as verses f. This couplet can only allude to the Latin narrative into which it is inserted; isolated as "an English verse/poem," it would be senseless, unless one knew the little story to which it alludes.[35] One might especially emphasize the end of the Latin account; there the two verses are treated as if they were a biblical text to be glossed, subjected to exegetical phrasal analysis (which interestingly, does not require the *ipsissima verba* of their original citation). Strikingly, the least independent English statement in the entire set becomes most fully recuperable within a learned rhetorical mode befitting the Latinity within which the verses have been submerged. Most similar to this example are probably verses e; here the rhymes require marginal Latin and internal bilingual glosses to make the appropriate point—that the power of Christian mercy surpasses both Old Testament rigor and the classical cardinal virtues. None of these is ever mentioned in the English text, and indeed, the Latin, as recorded, only implicitly links them to the five counselors of the anecdote.[36]

Other verses, only liminally intelligible in a fully English context, provoke different and more complicated analyses. The couplet that forms appendix verses i could just about stand alone as a recognizable version of an English "(twelve) abuses" poem.[37] But this English couplet isn't at all independent of its context, since its terms have been set by an enigmatic set of initials, in the narrative requiring an oracle for decipherment, and signaling specific Latin words the English more or less reproduces.

---

[34] Wenzel's *Preachers, Poets . . .* (see n. 6) offers extensive discussions of Latin-English verse relations in recorded sermons.

[35] That great bone of 1950s New Critical/Exegetical contention, the lyric "Maiden in the moor lay" (*Index* 3891), very likely is of this type; see Wenzel, "The Moor Maiden—A Contemporary View," *Speculum* 49 (1974), 69–74, but also John Spiers, *Medieval English Poetry: The Non-Chaucerian Tradition* (London, 1957), pp. 59–64; and J. A. Burrow, "Poems without Contexts," *Essays in Criticism* 29 (1979), 6–32.

[36] The marginal "Fides" inexactly translates "trewth" in an appropriate Northern sense, but the verses clearly intend "trewth" here to mean "veritas." Cf. the meeting of Langland's female personifications Mercy and Truþe in *Piers Plowman* B 18, the latter given to starkly retributive justice.

[37] Cf., for example, *Index* 873, 884, 906, etc.; see the entry, *Index*, 740, s.v. "Abuses of the Age."

Moreover, I would suspect that the eight letters are related in another fashion—as a Latin anagram; seven of them (but not "P") could be joined to form "InVIDIa MORS." In the narrative, the rise of this vice has produced the downfall of Carthage.

In contrast to these examples, a number of the verses resemble Wilfrid's prayer to the Virgin (**a**), in that whatever their narrative embeddedness, they might well stand apart from the Latin surround as meaningful English verses. In some measure, such a distinction from the English bits I have been describing rests (like verses **i**) upon seeing the English verses as (a) relatively detached from the accompanying Latin narrative, as recorded; and (b) in content, addressing a universal imperative of the Christian life. Examples would include verses **c and d** (on mercy), **g**, **h** (although it is potentially an elaborate sermon division), and most marginally, **j** (legible as the commonplace comparison of Christ to a lover-knight).[38]

Yet even these instances, at least as they are recorded, rely upon the Latin to some degree. One could abstract the lover-knight verses **j**, but the resulting "lyric" would be shorn of the claim made in the Latin for these as explicitly "clothing verses." This detail may imply that the recorded exemplum in fact signals an extensive moralizing development of the Christ-knight's incarnational clothing along lines similar to *Ancrene Riwle*'s moralized shield. Similarly, verses **g**, attached to but a single member of a twelve-part alphabetical distinction, may well be the remains of something a good deal fuller, and with alphabetical attachment to the Latin, whose language the verse appropriates (cf. "ludus honestus non placent" and "turned es to sorow all oure play").[39]

These verses' status as "translation" is reminiscent of several other examples, notably Wilfrid's verses **a** and the most extensive English here, verses **b**. The translated verse can never quite be dissociated from the wit

---

[38] Cf. *Ancrene Riwle* 7, *Medieval English Prose for Women*, ed. Bella Millett and Jocelyn Wogan-Browne (Oxford, 1990), pp. 112–16; and another example, printed at "Jesus College" (n. 12 above).

[39] Verses **c** might be seen as rather marginal as well. There are actually two poetic scraps here, not a single text; they are only recognizable as such from the Latin's identification of each as being written on separate parts of a "cor scissum." Moreover, the location of the statue of Mercy with its severed heart in the "templum Veste" elides altogether the obvious homiletic point—that the severed heart is that of the crucified Christ, awaiting man's prayers. And the classical connections might imply that the verses, like those discussed in the next paragraph, actually translate Latin hexameters, here not reported.

involved in converting sequences of Latin leonine hexametres into English distichs. In some sense, verses like these exist precisely to indicate the adeptness that comes with bi- or polylingualism, the ability to shift between languages while conveying closely comparable content within closely comparable form. But even here, there are "varying degrees of freedom or boundedness."

Verses **b**, paralleled in Harley 7322, is particularly interesting in this regard. The Harley version is relatively sparse in detail and provides the bare outline "hora," "dieta," an "a . . . vsque ad" statement (sometimes more explicit than that in Lambeth 260), and "radius."[40] Most strikingly, the Harley version reports none of the Latin leonine hexametres included in Lambeth. But the inclusion of Latin renders the verses precisely liminal, and indicates that they might be recuperated in either language and could appear in either fully English or fully Latin form, depending on the desired audience.

Verses **b** involves a further complication; unlike other comparable Lambeth examples, its Latin and English verses are not equivalent. The two languages do not stand in any clearly "translational" relationship, and indeed, the Latin hexametres appear particularly labile, on their restatement at the end of each "hora" sometimes including elements not part of the formal statement of the full verse (cf. "quinta hora"). Moreover, the English verses often appear out of synch with the surrounding Latin content.

I should think that Lambeth's record of the Latin and English verses **b** provides yet another counterintuitive example of what might be postulated as the normative relation of the two languages. Not only has the relative fixity one might want to associate with Latin transmission vis à vis English disappeared, but the fullness of the Latin prose record here (and not in the Harley version) has frequently been achieved by rendering the English verses inconsequential and *not* like the Latin ones. This lack of parallelism between English verse and Latin surround invariably rests on a single copying technique Wilfrid chooses. He fills out the subsequent Latin record (as it appears in Harley 7322) on the basis of the

---

40 For example, for Lambeth's fairly elaborate account of the boy and his hoop, Harley offers only "a cuna et nutrice vsque ad trocum solacium." I'm grateful to Richard Beadle for offering me advice about this version of the poem. With the discussion in the next paragraph, cf. the extensive lyric printed at "Jesus College."

preceding English couplet; for example, "bow and lowte" under "tercia hora" suggesting to him "promocionem honoris et reuerencie" under "quarta hora." The plenitude one might presume associated with Latin has been programmed by the "vernacular" to the actual detriment of stating clearly the ten "diete" of man's life, as they appear succinctly (if less interestingly) in Harley 7322. Since there is certainly no "fixed text" here, one cannot describe this as "scribal error," although it resembles (and is similarly motivated to) many examples of scribal attraction to surrounding copy. The very temporality of textual reproduction, that something must come first and that it can exercise a magnetic attraction on what will follow, intrudes upon the copying.

Just as English appears within Latin in the Lambeth 260 exemplum book, Latin is not totally foreign to the in-column presentation of the English texts of the MS (as opposed to the marginal materials I have already discussed). At the end of *The Northern Homily Cycle*, the original text does not seem to have taken account of the variable number of Sundays after Pentecost. Lambeth 260 intrudes a brief Latin sermon for an apparently omitted homily for the twenty-fourth Sunday (fols 62vb–63ra), a treatment paralleled at various points in other copies.[41] But, if briefly, more flagrant Latinate activity intrudes on the English texts of Lambeth 260. Here the direction of temporal intrusion is reversed from what one sees in the preceding discussion of verses **b**. Rather than adjacently copied materials influencing what succeeds, Wilfrid's copying becomes driven by anticipation, his knowledge that he is engaged in creating a comprehensive sermon book and that the English preaching materials, the verse homilies that open the volume, will be reprised in a Latin Lenten collection to be provided later. The intrusiveness of temporality appears again in some sporadic gestures within *The Northern Homilies*.

As I have previously noted, Wilfrid's marginal activity in the volume is sporadic. But it is at its most intense over about a dozen leaves (fols 19^v–30), that section of *The Northern Homilies* that will correspond with later Latin materials. At this point in the English poem, Latin becomes an

---

[41] The incipit: "Secundum Mattheum [9:18–26]. . . . Loquente Ihesu ad turbas ecce princeps vnus. . . . Inter omnia miracula que Dominus noster per semetipsum ostendit in terris non legimus resuscitasse nisi tres viros. . . ." ["According to Matthew. . . As he was speaking these things unto them, behold a certain ruler . . . Among all those miracles Jesus personally showed, we find that he brought only three people back to life. . . ."]

integral part of its presentation, an activity that begins in the margins. In the sermon for Quinquagesima (*Index* 2971, on Luke 18:31–43; this entire section remains unprinted), the English preacher describes how Jesus

> ... fand be þe gate sytand
> A blynd man on hym calland;
> And Crist stod and gaf hym syght (89–91, fol. 22ᵛᵃ).

Wilfrid adds marginally a threefold Latin distinction, predicated upon the acts of sitting and begging described in the gospel.[42]

When this activity continues in the next sermon, for the first Sunday in Lent (*Index* 1862, on Matt. 4:1–11), it has become quite extensive. One note, again marginal, is carefully articulated with the English text, here describing Jesus's rejection of the temptation to turn stones into bread:

> Be Crist answere may we se
> Þat gastly° fode mare louys he;   *spiritual*
> Þat gers° man do ma gud-dedys   *causes*
> Þan bred þat mans body fedys.
> For Godys wordys es sall-fode°   *soul-food, spiritual sustenance*
> Þat gerys man kyth° costys° gode.   *display / manners, behavior*
> Forthi burd° chyldyre of Haly-kyrk   *it behoves*
> Here þis fode and aftyre it wyrk (107–14, fol. 23ᵛᵃ).

By the third line, Wilfrid adds, "*Mathei.* Sibi enim et non Deo ieiuniat qui hoc quod corpori subtrahit non pauperibus erogat, set sibi in posteruum

---

42 "*Cecus sedebat secum viam* [Luke 18:35]. Bene autem cecus iste secus viam sedere et mendicare dicitur, quia non sunt nonnulli qui nec secus viam sedent nec mendicant, id est qui nec Dominum credunt nec spirituales diuicias ab eo querunt. Sunt iterim et alij qui secus viam sedent set non mendicant, sicut peruersi et falsi Cristiani qui Dominum credunt set a bono opere torpentes spirituales diuicias querere non student. Ad huc et iterim sunt alij qui secus viam sedent et mendicant, id est qui Deum credunt et celestem gloriam assiduis oracionibus querere non cessant." [*A blind man sat by the wayside.* The text properly says that this blind man sat and begged, because there are many who neither sit by the wayside nor beg, namely those who neither believe in God nor seek spiritual riches from him. There are also others who sit by the wayside but do not beg, namely those who believe in God but, sluggish in their works, are not eager to seek spiritual riches. In addition, there are others who both sit by the wayside and beg, namely those who believe in God and who do not cease to seek heavenly glory through their constant prayers.]

reseruat" [*In Matthew*. A man who keeps for his own future use what he withdraws from his body, rather than giving it to the poor, fasts for his own benefit and not God's] (a statement conventional for this occasion; cf. *Patrologia Latina* 118:192, 155:1795).

But on three occasions in this homily (fol. 23ra–va, following lines 20, 90, and 126), Wilfrid's Latin annotations appear in-column, like the (authorial) quotations of biblical and authoritative *loci* in *The Prick*. The vernacular homily becomes filled out, for example, by a typical (here double-rhymed) Latin sermon division:

> For whare oure gospell sais today
> Þat Sathanas bad Ihesus say
> Þat stanes suld he torn to brede,
> Þare may we se þe feyndys rede°,   *counsel*
> Þat redd° hym to mak brede of stan   *advised*
> For he hym saw hongere as man.
> Triplex est ieiunium, primum corporis a cibo mali, secundum afflicionis a gaudio temporali, tercium spiritualis a peccato mortali. Hoc modo triplici ieiunio debemus castigare iumentum nostrum, id est carnem. [Fasting is threefold: first, of the body, withdrawing from evil food; second, of affliction, withdrawing from worldly joys; third, spiritual, withdrawing from mortal sin. Likewise, we ought to chastise that ox of ours, our flesh, with this triple fasting.]
> For ryfly° when men hongeres sare   *frequently*
> Þai pas mesor° and etys mare   *moderation*
> Þan dos þam gud to þer body
> And fals so in glotony (85–94, fol. 23rb).

The material, while not verbally exact, at least generally corresponds to (and would help fill out) the discussion of "ieiunium" in the later Latin outline sermon for this occasion.[43] In all these cases, Wilfrid's Latin edi-

---

[43] Most verbally proximate is part of the comment following line 20 (fol. 23ra): "Permisit tamen se a maligno spiritu temptari vt nobis exemplum pungnandi ostend(er)et" [Nevertheless, he allowed himself to be tempted by an evil spirit, in order to display for us an example of spiritual warfare]; cf. "Qui ieiuniat temptatur. Vnde et diabolus statim post ieiunium temptauit Cristum. In quo edocemur quod qui aliqua bona incipiunt, ut ieiunia vel huiusmodi, statim a diabolo impungnantur" (fol. 86rb). [The man who fasts is tempted. Therefore the Devil tempted Christ immediately after his fasting, through which we learn that anyone who begins any good works, fasting or such like, is immediately attacked by the Devil.]

torial work indicates the necessity of supplementing the English with the Latin. For whatever desired homiletic effect, the two must work in tandem.

Wilfrid's anticipatory copying implies that he had at least a vague plan before he began copying the first part of his volume. He knew, perhaps in a rather fuzzy way, that he would later include in his volume Lenten portions of a Latin "de tempore" cycle in abbreviated form. At the point he was engaged with *The Northern Homilies*, he may not have been either fully aware of or fully determined about the extent of these materials, but he could at least be certain they would include 1 Lent. Thus he attempted some pump-priming; he could see ways of accommodating his English text to the probable emphases of any sermon for 1 Lent (which would address the same gospel lection, the temptation in the wilderness, whatever its language). In essence, the English and the Latin might be "concorded" and useful detail cribbed from either the next time he or his patron was confronted with producing a sermon for this occasion. Indeed, the emphasis upon triple divisions in the Latin inserts here implies a readiness to construct a sequence of diversely structured sermons for the same occasion, relying on varying materials from both languages. The brief space for which Wilfrid adopts this procedure (like the partially present column-divisions mentioned in n. 27) probably indicates that he found the process too difficult to sustain. It is, after all, hard enough to copy a text in one language, without having to interrupt the procedure to check one's own sermon notes for relevant oddments and to reach some decision about the optimal position to insert them within a separate English exemplar from which one is copying.

But in this manuscript (as the "tabula" to *The Prick* also indicates), neither set of sermons can be construed as a truly self-substantial entity (as *The Northern Homily Cycle* customarily exists elsewhere), discretely bound within the linguistic categories "Latin/vernacular." The two simply interpenetrate—the Latin perhaps more useful for its customary categorical and exegetical precision, the English for its development of bare biblical narrative (indeed in some way replacing the august Latin Vulgate account). The two versions supplement each other, the English valuable perhaps precisely because it is *not* concise but in some measure evocative or suggestive (cf. my discussion of appendix verses **b** above).

I do not want here to offer—as rhetorical prescription says that I should—any summary of this section. The materials I assemble from

Lambeth 260 should simply sit here, in their full and utter messiness, in all the variousnesses of Wilfrid's and Peter Tollar's negotiations between English and Latin. Only by internalizing the detailed, multiform, and unstable bilingual engagement inscribed in Lambeth 260, one that I would argue is exemplary of a wide variety of other contexts, does one get any sense of what "the situation of the vernacular" in late medieval England might have been like.

So what is one to say, in the context of Lambeth 260, about discussions of "English vernacularity"? My analysis enters a discussion that seems to me limited for two reasons. First, vastly too many studies rely on notions of a self-enclosed English archive as I have outlined it in part I—that medieval language usage could be recuperable on the basis of discrete texts, and particularly of discrete printed texts. As my discussion will have made clear, modern edited volumes have been deliberately sanitized to reduce, if not obliterate, signs of polylingual usage. Middle English is the province of "Anglistik," and editors, following convention, have often suppressed oddments in other languages. But the world in which medieval texts actually exist, the manuscripts frequently misreproduced in the visible archive, tells a rather different story.[44]

Second, many discussions appear to have been authored by persons with only a theoretical knowledge of operative bilingualism. At the best, many who have addressed this subject have conned up their languages through *grammatica* and for, as graduate school regulations have it, "reading knowledge" alone. They simply do not have the experience of how bi- or polylingualism operates in practice or what it might mean to someone habituated to interactions, often with the same people, in more than one language.[45]

---

[44] I think here of some of the essays collected in Fiona Somerset and Nicholas Watson, eds., *The Vulgar Tongue: Medieval and Postmedieval Vernacularity* (University Park, Penn., 2003). Similarly, Christopher Cannon, *The Grounds of English Literature* (Oxford, 2004), against considerable counter-evidence, argues implicitly for his authors' monolingualism.

[45] This was an experience available to my father in New Mexico as recently as 1911–17. At home, he listened to and spoke in two closely related mother tongues, German and (standard) Yiddish. When he ventured on the street, he spoke Spanish like everyone else (always dialectal Spanish, and on some occasions mixed with Mescalero Apache). His only "grammatically" acquired language was English, which he learned at age six on entering the U.S. public educational system. This, even years

Thus, I think the issue of "the vernacular" is in need of substantial reformulation, beginning with some consideration of "the situation of literature in the English later Middle Ages." This is, of course, the only way in which the "vernacular" initially becomes visible to us, as a written (printed) text of interest to someone in an English department. Whatever may be said about the growth of "literacy" in the later Middle Ages,[46] if one is considering literary culture, it extends to only a tiny subset of those somehow "literate." Were one to accept the usual estimates of English population *c.* 1400 of about three million, one would probably be discussing a "literarily literate" community of something like 5 percent (an estimated 2 percent adult males in orders), 150,000 people, dispersed throughout the country. Testimony to such a thin or narrow potential reading community is provided by the apparent poverty of manuscript remains from the fourteenth century, particularly books in English, as well as by what one can gauge of the nature of literary communities that used these books or patronized their authors.[47]

---

later, he resented as one of several impositions inherent in this citizenly formation; until the advent of "bilingual education" in the 1970s, schoolchildren across the Southwest were allowed to speak Spanish, if at all, in furtive groups on the playground during recess. Cf. a discussion to which I will return, Gloria Anzaldúa, "How to Tame a Wild Tongue," *Borderlands/La Frontera: The New Mestiza* (San Francisco, 1987), pp. 53–62.

[46] The standard study is M. L. Clanchy, *From Memory to Written Record, England 1066–1307*, 2nd ed. (London, 1993); see also Brian Stock, *The Implications of Literacy* (Princeton, 1983). One might emphasize some of the constraints on which Clanchy touches, further developed in various essays by Margaret Aston, *Lollards and Reformers: Images and Literacy in Late Medieval Religion* (London, 1984): during this period, reading and writing constituted different literate skills, not necessarily conjoined; contemporaneously, an "oral literacy," especially associated with depictions of women (the Wife of Bath, Lollard women, Margery Kempe), exists— involving no ability we would identify as "literate," but including the capacity to perform sophisticated literary operations on a text absorbed through the ear. There are also useful comments in Parkes, "The Literacy of the Laity," *Scribes, Scripts . . .* (see n. 20), pp. 275–97.

[47] Here the classic studies are Paul Strohm, "Chaucer's Audience," *Literature and History* 5 (1977), 26–41; and "Chaucer's Fifteenth Century Audience and the Narrowing of the 'Chaucer Tradition,'" *Studies in the Age of Chaucer* 4 (1982), 3–32. Cf. the wise comments of the most gifted and intense modern student of Anglo-Norman language, William Rothwell, on the kind of "laypeople" Pierre d'Abernon of Fetcham imagined as the audience for *La Lumere as lais*, "Henry of Lancaster and Geoffrey Chaucer: Anglo-French and Middle English in Fourteenth-Century

Moreover, if one considers this group of "literary literates," one should immediately become aware of the power relations that run in tandem with literary sophistication. For literacy of this stripe can be variously and directly associated with those social groups one might identify as those likely least "progressive." Among the literarily privileged 150,000, one must include royalty and aristocracy, with their vested interests in the law and its administration; clerical figures, in many cases administrative "servants" of the first but otherwise engaged in acts of moral discipline, from the parish level up; and mercantile groups generally committed to trade in luxuries and to trade protectionism (hence also complicit with royal and magnatial activities) and suppression of anything like working persons' organizations.[48] In short, there is no reason to expect from the practitioners of medieval "literary literacy" anything that smacks of emancipatory narrative. The capacity for literary interest belongs to what one might call a domestic governing class; sophisticated literacy is more apt to be coterminous with a capacity for "social guidance" than not.

Moreover, one can probably stipulate that the linguistic training and the language competence of this cadre are broadly comparable, and that they are entirely trilingual. Here I run over some commonplace ground often obscured in discussions. By the fourteenth century, in England (but not Cornwall), virtually everyone native-born spoke English as a birth tongue, and they had done so, whatever their status, since at least *c.* 1175. The loss of native ability to speak (Anglo-)Norman at this date corresponds to a rising chorus of late twelfth- and early

---

England," *Modern Language Review* 99 (2004), 313–27 at 316 (the article contains abundant references to Rothwell's earlier seminal studies).

[48] I here elaborate an argument I also make at *London Literature, 1300–1380* (Cambridge, 2005), pp. 157–63, 166–72, offering a more general model for interlingual relations than I did there, where I concentrated upon an earlier period and the specific situation of commented biblical texts. An analysis like this one may highlight the social uniqueness of Lollardy—not the test case of "vernacularity" but a particularly overdetermined form of social challenge; cf. "The Difficulty of Ricardian Prose Translation: The Case of the Lollards," *Modern Language Quarterly* 51 (1990), 319–40. In their principled devotion to a specific version of parochial catechesis, the heretics sought to take "literary literacy" into areas where it had been absent and worked pragmatically with the tool at hand, universal English competence. This, not so coincidentally, reinforced a general rhetoric emphasizing clerical disinterest in teaching and preaching (which the heretics would provide) and concomitant clerical interest in a privilege associated with Latinate secrecy.

thirteenth-century complaints about the loss (alternatively, the quality of) English French.[49]

One should further note recent studies that suggest that, following the traumas of the Norman "monastic plantation," clerical culture allowed the most noncontentious and cooperative integration of English and Norman.[50] Latinity had been integral to Anglo-Saxon culture (and not simply clerical culture) since c. 600, with a major boost from Continental sources from the mid-tenth century. And the use of Latin in England was to expand exponentially over subsequent centuries with the growth of governmental systems, civil and ecclesiastical, all typically using Latin as their language of record. In the Middle Ages, clerical careers form the single widespread and dispersed socially leveling activity, always dependent upon achieved Latin competence, necessary for the work of administration. While this may appear a coercive imposition on native language use (comparable to the native colonial functionary), one might equally think administrative Latinity a symbiotic function. Perhaps suborned into administrative "service," competent clerical skills are integral to efficient governmental function, ecclesiastical and civil, and,

---

[49] The locus classicus is Richard Fitznigel, *Dialogus de scaccario*, ed. and tr. Charles Johnson (Edinburgh, 1950), p. 53 (composed in the later 1170s). The primary relevant documents have long been discussed, beginning with R. M. Wilson, "English and French in England, 1100–1300," *History* 27 (1943), 37–60. While one doubts that the modern situation is analogous in all respects, this dating roughly corresponds to the traditional modern American immigrant experience (that of the great wave of 1870–1920), in which the first generation remains fairly monolingual in the tongue of "the old country," the second generation is fully bilingual, and the third usually monolingual in the language of residence. For what follows, see also the important discussion of English language relations, Serge Lusignan, *Parler vulgairement: Les intellectuels et la langue française aux XIIIe et XIVe siècles*, 2nd ed. (Paris, 1987), pp. 91–127. "Native-born" in the main text above is intended to draw attention to various immigrant communities, mostly mercantile and courtly, largely French, Italian, and Dutch.

[50] See Hugh M. Thomas, *The English and the Normans: Ethnic Hostility, Assimilation, and Identity 1066–c. 1220* (Oxford, 2003), esp. pp. 200–35. With regard to the next sentence, a substantial amount of work needs to be done to de-Germanicize reports of Anglo-Saxon literary culture, most of which we know only through behaviors stimulated by "the Benedictine revival," fruit of cross-Channel contacts c. 950–1050 (the "purity" of indigenous folk can be much overrated); cf. the intriguing blend of Germanic historical practice with insistence upon continental Latinity at the head of Ælfric's "Life of St Edmund," for example.

in return for such competence, offer paybacks to the talented, the open opportunity for advancement.

But paradoxically, one prerequisite for post-Conquest Latin literacy was, until the mid-fourteenth century at least, Anglo-Norman. As I have mentioned above (n.16), Latin was normally approached through French. From the time this language had ceased to be a living birth tongue, it had become (as Latin always was) a grammatically learned language, one taught children in upper-class environments from an early age. Moreover, by this time, its social usefulness had been institutionally insured, and Anglo-Norman might be seen, even if learned, as central to any literate social intercourse. At just the time it was dying out as a birth tongue, in the reign of Henry II, Anglo-Norman became established as the language of legal pleading, and this position was consolidated, late in the reign of Henry III, by its customary use for legal instruction in (oral) classroom and textbook, as well as the customary language of statute from 1275. Anyone with serious legal interests (e.g., holding property) had to be conversant with it. Moreover, from the "plantation" onwards, all institutions in any broad way educative, monastic, or collegiate discriminated against conversation in English but allowed that in either Latin or French. If one hadn't learned French from a tutor at home, one needed, I would suppose, to pick it up conversationally from the other boys in one's grammar school.[51]

Moreover, one must understand that Latin grammatical training did not use Anglo-Norman just in passing, or simply as a written convention. As early as the last third of the twelfth century, a copy of Ælfric's Old English/Latin grammar and glossary was supplemented with Middle English and Anglo-Norman glosses as well as explanations of a type implying

---

[51] On the language of the law, see *London Literature*, ch. 1 (with further references), and for one example of regulated institutional conversation, 213 n.13. On French usage in an educational context (both books also include good general discussions), see Nicholas Orme, *English Schools in the Middle Ages* (London, 1973), pp. 73–74, 95 (and note Thomas Cranmer's appeal for French teaching, 1539 at pp. 263–64); *From Childhood to Chivalry: The Education of the English Kings and Aristocracy 1066–1530* (London, 1984), pp. 123–24. For copious exemplification, see Hunt, *Teaching* (n. 6 above); Hunt discusses the twelfth-century example I mention in the next paragraph, British Library, MS Cotton Faustina A.x (I), at 1:23–26. For the culture of "vulgaria" (here fifteenth- and sixteenth-century anglicized versions), see "School and Scorn: Gender in *Piers Plowman*," *New Medieval Literatures* 3 (1999), 213–27.

a trilingual classroom. But most importantly, fundamental to training in grammar (and the use-area of surviving "vulgaria"), was "opposing," instruction through *viva voce* performance. In this process, conducted publicly in front of all the other boys, the student would be given a sentence, orally and in French, and had to produce the Latin equivalent. Given that "vulgaria" tend to emphasize picky questions of language use (the subjunctive, sequence of tenses), success in the enterprise required the student's command of difficult spoken French, as well as the ability to convert this into comparably sophisticated Latin.

On this basis, literary competence, inherent in socially efficacious education at all levels (not simply the clerical), must represent achieved trilingualism. Moreover, this skill is not limited to reading knowledge alone but forms a full compositional and conversational capacity. "Literate literacy" at all levels draws on all three of England's languages, and "English" literary audiences are constructed as such through a common educational formation. That thin upper social layer with which I have associated literary activity in England is essentially "convened," beyond its power relationships, as an audience of literary sophisticates precisely by its capacity to respond with familiarity to three languages on some ad lib basis. English polylingualism provides the substantial basis of a literary coterie.

It thus should not be surprising that the emergence of substantial English literary writing in the thirteenth century almost invariably occurs in trilingual contexts. The best known of these is the latest, British Library, MS Harley 2253 (*c.* 1340).[52] By the same token, cessation of grammar-school Anglo-Norman usage may well have been a major contributor to the demise of literary composition in the language (by *c.* 1405) and the

---

[52] See *Facsimile of British Museum MS. Harley 2253*, introd. N. R. Ker, EETS 255 (1965); and Susanna Fein, ed., *Studies in the Harley Manuscript: The Scribes, Contents, Social Contexts of British Library MS Harley 2253* (Kalamazoo, 2000), particularly the contributions of Carter Revard, John Thompson, and Barbara Nolan. The earliest examples involve *Ancrene Riwle* and related texts. These are in English, but with instructions for Latinate "liturgical literacy" and a reference to the addressees' French books; for the latter, see *Ancrene Wisse . . . Vol. 1*, ed. Bella Millett, EETS 325 (2005), 18, line 394. Cf. also British Library, MS Cotton Caligula A.ix (1270s), with Laȝamon (whose resolutely English form is in constant dialogue with his carefully named Latin and French sources), but also *The Owl and the Nightingale*, in juxtaposition with Anglo-Norman texts, including another dialogue, Chardri's *Le petit plet*, ANTS 20 (1970 for 1962), ed. Brian S. Merrilees.

retraction of Anglo-Norman usage to the legal and administrative/business spheres.

One should insist that such a linguistic situation is far from unparalleled. It was widespread in the late classical world, both east and west. In the latter, Greek, Latin, or both provided an "educated" and international means of communication, but in informal situations, speakers relied upon regional (romance) vernaculars. In the east, Hebrew competed with other languages, most notably vernacular Aramaic, which actually displaces it as "sacred language" in the most recent books of "the Hebrew Bible." The language situation of modern India offers complicated analogous instances.[53]

With the decline of English philological studies, scholars often seem to have forgotten that operative multilingualism is everywhere marked in basic features of the history of English. The huge influx of Anglo-Norman "loan words" into English (I must rely on traditional locutions, badly in need of reformulation), first extensively evidenced in *Ancrene Riwle* and its satellites and reaching spate-proportions *c.* 1250–1400, relies absolutely on bilingual capacity. Generally, a loan word cannot function (be intelligible) unless it is lexically recognizable in its speech community; such items absolutely presuppose knowledge of "source-language" lexicon and usage. In an as yet untheorized way, Anglo-Norman occurs in English contexts because bi- or polylingual speakers carry over habits, in the narrowest grammarians' sense appropriate only in one language, into their usage in a second that they (and their interlocutors) know equally well. This process is as (or more) apt to occur orally, in conversation, as it is in writing.[54]

The best-known example of such behavior does not involve Anglo-Norman usage but an earlier behavior that may have already inured

---

[53] For the first, see John F. A. Sawyer, *Sacred Languages and Sacred Texts* (London, 1999), esp. pp. 9–12, 18–22, 31–35, 37–39; for the second, John Gumperz, "Speech Variation and the Study of Indian Civilization," *Language in Culture and Society: A Reader in Linguistics and Anthropology*, ed. Dell Hymes (New York, 1964), pp. 416–23, esp. 420–22.

[54] Cf. Rothwell, "Henry" (n. 47 above), pp. 314–15. There is a commonplace manuscript analogue; scribes, who routinely write more than one script, frequently carry habits from one across into the writing of a second (defined by its different script habits). The most prevalent, although far from unique, English example would be the blending of anglicana and secretary features in many scripts after 1440.

English speakers to bilingual interchanges. Many Scandinavianisms (not limited to lexical items) begin to appear in the earliest recorded Northern texts *c.* 1275–1300, but in archaic forms that indicate their presence in an Anglo-Scandinavian oral-conversational context for perhaps as long as four centuries. (E.g., *fell* ("mountain") is so familiar as to be a commonplace toponym, but the word had developed to *fjáll* in Scandinavian a long time before the English record.) Norse examples may actually represent not functional bilingualism but an unusual case of exchange between two mutually intelligible "different languages," from 850 on. But certainly testimony to interlingual exchange between polylingual speakers are frequent examples, predating or contemporary with *OED* first citations (and thus presented there in brackets), of English words that appear, often with inflections appropriate to their linguistic surround, as "loan-elements" in Latin and Anglo-Norman legal and business records.[55]

Just as in my preceding discussions, the vernacular always at some point begins to disappear, to recede into some broader spectrum of usage and to be constantly a product of interlingual negotiations, among a free-flowing stream of options. This implies that one might not view English "vernacularity" as a separate or separable option but engage in a narrow consideration of trilingual usage, local and peculiar. For example, one might point out that in Laura Wright's Thames documents (see n. 6) English usage is overwhelmingly nominal, while Latin and Anglo-Norman, in varying combinations, provide the ongoing grammatical language of entries. The situation here exemplifies that described at the end of my last paragraph; the creators of record plainly considered their "business" in English, but generally recorded it otherwise.

In such situations, like the varying relations of Latin and English I have described in Lambeth 260, terms like "code-switching" or "shift of stylistic register" are utterly nondescriptive. Modern models of bilingual oral communication, on which such analytic terms are predicated, identify a series of features as inherent in such discourse. John J. Gumperz, along with more recent practitioners such as Carol Myers-Scotton, Shana Paplock, and Herbert Schendl, identifies three features common to all: (a) monolingual utterances within bilingual oral discourse are typically full statements, sentence- or clause-bound; (b) the utterances are

---

[55] See, for example, Rothwell, "The Trilingual England of Geoffrey Chaucer," *Studies in the Age of Chaucer* 16 (1994), 45–67 at 62–65.

typically iterative or paraphrasal, reproductions of the same content in two languages; (c) alternation between different languages can be associated with "stylistic" choices within conversation. Gumperz especially notices the prevalence of alternation in contexts he identifies as involving "appeal" or "argument."[56]

But a single example will indicate that linguistic models predicated on modern instances, perhaps artificially constructed ones, do not describe anything resembling received (and thus written) medieval usage. Something a great deal more intimate and flexible, what I would identify polylingually and dialectically as "coplas" (improvisation) is going on here:

> Lex nature dampnavit Christum morti per eos qui erant de lege nature. Duo placitores de curia erant **trewthe and nede**. Set **trewthe** probavit quod Christus non debet mori per istam rationem: **It is no trewthe þat o man trespace** et alius **schul be for his gilte**. Set Adam forisfecit, Christus autem nuncquam; ideo Christus non debet mori, et hoc **thorgh trewthe**. E contra fuit alius placitor, videlicet necessitas, qui dixit: **Nedfull mot mankynd be saued** quia **man wolde hymselfe** set non potuit. **God my3t but hym sell no3te**. Set Christus Dei filius, qui fuit deus et homo, deus qui potuit, homo qui debuit saluare genus humanum. Et sic necessitas ostendit **þat he shal dye** et sic saluabitur homo; et sic iste aduocatus habuit magisterium et plus de fauore. **The quest of xij.** fuerunt xij. patriarche. **Þe spekere** eorum fuit **Ioseph** qui dixit: **I was solde to Egipte** pro 30. denariis

---

[56] See Gumperz, *Discourse Strategies* (Cambridge, 1982), as well as such representative publications as Myers-Scotton, *Duelling Languages* (1993); Paplock (with M. Meechan), "How Languages Fit Together in Code-Mixing," *International Journal of Bilingualism* 2, no. 2 (1998), 127–38; Schendl, "Mixed Language Texts as Data and Evidence in English Historical Linguistics," in *Studies in the History of the English Language: A Millenial Perspective*, ed. by Donka Minkova and Robert Stockwell (Berlin and New York, 2002), pp. 51–78. For Gumperz's discussion of clause or sentence bounds, see pp. 59, 86; of iterativity, pp. 82, 84 ("two alternative realisations of the same message"); of the stylistic function of language variation, pp. 48–50, 72; of in-group and more public languages ("we" and "they" codes), pp. 65–66. Gumperz addresses a topic I discuss above, the difficulty of distinguishing linguistic borrowing from "language switches." at pp. 66–68, 72. On the whole, I am dubious about the descriptive validity of Gumperz's analysis even for modern instances; his English-Spanish examples resemble no conversation I have heard in Tex-Mex or read in literary *caló*, and I suspect the presence of the observer may have constrained the behavior of his subjects.

and saued all myn kynde et sic faciet De[i] filius **be solde in Iuda** Iudeorum et postea mori et sic saluabit genus humanum. Hic questa fuit contra deum.[57]

Quite simply, none of the descriptive categories invoked by Gumperz and other researchers obtain here. Far from clause- much less sentence-bound statements, Nicholas Phillip here frequently embeds phrases and single words from one language in another. Moreover, he shows no consistent pattern as to whether he embeds English in Latin, or the reverse, for example, "thorgh trewth" [6], "pro 30. denariis" [13]. Particularly disconcerting from Gumperz's perspective would be odd and logically inconsequent brief intrusions, for example, "et alius" [4], "quia" [7], "eorum fuit" [13]; in each example, maintaining a single-language statement might have seemed more economical (for example, "Þaire spekere fuit"). Further, what appears as English and what as Latin shows no particular consistency; "trewth" is always English, but "nede" alternates with "necessitas," for example—as also "man/homo," "God/Deus," "curia/quest." Moreover, a few items are at least potentially French—"plus de fauore" certainly so as a construction (not "plurem fauorem"), and "questa" as Latinized French legalism (also evident in English "quest").

Further, even when statements are clause-bound, they can scarcely be conceived as iterative or as paraphrasing one another. The entire passage presents an ongoing argumentative movement, broadly an extended metaphor of Christ having been condemned through three laws—here Old Testament history as involving the "lex nature"—and thus Christ's sacrifice is conducive to analysis as a court case. Although certainly argumentative, a situation Gumperz associates with language-variation, the passage exfoliates rather than repeats. Rather than hover about an argumentative point, switching from English to Latin or vice versa, insofar as

---

[57] From the first macaronic sermon published, apparently preached by Nicholas Phillip, Franciscan of King's Lynn, in Newcastle, Good Friday 1433. I cite A. G. Little, "A Fifteenth-Century Sermon," in *Franciscan Papers, Lists, and Documents* (Manchester, 1943), p. 248, with some adjustment of punctuation. This is the forty-second sermon in Alan J. Fletcher's description, "The Sermon Booklets of Friar Nicholas Phillip," *Medium Ævum* 55 (1986), 188–202; see further Wenzel, *Macaronic*, pp. 40–43, 165–73. (I construe "schul be" in the 4th line as "ought to atone" and "hym sell noȝte" in the 7th as "it is not appropriate for him," according with various uses of "debere.")

[From the beginning to the present, the divine wrath, which attacks the faithful but also judges the impious, has set five plagues upon Britain. The first came with the Romans, who conquered Britain but afterwards withdrew. The second involved the Picts and Scots, who grievously beset the land with wars, yet never conquered it. The third plague was the English, who subdued and won the land. The fourth, the Danes, won Britain in battle but later died off. The fifth plague, the Normans, conquered the place and still rule the English.]

This account, which structures Henry of Huntingdon's history, draws its deepest resonances from a fractured biblicism. Following on Henry's quite standard appropriation of Bede—Britain as Eden or Promised Land "ab exordio"—the account turns, as does the biblical history of faithless Israel, into an inverted Exodus narrative. The British, or their various violent successors, all turn Pharaonic, not Hebrews but Egyptians. The apparently faithless abuse of the wealth and power they have received (cf. the alternate account, 1.10 at 28) merits "plagas" (the biblical ten to be anticipated *in plenitudine temporis?*); rather than exodus *to*, Henry's

---

thirteenth- and fourteenth-century circulation, see *London Literature*, pp. 86–87. The "official narrative," Geoffrey of Monmouth's *Historia regum Britanniae*, renders conquest unproblematic, an explorer's entry into emptiness; cf. Diana's prophecy to Brutus:

> Insula in occeano est, habitata gigantibus olim,
> Nunc deserta quidem gentibus apta tuis. . . .
> Hic erit et natis altera Troia tuis
> Hic de prole tua reges nascuntur . . . (ed. cit. ¶16 [1.11] at 9).
> [There is an island in the Ocean, although once inhabited by giants, now deserted and suitable for your people. Here will be a second Troy for your offspring; here kings will be engendered of your descendants.]

The account of the later Anglo-Norman *Brut* renders this downright emancipatory. The Middle English version, drawing from a prologue, *Des grantz geanz: An Anglo-Norman Poem*, ed. Georgine E. Brereton, Medium Ævum Monographs 2 (Oxford, 1937), begins with the diabolical generation of those giants and has Brutus exterminate them (in this account, they are still in place as sole inhabitants); see *The Brut, or the Chronicle of England*, ed. Friedrich W. D. Brie, 2 vols., EETS 131, 136 (1906–8), 1:1–4, 10–11.

history narrates a succession of punitive incursions *into* by those not-chosen, who in their turn repeat the cycle.

One form of repetition will draw the argument back to a linguistic perspective on an idea I have glanced at earlier, domestic colonization. A prominent feature of the late Old English period was the development of something like a linguistic standard, "late West Saxon." The product of the tenth-century Wessex Reconquest, in conjunction with the "Benedictine revival," this developed largely through refoundation and repopulation of monastic houses from Wessex centers; it was dispersed in the chaos after 1066. Of course, historical narratives of the English language always investigate standardization—the imposition of a properly "fixed" and grammatical language—as a feature of national cultural maturity. But the process can scarcely be seen as so benign, since it is always complicit with centralizing efforts that intend the reduction of local difference— indigenous oral autonomy—in the interests of some broader imagined or projected unit.

In these terms, as English speakers became increasingly, if belatedly, aware,[60] there was no single vernacular, even if separable from Anglo-Norman and Latin. The Norman linguistic legacy, following subsumption of those centers propagating West Saxon *koiné*, was thorough localism. Lambeth 260, which has prompted this discussion, provides an excellent example from a legion that might be cited. The book provides English texts whose early dissemination was limited to the North, where the works had been composed, and always, in this form, in a frankly off-putting, localizable form of English. Nor are the two texts of Lambeth 260 unique examples, only a single testimony to a thriving local culture that did not, until the early fifteenth century, easily associate with anything else and that was communicated in the language of its origin.[61]

In essence, the history of Middle English (and of its literature) at a certain point begins to replay in a different modality the hegemony of Wessex English in the late Old English period. At least in part, this should be seen

---

[60] The most emphatic statement comes from early print (which required some standardization for marketing), Caxton's prologue to his *Eneydos*; see *The Prologues and Epilogues of William Caxton*, ed. W. B. Crotch, EETS 176 (1928), 107–10 at 108.

[61] See "Yorkshire Writers," *Proceedings of the British Academy* 121 (2003), 91–109, which presents a theory of the demise of local cultures like these, paralleled elsewhere. For another example, see "Sir Thomas Berkeley and His Patronage," *Speculum* 64 (1989), 878–916 at 909–13.

as a "Lancastrian" project, perhaps specifically a Henry V one, and as an appeal to national endeavor and hegemony in dialogue with another version of Henry of Huntingdon, the narrative of usurpation (both internal and overseas). But Lancastrianism and fifteenth-century literary culture generally differ from traditional English trilingualism through having shut down one option, the Anglo-Norman. Between the combined pressures of grammatical instruction in English and eighty years of identifying Frenchness with an inimical and usurping culture, literary production in the language ceased in the fifteenth century. The result, as John Trevisa, historian of English grammatical education, had predicted, *c.* 1380, was in fact a pauperized literary coterie. While more people may have read English literature in the fifteenth century than the fourteenth, their competences were different and, to a degree, significantly reduced. Literary French competence, now exclusively in one or another Continental dialect, had to be acquired by new means, much perhaps through one or another form of (vocational) tourism, and the growing volume of translation from nonlearned Continental French sources indicates that it may have been a skill far from so widely dispersed as Anglo-Norman literacy had been previously.[62]

Yet long after this moment, locality remained functionally alive, English a myriad succession of formal and lexical alternatives. Depending on what feature one would choose to rank first, medieval England linguistically is a continuous succession of usage boundaries and internal frontiers. These include frontiers that overlap not just the traditional governmental shires but conventional national boundaries (in southern Scotland, for example).[63]

The perpetually shifting linguistic frontier that lies beneath the imposed boundaries of governance returns me, as a concluding move,

---

[62] Cf. Trevisa's discussion, Sisam, ed., p. 149 lines 37–42. Trevisa's "Dialogue between a Lord and a Clerk" makes clear that competent Latin literacy (which Trevisa's Lord certainly had) did not necessarily include the ability to cope with sophisticated literary texts.

[63] The monumental demonstration appears in Angus McIntosh et al., *A Linguistic Atlas of Late Mediaeval English*, 4 vols. (Aberdeen, 1986), in which well over one hundred features are put in play as a means of identifying specific local usage. One might do worse than read the opening pages of Simon Armitage, *All Points North* (London, 1998), particularly his opposition of the strange vowels used by people over the hill (the ten villages of Saddlesworth) to the civilized usage of Marsden (West Yorks.).

to Gloria Anzaldúa.[64] As she was well aware, if we shift from inner to outer, *la frontera* is always double. On the one hand, it is the edge, the boundary that defines nationhood, the limit that distinguishes some We from another Them. Equally, as an edge, *la frontera*, like the internal differentiation that constructs medieval English, always proves mobile, permeable, osmotic. The center—the nation—may believe it somehow fixed and surrender its exact demarcation to the locals (marcher lords like the Percys who ceaselessly fought it out on the ground), but in fact frontier relations provide the most palpable sign of that instability that always coexists within unific national mythology.

Anzaldúa offers an analysis of her own linguistic usage (formed in *la frontera* of the Rio Grande valley), in which she finds herself competent in eight separate languages (55–56). These she describes as socially determined by context of utterance. While this represents an accurate reading of her own situation, from the standpoint of English studies it reflects an "Old Historicist" argument about linguistic relations that I hope this paper will substantially have queried. Although Anzaldúa demonstrates clearly her own constant mediation into selective monolingualism on the basis of social occasion, this activity always occurs in the context of partially overlapping (but never fully reflective) multiple speech communities. All these thus have the potential for active bi- or polylingualism of some type, inhibited only by social conditioning.[65]

More interesting is the language that "comes most naturally to me," Tex-Mex (56–57, 59). "I may," Anzaldúa continues, "switch back and forth from English to Spanish in the same sequence or in the same word." (The last phrase presumably refers to bilingual compounding, to the

---

[64] See n. 45; Anzaldúa's work is also invoked by Jeffrey J. Cohen, "Hybrids, Monsters, Borderlands: The Bodies of Gerald of Wales," in *The Postcolonial Middle Ages* (Basingstoke, 2000), pp. 87–104. Cf. some interesting comments on frontier landscapes in Christopher Cannon, *The Grounds*, pp. 142–50. I follow out the linguistic emphasis of Anzaldúa's argument, but one should note her interest in internal cultural frontiers as well (e.g., the discussion of *conjunto*, pp. 60–61).

[65] In modern linguistic terminology, Anzaldúa does not describe polylingualism but an extreme instance of "diglossia," the use of single linguistic codes, selected from various options on the basis of setting, social activity, or person addressed. The great theorist of such usage is Charles A. Ferguson, e.g., "Diglossia," in *Language in Culture and Society*, ed. Dell Hymes (see n. 53), pp. 425–37.

imposition of grammatical forms from one language on words derived from another, or to both.) Anzaldúa's principal discussion of Tex-Mex addresses codes of grammatical propriety. She seeks to debunk the purist view that this language is "mongrel" or "bastard," a creole to be exorcised or repressed as No-language. Nor can, in her telling, Tex-Mex be reduced (the sentence I have quoted, with its implicit reference to "code-switching," is a descriptive misstatement, like the language I am forced to adopt in my discussion of lexical transfer above). The language can be neither reduced nor etymologized into its constituent elements, Spanish fragments mixed with English ones. Tex-Mex is a "natural" language, one that in Anzaldúa's argument of ethnic identity is specifically appropriate to a *mestiza*, a woman of *la frontera*.

But Anzaldúa has a more interesting view to offer than this attack on the anticreole linguists, as well as the teachers who forced her into participation in English-only classrooms—her sheer joy in Tex-Mex. What matters for her, in the sentence I have cited, is the exuberance of unprogrammed improvisational speech, an extended expressive competence she feels as she speaks in this language. I think her analysis may understand, perhaps better than most, the power Nicholas Phillipp may have felt as he recorded the macaronic sermon I have cited above. Knowing a language polylingually in this way is not knowing etymological separateness, but knowing that some alternatives, regardless of where grammarians say they came from (and maybe even *should* belong), have a local expressive power and that a competent polylingual speaker can draw upon this richness as a form of eloquence.

Anzaldúa's attack on the grammarians and teachers also suggests salutary lessons for thinking about the vernacular. As I have tried to indicate, vernacular English studies have always, too seldom uncomfortably, been complicit in a triumphalist narrative of national identity. Thus, its practitioners have tended to resemble the figures Anzaldúa constructs as her enemy—spokespersons for the legal (Anglo) frontier, the hegemony of nation. But Anzaldúa, conscious of the experiences of *braceros*, *pachucos*, and others who seek *el Norte* or *Atzlán* for tactical and personal negotiations, knows there is a power, both politically and comradely, to be unleashed in a language that isn't one. Conventional discussions of English language relations, including those of "vernacularity," need to attend to her message, analogous to that which I have argued one might also find in Lambeth Palace MS 260.[66]

[66] I am grateful for argumentative and bibliographical suggestions to a large number of readers: Anne Middleton, Roger Dahood, two anonymous journal readers, and especially Laura Wright and Simon Meecham-Jones. None, of course, is responsible for the blindnesses that remain. Justin Wilson, whose name you will not pronounce correctly, should get the last bilingual word, "Mais yeah, mon."

Appendix

English Verses from
Lambeth Palace Library, MS 260

The following texts represent the "final form" of the MS, with no identification of cancellations and expunctions. I have silently expanded all
abbreviations. When writing English, the scribe (as customary in Yorkshire) uses the same grapheme for *y* and *þ*; where manuscript *y* represents
þ, I have printed *þ*. I use the conventional symbols, \left and right slashes/
to indicate interlineations and (parentheses), to correct scribal lapsus
calami; all other emendations are bracketed and explained in footnotes.

Verses a, *fol. 66*ᵛᵇ *= Index 2248, unpub. and unique*

O spes in morte, me salua, Maria, precor te.
Hanc animam posco quam plenam crimine nosco.
 My hope mayden I ask and crafe,
 In þis caus[1] þat þou me safe.
Quis peccauit, nece pressus opere, rogitauit.
 þis sawle I ask þe, qwylk within
 I knaw it es fyled with syn.
 If þat þis body syn has wroght,
 In perell of dede help he besoght.
Hec quia suxisti, fili, veniam precor isti.
 For þies pappes þat þou sowked has,
 My son, forgyf hym hys trespas.
Wlnere queso, pater, fac quod rogitat mea mater.
 Fadyr, for my wondes wyde
 My modyr here bon I pray þe þis tyde.
Nate, petita dabo quod bis volo nulla negabo.
 I grante þe, son, all þine ꝫernyng;
 we will b[e] at[2] ane withoutyng werny(n)g.

---

[1] MS apparently trans.
[2] MS bat.

Wilfridus clamidem quam suscepit per attridem[3]
Seruauit pridem; casus dedit, abstulit idem.

[Wilfrid served previously for the black robe he received; chance gave it, and the same (i.e., chance) carried it away. (The black robe is presumably an allusion to a Dominican habit.)]

Verses b, *fols 79vb–80ra = Index 3858 (s.v. waith)*

Also appears at Harley 7322, fol. 163^v, ed. EETS 15 (rev. edn, 1893), p. 267.

Secundum commentatorem Macrobij *de sompno Ciponis* i(n) 3. volu-minibus: declarat quomodo tota vita mundana decurrit dietis secundum x^{cem}. horas principales diei, et secundum x. radios rote fortunalis. Prima hora diei est aurora, et secundum illam primam horam in primo radio rote fortunalis. Et domina Fortuna scribit super caput eius versiculum, "Lacte cubat salmus[4] tibi iure fuerat almus"; Anglice:

[According to the commentator on Macrobius's *Somnium Scipionis* in three volumes: He shows how all life in this world passes away by regi-mens in accord with the ten principal hours of the day and with the ten spokes of the wheel of Fortune. The first hour of the day is dawn, and it accords with the first hour in the first spoke of the wheel of Fortune. And Lady Fortune writes upon a man's head this verse, "The creature beds down in milk which a nurse had properly poured out for you"; in English:]

Wayke and wryched þou ert in syght;
Of alkyns beste leste es þi myght.

---

[3] As other readings, e.g. "salmus/a" (discussed in the next note), testify, the hex-ameters sometimes require excessive cleverness. Here the rhyme in -*idem* provokes a nonce-coinage, *attris, -idis* (rather than commonplace *attram*).

[4] For "psalmus," a metathesized form of "plasmus"; cf. Anglo-Latin psalmare "to form, create." The noun is usually feminine, and the line should probably read with rhyming "salma . . . alma."

Tradunt auctores quod dum puer est in vtero matris, alitur sanguin(e) m[e] nstruo[5]; quando autem nascitur, alitur sanguine nutricis. Et idem[6] domina Fortuna scribit super caput eius sic, "Nati et reclinati lacte cubat etc."

[Authors assert that while a child is in its mother's womb, it is fed with menstrual blood. But when it grows, it is fed with a nurse's blood. And thus Lady Fortune writes on his head, "You youths born and lying abed, he beds down in milk," etc.]

Secunda hora diei est mane, et secundum illam horam facit homo [quo]que[7] secundam dietam. Et est a cuna innocencie vsque ad pilam lasciuie, quia dum puer ludit cum pila est in secundo radio rote Fortune. Et domina rote scribit super caput eius sic, dicens versus, "Est pila vita mea perila[8] perdita mortis ydea."

[The second hour of the day is morning, and, in accord with this hour, a man enters his second regimen as well. This is the passage from the crib of his innocence to the ball of his delight, for while a boy plays with a ball, he is in the second spoke of the wheel of Fortune. And the Lady with the wheel writes this verse on his head, saying, "The ball is my perilous life; once lost, it is an image of death."]

All þis werld es turned to play;
þe mare þou plays, þe mare þou may.

Experimentum est quod si puer posset ludere cum pila sua, iam habet quicquid wlt habere de solacio et gaudio. Si autem pila perdatur uel ab eo auferatur, corruit in terram pre dolore cum lacrimis et gemitibus, ac si in breui esset moriturus. Et ideo domina Fortuna scribit super caput eius ludenter, "Est pila etc."

[It's well known through experience that if a boy can play with his ball, he then has all the joy and delight he wants to have. However, if his ball

---

[5] MS monstruo.

[6] So MS, but probably a mistake for "ideo," as elsewhere.

[7] MS que.

[8] Presumably latinized French, the word is a derivative of synonymous Latin "periculosus." Similarly, in the tenth verse, "guerra" is a commonplace latinization from French.

is lost or taken away from him, he falls to the ground sorrowfully, with tears and sighs, as if he were actually about to die. And therefore Lady Fortune writes playfully on his head, "The ball is etc."]

Tercia hora diei est prima, et secundum illam horam facit terciam dietam. Et est a pila lasciuie vsque ad studium sapiencie, et dum occupatur citra actus scolasticos, est in tercio radio rote Fortune. Et domina Fortuna scribit super caput eius et dicit versum, "Inclite viuenti dux est ars visita[9] menti"

[The third hour of the day is Prime, and, in accord with that hour, a man enters his third regimen. He passes from his ball of delight to the pursuit of wisdom, and while he is engaged in scholarly acts, he is in the third spoke of the wheel of Fortune. And Lady Fortune writes this on his head and speaks the verse: "Renowned exemplar, learning has frequented your lively mind"], þat

 Ryches mase° man behald abowte,   *makes*
 For to þe ryche will men both bow and lowte.
Secundum Macrobium *libro de saturnalibus* ad hoc ordinatur ars vt homo seipsum sciat ducere et regere.

[According to Macrobius, in his *Saturnalia*, learning is organized so that a man may learn to control and rule himself.]

Quarta hora diei est tercia, et secundum illam horam homo facit 4. dietam, id est a studio sapiencie vsque ad promocionem honoris et reuerencie. Et quando profertur homo ad gradum honoris etc. est in [quarto][10] radio rote et domina Fortuna scribit sic, "Hic honor est onere[11] vbi stultus fulget honore."

[The fourth hour of the day is Tierce, and, in accord with that hour, a man enters his fourth regimen, i.e., from the pursuit of wisdom to his advancement to honor and respect. And when a man is advanced to a

---

 9 For "visitata."
 10 MS quatuor.
 11 MS oneres; the rhyme requires the awkward ablative, literally "with a burden."

position of honor etc., he is in the fourth spoke of the wheel, and Lady Fortune writes, "This honor is burdensome, when a fool is resplendent in honor."]

> Now has þou fonden þat þou has soght,
> Bot be wele ware it lastis noght.

Vbi honor ecclesie sine sanctitate et sciencia, ibi honor seculi est in onus confusionis extreme. Et ibi domina Fortuna scribit super caput eius sic, "Promoti hic honor etc."

[And where clerical honor exists without holiness and wisdom, it is merely worldly honor and a burden of excessive anxiety. And there Lady Fortune writes on his head, "O you advanced to honor, this honor etc."]

Quinta hora diei est sexta, et secundum illam horam diei homo facit dietam quintam, id est ab officio honoris vsque ad consummacionem sue glorie. Et quando homo deicitur a gradu honoris, tunc est in quinto gradu[12] radio rote Fortune. Et domina Fortuna scribit super caput eius vt hic, [fol. 80ra] "Tangit; ita defluit et dolor angit."

[The fifth hour of the day is Sext, and, in accord with that hour, a man enters his fifth regimen, i.e., from a position of honor to the end of his glory. And when a man is cast down from a position of honor, then he is in the fifth spoke of the wheel of Fortune. And Lady Fortune writes on his head, "It affects you; so it flows away, and sorrow afflicts you."]

> Strang þou ert; now fayles þi myght;
> þou waxes full hewy þat was full lyght.

Secundum beatum Gregorium, nichil perditur sine dolore quando retinetur cum amore. Et ideo domina Fortuna sic scribitur, "Vt decus etc."

[According to blessed Gregory, nothing is lost without sorrow when it is clutched with love. Therefore Lady Fortune writes, "As is appropriate etc."]

---

[12] Probably to be deleted.

Sexta hora diei est octaua, et secundum illam horam homo facit 6. dietam, id est ab ortu solis vel glorie vsque ad senectutem miserie. Et quando homo incipit deficere in ualore et uigore etc. est in 6. radio rote. Et scribit super caput eius et dicet, "Flectet \ad/ obcena redolens caro mortis aliena."

[The sixth hour of the day is "Oct," and, in accord with that hour, a man enters his sixth regimen, i.e., from the rising of the sun or of his glory to his miserable old age. And when a man begins to decline in strength and vigor etc., he is in the sixth spoke of the wheel. And Fortune writes on his head and she will say, "The flourishing flesh will change to the disgusting and estranging things of death."]

> All þi lyfe es sorow and kare,
> And dede es nere that nane will spare.

Secundum Tullium, *De senectute*, senectus propter multa incomoda dice-batur morbus incurabilis. Et ideo domina scribit[13] super caput eius sic, "Deficientis flectet ad obcena etc."

[According to Cicero, *On Old Age*, age is called an incurable disease for its many troubles. And therefore the Lady writes on his head, "Your flesh, when you are declining, will change to disgusting things etc."

Septima hora diei est nona, et secundum illam horam facit homo 7. dietam et [est][14] in 7°. radio rote Fortune. Et scribit super caput eius sic, dicendo versum, "Nescio nunc quid ago quia senit mortis ymago."

[The seventh hour of the day is Nones, and, in accord with that hour, a man enters his seventh regimen and is in the seventh spoke of the wheel of Fortune. And she writes on his head, while saying the verse: "I now do not know what I do, for the likeness of death grows feeble."]

> Lorn þou hase bath tong and mynde;
> Als þou hase lyued sall þou now fynde.

---

13 MS scribit sic. The scribe has corrected his own similar error in the preceding "dieta" by expunging "sic" before "Vt decus etc."

14 MS omits, probably haplography.

Octaua hora diei est vespera, et secundum illam horam homo facit octauam dietam, id est a perdicione sensus et loquele vsque ad vltimum punctum vite sue. Et quando homo moritur est in octauo radio rote Fortune. Et ideo domina scribit super caput eius et dicit uersus, "Obruta morte caro flatu laxatur amaro."

[The eighth hour of the day is Vespers, and, in accord with that hour, a man enters his eighth regimen, i.e., from the loss of his senses and ability to speak into the last moment of his life. And when a man dies, he is in the eighth spoke of the wheel of Fortune. And therefore the Lady writes on his head, while saying the verse, "Buried in death, the flesh is undone with a bitter breath"]

    All þis werld þou sall forsake
    For dede es comen and will þe take.
Maxima pena est anime a dissolucione sua a corpore, propter magnum appetitum quem habet ad corpus. Ideo domina scribit [super][15] caput morientis et dicit, "Obruta etc.."

The greatest torment of the soul comes from its separation from the body, since it has a great desire for the body. Therefore the Lady writes on the dying man's head and says, "Buried etc."

Nona hora diei est completorium, et secundum illam horam homo facit nonam dietam, id est a morte vsque ad foueam sepulture. Et dum homo portatus est ad sepulcrum est in nono radio rote Fortune. Et domina scribit super caput eius versus, "Ad foueam pergit quem sarcina terrea mergit."

[The ninth hour of the day is Compline, and, in accord with that hour, a man enters his ninth regimen, i.e., from death to the pit of his grave. And while a man is borne to his tomb he is in the ninth spoke of the wheel of Fortune. And the Lady writes on his head the verses, "The man proceeds to the pit where an earthy load buries him."]

---

[15] MS omits; Wilfrid here abbreviates his repeated phrase as a series of initial letters, and wrote "s.," rather than "s. s."

Man and woman hafs ane ende:
Fra erth þai com, till erth þai wende.
Decima hora diei est nox, et secundum illam horam homo facit x. dietam,
id est a sepulcro vsque ad escam vermium. Et quando misera caro
anima[16] corodetur a vermibus etc. est in x. radio rote Fortune. Et domina
scribit super caput eius sic dicendo, "O cinis et terra cum vermibus est
tua guerra."

[The tenth hour of the day is night, and, in accord with that hour, a
man enters his tenth regimen, i.e., from the tomb to worms'-meat. And
when the poor flesh gets gnawed by worms etc., he is in the tenth spoke of
the wheel of Fortune. And the Lady writes thus on his head, while saying,
"O, dust and ashes, your struggle is now with the worms."]

Off þi lyfe lityll þou lete
For þou ert grauen to wormys mete.
Vita hominis transit per x. horas et x. dietas et decem radios rote
fortunalis:

[The life of man passes through ten hours and ten regimens and ten
spokes of the wheel of Fortune]:

In ten tymes of þe day,
In ten iorneys of hys way,
In ten spekes þat turnes ay. Amen.

Verses c, *fol. 80rb* = *Index 2155*

Also appears at (a) Harley 7322, fol. 158, ed. EETS 15 (rev. ed., 1893), p. 263;
and (b) Advocates 18.7.21, fol. 85, ed. Brown, *Religious Lyrics*, p. 81 and
265n, with four extra lines; and Edward Wilson, *A Descriptive Index of
the English Lyrics in John of Grimestone's Preaching Book*, Medium Ævum
Monographs ns 2 (Oxford, 1973), no. 107 (p. 22, s.v. Misericordia).

---

[16] Conceivably ablative of accompaniment, but perhaps to be dropped. The
word may be the remnant of a fuller body-and-soul statement resembling that under
the eighth hour.

Misericordia depingebatur in templo dee Veste vt homo habens cor in manu sua scissum in duas partes, quarum prima parte scriptum erat sic:

[Mercy was represented in the temple of the goddess Vesta as a man holding in his hand a heart cut into two parts, on the first part of which was written]:

> Mercy bydes and lukes allway
> When men leuys syn and turnes away.

In alia parte scriptum erat sic:

> þof syn ware [and][17] mercy ware nane,
> Ask mercy—it comys anane.
> For mercy es redy þer syn es mast,
> And mercy es lityll þer syn es lest.

Legitur in gestis Anglorum de quodam rege quem Saxones cogitabant interficere [by poisoning a fountain from which he drank]; this is moralized:

Verses d, *fol 80^{rb-va} = unpub. and unique*

Per illum regem intelligo Adam primum parentem, cui subiecte erant omnes creature in mundo, vt habetur *Genesis* [cf. 2:19–20]. Demones igitur querebant illum regem interficere, vt venenum infundere(n)t in fonte qui regi placuerat. Iste fons est cor, quia riuuli a fonte mana(n)t, ita cor influit vitam in omnes partes corporum. In fonte illo infusum fuit venenum quando primus parens suggestionem diaboli suscepit, vt faceret contra preceptum diuinum. Et dum assensum prebuit, quasi de fonte illo bibit et statim morti subiectus est, et post illum mortui sunt alii, quia omnes homines vsque ad mortem Cristi propter illud [fol. 80va] venenum ad infernum descenderunt. De illo fonte adhuc fluunt riuuli in nobis, quia racione illius peccati pronitatem habemus ad malum. Proni enim sunt sensus ad malum ab adolescencia. Sic igitur maliciam huius veneni vitare velimus. Oportet quod cumulum terre isti fonti supponamus, id est cum motus peccatorum in nobis insurgunt, habeamus memoriam quod terra sumus et terram reuertemur, secundum illud *Ecclesiastis* [3:19] quia

---

[17] MS ne ware.

omnia subiacent vanitati et omnia pergunt ad vnum locum etc. Ergo "memorare nouissima et in eternum non peccabis" [Ecclus. 7:40].

[I understand through this king Adam our first parent, to whom all the creatures in the world were subject, as it says in *Genesis*. Therefore devils sought to kill this king and poured poison into the spring he found pleasing. This spring is the heart, for just as brooks flow out from a spring, so the heart infuses life into all parts of bodies. Poison was poured into this spring when our first parent took up the devil's suggestion, that he should act against God's precept. And when he consented, it was as if he drank from that fountain and was immediately subject to death, and, following him, all others have died, for all men until the death of Christ descended to hell because of this poison. Brooks flow in us from this spring, since we have a propensity to evil because of Adam's sin. Our senses are bent to evil from our youth. Thus, we wish to avoid the evil of this poison. To do so, it is necessary for us to place a heap of earth on top of this fountain. That is, when the motions of sins surge up in us, to remember that we are earth and will return to earth, according to the verse in *Ecclesiastes* that says, "All things are subject to vanity, and all things go to one place." Therefore, "Remember thy last end, and thou shalt never sin."]

Dede es dete of mans kynde;
Dede es dole of mans mynde;
Dede refes ilk man fra hys,
and dede ledys bath to sorow and blys.[18]

Verses e, *fol. 80ᵛᵇ = Index 3729, unpub.*

Also appears in a similar exemplum at Bodleian Library, MS Bodley 649, fol. 183ᵛ.[19]

---

18 Marked marginally "Mors."
19 This book was compiled by John Swetstock 1417x1421; see Roy M. Haines, "'Wilde Wittes and Wilfulnes': John Swetstock's Attack on Those 'Poyswunmongeres,' the Lollards," *Studies in Church History* 8 (1972), 143–53; Wenzel, *Macaronic*, pp. 160–65. Sweetstock was a monk of St. Albans; some of the sermons in his collection also appear in Bodleian, MS Laud misc. 706, copied by John Pauntley, monk of Gloucester. On this book, see Wenzel, *Macaronic*, pp. 173–77.

Romulus in annalibus Iudeorum: Hic enim transtulit annalis Iudeorum,
Grecorum etiam, in Latinum et omnes fabulas Ysopi et misit Tibirio filio
suo. Narrat quod [fol. 81[ra]] in Iudea fuerunt leges tres. Prima lex quod rex
semel in anno cum magna nobilitate omni populo se ostenderet et racio[20]
legis [cf. Deut. 17:18], ut populus eum agnosceret ac propter suam nobili-
tatem ut eum timeret. Secunda lex fuit quod lex et regnum regi deberent
per quinque consiliaros, et hec racio legis, ut in omni suo regno vigeret
sapiencia. Tercia lex quod perditores deberent exulari, et hec racio, ut rex
sine timore quiesceret in regno et ne tales regi uel regno iterum moles-
tiam inferent.

Accidit quod vnus magnus dominus regi valde specialem perdi-
cionem fecit, qui deprehensus ut perditor regni, secundum legem exula-
tur. Qui tempore exilij literas quinque consiliariis direxit deprecotorias
ad patriam posset remeare. Et primus conciliarius sic scripsit literam ista
contentem; similiter et omnes consequenter rescripserunt:

[Romulus, in the annals of the Jews: He translated both these annals
and those of the Greeks into Latin, as well as all Æsop's fables, and sent
them to his son Tiberius. He tells that there were three laws in Judea. The
first law was that once a year the king, in all his splendor, should show
both himself and the sense of the law to the whole populace. In that way,
the people would acknowledge and fear him because of his nobility. The
second law was that both the law and the kingdom should be directed by
five counsellors, so that that wisdom should thrive in the whole kingdom.
The third law was that traitors ought to be exiled, so that the king might
rule peacefully and without fear in his kingdom and so that such men
should not again cause injury to the king or the kingdom.]

[It befell that a great lord caused an especially grievous injury to the
king. When he was captured, he was, according to the law, banished as a
traitor to the kingdom. But he, while he was exiled, sent letters to the five
counsellors, entreating that he might return to his homeland. In return,
the first counsellor wrote him a letter saying these things; likewise, all the
others wrote back to him in turn:]

þi dome es skylfull and eftyre þe laghe;

---

[20] Should read "racionem," but probably haplography for "[racionem legis, et
hec] racio legis," as in the following members.

how myght I help agayns my saghe°?   *oath*
Litera primi conciliarij, vocatur Trewth.[21]
    þi syn es grete, and þat is rewth;
    Recouere es non, and þat is trewth.
Littera secundi conciliarij, vocatur Wysdom.
    In me grace ne hope þou noght,
    For þou sall hafe as þou has wroght.
Littera tercij conciliarij, vocatur Ryght.
    How suld \be/ reson[22] þe forgyfe,
    Sen þou wald noght in trewth lyfe?
Littera iiii[ti]. conciliarij, vocatur Might.
    I may noght thole° þat þou be spylt;   *suffer, allow*
    I will gyf mercy for þi gilt.
Littera quin[ti][23] conciliarij, vocatur Mercy.
    Per illum regem intelligo Deum; per quinque regis uel regni conciliarios intelligo ista: primus conciliarius est Trewth, secundus Wysdom, tercius Ryght, iiij[tus]. Myght, quintus Mercy. Per perditorem qui fuit magnus dominus in celo intelligo Adam, qui fecit contra legem et conciliarios, et quantum in ipso fuit, perdidit quando diabolo consensit dicenti, "Eritis sicut dij etc." [Gen. 3:5]. Et ideo fuit exulatus de paradiso usque in uallem miserie. Iste scripsit litteras conciliarijs, et nullus uoluit subuenire nisi Cristus, qui secundum suam inaquam[24] misericordiam saluos nos fecit. Qui scripsit istam litteram, "I may noght etc.," et hoc fecit feria vj[a]. in Parasceue, quando in ara crucis se ipsum optulit.

[By this king, I understand God; by his and the kingdom's five counsellors, Trewth, Wysdom, Ryght, Myght, and Mercy. By the traitor, who was a great lord in heaven, I understand Adam, who acted counter to the law and the counsellors' advice, and in so far as he was capable, was treasonous, when he consented to the devil, who said to him, "You shall be as gods." And for that reason, he was exiled from paradise and entered this vale of tears. He wrote letters to the counsellors, and none of them wanted to help him except Christ, who, following his unsurpassed mercy,

---

21 Each of the verses is also marked marginally: "1. de fide," "2. Sapiencia," "3. Iusticia," "4. Potencia," "5. Reduccio" (i.e., introducing the "moralitas"), respectively.
22 One might add "Y," possibly lost by haplography.
23 MS quinque.
24 Presumably for "inequam."

saved us. Christ wrote him the letter, "I may noght etc.," and he did what he promised there on Good Friday, when he offered himself upon the altar of the cross.]

Verses f, *fol. 81va* = *unpub. and unique*

Estimo quod communiter accidit et de superbo et diabolo sicut quondam accidit de quodam ioculatore et armigero. Ioculator vidit armigerum equitare super bonum equum. Ioculator fecit sibi equum vnum de vno pessewyspe, ac si esset bonum palfridum. Dixitque ioculator armigero, "Vis tu comutare equum tuum cum equo meo?"

[I think that what commonly happens between a proud man and the devil resembles an exchange once between a certain jester and a knight. A knight riding a fine horse met a jester who, having seen the knight, had constructed for himself what looked like a fine horse out of a "pessewyspe."[25] This he offered to trade with the knight for his horse. They do exchange, the jester telling the knight that the horse will neither jump walls nor cross rivers. The knight, fearing a bridge, plunges the horse into a river, at which point the horse becomes a "pessewyp"[25] again.]

Tunc videns armiger quod illusus esset arte callida et tunc prorupit in hec verba:

[Then the knight, seeing that he had been deceived through his own rashness, burst into speech]:

Off perell am I gretely ferde;
Mi hors es changed; myn ey es blerde.

The subsequent moralization identifies the minstrel with the devil, the knight with a good man, his horse with his good works, but the jester's palfrey with pride (which returns to the "nichil" of a peyssewysp[25]). The bridge represents death and the river "tribulacio et angustia." Near the end, this formulation is used to interpret the verses, cited in a slightly different form:

---

[25] The paraphrase follows the variant manuscript spellings of "pessewyspe."

[fol. 81vb] Et tunc potest dicere bene, "Of harme am I sore aferde," videlicet de perpetua dampnacione, nisi habeat graciam de consolacione. "My hors es chaunged," valde mala mutacio glorie celestis pro mundana superbia. "Myn ey es blered": credit suam gloriam durasse vsque infinitum; iam quasi reducitur ad nichilum. Vidistis enim multos ad predictum pontem, id est per mortem transire.

Verses g, *fol. 81vb = Index 221 (s.v. "Al ande ioʒe")*

This tag, based on Lam. 5:15–16, ed. F. A. Patterson, in his review of Brown's *Register, Journal of English and Germanic Philology* 20 (1921), 270–75 at 275 (this copy has reversed the first two lines), also appears at Advocates 18.7.21, fols. 25^v and 69^v; see Wilson, nos. 39 and 92 (pp. 9 and 20, s.v. "De contricione" and "De inferno"); and (b) Harley 7322, fol. 153^v, ed. EETS 15 (rev. ed, 1893), p. 261.

Tradunt historie quod Cartaginenses fabricauerunt aram maximam deo Priapi. Querens preses ciuitatis ab eodem deo suo quamdiu hec ara perduraret, responsum accepit metrice per hos versus:

A C triplicando, D et E simul asociando
Possunt signa capi quod corruet ara Priapi.

Qui versus a sapientibus taliter exponuntur: quod cum triplex A eueniret, triplex C et triplex D etc. ara destruetur. Triplex A Auaricia sine mensura, Adulacio sine fide, Astucia sine lege [with similar identifications for C and D] . . .

Placent triplex E; elemosina liberalis, equitas legalis, eutrapelia militaris non placent. Eutrapelia idem est quod ludus honestus.

[Historians tell us that the Carthaginians built a huge altar to the god Priapus. The ruler of the city asked this god of theirs how long the altar should last; he received a reply in verse:

["You can understand the portents that will lead to the fall of Priapus's altar, if you repeat three times A and C and join D and E three times with them."

[Wise men explained these verses as indicating that when a triple A, a triple C, a triple D, etc. occurred, the altar would be destroyed. The triple A is avarice without moderation, flattery without good faith, cunning without law . . .

[While the triple E should please, actually liberal almsgiving, equity at law, and martial "eutrapelia" will not please. "Eutrapelia" means the same thing as virtuous play. (i.e., these are great things, but the triple E won't please when the people have become so nasty that Priapus is going to desert them and his altar fall down.)]

> þe ioy of oure hertes es went away;
> Turned es to sorow all oure play;
> þe croun of our hede fallen it es to ground.
> þat we euer synde sa, wa worth þat stound.

Verses h, *fol. 82ra* = *unpub. and unique*

The exemplum begins: "Diligere inter omnia que sunt uel tantum prodest homini. . . ." [fol. 81vb]. The English is presented in a fashion unique here, within the prose and not as bracketed verses.

Necessaria est cuilibet uiuere apparenti dileccio. Set tria sunt que dilegere debes: Deum in quo est requies viatoris; proximum propter premium laboris; mundum ut peregrinum mereris.

[Love is necessary to anyone who wants to show he's alive. There are three things you ought to love: God, in whom is rest for the worldly pilgrim; your neighbor on account of the reward gained by the act of loving him, and the world, so you can earn your pilgrimage from it.]

> Loue god suffrandly°   *patiently*
> In qwham is all þi rest;
> Loue þine euencristen laustandly°,   *with perseverance*
> For þat es next þe best;
> Loue þe werld passandly,
> For he es bot a gast.

Verses i, *fol. 82va-vb = unpub. and unique*

Inter an[n]alia[26] Romanorum: ipsi de ciuitate Cartaginensi fuerunt in magna quiete, et operabatur secundum consilium comune et non | [fol. 82vb] erat inuidia inter eos. Rebus sic habentibus, quicunque pungnare contra eos attemptauerunt ab ipsis de ciuitate fuerunt deuicte. Cernentes hij de ciuitate quod in annum superiorem semper obtinerent, superbia cordis percussi, adinuicem inuidebant. . . .

[Among the annals of the Romans: the people of Carthage were at peace, and they carried on their affairs with a single will, and they showed no envy. While things went in this way, those who tried to fight against them were conquered. But the Carthaginians, perceiving that they had always achieved their goals in the past, were struck by pride of heart and began to envy one another. . . .]

Thus, the Carthaginians lose the war, and four golden rings are found in the ruins of the fallen city. Each has two letters inside it, and priests are called upon to sacrifice in order to discover their significance.

Finitoque sacrificio, vox quedam miro modo delapsa que ita dicebat: "Causa destruccionis ciuitatis istius est circulorum scriptura. In primo circulo, S et R, silicet 'superbia regnat.' In 2°., V et I, id est 'voluntas imperat.' In 3°. [P] O, \id est/ '[p]eccatum[27] oritur.' Et in 4°., D et M, id est 'Deus moritur,'" Anglice:

[When the sacrifice was done, a voice miraculously came down and said, "The cause of destruction of this city is written on the rings. On the first ring, S and R, namely 'pride rules.' On the second, V and I, that is 'desire commands.' On the third, P O, that is 'sin rises up.' And on the fourth, D and M, that is 'God dies,'" in English]:

Pryde es kyng, and wyll es rede;
Syn es on liue, and Gode es dede.

---

26 MS aialia, i.e., animalia.
27 MS O \id est/ per peccatum.

Verses j, *fol. 83va* = *Index 2260*

Also appears at Advocates 18.7.21, fol. 125^v, ed. Brown, *Religious Lyrics* 90; see Wilson no. 208 (p. 53, s.v. Lamentacio dolorosa).

Qvidam miles vnam gloriosam virginem siue puella(m) dilexit, pro cuius amore hastiludia proclamare fecit, partem contra omnes super-uenientes tenens. Consuetudo est quod qui talibus ludis wlt interesse in apparencia propriorum armorum accepit de puella quam dilexit, et in anteriori parte talem ludum non debet excercere.[28] Et ideo miles vnum signum acepit de puella quam dilexit, et in anteriori parte illius vestis scribebatur, "Puella quam diligo, pro cuius amore hodie certare volo."

[A certain knight loved a splendid young maiden, and to display his love he had a tournament proclaimed, in which he would stand against all comers. Now it's customary that whoever wants to take part in such games takes from the maiden he loves a token as the apparent form of his own arms, and unless he has that in front of him [like a shield], he ought not engage in such a game. Therefore, this knight took a token from the maiden he loved, and there was written in the front part of this clothing, "The girl whom I love, for whose love I want to do battle today."]

> My loue es fallen on a may;
> For hyre loue will I feght today.

In parte posteriori sic scribebatur, "Amor fortunatus neminem fugit, set fortis est vbi se tenet," Anglice:

> Loue anterous no man forsakys;
> Loue es stalworth þer he hym takys.

---

[28] So the MS, with considerable problems. The simplest solution, which I adopt in the translation, would involve two rather speculative emendations: (a) to insert *signum* before *accepit* (paralleling the next sentence); (b) to emend *et* in the same line to something like *et* [*nisi eam habet*]. But I would still find *in apparencia* somewhat problematic and suspect that the first use of *in anteriori parte* might be a scribal echo of the second.

In parte dextra scribebetur, "Amor fortunatus neminem parcit; ideo quinque suis sequacibus dira wlnera infligit."

> Loue anterous no man will spare
> þerfor to suffyre wondes sare.

In parte sinistra scribebatur sic, "Amor fortunatus requiem non possidet, set semper nouus est vbi fideliter residet."

> Loue anterous may haue non rest;
> My loue es n[e]w[29] þer loue es fest.

Ad propositum, iste miles est Cristus qui supramodum dilexit vnam puellam, id est animam humanam. Set in propriis noluit ludum adire, id est in deitate, set accepit signum de puella, id est carnem de uirgine Maria, et in anteriori parte scribebatur sic, "Puella quam diligo etc." Et bene apparuit quod istam puellam dilexit quando de tanta gloria ad tantam miseriam descendit. In parte posteriori sic scribebatur, "Amor fortunatus neminem fugit," et bene potuit dici fortunatus miles, quia a multis erat incognitus. Et neminem fugit, quia contra diabolum, mundum, et carnem pungnauit viriliter—contra mundum, penitencia et tribulacionibus; contra carnem in fame et siti et diris wlneribus; contra diabolum cum morte, ut patet in euangelio cum multis increpacionibus. In parte dextra scribe(ba)tur sic, "Amor fortunatus neminem parcit etc." Ipse passus est multa dira wlnera, quia secundum propheciam "dinumerauerunt omnia ossa mea" [Ps. 21:18]. In parte sinistra scribebatur sic, "Amor fortunatus requiem non possidet." Quamdiu Cristus fuit in hoc mundo semper fuit in labore continuo, et ad hec suus amor erg[a][30] nos est ita nouus sicud vnde quam fuit, quia quandocunque aliquis p(re)mere[31] proponit, Cristus paratus est eum recipere. Tale pro nobis Cristus sustinuit torneamentum, et tale pro nos fecit commercium. Omne contrarium Cristus sustinuit in sua passione.

[Now the explanation: this knight is Christ, who loved, beyond all moderation, a maiden who is man's soul. But he did not wish to go to the

---

29 MS now.

30 MS gº, i.e., "ergo."

31 MS pereu'ie or perm'e.

tournament in his own clothing, that is in his divinity, but he accepted a token from the maiden, that is flesh from the Virgin, and in its front part was written, "The girl whom I love, etc." And it certainly appeared that he loved this girl when he descended from such glory to such misery. In the back part was written, "Love willing to undertake risk flees no one," and he might well be called a knight willing to undertake risks, since he was unknown to many. And he fled no one, since he fought with valor against the devil, the world, and the flesh—against the world, through patience and tribulations; against the flesh, in hunger and thirst and horrible wounds; against the devil with death, accompanied by many reproaches, as is evident in the gospel. In the right side was written, "Love willing to undertake risk spares no one." He suffered many horrible wounds, since, as the prophecy says, "They have numbered all my bones." In the left part was written, "Love willing to undertake risk has no rest." As long as Christ was in this world, he always labored, and for this reason, his love for us is every bit as new as it once was, because whenever anyone proposes to attack, Christ is ready to take him on. Christ endured such a tournament for us, and he undertook such a bargain for us. He endured every adversity in his crucifixion.]

[The moralization concludes with an extended comparison of Eve, at the moment of the fall, and Christ on the cross.]

GAME IN THE MEDIEVAL ENGLISH DIET

Robin S. Oggins
Binghamton University

WHEN ONE THINKS of medieval feasts, one thinks of game: haunches of venison, whole roast swan, the boar's head "bedecked with bay and rosemary" on the Christmas table. Medieval cookbooks invariably contain recipes for game, some unfamiliar to modern palates: nombles (organ meat) of venison and roast peacock or bittern. Then there are the "four and twenty blackbirds baked in a pie" of the nursery rhyme. Among animals that might be eaten were porcupines, hedgehogs, badgers, and dormice, though there is doubt as to whether the last constituted "game."[1]

Certainly at one time or another some medieval English tables included most or all of the above. But what kinds of game were ordinarily eaten? And who ate game, when, and why? Referring to a range of medieval records, this paper attempts to answer these questions.

Game, according to Webster's, is "wild animals hunted for sport or food."[2] But the distinction between wild and domesticated animals was

---

[1] *Two Fifteenth-Century Cookery-Books*, ed. Thomas Austin, Early English Text Society, o.s., 91 (London, 1888), pp. 70, 78–79; Constance B. Hieatt, *An Ordinance of Pottage* (London, 1988), pp. 42, 91–92; Platina, *On Right Pleasure and Good Health*, ed. and trans. Mary Ellen Milham (Tempe, Ariz., 1998), pp. 236–39.

[2] *Merriam-Webster's Collegiate Dictionary*, 10th ed. (Springfield, Mass., 1993), p. 478.

not as clear in the Middle Ages as it is today. Deer ran free in the forests, but they were also kept in parks,[3] and there are even references to tame deer. According to a fourteenth-century tale, a "tame stag in England, accustomed to eat bread and drink beer, falls into a pit when drunk, and breaks his leg; he refuses beer ever after."[4] Wild swine are said to have become increasingly rare after 1260, and many of the boars listed in accounts after that date were probably domesticated.[5] Game that can be characterized as "semi-domesticated" included swans, rabbits (kept in warrens), and pigeons (kept in dovecotes).[6] Other birds considered wild today, such as cranes, herons, and egrets, were sometimes kept. I have regarded as game all the birds and animals previously mentioned, but, as we shall see, the most important distinction was not that between game hunted and game raised or purchased but between more and less prestigious kinds of game.

The most lavish medieval English feast may well have been that celebrating the enthronement of George Neville as archbishop of York in 1466. Among the creatures reportedly served were six wild bulls, more than five hundred deer, four thousand rabbits, four hundred peacocks, four hundred swans, eight hundred cranes, four hundred herons, one thousand egrets, eight hundred bitterns, two hundred pheasants, five hundred partridges, twelve hundred quail, four hundred woodcocks, four hundred plovers, four thousand mallards and teals, and four thousand

---

[3] In 1512, there were 5,571 deer in "the Parks and Forests in the North belonging to the Earl of Northumberland . . . exclusive of those in Sussex and other Counties in the South" (*The Regulations and Establishment of the Household of Henry Algernon Percy, the Fifth Earl of Northumberland at His Castles of Wressle and Leckonfield in Yorkshire,* new ed. [London, 1905], pp. 409–10; henceforth cited as *Northumberland Household Book*).

[4] J. A. Herbert, *Catalogue of Romances in the Department of Manuscripts in the British Museum,* vol. 3 (London, 1910), p. 646.

[5] Oliver Rackham, *Ancient Woodland: Its History, Vegetation and Uses in England* (London, 1980), p. 133.

[6] Such game might be kept in large quantities. In 1295 Robert de Tateshale, while on the king's service in Scotland, had forty swans carried away by poachers (Great Britain, Public Record Office, *Calendar of the Patent Rolls Preserved in the Public Record Office, Edward I* [London, 1893–1901], 2:161), and in 1245, during a vacancy at Chichester, Henry III had five hundred rabbits and two hundred hares sent from the estates of the bishopric for the queen's purification (Great Britain, Public Record Office, *Calendar of the Liberate Rolls Preserved in the Public Record Office* [London, 1916–64], 2:289).

pigeons.[7] Neville was the brother of Warwick "the kingmaker," and the feast's lavishness was no doubt a political as well as a social statement.

English kings also consumed game in substantial amounts. As one would expect, much game might be served at feasts, whether seasonal, to mark important occasions, or for important visitors. Before Christmas 1248, Henry III ordered the sheriff of Hampshire to send one hundred does and the sheriff of Nottingham to provide six hinds. Thirteen men were instructed to procure a total of 72 boars, 40 sows, 10 (wild?) pigs, more than 40 swans, more than 46 peacocks, 700 partridges, 420 hares, 400 rabbits, 24 pheasants, 60 sheldrakes, and unspecified numbers of mallards and birds of the river. For the feast of St. Edward the Martyr on the following January 5, the total was 15 does, 26 boars, 300 partridges, 270 hares, and 500 larks, in addition to cranes, peacocks, swans, sheldrakes, mallards, and birds of the river.[8] For Christmas 1251, 812 deer were ordered, more than half the 1,598 deer ordered to be taken for the entire year.[9] Amounts of game varied from year to year[10] and from holiday to holiday.[11]

---

[7] John Leland, *Joannis Lelandi antiquarii De rebvs Britannicis collectanea*, ed. Thomas Hearne (1774; reprint, Farnborough, Hants, 1970), 6:2.

[8] For the deer, see *Liberate Rolls*, 3:210, 213; Great Britain, National Archives, E372/93. For the other game, see *Liberate Rolls*, 3:212, 215–16; Great Britain, Public Record Office, *Close Rolls of the Reign of Henry III Preserved in the Public Record Office* (London, 1902–38), 6:96.

[9] *Close Rolls Henry III*, 6:407–52l; 7:1–23; *Liberate Rolls*, 3:333–76; 4:1–9.

[10] Total surviving royal orders for deer in Henry III's reign range from 1,790 in 1256 to none in 1222, and for Edward I from 460 in 1301 to none between 1294 and 1296. Between 1240 and 1263, Henry III ordered more than five hundred deer yearly and in six years the totals of deer ordered were more than a thousand, in addition to other game (1,250 hares and 1,080 rabbits in 1245, etc.). For Henry's entire reign the percentage of deer explicitly ordered for specific feasts was 43 percent of the total ordered. Unfortunately, many royal commands have not survived, some that have do not specify an occasion, and others simply request as many of the specific game as possible.

[11] For Christmas 1249, for example, 120 does, 26 boars, 120 (wild?) swine and sows, 6 swans, 40 peacocks, 52 pheasants, 350 partridges, and 200 hares plus rabbits, mallards, and birds of the river were ordered. For the feast of St. Edward following, 40 does, 36 roebucks, 19 boars, 40 (wild?) swine and sows, 22 swans, 38 peacocks, 108 pheasants, 288 partridges, 200 hares, and 190 rabbits. (*Liberate Rolls*, 3:270, 272, 275; *Close Rolls*, 6:239, 247–48, 250). In the surviving documents, the major feasts for which game was ordered were Christmas, Easter, Whitsun, and the two feasts of St. Edward—the deposition on January 5 and the translation on October 13, but

But were the amounts of game that were ordered the quantities actually supplied? The limited available evidence suggests they were not. In theory, when the king ordered a sheriff or other official to purchase game (or anything else, for that matter), the amount expended might be listed as a credit on a Pipe Roll, or the sheriff might be reimbursed through a command entered on a Liberate Roll. In most cases for which royal orders for game are recorded, no corresponding credits or reimbursements have survived. While this could be because the sheriffs had made no purchases, several instances in which sheriffs received credits or payments for purchases for which no orders survive suggest that some discrepancies were the result of either inadequate accounting procedures or lost records.[12] If one looks at cases for which there are both royal orders and numbers of game actually purchased, one finds that the quantities provided were often smaller than those ordered. For example, for Christmas 1240 twelve officials were ordered to buy and send to Westminster 40 roebucks, 68 boars,[13] more than 30 swans and 50 cranes,[14] 60 herons or bitterns, 110 peacocks, 312 pheasants, 1,230 partridges, 1,000 hares, and 500 rabbits. Of these the sheriff of Essex was responsible for 6 boars, 10 peacocks, 48 pheasants, 120 partridges, and 100 hares. He actually provided three boars (50 percent of the number requested), two peacocks

---

in various years significant quantities of game were also specifically ordered for the Nativity, Purification, and Ascension of the Virgin Mary; the decollation of St. John the Baptist; Michaelmas; All Saints; Henry III's and Edward I's coronation feasts; the marriage of Edward I's daughter Eleanor; purifications of Henry III's queen Eleanor of Provence and of Henry's sister Eleanor countess of Pembroke; and in advance of a meeting of Parliament in 1260.

[12] For example, in the Pipe Roll of 1241–42 the sheriff of Nottingham received credit for the cost of 9 swans, 20 hares, 10 peacocks, and 118 partridges for which there are no extant orders (Henry Lewis Cannon, ed., *The Great Roll of the Pipe for the Twenty-Sixth Year of the Reign of King Henry the Third: A.D. 1241–1242* [New Haven, 1918], p. 307); in the Pipe Roll for 1245 the sheriff of Surrey and Sussex received credit for the cost of twenty-four roebucks for which there is no corresponding order (National Archives E372/93; *Liberate Rolls*, 3:12).

[13] William de Munceals, keeper of "the lands late of W. earl Warenne," was instructed to provide "12 boars (*braones*) with their heads, the heads to be cut clean off and the brains taken out, and [the heads] to be cooked and well soused (*susciri*)" (*Liberate Rolls*, 2:11).

[14] The sheriff of Northampton was ordered to buy "as many swans and cranes as possible," and William de Munceals "as many swans as possible" (*Liberate Rolls*, 2:11).

(20 percent), eleven pheasants (23 percent), seventy-three partridges (61 percent), and sixty hares (60 percent). The sheriffs of London came up with all ten of the peacocks they were ordered to send (100 percent), but there is no mention in the Pipe Roll of the requested three hundred partridges or two hundred rabbits. In addition to the above, royal huntsmen were sent to take 180 deer and 60 (wild?) swine and sows, but there is no information on how many were actually delivered.[15]

If one averages results for the limited number of cases for which numbers of game ordered and of game delivered survive, the range is from 42 percent (percentage of hares ordered that were actually delivered) to 74 percent (pheasants and swans) with an overall average (for eight different kinds of game) of 64 percent.[16] But even though everything ordered may not have been sent, the records still indicate that substantial numbers of game were consumed on the occasions in question and, by implication, at royal feasts in general.[17]

---

[15] *Liberate Rolls*, 2:11–12; National Archives E372/85, Essex, London; *Close Rolls Henry III*, 4:251–52, 257.

[16] The overall totals compiled from available figures for twelve years between 1240 and 1256, in order of declining percentages of kinds of game actually received, are as follows: swans, 90 ordered, 67 received (74 percent); pheasants, 192 ordered, 142 received (74 percent); rabbits, 1,172 ordered, 862 received (73.5 percent); peacocks, 101 ordered, 71 received (70 percent); boars, 163 ordered, 104 received (64 percent); partridges, 1,768 ordered, 1,104 received (62 percent); cranes, 12 ordered, 6 received (50 percent); and hares, 731 ordered, 310 received (42 percent). Because of the discrepancies in numbers of particular kinds of game, I have averaged the percentages for the kinds of game ordered and received. For the orders for game see *Liberate Rolls*, 2:11-12, 95–97; 3:12–13, 93–94, 251; *Close Rolls Henry III*, 6:96; 7:259, 427–28, 503; 8:156; 9:149, 166, 377, 432–33; 12:10, 106, 280. For the credits for game actually received see National Archives E372/85, Essex; Cannon, *Great Roll of the Pipe*, pp. 259, 276, 307; E372/90, Cambridge and Huntingdon, Kent, Northampton, Surrey and Sussex, Bishopric of Chichester; E372/91, Hampshire, Oxford and Berkshire, Account of William de Breause, Surrey and Sussex, Wiltshire; E372/93, Surrey and Sussex, Essex and Hertfordshire, Somerset and Dorset, Kent, Oxford and Berkshire, Wiltshire, Buckingham and Bedford; E 372/96, Surrey and Sussex; E372/97, Northampton, Hampshire; E372/98, London and Middlesex, Surrey and Sussex; E372/99, Norfolk and Suffolk, London and Middlesex; E372/100, Wiltshire; E372/101, Oxford and Berkshire, Essex; E372/102, Cambridge and Huntingdon.

[17] For Christmas 1254 the sheriffs of London sent the king ten boars, twenty-nine hares, sixty-six rabbits, nine pheasants, fifty-six partridges, sixty-eight woodcocks, thirty-nine plovers, six lapwings, and a heron (*Liberate Rolls*, 4:198). The king also received ten swans as a gift from Roger de Turkelby (*Liberate Rolls*, 4:187). There

There is one surviving thirteenth-century royal diet account: a daily roll of kitchen expenditures for 21 Edward I (1291–92). The manuscript is difficult to read in places and any attempt to compile totals would be questionable at best. But even a listing of items purchased can give one an idea of game normally consumed by the royal household. Rabbits, partridges, mallards, woodcock and teal (generally listed together), and larks (sometimes purchased in the hundreds) appear regularly in the account. Hares and pheasants appear somewhat less frequently and in smaller numbers. Sheldrake, plover, and doves appear on occasion, while swans, cranes, herons, and bitterns were purchased only a few times, but then in some quantity (e.g., eight swans, six cranes, twenty-three bitterns and herons)—no doubt for feasts.[18] The variety of game is roughly similar, as we shall see, to that consumed by well-to-do private households, although the quantities of game and the number of feasts are much greater.

Two documents of Henry VIII's reign, sumptuary regulations from 1517 and a household ordinance of 1525–26, provide additional information as to the quantities of various kinds of wildfowl served in a single dish, the variety of game that might be eaten, and the different kinds of game ordained for the king and queen and for various ranks of royal servants.

The purpose of the sumptuary regulations was "putting apart the excessive fare, and reducing the same to . . . moderation." People of various ranks were limited as to the numbers of "dishes" to be served at a meal:

> Item, cranes, swan, bustard, peacock, and all other fowls of like greatness, but one dish.
>
> Item, partridge, plovers, woodcocks, and all other wildfowl of like greatness, but six in a dish for a cardinal only, and four in a dish for all other lords.
>
> Item, quails, dotterels, snites, and all other fowls of like greatness, but eight in a dish.

---

is no indication as to how much of the additional game ordered by the king (100 does, 100 boars and lays, a further 16 boars, 12 cranes, 16 peacocks, 26 more swans, 450 rabbits, 270 hares, 96 partridges, 24 pheasants, 50 mallards, and 12 sheldrakes) was delivered (*Close Rolls Henry III,* 9:10, 149–50).

[18] National Archives E101/353/2, *passim.* Because deer were not purchased, they were not listed on the account.

Item, pheasants, gulls, and all other fowls of like greatness, but two in a dish.

Item, larks and all other fowls of like greatness, but 12 in a dish.[19]

In the ordinances, the dinner menu for a flesh day's "Diett for the King's Majesty and the Queen's Grace, of like fare" was to include two kinds of venison; swan (or?) stork; and coneys in the first course; pheasant, heron, bittern, shoveler [duck]; partridges, quails, or "Mewz" [seagulls];[20] cocks, plovers, or gulls; kid, lamb, or pigeons; larks or rabbits; and venison in paste in the second course. For the first supper course there were to be stewed larks, sparrows, or lamb; gigot of mutton or venison; coneys; pheasant, heron, or shoveler; and cocks, plovers, or gulls. In the second course there were to be partridges or quails; godwits or teals; rabbits or larks; and venison or other baked meats.[21] Again one is struck by the variety of game, but also noteworthy is the interchangeability not only of various kinds of game but of game and domestic meats or birds.

The Great Master was to be served swans, herons, bitterns, curlews, plovers or gulls, snipe, coneys, rabbits, and larks—but not venison, pheasant, or partridge. The Lord Privy Seal, king's and queen's Lord Chamberlains, the Captain of the Gentleman Pensioners, the Secretary, the Treasurer, and the Comptroller received much the same fare as the Great Master, though in smaller quantities—one "mess" rather than two, one heron rather than four, etc. The gentlemen of the privy chamber and the "ladies in presence" were served coneys, pigeons, and plover for dinner; and coneys; lamb, chicken, or rabbits; and plovers and(?) teal for supper. Pigeons were the only game received by the physicians and surgeons; the Wardrober of the Beds, groom, porter, yeomen, and officers of the house were limited to coney; and the maids, servants, children of officers, porters, and "skewerers" were served no game at all.[22]

The importance of game was shown in ways other than consumption. English kings both gave and received presents of game, particularly

---

[19] *Tudor Royal Proclamations*, vol. 1, *The Early Tudors (1485–1553)*, ed. Paul L. Hughes and James F. Larkin (New Haven, 1964), pp. 128–29.

[20] W. B. Lockwood, *The Oxford Dictionary of British Bird Names* (Oxford, 1993), p. 103.

[21] Society of Antiquaries of London, *A Collection of Ordinances and Regulations for the Government of the Royal Household* (London, 1790), pp. 174–75.

[22] *Ordinances and Regulations,* pp. 177–91.

of deer. In his fifty-six-year reign, Henry III made more than 3,200 gifts totaling almost 17,500 deer, 54 boars, 70 wild sows, 395 rabbits, and 2 flying swans. Edward I's recorded totals over thirty-five years were 613 gifts of 4,841 deer, 6 boars, and 3 wild swine.[23] While the reasons for royal gifts of game were generally not specified, some were, and those were usually for festive occasions. Archbishops-elect and bishops-elect might receive gifts for the feasts of their consecration.[24] The abbot of Waltham was given four stags for the feast of his institution, the abbot-elect of Cerne seven stags to celebrate his benediction, and the abbess of Wherwell two deer for the feast of her institution. The abbot of Evesham and the abbess of Romsey received seven and five deer respectively for feasts they were holding. William de Longespee and Gilbert Marshal served royal deer at the feasts of their knighting; Master John Wiche, clerk of the bishop of Carlisle, was given two stags for his inception at Oxford lecturing in law; two sons of Sibyl Giffard received three stags for their inception in the art of dialectic at Oxford; Ela countess of Salisbury was given a buck for the marriage feast of Marie, daughter of the former earl of Salisbury; Johanna de Valence was given three deer and one stag for her lying-in; and the wife of Nicholas de Haudro three deer for her churching.[25] Henry III gave deer to celebrate Christmas, Easter, Whitsun, the Assumption of the Virgin, the feast for the translation of St. Thomas Martyr, the feast of St. Benedict (to the abbot of Ramsey), the feast of St. Peter Chains (to the

---

[23] The actual recorded totals for Henry III are 3,289 gifts of 17,473 deer, but quantities given were not always specified (e.g., Great Britain, Public Record Office, *Calendar of the Close Rolls Preserved in the Public Record Office, Edward I* [London, 1900–1908], 1:401), some gifts were by word of mouth (2:210), and not all such gifts may have been recorded. Deer illegally taken but pardoned for (which I have not counted) amounted to gifts as well. The main source for royal gifts is the Close Rolls, but some orders are recorded in the Liberate Rolls, and occasionally relevant information can be found in the Patent Rolls.

[24] Great Britain, Record Commission, *Rotuli litterarum clausarum in turri Londinensi asservati*, ed. Thomas Duffus Hardy (London, 1833–44), 1:406, 592, 593; *Close Rolls Henry III*, 1:201; 3, 90; 5:222, 342; 6:214, 519; 8:54. Gifts of deer were made to ten of the seventy-four archbishops and bishops consecrated or translated during Henry III's reign.

[25] *Close Rolls Henry III*, 6:61 (Waltham); 5:179 (Cerne); 10:376 (Wherwell); 3:398 (Evesham); 3:445 (Romsey); 2:210–11 (Longespee); 2:444 (Marshal); 3:446 (Wiche); 6:459 (Giffard); *Rotuli litterarum clausarum*, 2:200 (Salisbury); *Close Rolls Henry III*, 12:351–52 (Valence); 11:108 (Haudro).

abbot of Westminster), and the feast of St. Edmund.[26] One royal gift of game for which there seems to have been no special occasion was the six cranes' heads Edward I sent his mother, then a nun at Amesbury. But this was noteworthy enough to lead the queen to write, thanking her son.[27]

The kings also received presents of game. From July 12, 1338, to May 27, 1340, Edward III received recorded gifts of 124½ deer, 2¼ boars, 4¼ wild sows, 2 swans, and 22 rabbits.[28] Thirteenth-century sovereigns were given swans, cranes, herons, and birds of the wood (*aves silvestris*).[29] One gathers that almost any kind of game might be a present for a king. Wild animals were more valued than their domestic counterparts: the price in a London ordinance of 1378 for "best roast river mallard" was 4½ pence, while the price for domesticated duck "best roast dunghill mallard" was a penny less.[30] And a late fourteenth-century Parisian bourgeois included in a book of instructions for his young bride a brief section on how "to give the flavour of game to capons and hens."[31] Game might also be served in spectacular fashion. We have noted the boar's head. One way of presenting peacocks, swans, and pheasants was to skin them "so as to

---

[26] *Rotuli litterarum clausarum*, 2:87 (Christmas); *Close Rolls Henry III*, 3:251 (Easter); 2:444 (Whitsun); 12:352 (Assumption); *Rotuli litterarum clausarum*, 2:122 (Thomas); *Close Rolls Henry III*, 7:30 (Benedict); 5:441 (Peter Chains); 7:30 (Edmund).

[27] National Archives SC1/16/172. Other noteworthy gifts include the "hundred bucks of his English venison" Edward I sent Pope Clement V in 1306 (*Close Rolls Edward I*, 4:461) and Edward's gift to "Sir Francis de Bonon[ia], LL.D. (*legum professori*)," [of] two young bucks and four young does for the present year, [and?] four live hares and six live rabbits to be placed in the king's garden at Oxford" (1:296).

The importance of deer can be seen in the fact that although the archbishopric of Canterbury had its own deer parks (e.g., *Rotuli litterarum clausarum*, 1:154), Archbishop Boniface of Savoy (1241–70) made a compact with John Fitz Alan to be provided annually with thirteen bucks and thirteen does from the latter's forest of Arundel (*Close Rolls Edward I*, 1:34–35; 2:6).

[28] Mary Lyon, Bryce Lyon, and Henry S. Lucas, *The Wardrobe Book of William de Norwell: 12 July 1338 to 27 May 1340* (Brussels, 1983), pp. 204–5.

[29] For a gift to King John of two cranes see "Rotulus Misæ anni regni Regis Johannis quarti decimi," in Great Britain, Record Commission, *Documents Illustrative of English History in the Thirteenth and Fourteenth Centuries*, ed. Henry Cole (London, 1844), p. 257; for ten swans given to Henry III, see *Liberate Rolls*, 4:187; for the other birds, given to Edward I, see National Archives E101/357/9.

[30] Henry Thomas Riley, *Memorials of London and London Life in the XIIIth, XIVth, and XVth Centuries . . . .* (London, 1868), p. 426.

[31] *The Goodman of Paris*, trans. Eileen Power (London, 1928), p. 224.

keep the skin whole and complete with feathers." After roasting the "skin [was] replaced and the bird presented as though still alive."[32]

But while game was consumed in substantial quantities at the feasts of the great, what part did it play in the diet of the less exalted? Certainly members of all medieval English social classes consumed at least some game. Although most royal gifts of game were to the great, to important people, or to the well connected, humbler individuals received gifts as well. Among those given deer were such royal servants as the tailor of the wardrobe; royal clerks; John de Spigurnel, servant of the chapel; the royal physician and surgeon; and royal huntsmen. Henry III gave John Fitz Bernard, marshal of the king's hawks, twelve live deer to put in his park, while the falconer Thomas de Hauvill similarly received fifteen live deer from Edward I.[33] Other recipients of deer included the clerk of Richard Longespee, Robert parson of Appleton, sick monks at Westminster and Malmesbury, and the poor in the hospital of Bindon.[34]

Peasants might capture unprotected game, and some undoubtedly poached. In the period from 1268 to 1272 Thorold Rogers found prices for 121 hawks ranging from a penny and a half to three pence. Both the number and the low prices suggest that a fair number of peasants hawked. In a single season in the late fifteenth century, a hawk of a vicar of Watford caught for his table some sixty fen birds and mallards. And the previously mentioned London ordinance set prices not only for mallards, but for teal, snipe, larks, woodcock, partridge, plover, pheasant, curlew, thrushes, finches, heron, bittern, and pigeons.[35] The lower classes, however, did not keep records of what they consumed or when,

---

[32] P. W. Hammond, *Food and Feast in Medieval England* (Gloucestershire, 1993), p. 138; Hieatt, *An Ordinance of Pottage*, pp. 109–10.

[33] *Close Rolls Henry III*, 2:93 (tailor); 3:302; 6:312, 478, etc. (clerks); 4:251 (Spigurnel); 10:249 (physician); 10:166 (surgeon); *Close Rolls Edward I*, 2:104 (huntsmen); *Close Rolls Henry III*, 10:25 (Fitz Bernard); *Close Rolls Edward I*, 2:307 (Hauvill). Henry's gift to stock the park of a hawker and that of Edward to a falconer may be a reflection of their different sporting tastes; see Robin S. Oggins, *The Kings and Their Hawks: Falconry in Medieval England* (New Haven, 2004), p. 82.

[34] *Close Rolls Henry III*, 4:161 (clerk); 14:201 (parson); 10:259 (monks of Westminster); 13:70 (monks of Malmesbury); 4:16 (poor at Bindon).

[35] See Jean Birrell, "Peasant Deer Poachers in the Medieval Forest," in *Progress and Problems in Medieval England: Essays in Honour of Edward Miller*, ed. Richard Britnell and John Hatcher (New York, 1996), pp. 68–88; Oggins, *The Kings and Their Hawks*, pp. 120, 124, 190, 192; Riley, *Memorials of London* , p. 426.

so any detailed account of medieval English diet must be based on the consumption of the well-to-do.

The regulations drawn up in 1512 for the fifth earl of Northumberland (the *Northumberland Household Book*) give good insight into the theoretical consumption of a great nonroyal household. The regulations provided for forty-nine deer—twenty-nine does and twenty bucks—to be consumed yearly: the does between All Hallows (Nov. 1) and Lent, the bucks from the week following May Day to All Hallows. Does were specified for a number of feasts: two for All Hallows, two for Christmas, one for St. Stephen's Day (Dec. 26), two for the holy days between St. Stephen's and New Year's, two for New Year's Day, two more for between New Year's and Twelfth Day (Jan. 6), and three for Twelfth Day itself. The remaining fifteen does were allotted weekly for the eight weeks between All Hallows and Christmas and the seven weeks from Twelfth Night to Shrovetide (Lent). Nineteen of the twenty bucks were scheduled for the nineteen weeks between May Day and All Hallows with one buck specified for Whitsun (the seventh Sunday after Easter).[36]

Game other than deer were divided under four headings according to the times they were to be "provided and ordeyned to be served": "at principall feestes," "yerely," "mounethly," and "weekely."[37] For most items maximum prices were set, though in some cases there is the proviso "except my Lordes comaundment be otherwise."[38] Twenty swans per year were to come from the earl's own stock, eighteen for the Christmas season—five for Christmas, two for St. Stephen's Day, two for Childermass (Dec. 28), two for St. Thomas's Day (Dec. 29), three for New Year's Day, and four for Twelfth Night—and two for St. John's Day (June 24).[39] Game that might be provided at principal feasts included cranes (at 16*d.* each); bitterns, curlews, heronsews (herons), pheasants, and peacocks— but not peahens (12*d.*); shovelers (6*d.*); "reys"—female ruffs (2*d.*); redshanks and widgeons (1½*d.*); knots (1*d.*); dotterels (½*d.*); terns (four for

---

[36] *Northumberland Household Book,* pp. 112–14, 202–4. For the seasons for hunting deer, see Jean Birrell, "Deer and Deer Farming in Medieval England," *Agricultural History Review* 40 (1992), 126.

[37] *Northumberland Household Book,* pp. 102–8, 169, 176–78, 183–85, 196–97.

[38] *Northumberland Household Book,* pp. 106–7. Exceptions are made for widgeons, knots, bustards, and terns. Teals are "to be bought bot if so be that other Wyldefowll cannot be gottyn" (104).

[39] *Northumberland Household Book,* pp. 108, 197.

1*d*.); and bustards and "see-pyes" (oystercatchers—no price given). While plovers (1*d*., at most 1½*d*.) are put in the monthly category, the text under the heading states that they should only be bought at Christmas and for principal feasts. Other "mounethly" birds were mallards, quail, and partridges (2*d*. each); seagulls and woodcock (1½*d*. at most); teal and "wipes" (lapwings—1*d*.); snipe (three for 1*d*.); "great birds" (four for 1*d*.); larks and stints (six for 1*d*.); "small birds" (twelve for 1*d*.); and "all manar of wyldfewyll" (no price given). The only game in the weekly category were rabbits—"cunys"—(2*d*.) and pigeons (three for 1*d*.), and these were the only game designated for the Master Chamberlain and the Steward's mess.[40] There is no mention in the regulations of boars or hares. Informative as it is, the *Northumberland Household Book* does not tell us what was actually consumed. For that one must go to household accounts—a limited number of which, covering extended periods of time, have survived. Christopher Woolgar has summarized his work on a number of such accounts from East Anglia. He notes the scarcity of boars, seasonal variations in eating rabbits and pigeons, the frequency and varieties of wildfowl consumed, and the receipt of twenty-six swans as gifts by Joan, duchess of Brittany and half-sister to Richard II.[41]

To describe what game contemporaries actually ate, I will summarize in detail accounts for the households of Richard de Swinfield, Bishop of Hereford, for the years 1289–90; of Richard Mitford, Bishop of Salisbury, for 1406–7; of Dame Alice de Bryene for 1412–13; along with the fragmentary account of Ralph of Shrewsbury, Bishop of Bath and Wells, for 1337–38. In considering these records several general circumstances should be noted. In all cases meat was not normally eaten on Wednesdays, Fridays, Saturdays, or during Lent, and meat and fish were seldom

---

[40] *Northumberland Household Book.* For "reys," "see-pyes," and "wipes," see Lockwood, *Oxford Dictionary of British Bird Names,* pp. 128, 136, 169. The monks of Westminster Abbey (c. 1495–c. 1525) also on occasion ate pigeon and cony as part of their normal diet, and on feast days might be served venison and such game birds as swan or cygnet, teal or snipe (Barbara Harvey, *Living and Dying in England, 1100–1540: The Monastic Experience* [Oxford, 1993], pp. 52–53). One surmises that Northumberland's Master Chamberlain and Steward also received a greater variety of game at feasts.

[41] "Diet and Consumption in Gentry and Noble Households: A Case Study from around the Wash," in *Rulers and Ruled in Late Medieval England: Essays Presented to Gerald Harriss,* ed. Rowena E. Archer and Simon Walker (London, 1995), pp. 21–23.

eaten on the same day. All four households fed substantial numbers of people daily, some kept records of how many and whom they fed, and amounts of food recorded were for the entire day. In all cases the choicest food would no doubt have been reserved for the head of the household and important guests, though this is not specified in the accounts.

According to the papal taxation of 1291, the annual income of the bishop of Hereford was £469 1s. 5d.—the equivalent of a comfortable baronial income.[42] Swinfield's surviving household account lists daily consumption and expenses from September 30, 1289, to July 23, 1290. Between September 30 and April 9 game was eaten on sixty-five of the seventy-seven days on which meat was consumed (84 percent). From April 10 to July 23 the number of days on which game was eaten dropped sharply, but deer was consumed on five of the six days on which game was eaten. Swinfield employed huntsmen and a fowler, a fact reflected in his diet. During the ten months, about 40 deer and 392 partridges were consumed, substantially more of both than in any of the other accounts. Herefordshire is a hilly, wooded area bordering Wales, and game seems to have been plentiful there. In other households, deer tended to be reserved for festive occasions, and while this was also true for Swinfield, deer was eaten at other times as well. Between November 20 and December 13, during the fall hunting season, deer was on the table for eleven of the twelve days on which meat was eaten. On June 29, after a two-day hunt, two of the three does taken were eaten, and on June 4 and July 16 salted venison from the previous winter was consumed. Boar, however, seems to have been saved for special occasions. It is unclear why a boar was purchased for Sunday, October 16, but one was served at Christmas and two were on the table at Easter. Half a boar and some pheasants (the only pheasants consumed that year) were eaten on January 10, while the bishop was in London. Hares were served only twice: during the London visit and on January 2, when the bishop entertained the abbot of Ramsey, with whom he had been staying (three deer were also part of that banquet). Rabbits were eaten on four days, and hares and rabbits, except for a gift of six rabbits, were bought. Partridge was a staple of diet from October

---

[42] Webb, who provides a full account of the bishop's resources, believes his annual income was more than £520 (*A Roll of the Household Expenses of Richard de Swinfield, Bishop of Hereford,* 2 vols., ed. John Webb, Camden Society, o.s., 59, 62 [London, 1853–55], 2:xxvii).

until the beginning of January, during which time 365 were eaten. Of the total of 392 partridges, 43 were gifts, the rest were either raised or trapped by Harpin the fowler. Other birds, however, were bought. Mallards were eaten on four days, larks on five, and small birds (*volatilia*) every day but one on which game was eaten in January, but only twice in other months. Pigeons were eaten fairly frequently in October, twice in November, and then not again until April, when on Easter Sunday 88 were consumed, followed by 110 the day after and 50 more on two days later in the week. Then no more pigeons until July 23, when 46 appear in the account. There is no record of any of the prestige birds—crane, swan, heron, or peacock—being eaten.[43]

According to Christopher Dyer, Bishop Mitford's annual income was more than £1,000, but the Taxation of 1291 gives the total for the diocese as £531 19*s*. 5*d*.[44] Mitford's surviving household account lists daily consumption from October 1, 1406, to June 10, 1407[45]—although Mitford died on May 3.[46] As in Swinfield's case, game was a regular part of diet before Easter and was eaten on seventy of the seventy-four days (95 percent) on which meat was recorded. From Easter on, game was consumed less than half the time (twenty of forty-eight days), being replaced by veal, mutton, and lamb. Mitford employed two huntsmen,[47] and the total number of deer eaten was twenty-four—eighteen-and-a-half between Christmas and Epiphany. Fifteen of the twenty-four swans eaten were consumed in the same period, as were 2¾ of the 4¼ boars. Herons, however, were eaten in the spring: eleven between April 21 and May 1 and twenty-seven, plus eight egrets, at the great feast held on June 7 (more than a month after Mitford's death), at which the bishop of Norwich, the clergy of Mitford's diocese, various nobles, and the mayor and burgesses of Salisbury were present. Rabbits were a staple for much of the year, but not between Lent

43 Webb, *Swinfield*, 1:3–108.

44 "The Consumer and the Market in the Later Middle Ages," *Economic History Review* 42 (1989), 306, citing "B.L., Harley MS 3755"; S. L. Ollard and G. Crosse, eds., *A Dictionary of English Church History* (London, 1912), p. 540.

45 "Accounts for the Household of Richard Mitford, Bishop of Salisbury, October 1406 to June 1407," in *Household Accounts from Medieval England*, 2 vols., ed. C. M. Woolgar, Records of Social and Economic History, n.s., 17–18, (Oxford, 1992), pp. 264–405.

46 E. B. Fryde, D. E. Greenway, S. Porter, and I. Roy, *Handbook of British Chronology*, 3rd ed. (London, 1986), p. 271.

47 Mitford, "Accounts," pp. 416–17.

and the beginning of June. In all 501 rabbits were consumed, 126 on June 7. Pigeons too were eaten in large numbers (990) and were seasonal: none were eaten between November 21 and April 21. During that period, however, other kinds of birds were consumed: woodcock most frequently (on twenty days—106 were eaten in all), but the greatest number eaten in the entire period were "large birds" (558) followed by "small birds" (245), snipe (129), woodcock, and larks (89), with smaller numbers of pheasants (only 7), partridges, plovers, mallards, teal, and quail. While deer, pheasants, and partridges were captured, and there were some gifts, most of the other birds and the boars and rabbits were purchased.[48]

Dame Alice de Bryene was the widow of the eldest son of a minor baron. In her later years she lived in Suffolk; her annual income has been estimated at about £400.[49] A detailed account of her household has survived that covers the entire year from September 29, 1412, to September 28, 1413. Dame Alice had the smallest income of any of those considered, and her diet contained the smallest variety of game. In all, her household consumed 1,713 pigeons, 116 rabbits, 15 partridges, 6 swans, and 5 herons. Not a single one was recorded as purchased. Game was eaten on 149 of the 173 days on which meat was consumed (86 percent); thirteen of the twenty-four gameless days fell between June 26 and July 20. Pigeons were eaten daily from September 29 until November 20 (an average of 18½), then only once (four on March 6) until Easter (April 23), after which they were eaten on every day but one on which game was consumed until the end of the account. When no pigeons were eaten, rabbits took their place, served on all but two days on which game was eaten from November 21 to February 21, and then only once more—two rabbits on September 4. Except for New Year's Day, on which seventeen rabbits were served, the average was roughly two rabbits per day.[50] Swans were served on five occasions: two for Christmas and three on days when there were important guests. Two herons were served for important guests and two on the

---

[48] Ibid., pp. 264–405.

[49] Ffiona Swabey, *Medieval Gentlewoman: Life in a Gentry Household in the Later Middle Ages* (New York, 1999), pp. 1, 67.

[50] *The Household Book of Dame Alice de Bryene*, ed. V. Redstone, trans. M. K. Dale (Ipswich, 1931), pp. 1–102. For 1418–19 the totals of game consumed were 1,216 pigeons, 102 rabbits, 13 partridges, 7 pheasants, 5 swans, 5 herons, and 3 boars. Only one of the boars was bought (pp. 131, 133–35).

Monday and Tuesday before the beginning of Lent. All the herons were served between February 16 and August 10.[51]

The income of the bishop of Bath and Wells, according to the Taxation of 1291, was £551 13s. 11d.[52] A fragment of Ralph of Shrewsbury's household account for the period from November 2, 1337, to March 10, 1338 has survived, but the entries from December 5 to 28 and January 11 to February 12 are missing, and there are small gaps elsewhere.[53] Game was eaten on thirty-two of the thirty-four meat days for which entries are recorded (94 percent). Only two kinds of animals (deer and rabbits) were eaten, and not many of those (three and five), but fourteen different kinds of birds were served and there are additional separate entries for "wood birds," "birds," and "small birds." Two birds not recorded elsewhere are listed: a single wild goose, served on New Year's Day, and a bullfinch. The greatest number of birds in a single category consumed was more than eighty "small birds," eighty on a single day (Jan. 4). On nineteen days partridges were eaten (sixty-five in all); on sixteen days mallards (thirty-three plus); teal (thirty-five) and woodcock (twenty-four) were each consumed on nine days, only once on the same day; and on one day (Nov. 9) seven different kinds of birds graced the bishop's table.[54]

To summarize and to answer the initial questions: Clearly the specific kinds of game eaten were determined by availability, cost, seasonal factors, and, no doubt, by personal preference. Serving different kinds of

---

[51] The guests served swan were Sir John Howard (Oct. 20); Morgan Gough, Dame Alice's receiver for her West Country estates (Nov. 20); and Dame Alice's sister-in-law, the Lady Waldegrave (Feb. 16), who was also served heron. The remaining swan was eaten on March 5, the Sunday before the beginning of Lent. One of the unaccounted-for herons was served to Sir Andrew Boteler (Aug. 10). On some of the people mentioned, see Swabey, *Medieval Gentlewoman,* pp. 55, 125–26, 107–8. Joop Witteveen, writing about the Netherlands, notes: "In a heronry, the breeding season started in late February and early March, but not all herons hatched at the same time. Consequently, edible herons were available from early May until the end of July. . . . At this time of year other game birds weren't yet available; herons were the first game after the winter season" ("On Swans, Cranes, and Herons: Part III," *Petits propos culinaires* 26 [July 1987], 68).

[52] Ollard and Crosse, *Dictionary of English Church History,* p. 44.

[53] J. Armitage Robinson, "Household Roll of Bishop Ralph of Shrewsbury (1337–8)," in *Collectanea I: A Collection of Documents from Various Sources,* ed. T. F. Palmer, Somerset Record Society, 39 ([London], 1924), pp. 85–157.

[54] Small birds were also eaten on December 1, but no quantity was given.

game seems to have been desirable, albeit less so for Dame Alice. Game eaten can be put into two main categories. The first is high-status food, served on special occasions, often to honor guests,[55] though not exclusively so. In this category are deer, boar, peacocks, cranes, swans, herons, and egrets. To some extent, different species seem to have been interchangeable: one served high-status game at feasts, although not necessarily a particular kind. The second category includes game served as part of the ordinary diet. Sometimes the birds or animals might be staples—pigeons and rabbits for Mitford and Dame Alice, pheasants for Swinfield—but more often were not. Game provided variety in diet, especially in the fall and winter, but if one kind was not available, another would do. In the final analysis, one gets the feeling that social expectations were at least as important as gastronomical considerations.[56] If in the modern world, as the saying goes, "You are what you eat," in the medieval world what you ate showed who you were.

---

[55] Birrell, "Deer and Deer Farming," p. 126.

[56] "Game symbolized the aristocratic style of life" (Christopher Dyer, *Standards of Living in the Later Middle Ages: Social Change in England c. 1200–1520* [Cambridge, 1989], p. 61). Dyer notes that "When it is recorded, the quantities [of game] seem small compared with the meat of domesticated animals" (60). But Dyer bases his statement on overall meat consumption (59–61) while at the same time noting that venison would be consumed "only at the top table" (61). Presumably the same would be true for other high-prestige game and probably for other game as well. While Dyer's overall analysis may be correct, the elite no doubt ate a higher proportion of game than he gives them credit for. And, of course, the importance of the social distinction, that they were eating different food from that of the rest of the household, must also be considered.

Talking with the Taxman about Poetry: England's Economy in "Against the King's Taxes" and *Wynnere and Wastoure*

Brantley L. Bryant
Sonoma State University

"THE LAW THAT makes my wool the king's is no just law" ("Non est lex sana quod regi sit mea lana"), proclaims the anonymous Anglo-Norman and Latin poem whose editorial title, "Against the King's Taxes," reflects the depth of its antipathy to royal exactions.[1] This eighty-five line macaronic poem, probably composed in the late 1330s, rails against the extortions of wool collectors, the pride of the great, and the process of tax granting.[2] Addressing itself directly to God and implicitly to an already

---

This essay has benefited from generous readings by Paul Strohm, Susan Crane, Clementine Oliver, Laura Wolfram, and the Columbia University Medieval Guild. I am especially grateful to Roger Dahood and to the anonymous readers of *Studies in Medieval and Renaissance History* for their suggestions for revision. Thanks also to Jonathan Newman, David J. Seipp, and Steven A. Schoenig, S.J., for references.

[1] Isabel Aspin, ed. and trans., *Anglo-Norman Political Songs*, Anglo-Norman Texts XI (Oxford, 1953), pp. 105–15. I have used modified versions of Aspin's translations throughout. I have also consulted *Facsimile of British Museum MS. Harley 2253*, introduced by N. R. Ker (London, 1965).

[2] On the dating of "Taxes," see Aspin, *Anglo-Norman Political Songs*, pp. 104–7; Carter Revard, "Scribe and Provenance," in *Studies in the Harley Manuscript: The Scribes, Contents, and Social Contexts of British MS Harley 2253*, ed. Susanna

---

agitated and alienated readership, the poem begs for justice in a series of prayers and curses, evoking the image of Doomsday as an apocalyptic corrective to social injustice. It opposes the allegedly corrupt system of parliamentarily sanctioned royal taxation to the transcendental truths of Christian morality.

Written at least a decade later,[3] the Middle English *Wynnere and Wastoure* imagines England's economy more expansively.[4] While "Taxes" bases its polemic arguments on Christian eschatology's threats and rewards for individual souls, *Wynnere and Wastoure* invests itself in the collective economic good of the realm. Imagining England's wealth as a single shared treasury, the later poem seamlessly integrates moral and economic principles in an enactment of the political *status quo*. Whereas "Taxes" laments the injustice of parliamentary tax grants, *Wynnere* presents us with an idealized poetic representation of the same process.

These two texts provide some of the most richly detailed poetic treatment of the English economy in the fourteenth century, but they tell us the most when put in comparison. Their marked differences provide insight into the genre of political poetry and the relationship between political thought and poetic creation in this period. Each poem has been identified with national economic distress; "Taxes," with relative certainty, has been connected to the discontent over Edward III's war finance in the late 1330s, and *Wynnere and Wastoure*, less precisely and with significantly more scholarly disagreement, to later fourteenth-century debates over

---

Fein (Kalamazoo, 2000), pp. 21–109; John Scattergood, "Authority and Resistance: The Political Verse," in *Studies in the Harley Manuscript*, pp. 163–201, especially 163–69.

[3] Debates on the dating and context of *Wynnere and Wastoure* are discussed by Stephanie Trigg in her edition for the Early English Text Society (Oxford, 1990), pp. xviii–xxvii. For more detail, see notes 4 and 5. Throughout, I will refer to the poem itself as *Wynnere and Wastoure*, occasionally shortened to *Wynnere*, and to its titular characters in modern spelling as "Winner" and "Waster."

[4] My discussion of *Wynnere*'s conception of national economy draws from Lois Roney's in "Winner and Waster's 'Wyse Wordes': Teaching Economics and Nationalism in Fourteenth-Century England," *Speculum* 69 (1994), 1070–1100. I clarify my relation to Roney's argument below and in note 49. D. Vance Smith has recently noted the overlap of household and national economic concerns in the poem in *Arts of Possession* (Minneapolis, 2003), pp. 72–107. In relation to post-plague labor regulations and the poem, see Kellie Robertson, *The Laborer's Two Bodies* (New York, 2006), pp. 39–45.

royal expenditure and post-plague control of wages.[5] Such topical identifications can partially locate our readings of the poems, but the poems
do more than react to given circumstances or comment upon crises; this
paper stresses that "Taxes" and *Wynnere* themselves provide insight into
the perception of national issues in this period. Their contrasting por-
trayals of England's economy, achieved through fundamentally different
configurations of the eschatological and the worldly, evince two distinct
poetic reactions to parliamentary control over England's trade and public
finance. "Taxes" has been identified by J. R. Maddicott as a poem of "social
protest," a polemic, vituperative form of political poetry prone to harsh
moral criticism of authority.[6] To Maddicott's assessment, we can add
that "Taxes" is particularly opposed to the national economic interven-
tions authorized in Parliament; as we shall see, it characterizes taxation
as pillaging of the poor and parliamentary tax granting as a sham.[7] On
the other hand, *Wynnere* discusses national economy less divisively. The
later poem is shaped by an alternate set of expectations and assumptions
that can be called "Public Wealth." This emergent mode of economic discussion opens broad imaginative and argumentative possibilities, comprehensively imagining England's wealth as a shared storehouse whose
stewardship imposes moral obligations.

   Tied to the parliamentary compromise between Crown and populace
that "Taxes" so vigorously attacks, Public Wealth could best be described

---

   [5] On the context of "Taxes," see Janet Coleman, *Medieval Readers and Writers, 1350–1400* (London, 1981), pp. 79–84; G. L. Harriss, *King, Parliament, and Public Finance in Medieval England to 1369* (Oxford, 1975), pp. 250–52; Scattergood,
"Authority and Resistance," pp. 163–69. On that of *Wynnere*, in addition to Trigg,
above, see Thomas H. Bestul, *Satire and Allegory in* Wynnere and Wastoure (Lincoln,
Nebr., 1974), 46–81; Scattergood, "*Winner and Waster* and the Mid-Fourteenth-Century Economy," in *The Writer as Witness*, ed. Tom Dunne (Cork, 1987), pp. 39–57.
In this paper I accept these scholars' more general contextualizations of *Wynnere*
rather than Thorlac Turville-Petre's argument that *Wynnere* refers specifically to the
Black Prince's negotiations with Cheshire in 1352–53, put forth in "*Wynnere and
Wastoure*: When and Where?" in *Loyal Letters*, ed. L. A. J. R. Houwen and A. A.
MacDonald (Groningen, 1994), pp. 155–66.
   [6] J. R. Maddicott, "Poems of Social Protest in Early Fourteenth-Century England," in *England in the Fourteenth Century: Proceedings of the 1985 Harlaxton Symposium*, ed. W. M. Ormrod (Dover, 1986), pp. 130–44.
   [7] The intensity of the attack on Parliament in "Taxes" is brought out in David R.
Carlson's reading of the poem in *Chaucer's Jobs* (Palgrave, 2004), pp. 20–22.

as an imaginative matrix. An "imaginative matrix" is a formulative force in the production of texts, not a specific theory or concept. J. G. A. Pocock defines "languages" as the linguistic possibilities for the discussion of a given topic in a given period and thus "the matrices within which texts as events occur."[8] To follow Pocock, the imaginative matrix of Public Wealth is an idiom within the larger language of fourteenth-century politics, a particular way of discussing economic concerns in poetic creation and political debate. It draws equally upon what we would label economics, politics, and ethics and is shaped by the institutions and practices of fourteenth-century English representative government. Public Wealth's core is the assumption that the varied resources used in the economic activity of the realm—coin and bullion, agricultural production, commodities—constitute a common treasury whose status directly affects England's fate. If these resources are protected, the realm prospers; if the resources are damaged, the realm suffers. These resources are seen as belonging to the realm as a whole, prone to abuse by sectional or factional interest, even by the Crown; the Crown can legitimately lay claim to these resources only to act for the common good. Every agricultural, military, or commercial action affects the realm's wealth for good or ill—by augmenting it, properly using it, or wasting it. Those who protect these resources act for the good of the realm, while those who squander or damage them are dangerous to the polity.[9]

Public Wealth shapes a range of fourteenth-century texts, from intricately literary poems that imagine economic issues to ostensibly objective parliamentary petitions that demand policy change (while implicitly performing imaginative work through their evocation of the realm's

---

[8] J. G. A. Pocock, "Texts as Events: Reflections on the History of Political Thought," in *Politics of Discourse*, ed. Kevin Sharpe and Steven N. Zwicker (Berkeley: University of California Press, 1987), pp. 21–34, 28. My method in this essay also owes much to Helen Barr's discussion in *Socioliterary Practice in Late Medieval England* (Oxford, 2001), pp. 1–9 and *passim*.

[9] Discussing fifteenth-century mercantile texts, notably the *Libelle of Englysshe Polycye*, J. L. Bolton identifies an "[i]dea of national prosperity," an assumption present in "the welter of debate and polemic about the [English] economy in the Later Middle Ages" that "[prosperity] was not a question of an individual or group benefitting from this or that action, but that the country's wealth might be increased." My argument observes an earlier, less specifically mercantile manifestation of this kind of thinking, and conceives of it as a generative force for texts. J. L. Bolton, *Medieval English Economy 1150–1500* (London, 1980), pp. 329–31.

economy). Texts shaped by Public Wealth analyze and evaluate economic policies, surveying the realm's prosperity. Public Wealth enables such texts to imagine a wide and confusing variety of developments—in trade, diplomacy, finance, and taxation—as parts of a comprehensible whole and to measure economic policies against the apparently objective standard of the common good. Through comprehensively depicting the realm's economy, texts of Public Wealth imply their authority in economic decisions. Such a discursive formulation accepts and engages with the assumptions about representation and national finance at the heart of parliamentary practice in this period.

Political Society, Parliament, and Poetry

As G. L. Harriss has argued, an emergent "political society" played a key role in government, state finance, and law in England's later Middle Ages.[10] This society was made up of what we can, as a term of convenience, label the "middle strata," those English subjects above the peasantry but below the magnates. Harriss numbers among them "middling landowners" and those "on their way" to that status, the "gentleman bureaucrats" who administered law and government, "clergy and their officials," and "urban merchants and substantial citizens." Though the groups that made up these strata had a range of political and economic interests, they were united by their common participation in government, service as officials or parliamentary representatives, and vested interest in law and policy.[11] The middle strata of late medieval English society are also closely associated with the production and consumption of much of the literature remaining to us from this period—Geoffrey Chaucer being perhaps the most notable example of a middle-stratum writer.[12] Members of these groups were the

---

[10] G. L. Harriss, "Political Society and the Growth of Government in Late Medieval England," *Past and Present* 138 (1993), 28–57. For a classic assessment of the middle strata, see Sylvia Thrupp, *The Merchant Class of Medieval London*, paperback edition (Ann Arbor, 1962), pp. 288–319.

[11] Harriss, "Political Society," 33–34.

[12] Key studies on this topic include Anne Middleton, "The Audience and Public of *Piers Plowman*," in *Middle English Alliterative Poetry and Its Literary Background*, ed. David Lawton (Cambridge, 1982), 101–54; and Paul Strohm's chapter "Chaucer and the Structure of Social Relations," in *Social Chaucer*, paperback edition (Cambridge, Mass., 1994), pp. 1–23.

consumers of both "Taxes" and *Wynnere*. If we accept Carter Revard's conclusions, British Museum MS Harley 2253, in which "Taxes" appears, was the household book for the Ludlow family of Stokesey, Shropshire. During the time when the poem was copied into the manuscript, the family's head, Sir Laurence, was a former MP and collector of the wool subsidy.[13] A similar kind of middling landowner with a career in service, Robert Thornton copied *Wynnere* into British Library MS Additional 31042 for his own use some time before his death in 1468.[14] Though his involvement in office and government is less extensive than Ludlow's, Thornton also served as a collector of a Parliamentarily imposed exaction, a fifteenth and a tenth of movable property, in 1453–54.[15] Just as these middle-strata consumers of texts were involved in the surveillance and control of England's financial systems, the poems associated with them show intense interest in economic questions. "Taxes" rejects, whereas *Wynnere* embraces, the terms of the public discussion of national finance in Parliament.

The role of the parliamentary Commons—representatives of the shires and boroughs of England—developed irregularly and gradually from the late thirteenth century on, but the aggregate result was greater involvement of the middle strata in questions of national finance.[16] By 1340, it was formally recognized that the Crown needed the consent of the Commons in Parliament to exact the large national levies on movables, customarily set in 1334 as a fifteenth from shires and a tenth from specified taxation boroughs and royal demesne lands.[17] The parliamentary Commons also struggled to assert their control over the granting of indirect taxation on trade, such as additional customs and subsidies on commodities.

---

[13] Revard, "Scribe and Provenance," pp. 63, 78–79.

[14] George R. Keiser, "Lincoln Cathedral MS. 91: Life and Milieu of the Scribe," *Studies in Bibliography* xxxii (1979), 158–79; John J. Thompson, *Robert Thornton and the London Thornton Manuscript* (Cambridge, 1987), pp. 1–5; Trigg, *Wynnere and Wastoure*, xiii–xviii.

[15] Keiser, "Life and Milieu," p. 164.

[16] In this broad sketch I follow the theses of Harriss from *King, Parliament, and Public Finance* and T. H. Lloyd, *The English Wool Trade in the Middle Ages* (Cambridge, 1977). In this section, I am especially grateful for the suggestions from the readers for *Studies in Medieval and Renaissance History*.

[17] A. L. Brown, *The Governance of Late Medieval England 1272–1461* (London, 1989), pp. 70–77; Harriss, "The Formation of Parliament, 1272–1377," in *The English Parliament in the Middle Ages*, ed. R. G. Davies and J. M. Denton (Manchester, 1981), pp. 29–60; W. M. Ormrod, *The Reign of Edward III* (New Haven, 1990), p. 164.

In exchange for these grants of taxation, the Commons fought for and attained the right to redress of grievances from the Crown. It became routine for the Commons at Parliament to submit lists of *commune* petitions: formal requests for the correction of legal or financial problems, given in the name of the Commons as a whole for the good of the realm, that were answered by the king and council.[18] In this regard as well, 1340 was a turning point. During a "parliamentary crisis" over Edward III's war taxation, Harriss argues, the Commons "first emerg[ed]" as political actors who used their powers of tax-granting to assure redress of grievances in their interest.[19]

In the 1350s, post-plague labor shortages led to an even more open acceptance of the routines of taxation among the middle strata that constituted the parliamentary Commons. The Commons aligned their financial interests with those of the Crown against newly mobile and assertive peasants and artisans.[20] During this period, as Harriss observes:

> [The Commons were] coming to regard taxation not so much as something grudgingly paid to the King under an inexorable obligation for purposes which he determined, but as a charge on communities in the interests of government and the governing class.... *The taxes became, in a sense, theirs as well as the King's*; in granting them they participated in government and they were beginning to take a greater interest in their disposal.[21]

The parliamentary Commons varied their strategies, interests, and affiliations considerably throughout the fourteenth century, but their actions show a consistent acceptance of the central parliamentary arrangement of grants of taxation adjudged necessary for national good given in exchange for redress of grievances.

---

[18] Harriss, *King, Parliament, and Public Finance*, pp. 358–75; Maddicott, "Parliament and the Constituencies," in *The English Parliament in the Middle Ages*, pp. 61–87; Ormrod, *The Reign of Edward III*, pp. 61–63; Doris Rayner, "The Forms and Machinery of the "Commune Petition" in the Fourteenth Century," *English Historical Review* 56 (1941), 198–233, 549–70.

[19] Harriss, *King, Parliament, and Public Finance*, p. 259.

[20] Ibid., pp. 333–34.

[21] Harriss, *King, Parliament, and Public Finance*, p. 343 (my emphasis). On acceptance of taxation, also see W. M. Ormrod, *Political Life in Medieval England* (London, 1995), p. 92, who also remarks on the oppositional stance of "Taxes."

This routine of parliamentary taxation was justified by appeal to shared assumptions about community and representation. The political attitudes of the thirteenth century, in which national taxation developed, dictated that the king could not request taxation from the entire realm without gaining the realm's assent, according to the Roman Law maxim "quod omnes tangit ab omnibus approbetur" ("what affects all must be approved by all").[22] To gain this assent, the king summoned the Commons as representatives of their localities. The ideological identification of parliamentary representatives with the *communitas* of the realm would remain crucial for the validation of parliamentary decisions. As J. G. Edwards has observed, late-thirteenth-century summonses to Parliament used a variety of formulae to stress that the parliamentary Commons would be answering authoritatively for all of the inhabitants of their counties or boroughs.[23] By the early fourteenth century, the standard wording of parliamentary summonses requested that MPs come with "full power" (*plena potestas*) to commit their localities to taxation. A fourteenth-century legal-procedural parliamentary handbook, the *Modus tenendi parliamentum*, clearly illustrates the assumptions about representation and community that were imagined to legitimate parliamentary process.[24] The *Modus* states that two shire knights of the parliamentary Commons "qui veniunt ad Parliamentum pro ipso comitatu, maiorem vocem habent in Parliamento in concedendo et contradicendo, quam maior comes Anglie" ("who come to parliament for the shire have a greater voice in granting and denying [aids to the king] than the greatest earl of England") because of their representative power. It goes on to say that all things granted or denied in Parliament must be confirmed by the Commons, "qui representant totam communitatem Anglie" ("who

---

[22] Harriss, *King, Parliament, and Public Finance*, p. 3–48, "The Formation of Parliament," pp. 40–43.

[23] J. G. Edwards, "The *Plena Potestas* of English parliamentary Representatives," reprinted in *Historical Studies of the English Parliament*, ed. E. B. Fryde and Edward Miller (Cambridge, 1970), pp. 136–49; Michael Prestwich, *The Three Edwards: War and State in England 1272–1377* (London, 1980), pp. 119–20.

[24] Nicholas Pronay and John Taylor maintain the *Modus* is an uncontroversial encapsulation of widely held assumptions about Parliament, in opposition to an earlier view that saw the *Modus* as a biased, factional treatise. They suggest it is a legal treatise that saw "complete acceptance" during the period in *Parliamentary Texts of the Later Middle Ages* (Oxford, 1980), pp. 25–30, 30. On the *Modus*'s discussion of the parliamentary Commons, see Pronay and Taylor, pp. 38–41.

represent the whole community of England") and not by the magnates, "quia quilibet eorum est pro sua propria persona ad Parliamentum et pro nulla alia" ("because each of these [magnates] is at parliament for his own individual person and for no one else").[25] In practice, the public involved in economic discussion was only slightly expanded through the growing participation of the middle social strata in Parliament, but in the routines of Parliament the imaginary public came to include the entire realm.

With the parliamentary Commons drawing their power as grantors of taxation from representative ideals, the Crown, the magnates, or factions within the Commons themselves had to phrase requests for their support in terms of the good of the nation.[26] When considering demands for direct taxation, the Commons (or those seeking to influence them) were called on to weigh the needs of the realm and the available wealth of their constituents. This arrangement encouraged them to conceive economic issues in a broadly collective sense, even when their motivations remained grounded in private interest. Discussion of indirect taxation through customs, depending as it did on patterns of trade, necessitated a similarly collective conception of economic relationships with other countries. Through petitions, the Commons not only reacted to questions of taxation, but made their own demands and suggestions about the regulation of economic activity.

This brief account of parliamentary ideals leaves aside many questions about the actual practice of Parliament that are open to debate by historians: to what extent did the Commons actually wield power? Were they simply a "rubber stamp" for royal policies? Did the Commons act independently or were they guided by the Lords?[27] But what is clear, and most at stake for our interpretation of "Taxes" and *Wynnere*, is the availability of Parliament as an institutional occasion for thinking nationally about economics. The increasingly public nature of discussions of national finance—spoken in the name of the realm, for the good of the realm—made space for a discursive formation like the Public Wealth of *Wynnere*, with its panoramic view of national economy. "Taxes," on the other hand, strains against these parliamentary conceptions through its zealous dismantling of representative rhetoric.

---

[25] Pronay and Taylor, *Parliamentary Texts,* p. 77; translation on pp. 89–90.

[26] Harriss, *King, Parliament, and Public Finance,* pp. 314–20.

[27] On questions about the actual power of the Commons, see, for example, Prestwich, *Three Edwards,* pp. 119–22.

Death and Taxes

Social protest poetry is deeply engaged with the particulars of political life; in contrast with other kinds of complaint poetry, the attacks of social protest poems are detailed and precise.[28] Yet social protest poetry's political engagement also amounts to a kind of disengagement; its divisive and inflammatory rhetorical moves are quite different from the unifying and consensus-seeking formulations shaped by Public Wealth. Social protest poetry's angry tone, its refusal to accept the ideological foundation of taxation, and its tendency to think at the level of universal Christian morality rather than the good of the realm all indicate the fractious, oppositional relation this poetry adopts towards the parliamentary routine. Poems of social protest do not speak in the name of an idealized conception of England's collective good; rather, they imagine an England divided between, on the one side, the righteous poor and their pious benefactors and, on the other, the damnation-bound rich and their lackeys.

"Taxes," exemplifying these tendencies, depicts the taxation for Edward III's wars as an unjust and damaging series of abuses.[29] Preparing for his bid for France, Edward attempted to "mobilize the financial resources of the realm on a massive scale."[30] In 1337 Parliament granted him a tenth and fifteenth for three years. Edward also arranged to exploit indirect taxation by giving a wool monopoly to English merchants in return for a loan.[31] But the various systems of wool collection set up by Edward before his 1338 departure for the Continent proved difficult to sustain once he was abroad, especially with subjects already agitated by the "unprecedented" three continuous years of taxation.[32] This breakdown sparked a political controversy in Parliament from 1339 to 1341. On one side Edward and the courtiers who accompanied him to war pressed for further tax collection to answer the urgent needs of a military campaign, while on the other the lords of the governing home council urged Edward to refrain from imposing more burdens on the discontented populace.

---

[28] Maddicott, "Poems of Social Protest," pp. 140–42.

[29] For taxation and crisis in the late 1330s, see Harriss, *King, Parliament, and Public Finance*, pp. 231–312; May McKisack, *The Fourteenth Century 1307–1399* (Oxford, 1959), pp. 152–81; Scattergood, "Authority and Resistance," pp. 164–65.

[30] Harriss, *King, Parliament, and Public Finance*, p. 235.

[31] Ibid., pp. 235–36.

[32] Ibid., p. 234.

The restrained financial policies of the lords of the home council drew the support of the parliamentary Commons, and both groups united to resist royal exactions. "Taxes" has been seen as sympathetic to the cause of the Commons and the home council, since it decries the damages done by taxation; the Harley scribe may have interpreted it as such when copying it into the household book of a middle-strata family with ties to Parliament.[33] But the poem's attacks on parliamentary representation would still be potentially unsettling to those with a vested interest in government, in contrast to the uncontroversial acceptance of the national economic *status quo* we see in *Wynnere*.[34]

"Taxes" begins by lamenting that Edward III has crossed over the sea to pursue his wars. Subsequent stanzas complain about the high level of taxation and also about the rampant corruption that aggravates its effects. The poet then warns the rich ("les grantz") who avoid paying the tax that they will be punished at Judgment Day for their actions. The poet finishes his discussion of taxation by praying for the deliverance of the common people, warning that they will soon have nothing left and be moved to revolt. Two stanzas then note the trouble caused by the lack of coin in the kingdom, another complains of the expenses of the king's army abroad, and a final stanza begs God to intervene.

Although social protest poetry draws from the long-established genres of estates and venality satire, it eschews abstract statements in favor of detailed discussion of contemporary abuses.[35] Maddicott notes the contrast between the long tradition of "world upside down poetry," with its ambiguous pronouncements such as "Vulneratur karitas, amor egrotatur, / Regnat et perfidia, livor generatur" ("Charity is wounded, love is sick, perfidy reigns and hatred is born"), and the specific grievances named in "Taxes."[36] Its third stanza describes contemporary national taxation and the damage it causes to the "commune" people:

---

[33] Revard, "Scribe and Provenance," p. 74.

[34] Harriss, *King, Parliament, and Public Finance*, pp. 250–52.

[35] Maddicott, "Social Protest," p. 142. Also see Coleman, *Medieval Readers and Writers*, p. 67.

[36] The quotation is from "Vulneratur Karitas," in Aspin, *Anglo-Norman Political Songs*, pp. 149–56, probably from the thirteenth century, cited in Maddicott, "Social Protest," p. 141; translation mine.

Ore court en Engletere de anno in annum
Le quinzyme dener, pur fere sic commune dampnum;
E fet avaler que soleyent sedere super scannum,
E vendre fet commune gent vaccas, vas et pannum
Non placet ad summum quindenum sic dare nummum. (11–15)

Now runs in England year after year / the fifteenth, and thus brings common harm; / And it makes those go low who used to sit on benches, / and makes the common people sell cows, vessels, and clothing. / It is not pleasing thus to give the fifteenth to the last farthing.[37]

"Taxes," as Maddicott observes, locates its complaint both in place ("en Engletere") and time ("ore").[38] It describes the taxation of those years, the repeated ("de anno in annum") fifteenth ("quinzyme dener"), and it draws attention to the financial hardship these taxes cause for the "commune gent" who are forced to sell their possessions.[39] It may also allude to the difficulties of a higher social class through its cryptic mention of the decline of "those who used to sit on benches."[40] The poem states other grievances with more pathos and shows little concern about the consequences for all of society (if indeed the "benches" comment can be taken as such); it concerns itself almost exclusively with the plight of the taxed. The collection of taxes is particularly unjust, the poem claims, because tax collectors embezzle the money and thus the people are oppressed ("gravatur") and damaged ("sincopatur") (16–20). According to the poem, the collection of wool in particular "burdens" ("greve") the "simple people," and through such collection the people are destroyed (21). The wool collection is described with an image capturing both the fraud of the wool collectors in measuring collections and the burden placed on the people: it is a "pondus . . . falsum" ("false weight") that is bitter ("constat amarum") to the unwilling donors (30).

---

[37] Aspin, *Anglo-Norman Political Songs*, p. 109; translation mine, based on Aspin's.

[38] Maddicott, "Social Protest," p. 141.

[39] Scattergood, "Authority and Resistance," p. 165.

[40] Maddicott, "Social Protest," p. 141; and Scattergood, "Authority and Resistance," p. 165, suggest that this line might refer to Edward III's widespread dismissal of officers in 1340.

These specific complaints serve as ammunition for an attack. "Taxes," like the other poems of social protest, is hardly interested in meekly expressing grievances in the hope of reform. With outraged laments and appeals to Christian eschatology, the poem angrily indicts the current system of taxation, questioning parliamentary assumptions about representation and consent. "Taxes" claims that since the rich ("les grantz") can avoid paying taxes through bribe and influence, their grant of taxation is "polluted with vices" ("viciis pollutum") and "wickedly done" ("male constitutum") (41–45). If other, more publicly minded texts back the representative assumption that equates the parliamentary Commons with all the people of the realm—the parliamentary Commons with the "common" people—the poet of "Taxes" stresses the difference between "les grantz" who go to Parliament and the inhabitants of the localities they purport to represent. "It does not grieve the great to grant the king such tribute," "Taxes" claims, "for the simple have to give all of it" ("Rien greve les grantz graunter regi sic tributum / Les simples deyvent tot doner. . . .") (41–42). Such lines show that the poem has no tolerance for the niceties of consent and necessity. Taxation is nothing more than coercion and theft: "[t]o take the goods of the poor against their will is plunder" ("Res inopum capta nisi gratis est quasi rapta") (60).[41] Since, in the poem's view, parliamentary grants of taxation do not express the people's decision, taxation itself is invalid and unjust. The poem refers to the current national taxation as "such perversity" ("talem pravitatem") (36). This taxation is a threat to the souls of those who enact it. "He who takes the silver of the needy without cause is sinning," the poet proclaims ("Qui capit argentum sine causa peccat egentum"), also implying in this line that Parliament improperly judged the war effort to be a worthy "causa" for taxation (35). "To say the substance of the case," the poet says, playing on legal language, "[all of this] is like robbery" ("A dire grosse veritee est quasi rapina") (59).[42]

"Taxes" claims that the wool collection is not "dear to God" ("Deo carum") (23). This line is characteristic of the poem's approach, for it is through comparison to strictly conceived Christian morality that "Taxes"

---

[41] Aspin's edition has "capita" for "capta," but the manuscript shows "capta" in facsimile.

[42] Aspin, *Anglo-Norman Political Songs*, 114, note to l. 27. *Anglo-Norman Dictionary*, s.v. *verité*, online at the *Anglo-Norman* online hub, http://www.anglo-norman.net/sitedocs/main-intro.html.

most aggressively attacks those whom it sees as responsible for the taxation (23). It disrupts political consensus by shifting it into a narrower register of penitential discourse.[43] The poem itself is a prayer, calling in its opening line on "God, King of Majesty" ("Dieu, roy de magesté") and continuing in this devotional vein throughout, begging God to right the injustices it describes; its last line incorporates the format of a prayer into its poetic structure, internally rhyming the "solamen" sought with the final word "amen." In this political prayer, "Taxes" works the language of legal reform and political action into series of curses and invocations. The tagline of its first stanza embodies the poem's hopes that devotional intensity and moral judgment will rectify political problems: "Let curses be given to the false, so that the king may be saved" ("Rex ut salvetur falsis maledictio detur") (5). The poem asks God to "take pity on your people, through divine grace / So that the world may be saved from such destruction" ("De vostre pueple eiez pitee, gracia divina, / Que le siecle soit aleggee de tali ruina") and to "have vengeance" ("vengeaunce en facez") on the people who oppress the poor (56–57, 83). These prayers are somewhat unnecessary, we might think, for the poem suggests that the rich are already set to receive punishment for their oppressive exactions. The "great judgment shall come, the great day of wrath" ("vendra le haut juggement, magna dies ire"), the poet says, and the rich who do not change their habit of living off of the goods of the poor will then be destroyed (53). Fracturing the assumed unity of parliamentary representation, the poet reminds us of the drastic separation soon to occur between England's worthy poor and her filthy rich, quoting Matthew 25:34–36, "The king says 'away' to the damned and 'come near' to the good" ("Rex dicit reprobis 'ite,' 'venite' probis") (55). The poem's repeated evocation of God's kingly and royal aspects, indeed, downplays the authority of the earthly king, who is depicted as something of a dupe, a young, guileless figure manipulated by evil counselors (36–40).

Consideration of the relation between the poem and the probable owner of its manuscript helps reveal the unusual political position of social protest verse like "Taxes." Sir Lawrence Ludlow, apparently the owner of MS Harley 2253 at the time of the poem's copying, would have

---

43 Tison Pugh, "'Falseness Reigns in Every Flock': Literacy and Eschatological Discourse in the Peasants' Revolt of 1381," *Quidditas: Journal of the Rocky Mountain Medieval and Renaissance Association* 21 (2001), 79–103, 91–92.

found parts of the project in "Taxes" congenial. Ludlow probably took the side of the home council during the constitutional crisis of 1340–41, as Carter Revard points out, because of his ties to the Earl of Arundel, one of that faction's stalwarts.[44] As such, the poem's criticism of bad royal counselors and poor financial decisions might have struck Ludlow as a useful expression of the home council's broad agenda to reduce royal exactions. However receptive Ludlow might have been to this aspect of the poem, he would less immediately have accepted the inflammatory statements in "Taxes" about parliamentary representation, statements that not only question the abuses of the system (in which case he could have imagined himself as one of the righteous) but that attack the system itself. The poem's claims that taxes are little more than theft and its rigid moralization of political action challenge the premises of financial distribution, representation, and collective good on which parliamentary authority, and Ludlow's public career, depended. Perhaps these claims were overlooked, since their virulent and rigidly moral aspects made the poem's attack on the court's policies more intense. Perhaps, even, the poem's religious questioning of the good of politics served a devotional purpose. "Taxes" appears near the end of the Harley manuscript, in a section composed largely of devotional material; it directly follows a series of Latin questions used to examine the faith of the dying. The questions, originally written for cloistered religious but available in Harley for lay use, end with the statement "The one to whom the above shall be said before death shall not taste eternal death" ("Cui hec premissa ante mortem dicantur mortem non gustabit ineternum").[45] "Taxes" could be read as serving a similar devotional purpose, encouraging meditation on the moral aspects of a political career.

But notwithstanding such possible uses, the tendencies of social protest poetry to pit rich against poor and to speak to an isolated audience of the morally justified render it strikingly inadequate for the creation, exploration, and imagination of political consensus that so often was the concern of middle-strata writers and readers. Social protest poetry's association with voicing the complaints of the poor would become more

---

[44] Revard, "Scribe and Provenance," pp. 78–81.

[45] Text transcribed in Ker, Harley *Facsimile*, xv. The second part of the line quotes from John 8:51. On the questions for the dying, see Michael P. Kuczynski, "An 'Electric Stream,'" in *Studies in the Harley Manuscript*, pp. 123–61, 146.

problematic throughout the century. The poetry of social protest was not written, of course, by the truly disenfranchised; "Taxes," cast in a traditional Latin satirical verse form, is probably the work of an educated ecclesiastic.[46] It seeks, nevertheless, to speak on behalf of, or even in the voice of, the "commune gent."[47] "Taxes" may have been a disturbing juxtaposition of the political and the penitential for a reader such as Sir Laurence Ludlow. Its identification with the poor and disenfranchised could only grow more disconcerting as the middle strata aligned with the Crown to control an increasingly assertive peasantry in the labor legislation of the early 1350s.

Imagined Economies

Another sometime tax collector, Robert Thornton, would have found no such oppositional stance in *Wynnere* as he copied it into his personal collection of romance and devotional materials, MS Additional 31042, near the middle of the fifteenth century. Scholars disagree on the poem's dating, extrapolating from a series of topical references. Some argue for a specific date of 1352–53, while others, notably Stephanie Trigg, have suggested the wider range of 1352–c. 1370.[48] It is generally agreed, though, that the poem addresses concerns of England's troubled post-plague economy. Treating a topic similar to that of "Taxes," and invested to a certain degree with the sense of urgency in "Taxes" and with its attention to Christian morality, *Wynnere* nevertheless imagines the English economy very differently. Lois Roney has drawn attention to the way that the poem depicts the interrelation of the various "economic transactions

---

[46] Maddicott, "Social Protest," pp. 134–36. Coleman, *Medieval Readers and Writers*, pp. 62–65. The poem is in the goliardic stanza *cum auctoritate*, a somewhat antiquated though still current form dating to the twelfth century, often used for satirical attacks on prelates; see Paul Gerhard Schmidt, "The Quotation in Goliardic Poetry: The Feast of Fools and the Goliardic Strophe *cum auctoritate*," trans. Peter Godman, in *Latin Poetry and the Classical Tradition*, ed. Peter Godman and Oswyn Murray (Oxford, 1990), pp. 39–55.

[47] Scattergood, "Authority and Resistance," p. 167.

[48] Trigg, *Wynnere and Wastoure*, xxv. On dating and context, see notes 3, 4, and 5 above.

of everyday national life."[49] We can pursue the implications of Roney's observation about the poem's totalizing economic vision to see how *Wynnere* is created within the politically charged matrix of Public Wealth.

The poem begins by lamenting the instability of society in abstract terms ("nowe alle es witt and wyles") (5) and predicting that the end of the world draws near (1–30).[50] By using the tropes of political prophecy, this prologue draws attention to the seriousness and social relevance of the poem's subject matter.[51] The prologue's tone, its castigation of moral failures, and its reminder that "Domesday" is nigh are all quite in line with "Taxes," but the poem's approach will soon change entirely. In the next section, the speaker recounts traveling through an idyllic landscape, in which he falls asleep and experiences a dream vision that takes up the largest part of the poem. This sequence of wandering and dream vision evokes the structure of a *chanson d'aventure*, a genre Anne Middleton has associated with instructive poetry offering a range of interpretations instead of one rigidly defined lesson, most notably employed in *Piers Plowman*.[52] *Wynnere's* initial pairing of stark jeremiad and serendipitous journey prepares the reader for its open-ended discussion of England's fate.

In his dream vision, the speaker observes two battle-ready forces: the army of Winner, composed of the pope, lawyers, the four orders of friars, and merchants; and the army of Waster, composed of squires, bowmen, and men-at-arms. This imminent battle draws the attention of a king, who summons the leaders of the armies to his tent. Asked to explain their quarrel, the leaders break out into debate. Winner objects to Waster's

---

[49] I draw on Roney's claims that *Wynnere and Wastoure* suggests a shared pool of resources, her observations about the presence of national and household levels of economy at work in the poem, her identification of the significance of the figures in Winner's army with the international flow of money, and her suggestion that the poem can be understood in comparison to English ideas about trade and bullionism.

[50] Citations are from Warren Ginsberg's edition from *Wynnere and Wastoure and the Parlement of the Thre Ages* (Kalamazoo, 1992), online at http://www.lib.rochester.edu/camelot/teams/ginwin.htm. See note 3 for the conventions of spelling in references to the poem.

[51] Bestul, *Satire and Allegory*, pp. 61–62; Scattergood, "*Winner and Waster*," p. 43.

[52] Middleton, "The Audience and Public of *Piers Plowman*," p. 115. Scattergood points out the relevance of Middleton's statement to *Wynnere and Wastoure* in "*Winner and Waster*," p. 46.

frivolous spending, while Waster attacks Winner's avaricious gathering of goods. At the end of their discussion, the king commands the two to separate, ordering Winner to settle at the richly appointed papal court and Waster to take his home in the bustling markets and taverns of London's Cheapside. The poem's action and the dialogue of its allegorical characters evoke the economic concerns of post-plague England: the regulation of expenditure, the cultivation of land, and the control of labor and wages. Eschewing the threatening theological maxims of social protest poetry, *Wynnere and Wastoure* makes many of its jabs at contemporary issues through the dialogue of its debaters, and through the disjunctions and ironies that arise as they disagree.[53] Since assessing the poem's perspective on specific policies depends on interpreting the cues given by the behavior of the dream-vision's central characters, scholarly interpretations have differed. Are Winner and his enemy meant to illustrate reprehensible economic abuses or contrary extremes that prove advantageous if properly harmonized? Does the king's ambiguous judgment on the two suggest an ideal example to be followed or give proof that the king cannot or will not reconcile the two enemies?

The poem's most important implications about economics, however, are conveyed through its vivid imagination of a national economy within which its king and disputants act and about whose flows and fluxes they debate. The poet, shaping his text within the matrix of Public Wealth, envisions the realm sharing a pool of resources, accessible to the king but primarily affected by the actions of Winner and Waster, who embody the interests and power of the middle strata. Scholars have disagreed about the precise identification of the two figures. Some have seen Winner as a merchant and Waster as a small landowner and war veteran, and the resulting debate as an expression of anxiety about growing mercantile influence.[54] But the two figures are not so easily separated into distinct classes: Winner discusses the husbandry of land, for example, while Waster becomes involved in the mercantile exchange of Cheapside.[55] The

---

[53] Bestul, *Satire and Allegory*, pp. 18–20.

[54] Bestul, *Satire and Allegory*, pp. 48–50; Scattergood, *"Winner and Waster,"* p. 50.

[55] Barr, *Socioliterary Practice*, pp. 20–21. Thomas L. Reed, Jr., recognizes the possibility of assigning the two characters to separate estates, but then notes that the identity of the two is in fact "a little too slippery to pin down"; *Middle English Debate Poetry and the Aesthetics of Irresolution* (Columbia, Mo., 1990), pp. 264–65.

blurred affiliations of the figures readily suggest the unwieldy range of groups in Harriss's "political society" who made up the Commons in Parliament, and the poem significantly puts these figures in control of England's resources.[56] The very framing of *Wynnere and Wastoure* is an economic argument: the assertion of the right and responsibility of middle-strata subjects to manage the nation's shared resources. The contrast with "Taxes" is striking. Gone is the authoritative voice of moral indignation and the division of England into righteous and sinners. *Wynnere* exemplifies a completely different mode of economic discussion, one whose willingness to imagine the distribution of England's wealth with all of its attendant practical problems, to extend its moral examination from the high principles of justice and charity to less theological questions of efficiency and conservation, bespeaks a comfortable acceptance of parliamentary routine.

The kingdom of the dream vision is clearly an analogy for England. Its king's tent bears the motto of Edward III's order of the garter, and the king, probably to be seen as Edward himself, wears richly decorated clothing that incorporates the order's "gartare of ynde" (94). As Roney observes, the description of the tent stresses English identity: the tent is decorated with "Ynglysse besantes" ("decorative coins") and the order's motto is written "appon Ynglysse tonge" (61, 67).[57] A "hathell" attends the king, probably Edward's son, the Black Prince; this character wears the heraldic expression of his father's dynastic ambitions: the quartered arms of France and England (77–81).[58]

As with the poem's evocation of its English identity, its examination of economy combines precise contemporary detail and suggestive allegory. The two armies drawn up for battle represent the dynamics of the realm's economy, evoking England's place within international trade and

---

[56] On the blurring of gentry and mercantile interests and identities, especially in Parliament, see Gwilym Dodd, "Crown, Magnates and Gentry: The English Parliament, 1369–1421," (PhD thesis, York, 1998), pp. 104–7; Ormrod, *Reign of Edward III*, p. 166; Smith, *Arts of Possession*, pp. 21–25; Thrupp, *Merchant Class*, pp. 292–94.

[57] I use glosses from the Ginsberg edition (n. 50, above) occasionally supplementing them with my own. On identification of the figures, see Bestul, *Satire and Allegory*, pp. 68–69. For Englishness in the poem, see Roney, "'Wyse Wordes,'" p. 1066.

[58] Note to lines 78–80 in Ginsberg.

personifying the flows of wealth into and out of the country.[59] D. Vance Smith, as part of an argument about heraldry and economics in the poem, notes that the armies are gathered in a clearly bounded "static field"; such a gathering of economic forces within this clearly defined area amounts to an act of accounting, grouping aspects of national economy together into a surveyable spectacle for the poem's speaker and the poem's readers.[60] The gathered armies, described in a monologue by the messenger sent by the king to stop the fight, are a virtual checklist of the country's military rivals and trading partners, an inclusion that demonstrates the poem's keen awareness of England's place within larger economic and political structures. Observing the armies, the messenger wonders at their size:

> For here es all the folke of Fraunce ferdede° besyde,   *assembled*
> Of Lorreyne, of Lumbardye, and of Lawe Spayne;
> Wyes° of Westwale°, that in were° duellen;   *men; Westphalia; war*
> Of Ynglonde, of Yrlonde, Estirlynges° full many.   *Hanseatic merchants*
> (138–41)

All of these groups play major roles in English trade and foreign policy; the Lombards are noted, even notorious, merchants and bankers, while the "Estirlynges" of the Hanseatic League are also important trade partners with England.[61] Notably, both Lombards and Hanse merchants resided within England, a situation clearly pointed to in the poem's picture of penetrated borders and a mass of aliens in England. The mixed makeup of the armies suggests that England is one participant in an international network of trade, inextricably tied to its allies, business partners and tributaries, even to its enemy, "Fraunce," just as the mention of "Ynglonde" is here included within the long list of nations.

If the messenger's initial remark evokes the broad context of international trade and competition, his description of units in the armies focuses

---

[59] Bestul, *Satire and Allegory*, pp. 70–72; Roney "'Wyse Wordes,'" p. 1093.

[60] Smith, *Arts of Possession*, pp. 86–87.

[61] For the Lombards, see Harriss, *King, Parliament, and Public Finance*; and Lloyd, *Wool Trade*, passim. On the Hanseatic merchants see Lloyd, *Wool Trade*, pp. 141–43, 191–92. For the residence of foreign merchants in England, see Alice Beardwood, *Alien Merchants in England, 1350 to 1377, Their Legal and Economic Position* (Cambridge, Mass., 1951), pp. 3–25. In general, see also Caroline Barron, *London in the Later Middle Ages*, paperback edition (Oxford, 2005), pp. 84–117.

on the specific flows of wealth within and outside of the kingdom. Looking at Winner's army, the messenger first sees the pope, whose banner bears bulls sealed with "a sad lede"—"sad" suggesting not only the weight of the lead seal but also the lamentable drain of wealth from England's church through papal letters of provision and ecclesiastical exactions (146).[62] The lawyers bear a banner that evokes the documentary vehicles of economic transactions; its "bende of grene" brings to mind the green wax used to seal documents requesting money for judicial penalties or debts (149).[63] The lawyers are a markedly domestic presence in Winner's otherwise boundary-crossing army, being "ledis of this londe that schold oure lawes yeme (protect)"(152). Their inclusion suggests the connection, perceived by contemporaries, between legal revenues and the collection of money for the king's war efforts.[64] Next follow the four orders of friars, whose banners evoke antifraternal tropes; the Franciscans in particular are presented as hungry for wealth in the messenger's aside, "I wote wele for wynnynge thay wentten fro home" (161). Last come merchants. As Roney observes, the section on merchants specifically mentions export trade (in wool) and import trade (in wine), drawing attention to the flow of wealth in and out of England.[65]

The list of Waster's army is short and, especially in contrast to the length of Winner's, striking in its brevity: "And sekere one that other syde are sadde men of armes, / Bolde sqwyeres of blode, bowmen many" (193–94). This brief description evokes the expenditure of national

---

[62] *Middle English Dictionary* online edition s.v. 'Sad' 4c. University of Michigan Digital Library Production Service, licensed through Columbia University, http://ets.umdl.umich.edu.arugula.cc.columbia.edu:2048/m/med (last updated 18 December 2001); William E. Lunt, *Financial Relations of the Papacy with England* (Cambridge, Mass., 1939–62), 2:334–37; W. A. Pantin, "The Fourteenth Century," in *The English Church and Papacy in the Middle Ages*, ed. C. H. Lawrence (Phoenix Mill, 1999), reprint, pp. 183–93; Ronald Butt, *A History of Parliament: The Middle Ages* (London, 1989), pp. 313–14.

[63] John Rastell, *Termes de la ley*, 1761 edition from *Early English Books Online*, page 98. Ginsburg, ed., *Wynnere and Wastoure*, ll. 149–55 n. Bestul, *Satire and Allegory*, p. 72.

[64] Certain fines and judicial fees were a traditional source of royal revenue, and Edward III "appreciated the contribution which the profits of jurisdiction could make to his war finances"; Harriss, *King, Parliament, and Public Finance*, p. 401. For a general discussion see Harriss, *King, Parliament, and Public Finance*, pp. 401–10.

[65] Roney, "'Wyse Wordes,'" p. 1096.

resources on war, the major drain of England's wealth throughout the century. The wording here used, "men of armes" and "bowmen," shifts from the language of romance to the technical vocabulary of the new contractual system of army-raising.[66] Repeatedly on indentures specifying wages and in the discussions of Parliament, troops to be hired are categorized as "men of arms," or "archers," two accounting categories for differently armed warriors who received different levels of wages. A clear late example comes in the Parliament of 1383. Hugh Despenser's offer to lead an army into Flanders (in what was to be the ill-fated "Despenser Crusade") mentions that if the king grants Despenser the revenues of various taxes and subsidies, he will be able to assemble ".iij. mille hommes d'armes et .iij. mille archers, bien mountez et arraiez" ("three thousand men-at-arms and three thousand archers, fully mounted and equipped").[67] On the poem's field, the forces that pursue profit ("winning") are marshaled under Winner, while the major source of national expenditure ("wasting") is associated with Waster.[68]

The description of the two armies, attentive to the flow of wealth through trade and other forces, sets up the context for the debate between Winner and Waster, in which the poet portrays the wealth of England as a set of goods shared by the two figures. Moving from international to internal flows of wealth, the poem now examines the particularities of domestic economy. Roney has drawn attention to several passages that,

---

[66] See Brown, *Governance*, p. 91; A. E. Prince, "The Strength of English Armies in the Reign of Edward III," *English Historical Review* 46 (1931), 353–71.

[67] Unless otherwise noted, all citations and translations from the Parliament rolls come from *The Parliament Rolls of Medieval England*, ed. Chris Given-Wilson, et al. CD-ROM. Scholarly Digital Editions (Leicester, 2005) (hereafter *PRME*). The Parliaments I cite are translated, edited, and introduced by Mark Ormrod (for 1337–77); Geoffrey Martin (for 1377–79); and Chris Given-Wilson (for 1380–1421). For ease of reference, I will cite the old *Rotuli parliamentorum* volume, page, and item numbers, which are also used in the CD-ROM edition. The Despenser passage is in *PRME* III.146.11. For other examples of the use of these categories in the Parliament rolls, see II.107.8 (on raising troops), II.352.168 (complaint of the behavior of Lord Neville's contractually raised troops), and III.91.18 (estimation of the size of English forces).

[68] Although Winner's army creates wealth through mercantile activity, Winner's and Waster's armies both do some damage to England's prosperity. Winner's army drains wealth through pursuit of profit by lawyers and church, whereas Waster's army drains wealth through profitless military expenditure. See Roney, "'Wyse Wordes,'" pp. 1093–94.

taken together, imply that Winner and Waster work as two sides of an economic "transaction," the one accumulating and the other consuming.[69] Winner complains, for example:

> All that I wynn thurgh witt he [Waster] wastes thurgh pryde;
> I gedir, I glene, and he lattys goo soone;
> I pryke° and I pryne,° and he the purse opynes.   *pin; stitch together* (230–32)

England's wealth, "all" that Winner gathers and Waster consumes, is conceived as a wide variety of agricultural goods, commodities, and precious metals. The poet's inclusive definition of the "wealth" or "goods" shared by the titular debaters is made clear in Waster's tirade against Winner's hoarding:

> And hase werpede° thy wyde howses full of wolle sakkes-   *filled*
> The bemys benden at the rofe, siche bakone there hynges,
> Stuffed are sterlynges undere stelen bowndes—
> What scholde worthe° of that wele if no waste come?   *become* (250–53)

"That wele," the wealth that Winner has amassed, is made up of traded commodities ("wolle sakkes"), agricultural produce ("bakone"), and coinage ("sterlynges"), perhaps also, by implication, the "wyde howses" in which these things are stored. The poem clearly conceives of a single, shared store of resources made up of various kinds of goods.

A later parliamentary record, also shaped within the matrix of Public Wealth, provides an analogue for this kind of holistic conception of the realm's wealth, attesting to the durability, adaptability, and utility of this mode of discussion. The Parliament of November 1381 was the first to be held after the Rising that summer; in it the king and council charged the Commons to identify the causes of the rebellion to avoid further disorder.[70] The Commons begin their answer by drawing attention to "the

---

[69] Roney, "'Wyse Wordes,'" p. 1085.

[70] *PRME* III.99.8. See Butt, *Parliament*, pp. 377–80. Also Given-Wilson, "Richard II: Parliament of November 1381, Introduction," in *PRME*. Smith's reading of the statute *De victu et vestitu* as analogous to *Wynnere and Wastoure* would seem to offer another example of the similar shaping of the poem and parliamentary texts by

great poverty in the kingdom at present, which is empty of riches and of all other wealth, considering what had been in the kingdom before, and this has come about for many reasons" (". . . avoir bone consideracioun al grant povertee dedeins le roialme au present, q'est tout voide de tresor et de tout autre bien a regarde de ce q'ad este en la dite roialme pardevant, et q'est avenuz par moultz encheson").[71] Among the reasons, the Commons name the drain of money from the realm through imbalanced trade, the expenses of the king's wars, and the French attacks on English property. They also cite the decline in the price of commodities such as wool, tin, and lead, "to the great impoverishment of the whole realm" (". . . a grant empoverissement de tout le roialme") and finally the great "expenses" ("coustages . . . plus outrageouses") of every estate of society. Taking on the role of advocates of the nation's wealth, the Commons engage in an imaginative project quite similar to that of *Wynnere and Wastoure*, conceiving of various economic activities, including trade, taxation, war finance, and even personal expenses ("coustages"), as interrelated parts of one process, all contributing to the increase or decrease of the nation's wealth.

Wynnere and Wastoure not only expansively portrays the realm's wealth but seeks to impose pragmatic standards on its production and control through appeals to religious principles. Unlike the relation of economics and morality in "Taxes," where economic oppression occasions a moral lesson of apocalyptic scale, the debaters in *Wynnere* bring their moral and religious arguments back to questions of economic mismanagement. Winner repeatedly accuses Waster of neglecting his lands. Wedding religious precepts to economic ones, he warns that this neglect will lead both to dearth in this world and pain in the next. He also blames Waster for selling his land to pay for his luxury and feasting, exclaiming "For siche wikked werkes wery the oure Lorde! (May our Lord curse you)" (285). Then he claims that God's precepts should encourage his bibulous opponent to

> Teche thy men for to tille and tynen° thyn feldes;   *fence in*
> Rayse up thi rent-howses, ryme up° thi yerdes,   *clear*

Public Wealth; Smith, *Arts of Possession*, pp. 104–6.

[71] I have changed the translation for *PRME* III.102.26. *PRME* has ". . . other wealth because of what has already occurred and arisen in the said kingdom for many reasons"—I take "a regard de" as a comparison of circumstances, not a causal.

Owthere hafe as thou haste done and hope aftir werse—[72]
That es first the faylynge of fode, and than the [hell] fire aftir,
To brene the alle at a birre° for thi bale° dedis.   *in an instant*;
  wicked
(288–92)

Waster for his part impugns Winner for his obsessive saving of goods:

Let be thy cramynge of thi kystes° for Cristis lufe of heven!   *chests*
Late the peple and the pore hafe parte of thi silvere; . . .
For and° thou lengare° thus lyfe°, leve° thou no nother, *if; longer;*
  live; believe
Thou schall be hanged in helle for that thou here spareste°;   *lock*
  up, confine
For siche a synn haste thou solde thi soule into helle . . . (255–60)

Winner claims it is a sin to neglect agriculture, while Waster says that
hell is the reward of those who hoard goods instead of distributing them
through charity. "With oure festes and oure fare we feden the pore,"
Waster claims (295). He presents his charity, however, as a pleasant corol-
lary to his imperative that goods and coin must be returned to the central pool of the kingdom's wealth through expenditure; it is a kind of
medieval trickle-down economics. Waster observes several times that
consumption maintains price levels and, thus, social hierarchy. He notes
that if no beasts or fish were killed, prices would drop and there "Schold
not a ladde be in londe a lorde for to serve" (388).[73] The two figures' views
about consumption and distribution are based on an integration of economic principles and Christian morality that removes the latter element's
potential for radical social critique.

While "Taxes" attacks the principles of parliamentary taxation, *Wynnere* works them into its poetic imagination of national economy. Except
perhaps for the reference to men-at-arms in the army catalogue, *Wynnere
and Wastoure* does not discuss taxation explicitly; rather, it symbolically
portrays the dynamic of national taxation in the relationship of the two

---

[72] "Otherwise, have what you have earned, and expect misfortune." My gloss,
based on Ginsberg's notes.

[73] This passage of course has bearing on post-plague control of labor; see Robertson, *Laborer's Two Bodies*, pp. 41–42.

titular figures and the king. The king functions as judge, peace-keeper, and war-leader while Winner and Waster are stewards of the wealth of the realm. Critics have stressed the close connection of the king with the two figures to further the argument that Winner and Waster are embodiments of Edward III's unwise (or unjust) economic practices,[74] but closer analysis suggests that this personal relationship is analogous to the ideal political relationship imagined between Crown and parliamentary Commons.

Each of the two rivals enjoys an affectionate and mutually beneficial relationship with the king. Early in the dream vision the king's messenger asks Winner and Waster to stop their fight and accompany him, and they respond:

> Wele knowe we the kyng; he clothes us bothe,
> And hase us fosterde and fedde this fyve and twenty wyntere.
> (205–6)

When they arrive before the king, they kneel. Taking their hands and asking them to rise, the king says, "Welcomes, heres, as hyne of our house bothen" (212). In this patron-client relationship, the king provides clothes and food for those who serve as his "hyne," or household servants. In return for the support of Winner and Waster, the king keeps the peace and adjudicates their disputes.[75]

The king's obligation to keep the peace, in fact, sets in motion the plot of the dream vision. Seeing the two armies on the field, the king tells his messenger to stop the fight, "For if thay strike one stroke stynte thay ne thinken" (107). The messenger informs the armies that by the "usage" of the realm no one rides in a warlike fashion ("with baner") except for the king (124–31).[76] The messenger's choice of words evokes contemporary

---

[74] Bestul, *Satire and Allegory*, pp. 73, 79–80; Scattergood, "*Winner and Waster*," p. 79.

[75] The relation evoked here is simplified, perhaps even rusticated, because the word "hyne" often referred to agricultural workers (*MED* online, s.v. "hyne").

[76] Scholars have suggested a relationship between this section and the 1352 statute of treasons, for example Scattergood, "*Winner and Waster*," p. 51. It is likely, however, that this section more generally invokes the king's role as peacekeeper instead of referring specifically to the 1352 legislation. On the topicality of the statute, see Trigg, *Wynnere and Wastoure*, xxiv–xxvi.

concerns over public order expressed in Parliament; no one, he says, should "lede rowte in his [the king's] rewme . . . / . . . his pese to disturb." "Rowte," *route* in Anglo-Norman, is the word commonly used in parliamentary records to complain of large, pseudo-military gangs of bandits and robbers. In the Parliament of 1348, for example, a Commons petition complains that it is "notoriously known throughout the counties of England that robbers, thieves, and other criminals travel and ride on foot and horse in great routs through all the land" ("notoirement soit conuz par touz les Countees d'Engleterre, que robbeours, larons, & autres mesfesours, a pee & a chival vont & chivachent a grant route par tote la terre").[77] The messenger's speech evokes the king's role as maintainer of public order. Although Winner and Waster seem eager to shed blood, readers from the middle strata of society would appreciate the king's prevention of conflict.[78]

If the dream-king's behavior suggests the role imagined for Edward III in the dealings of Parliament, his commands to Winner suggest the acknowledged role of the parliamentary Commons as the grantors of national taxation for the profit of the realm. The king tells Winner:

> And wayte° to me, thou Wynnere, if thou wilt wele chefe,   *look;*
>   *prosper*
> When I wende appon werre my wyes° to lede;   *men*
> For at the proude pales° of Parys the riche   *palace*
> I thynk to do it in ded, and dub the to knyghte,
> And giff giftes full grete of golde and of silver,
> To ledis° of my legyance that lufen me in hert. (496–501)   *men*

As Gardiner Stillwell long ago observed, the king's command to Winner to "wayte" to him metaphorically suggests a royal request for financial aid for the war effort, since Winner has been represented as a gatherer of

---

[77] *PRME* II.201.6. For later examples, see III.42.44, III.83.38. The *PRME* translators take "grant route" as "in rapid succession" (as per the *Anglo-Norman Dictionary* online, s.v. *rute* (2)); however, it is more likely to refer here to riding in a large, illegal grouping. See, for example, the Middle English uses in *MED* online s.v. "route (n.) 1."

[78] The parliamentary Commons' preoccupation with public order is stressed in most of the standard historical literature. See, for example, Ormrod, *Political Life*, pp. 119–29.

wealth throughout the poem.[79] The king's promises of titles and treasure may be the poet's depiction of an ideal application of national wealth: Winner's contribution to the king's enterprise will win him even more treasure and status. The wealth of the realm will "wele chefe" if it follows the king. Since the poem breaks off after two more lines, we are missing any final address that the king may have made to Waster, but it is possible that it might have been a similar request for aid. Thomas L. Reed, Jr. has suggested that the action of this section, the king's request for the appearance of Winner and Waster and his subsequent judgment, suggests "actual patterns of royal and parliamentary conduct," but we need not read the poem's depiction of parliamentary practice so literally.[80] *Wynnere* idealizes the central parliamentary compromise, the grant of resources and support in exchange for good governance—here personalized as economic contributions given in exchange for peace-keeping and the moderation of quarrels.

The dream vision of *Wynnere and Wastoure* thus offers an example of a narrative created within the matrix of Public Wealth. Winner and Waster conduct their debate about the merits of spending and saving in the context of a shared store of wealth composed of goods, resources, and coin. This store of wealth, manipulated by and exchanged between the two, can be only indirectly controlled by the king through his demands on its owners, made in tacit exchange for his wise judgment and governance. Public Wealth offers *Wynnere and Wastoure* the representational opportunities of imagining England's economy on a wide scale through symbolic action, and that imagination itself constitutes an implicit argument about the proper order of the kingdom. *Wynnere's* political intervention, unlike the indignant protests of "Taxes," takes the form of the detached observation—detachment enacted literally by the speaker's separation from the poem's central action—that the movement of England's wealth is the responsibility of the middle strata.

---

[79] Gardiner Stillwell, "Wynnere and Wastoure and the Hundred Years' War," *English Literary History* 8 (1941), 241–47.

[80] Reed, *Middle English Debate Poetry*, 266.

The Economics of Political Poetry

Observing the difference in the treatment of economic issues between "Taxes" and *Wynnere and Wastoure*, we can see their contrasting engagement with parliamentary conceptions of national economics. Such a difference could be related partially to their position within the chronology of developing parliamentary process; "Taxes" was written before the events of 1340 that Harriss identifies as a watershed for the political consciousness of the parliamentary Commons, before the plague and the subsequent social disturbances that, Harriss also argues, led the Commons to take a more proprietary attitude toward national taxation.[81] But such a strict relationship between context and poetic content does not adequately acknowledge the work the poems do in creating distinctive, forceful interpretations of England's economy. Although a more detailed examination of the specific political circumstances at work in the time of each poem's composition might give us a more precise understanding of the poems' particular references, the poems themselves already offer significant evidence. They demonstrate the sheer range of contemporary conceptions of parliamentary activity.

The poems' differences complicate our understanding of the category of political poetry. "Taxes" and *Wynnere* are part of a large body of anonymous verse over whose attribution, dating, and influence scholars have long puzzled.[82] Some have suggested that social protest poetry is the undeveloped, unsophisticated ancestor of later, more elaborate poetry touching on sociopolitical subject matter. Maddicott, though cautiously refraining from making a definitive statement about social protest poetry's further development, suggests an evolutionary view when he states

---

[81] See n. 19, 20, above.

[82] These are collected by Thomas Wright, *Political Songs of England: From the Reign of John to That of Edward II* (Camden Society, 1839) and *Political Poems and Songs*, 2 vols., (Rolls Series, London, 1859 and 1861); they are also collected in *Historical Poems of the XIVth and XVth Centuries*, ed. Rossell Hope Robbins (New York, 1959). For additional discussion, see Coleman, *Medieval Readers and Writers*, pp. 58–156; Thomas L. Kinney, "The Temper of Fourteenth-Century English Verse of Complaint," *Annuale Medievale* 7 (1966), 74–89; Rossell Hope Robbins, "Middle English Poems of Protest," *Anglia* 78 (1960), 193–203, and "XIII. Poems Dealing with Contemporary Conditions," in *A Manual of the Writings in Middle English 1050–1500*, vol. 5, ed. Albert E. Hartung (New Haven, 1975), pp. 1385–1536; John Scattergood, *Politics and Poetry in the Fifteenth Century* (New York, 1972).

that *Piers Plowman* will give protest poetry's topics "far more eloquent expression."[83] Janet Coleman more clearly suggests a linear development in her chapter on the subject in *Medieval Readers and Writers*. The poetry of "social unrest," as she terms some of these poems, is the first to show a strain of "realism," or "naturalistic reportage of events," in place of the abstract conceptions of earlier satire. In such an interpretation, this early political poetry functions as "a channeling medium, a tradition that is used but elaborated upon and then transformed by Gower, Langland, and Chaucer."[84]

In the case of "Taxes" and *Wynnere* proposed here, however, we can see a deep divide between two pieces of "political poetry." Examining the economic assumptions of these political poems reveals a heterogeneity in this body of texts, differences not just of chronology, intensity of complaint, or level of sophistication, but profound differences in how they conceive of the links between economy, morality, and political action. Distinctions as pronounced as those we have observed between "Taxes" and *Wynnere* emphasize the polyvocality of this massive topical grouping of texts. The poetry of social protest cannot be seen as part of an unbroken progression on the way to the poetry of the "common voice." Poems such as "Taxes" represent one way of poetically and conceptually negotiating the relationship between individual welfare and the common good. A significant conceptual break separates the poetry of social protest and poems such as *Wynnere and Wastoure* that are shaped by Public Wealth. The topical unity that leads to essays on "political poetry" should not mask the fundamental divisions between these texts. In contrast with "Taxes," *Wynnere and Wastoure* rests on, and promotes, assumptions about community and representation that social protest poetry ignores or denies.

---

83 Maddicott, "Social Protest," p. 144.
84 Coleman, *Medieval Readers and Writers*, pp. 67, 125.

Propaganda, Self-Interest, and Brotherly Love: Poverty and Wealth in the Pamphlets of an Early-Reformation Preacher

Jennifer Smyth
Trinity College, Dublin

THE LATE FIFTEENTH and early sixteenth centuries witnessed the initial stages of a transformation of both the image of the poor and the way in which they were treated in the towns, cities, and countryside of Western Europe. This latter development was characterized by an increase in urban ordinances dealing with poor relief and by the gradual removal of responsibility for the care of the poor from religious institutions. The change of image involved what has been termed a "new intolerance of poverty,"[1] and particularly of begging and vagrancy, which were increasingly viewed in the context of a fear of disorder. Poverty came to be seen not as a signifier of holiness and humility but as a shameful and possibly dangerous affliction that must be tackled on an official level. Charity as

This article is based on a paper given at the Reformation Studies Colloquium, held in Somerville College, Oxford, April 2006. I am grateful to the Irish Research Council for the Humanities and Social Sciences for their support in funding this research.

[1] Joel F. Harrington, "Escape from the Great Confinement: The Genealogy of a German Workhouse," *Journal of Modern History* 71, no. 2 (June 1999), 308–45, 310.

it was practiced in the Middle Ages was condemned, not entirely accurately, as an indiscriminate and individual gesture, made on the whim of the donor without serious consideration of the true level of the beneficiary's need. This phenomenon was subject to variations in both the pace of change and the type of provision made, and practical innovations could often lag decades behind their official approval on paper.[2] Broadly speaking, however, it involved the construction of centralized systems of civic poor relief, often with the establishment of a common chest, such as those of Nuremburg and Wittenberg (both 1522) and Ypres (1525).

Perhaps partly because of the relative contemporality of the two processes, these changes have for many years been associated with the sixteenth-century religious Reformation.[3] However, the degree to which the former development can be attributed to Protestant theology has been the subject of some debate since the late nineteenth century, and various scholars have shown its origins to be more complex than previous interpretations had allowed.[4] That a discourse regarding reform in this area predates the Reformation is evident in the social criticisms of figures such as the Strasbourg preacher, Geiler von Kaysersberg, who in his twenty-one articles of 1498 addressed the question of the proper distribution of alms by the city.[5] In 1968, Natalie Davis argued that the perception of Lutheran theology as the root of the new thinking on poverty had been unduly colored by the accusations of heresy that met Catholic attempts to

---

[2] Timothy Fehler has observed a "dramatic disconnection between the worlds of ordinances and of practical charitable provision," Fehler, *Poor Relief and Protestantism: The Evolution of Social Welfare in Sixteenth-Century Emden* (Aldershot, 1999), p. 72.

[3] The "confessional" Protestant historians of poor relief of the nineteenth and early twentieth centuries tended to credit an evangelically inspired rationalization with a significant improvement in the condition of the poor. One of the best-known examples of this approach can be found in Otto Winckelmann, "Die Armenordnungen von Nürnberg (1522), Kitzingen (1523), Regensburg (1523), und Ypern (1525)," *Archiv für Reformationsgeschichte* 10 (1912–13), 242–80.

[4] As early as the 1880s, Catholic historians had begun to challenge the perceived dominance of the Reformation in this context. Franz Ehrle, *Beiträge zur Geschichte und Reform der Armenpflege* (Freiburg im Breisgau, 1881), and Georg Ratzinger, *Geschichte der kirchlichen Armenpflege* (Freiburg im Breisgau, 1884).

[5] The thirteenth article (on begging) is reprinted along with part of Geiler's *Twelve Fruits of the Holy Spirit* on the subject of almsgiving in Christoph Sachsse and Florian Tennstedt, *Geschichte der Armenfürsorge in Deutschland,* vol. 1, *Vom Spätmittelalter bis zum 1. Weltkrieg,* 2nd ed. (Stuttgart, 1998), pp. 56–58.

introduce such changes in Ypres, and she pointed instead to the influence of Christian humanism (and particularly of Juan Luis Vives, whose *De subventione pauperum* appeared in 1526) on the civic administrators of Lyon, and the importance of the skills and knowledge of the administrators themselves.[6] Since then, a significant body of research has appeared, emphasizing not only the similarities between Catholic and Protestant systems of poor relief but also the shared factors that led to their adoption, ranging from the aforementioned humanist influence to the development of the medieval town and the increased administration of urban affairs during the Middle Ages by the citizens themselves, political motives, and the necessity of reacting to socioeconomic change.[7]

More recently, some historians have become concerned that this approach may have gone too far. Ole Peter Grell has noted a "near total removal of religion as a motivator and driving force behind the re-organization of poor relief which took place in the sixteenth century," and while admitting that one must look beyond the evangelical movement to find the sources of these reforms, argues that they owe both their extent and their rapid implementation to the growth of Protestantism and has called for a "revisionist interpretation of the reforms of poor relief in sixteenth-century Europe which emphasizes the significance of the Reformation for bringing about these changes."[8] The neglect of the Reformation lamented here has not been universal, and some historians have

---

[6] Natalie Zemon Davis, "Poor Relief, Humanism, and Heresy: The Case of Lyon," *Studies in Medieval and Renaissance History* 5 (1968), 217–75.

[7] On the reorganization of poor relief in the Catholic Reformation, see Brian Pullan, *Rich and Poor in Renaissance Venice: The Social Institutions of a Catholic State to 1620* (Cambridge, Mass., 1971). On the role of urban administration, see Sachsse and Tennstedt, *Geschichte der Armenfürsorge in Deutschland*, p. 24. The socioeconomic developments, particularly population movements, are described in Catherina Lis and Hugo Soly, *Poverty and Capitalism in Pre-Industrial Europe*, translated by James Coonan (Brighton, 1979).

[8] Ole Peter Grell, review article, "The Religious Duty of Care and the Social Need for Control in Early Modern Europe," *The Historical Journal* 39, no. 1 (1996), 257–63, 257, 262. Thomas Fischer, on the other hand, has argued that late-medieval poor-relief reforms determined those of the sixteenth century and that the specific role of the Reformation in the latter was limited to the speed at which they were introduced. Fischer, *Städtische Armut und Armenfürsorge im 15. und 16. Jahrhundert: sozialgeschichtliche Untersuchungen im Beispiel der Städte Basel, Freiburg i. Br. und Strassburg* (Göttingen, 1979).

continued to emphasize its importance in this area.[9] Grell makes a valid point, however, in that the existence of other factors and nuances does not negate the argument that the Reformation had a specific and verifiable influence on the shape and direction of poor-relief reform in those areas where Catholicism was replaced as the official creed. The emergence of the evangelical movement in Germany and Switzerland in the early 1520s saw an intensified discussion of the poor and their place in society, particularly noticeable in the emerging genre of pamphlet literature. The humanist and civic reforming values mentioned above were filtered through the general tenets of the new teaching, significantly affecting the experience and image of poverty.[10] The Reformation insistence on salvation through faith alone removed the incentive of almsgiving as a means to shortening the inevitable period in purgatory, either that facing the giver or that of a tortured soul already there. Poverty, therefore, served no purpose. The monastic ideal of poverty, in the form practiced by the mendicant orders, and particularly by the Observant Franciscans, could be condemned as a false, voluntary, and even self-serving condition, providing further evidence to its opponents of the degenerate nature of the Roman church. This distaste for mendicancy extended to all forms of idleness and begging, and a number of the early evangelical works on the subject of poverty addressed these issues.[11] Strong distinctions were made between the deserving and undeserving poor, and strategies for

---

[9] See, for example, Carter Lindberg, "Luther's Contributions to Sixteenth-Century Organization of Poor Relief," *Archiv für Reformationsgeschichte* 60 (1969), 222–34, and his more recent, comprehensive survey, *Beyond Charity: Reformation Initiatives for the Poor* (Minneapolis, 1993); Lee Palmer Wandel, *Always Among Us: Images of the Poor in Zwingli's Zurich* (Cambridge, 1990); and Fehler, *Poor Relief and Protestantism.*

[10] The need to recognize this continuity between evangelical and pre-Reformation ideas regarding poverty and charity has been discussed by Beat Kümin, "Reformations Old and New: An Introduction," in Kümin, ed., *Reformations Old and New: Essays on the Socio-Economic Impact of Religious Change c. 1470–1630* (Aldershot, 1996), pp. 1–17.

[11] Among the pamphlets written on this theme are Andreas Bodenstein von Karlstadt's *Von abtuhung der Bylder// Vnd das keyn Betdler// unther den Chri=//sten seyn soll.// Carolstatt. in der Christliche[n]// statt Wittenberg* (Wittenberg, 1522), and Wenzeslaus Linck's *Von Arbeyt vn[d] Bet=//teln wie man solle// der faulheyt vorkom-men / vnd yeder=//man zů Arbeyt ziehen* (Zwickau, 1523). See Carter Lindberg, "'There Should Be No Beggars among Christians': Karlstadt, Luther, and the Origins of Protestant Poor Relief," *Church History* 46 (1977), 313–34.

their identification and the limitation of charity to the former came to be a feature of the poor laws of Protestant cities. The deserving poor consisted of those too old or ill to work (excluding the "sturdy beggar" as well as the friar), but more narrowly referred to pious members of the community whose reputations could be ascertained, thus eliminating the possibility of foreign and possibly dangerous vagabonds flocking to the town to prey on its inhabitants. In 1520 Luther proposed the appointment in each town of an official ("ein vorweszer odder vormund") who could recognize the local, deserving poor and distribute alms accordingly.[12] This pattern was followed in the alms statutes of Nuremburg, of Zwinglian Zurich, and later in the office of deacon in Geneva and other centers of Calvinism.

The 1520s saw one of the most important phases of this process in German-speaking lands, and also the period of greatest activity of the ex-Dominican evangelical preacher, Dr. Jacob Strauss.[13] Born about 1485 in or near Basel and eventually receiving his doctorate in theology there and possibly at Freiburg, Strauss became influenced by reforming currents within a few years of Luther's initial protest of 1517. His early years as an evangelical preacher were generally itinerant; he is first recorded in this context in Berchtesgaden, and by 1521 was in Hall in the Tyrol, where he eventually obtained permission to preach. His sermons there appear to have gained a large following, and he is reported as having preached to crowds in the open air. This, along with the content of his teachings and particularly his condemnation of the practice of auricular confession to a priest, was unacceptable to local clerical and secular authorities.[14]

---

[12] *An den Christlichen// Adel deutscher Nation:// von des Christlichen// standes besserung* ([Wittenberg, 1520]), Iiijv–Iiiijr.

[13] The two most recently published accounts of Strauss's career are Hermann Barge, *Jakob Strauss. Ein Kämpfer für das Evangelium in Tirol, Thüringen, und Süddeutschland*, Schriften des Vereins für Reformationsgeschichte CLXII (Leipzig, 1937) and Joachim Rogge, *Der Beitrag des Predigers Jakob Strauss zur frühen Reformationsgeschichte*, Theologische Arbeiten VI (Berlin, 1957).

[14] The tone of these sermons can be gleaned from one of Strauss's earliest publications, a pamphlet that appeared the year after he had left Hall, supposedly at the request of his former parishioners: *Ain trostliche versten//dige leer über das wort sancti// Pauli. Der mensch soll// sich selbs probieren//// vnd also von dem// brot essen/ vnd// von dem// kelch// trincken.// Geprediget zü Hall im Intal/ // durch Doctor Jacob Strauß* ([Wittenberg], 1522); henceforth *Ain trostliche verstendige leer*. This work is a general instruction on confession and preparation for the Eucharist, the overall

Following the intervention of the bishop of Brixen, Strauss made an abrupt departure from Hall and moved north, and after a brief stint at Wittenberg in mid-1522 (his name being entered in the university's matriculation list for that year), Luther secured for him the post of preacher at the court of Wertheim am Main.[15] Strauss left this position after only a few months, his ideas once again proving unpalatable, and at the beginning of the following year began work as the resident preacher in the Georgkirche, one of three parish churches in the town of Eisenach in Thuringia. Here he enjoyed the protection of John, Duke of Saxony as well as the support of prominent townspeople, including civic leaders, and for the next two and a half years succeeded in introducing changes in ecclesiastical practice inspired by the new evangelical teaching. In 1525 John entrusted him with the task of conducting the first evangelical church visitation in Thuringia, an undertaking proposed by Strauss himself.

The theological basis for these reforms, however, while drawing much from Luther, cannot be described as strictly "Lutheran."[16] Strauss in his writings rarely acknowledges Luther's influence, and he would have seen himself not as a disciple of the latter but rather as a reformer in his own right. He rejected the existence of purgatory in a pamphlet dated 1523, long before Luther was willing to come to the same conclusion, at least in print.[17] Strauss pushed through reforms in outward, ceremonial matters,

---

message of which is that the Christian must simply recognize himself to be a sinner, thus removing any need of the "tyrannical butcher's stall, the invented, godless confession." *Ain trostliche verstendige leer*, B v.

[15] There is no evidence, however, that Strauss and Luther ever met, or that Luther gave any lectures that may have been attended by Strauss.

[16] Rogge sees Strauss's theology as dependent on, although inferior to, that of Luther. The possible influence of the South German and Swiss strain of reforming thought, as expressed by Zwingli, Oecolampadius, Bucer, and others, on Strauss has not yet been satisfactorily explored. This is all the more surprising, given Strauss's Swiss origins and Swiss and South German university experience.

[17] Luther did not definitively reject the idea of purgatory as an intermediate state until 1530. Even the radical Andreas Bodenstein von Karlstadt reconsidered, in his *On the State of the Souls of the Christian Faithful* of 1523, his denial of such an intermediate state, made in an anonymous collection of Latin theses published the previous year, and showed himself reluctant to go beyond a rejection of the possibility of intercession. The development of the theology of both Karlstadt and Luther on this subject has been traced by Craig M. Koslofsky, *The Reformation of the Dead: Death and Ritual in Early Modern Germany, 1450–1700* (Basingstoke, 2000), pp. 31–39.

most notably the use of oil and chrism in baptism, requiring no prior sanction or even advice from Wittenberg, and was consequently regarded by many of his contemporaries, including the earliest historians of the Reformation, not only as independent, but as impulsive and imperious. Myconius, in his account of the early years of the Reformation, wrote that Strauss left behind him in Eisenach "eggs and stink" for his successor, Menius, to clean up, and Justus Jonas described Strauss as a "pope," also portraying him as an associate of the reviled Thomas Müntzer, the latter seen by most of Luther's circle as the primary instigator of the Peasants' Revolt.[18] This depiction can to some extent be traced to the innovations described above, and also to a certain high-handedness as evident in the incident in which Strauss forbade a member of his Eisenach congregation, a vocal critic of the reformer, from attending *Gottesdienst*, thereby effectively performing an evangelical excommunication.[19] However, the most controversial aspect of Strauss's tenure at Eisenach was the furor caused by his condemnation of the practice of usury in a pamphlet of 1523, which emphasized not only the sin of the usurer, but also that of the creditor who agreed to the ungodly interest. These pronouncements, which were probably a distillation of various sermons on the subject, provoked an immediate and direct local response in the form of the "Eisenach usury controversy," during which many inhabitants withheld payment from their ecclesiastical creditors. The affected clergy complained to John of Saxony, who ordered the Eisenach council to ensure that the interest was paid. John's son, John Frederick, was particularly alarmed by the potential for rebellion displayed in Eisenach and expressed this in a letter to Luther, who in turn remonstrated with

---

[18] Friederich Myconius, *Geschichte der Reformation*, ed. Otto Clemen (reprint, Gotha, 1990), p. 53: "Herr Justus Menius, der hatt große Mühe, des Dr. Straußen hinter sich gelassen Eier und Stank auszukehren"; Justus Jonas, *Wilch die rechte Kirche/ Vnd dagegen wilch die falsche Kirch ist/ Christlich antwort vnd tröstliche vnterricht/ Widder das Pharisaisch gewesch* (Wittenberg, 1534), Jiijv, Or. Jonas's criticism of Strauss, in a work primarily dedicated to the vilification of the former radical preacher, Georg Witzel, may be the result of rumors that, like Witzel, Strauss returned to Catholicism before his death. On the other hand, of course, these rumors may have originated in an attempt to dissociate the evangelical movement from a perceived troublemaker.

[19] Strauss described this event in a short pamphlet, *Ein ernstliche handlung wider eyn freuenlichen widersprecher des lebendi//=gen wort Gottes beschehenn In sant// Jorgen kirchen zu Eyssennach*, (n.p., n.d.).

Strauss.[20] It was probably this intervention that led to the production of Strauss's second work on the subject, which explained his conclusions in more detail while not departing significantly from his original position. Strauss's behavior during this episode, particularly a perceived disregard for social order, may have damaged his standing in the eyes of the local authorities and certainly in those of John Frederick. This reputation may have been the principal reason for his arrest in the immediate aftermath of the Peasants' War, when Strauss was brought to Weimar and questioned about his involvement. Although he avoided the fate of his fellow prisoner, Müntzer, and was eventually released, he did not remain long in Eisenach. After another unsettled period, he managed to obtain another preaching position in Baden-Baden, and, despite two forays into the controversy over the real presence in the Eucharist in which he defended the Lutheran interpretation against that of the Swiss reformers, died in obscurity in or before 1532.[21]

Nevertheless, between 1522 and 1527 Strauss produced eighteen pamphlets, most of them written during his Eisenach period, and has been identified as one of the most prolific and reprinted pamphleteers of the German Reformation.[22] The pamphlet form provided both the evangeli-

---

20 Accounts of the controversy can be found in Rogge, *Der Beitrag des Predigers Jakob Strauss zur frühen Reformationsgeschichte*, pp. 71–86; and in Reinhold Jauernig, "D. Jakob Strauß, Eisenachs erster evangelischer Geistlicher und der Zinswucherstreit zu Eisenach," *Mitteilungen des Eisenacher Geschichtsvereins* 4 (1928), 30–48.

21 Strauss's works on the Eucharist: *Wider den unmilten Irrt//hum[b] Maister Vlrichs zwinglins/ So// er verneünet/ die warhafftig gegengwirtigkait// dess allerhailligsten leybs und blůts Christi im Sacrament* . . . , ([Augsburg: Melchior Ramminger], 1526); *Das der war// leyb Christi vnd seyn// heiliges blůt/ im Sacrame[n]t// gegenwertig sei/ richtige erkleru[n]g// auff das new büchleyn D. Johan//nes Haußscheyn/ disem zů wi=//der außgangen* (n.p., 1527).

22 Alejandro Zorzin in Mark U. Edwards, Jr., *Printing, Propaganda, and Martin Luther* (Berkeley, 1994), p. 26. Rogge has suggested, not without merit, that Luther's distancing himself from Strauss after the latter's arrest has resulted in Strauss's occupying a much more insignificant place in the historiography of the Reformation than warranted by his relative importance during his own lifetime. Rogge, *Der Beitrag des Predigers Jakob Strauss zur frühen Reformationsgeschichte*, p. 151. This neglect can only have been strengthened by the condemnations of Myconius and Jonas. A bibliography of Strauss's works has been compiled by Hermann Barge, "Die gedruckten Schriften des evangelischen Predigers Jakob Strauß," *Archiv für Reformationsgeschichte* XXXII (1935), 100–121, 248–52. Editions of all but two of these pamphlets

cal reformers and their opponents with a fast and relatively cheap means of transmitting their message to an extensive public, and pamphlets appeared in relatively vast numbers during the early and mid-1520s. They can be said to reflect most of the significant social and political as well as religious issues of the time, and it has even been suggested that they constitute a form of public opinion.[23] In any event, many of those written by clergymen were based on sermons, and it has been argued that ordinary people were "systematically" manipulated through pamphlets and sermons to spread the Reformation.[24] Apart from the two pamphlets on usury, with their apparently heartless condemnation of those forced to borrow money at interest, Strauss wrote no works specifically dedicated to the subject of the poor and does not appear to have been involved in any institutional reforms in Eisenach comparable to the common chests that were established in Leisnig, Wittenberg, and elsewhere. It is of course possible that the latter could simply be due to the relative brevity of his posts. Despite this apparent inactivity on a practical level, the themes of wealth and poverty make frequent appearances in those pamphlets written by Strauss before the outbreak of the Peasants' War.

In this article I examine how this preacher, during his attempts to introduce evangelical teachings in the early 1520s, wrote on money in general and specifically on the idea of responsibility toward the poor, and ask what this might reveal about the type of Reformation he envisaged. Strauss was an active preacher, giving weekly sermons, and the pamphlets are therefore unlikely to encompass all of his views and pronouncements

---

are included in the Tübingen Microfiche Project: Hans-Joachim Köhler, Hildegard Hebenstreit-Wilfert, and Christoph Weismann., eds., *Flugschriften des fruhen 16. Jahrhunderts: Microfiche Serie* (Zug, 1979–).

[23] This idea has been explored by Peter Matheson in *The Rhetoric of the Reformation* (Edinburgh, 1998), pp. 27–57. The research on the role of the pamphlet in the Reformation is extensive; the following is merely a tiny selection: the essays in Hans Joachim Köhler, ed., *Flugschriften als Massenmedium der Reformationszeit. Beiträge zum Tübinger Symposion 1980. Spätmittelalter und Frühe Neuzeit*, Tübinger Beiträge zur Geschichtsforschung XIII (Stuttgart, 1981), pp. 139–61; and Andrew Pettegree, *Reformation and the Culture of Persuasion* (Cambridge, 2005), particularly chap. 6, "Pamphlets and Persuasion."

[24] Hans-Jürgen Goertz, "'What a Tangled and Tenuous Mess the Clergy Is!' Clerical Anticlericalism in the Reformation Period," in *Anticlericalism in Late Medieval and Early Modern Europe*, ed. Peter A. Dykema and Heiko A. Oberman (Leiden, 1994), pp. 499–519, 500.

on these subjects. However, they could be said to be representative, and it is reasonable to assume that they would have included those aspects he considered to be most urgent and sufficiently important to warrant the trouble of publication. Although Strauss was not an unimportant figure during this period, his significance lies perhaps not so much in any concrete personal influence in the area of poor-relief reform, but in his role as one of the many voices of the early years of the Reformation. It has been suggested that the seven or eight years prior to the Peasants' War formed a period of *Wildwuchs*, or "wild growth," during which time Luther's initial ideas were digested and adapted in various ways by individual preachers and pamphleteers, leading to a relatively eclectic and diverse evangelical movement.[25] Strauss provides in this context an illustrative example of the manner in which a relatively minor figure promulgated teachings emanating from Wittenberg, to which, however, he added his own distinctive spin.

Having explored this material aspect of Strauss's writings, I also hope to reach some conclusions about his use of the pamphlet form. As a reformer, his primary aim was to turn people away from various practices that he believed had originated in invented, human teaching, were contrary to the word of God, and were therefore to be abolished. The pamphlets not only illustrate how Strauss used his chance to address a wider audience but may also give an indication of the methods used in his sermons to persuade his own congregation of the importance of his message. How might his treatment of wealth and poverty have played to an early sixteenth-century public? Finally, and more speculatively, it might be asked whether Strauss's decision to discuss socioeconomic concerns shows any conscious, perhaps even cynical awareness of a possible propagandistic value of this theme. Why do the poor and their problems appear in these works in the first place, given that the purpose of most of these pamphlets is ostensibly the instruction of the public in areas such as

---

[25] Bernd Moeller has used a selection of pamphlets, including Strauss's *Ain trostliche, verstendige leer* (see note 14, above), to argue in favor of the unity of the early Reformation, "Was wurde in der Frühzeit der Reformation in den deutschen Städten gepredigt?" *Archiv für Reformationsgeschichte* 75 (1984), 176–93. For the opposing side of this debate, see Susan Karant-Nunn, "What Was Preached in German Cities in the Early Years of the Reformation? *Wildwuchs* versus Lutheran Unity," in *The Process of Change in Early Modern Europe: Essays in Honor of Miriam Usher Chrisman*, ed. Phillip N. Bebb and Sherrin Marshall (Athens, Ohio, 1988), pp. 81–96.

the proper use of religious ceremonies and the role of the clergy?²⁶ What role, if any, did they play in Strauss's campaign of persuasion?

Although Strauss is (and was) best known for his two works on usury, it is necessary to examine his other pre-1525 writings to fully understand his views on economic matters.²⁷ Strauss tends to define "the poor" in its broadest and loosest sense, that of the financially oppressed "poor common man." The principal oppressors of this unfortunate figure are not difficult to identify. The avarice of the clergy is highlighted in all of these works: in the pamphlet based on the Hall sermons, the priests are described as having "their hearts, maws, and purses open for money, as long as you have a coin," and the mendicant orders are depicted as locusts, devouring all that has not been grabbed by the "claws" of the bishops and priests.²⁸ This theme resurfaces repeatedly, sometimes as a general denunciation of clerical greed and gluttony.²⁹ However, Strauss's

---

²⁶ This focus on Strauss and the reasons for which he may have chosen to address these issues does not imply that the role of the printer in this process should be ignored. However, an analysis of the influence of the (almost always profit-driven) motives of Strauss's printers on the type of pamphlets that they agreed to publish would be beyond the scope of this study.

²⁷ The usury pamphlets are *Hauptstuck// vnd artickel Christenlicher leer// wider den vnchristlichen// wucher/ darumb etlich// pfaffen zü Eysnach// so gar vnrüwig// vnd bemüet// seind.// Gepredigt zü Eysenach durch// D. Jacob Straussen.// 1523* ([Augsburg, 1523]); henceforth *Haubtstuck vnd artickel*; and *Das wucher zu nemen vnd gebe[n].// vnserm Christlichem glauben. vnd// brüderlicher lieb (als zu ewiger ver-damnyß reich=//ent) entgegen yst// vberwintlich leer/ vnd geschrifft. In dem auch die gemolete[n] Euange=//listen erkennet werden.// Auch wo dz gemein geschrey auffrur/ auffrur/ außgehet/ // am ende mit kurtzem guttem vnterscheidt angezeigt.* ([Erfurt], 1524); henceforth *Das wucher zu nemen vnd geben*. An edition of the former is reproduced in Rogge, *Der Beitrag des Predigers Jakob Strauss zur frühen Reformationsgeschichte*, pp. 167–72, and also in Adolf Laube, et al., *Flugschriften der frühen Reformationsbewegung (1518–1524)*, vol. 2 (Berlin, 1983), pp. 1073–76. Sections of the 1524 pamphlet have been reprinted in Adolf Laube, et al., *Flugschriften der Bauernkriegszeit* (Berlin, 1978), pp. 178–89.

²⁸ "Dann all ir hertz/ maul/ vnd beitel außgedent auffginet auff dein gelt/ weil du ain haller hast. . . . Also was der schaur der bischoff vnd der pfäffischen geytz nit erschlagen hat/ fressen darnach die Heüschrecken." *Ain trostliche verstendige leer*, Bijr, Bijv.

²⁹ For example, in his pamphlet on the Christian assembly, Strauss criticizes the wealth of the clergy, their possessions and endowments, "silver and gold," all of which, he says, are superfluous. *An den durchleüchtigistenn// hochgeborne[n] Fürste[n] vnd herrn herrn Johanßen// Friderichen hertzogen zu Sachssen/ Lant=//*

anticlerical invective usually appears in connection with the religious customs and rituals that he is attempting to abolish. Most of the practices he describes as "human and invented" or "false," and therefore inimical to salvation, have a monetary aspect, and he is always careful to introduce this. The consecrated chrism for baptism must be bought from the "insatiable money-jaws,"[30] a whole series of purchases can be made to reduce time spent in purgatory,[31] and the confessors demand the "confession-penny,"[32] all of this in service of the "idolatry of the belly."[33] According to Strauss, the clergy have turned the service of God into a flea market (*grempelmarkt*),[34] encouraging the poor common man to spend what

grauen in Dhöringen/ vnd Marckgrauen// zu Meyssen &c // Das nit herren aber diener eyner yedenn Christ=///lichen versamlung zugestelt werdenn/ beschluß=//reden und haupt artikel/ wem gelüstet/ mag sich// dar gegen hören lassen/ wirt im sunder zwey-fel// auff Euangelischer leer Christlich vn[d] brüderlich// gut bescheyd vnnd bewerung widerfaren.// ¶ Christus die warheit vberwindet.// D. Jacobus Straus// Ecclesiastes.// M.CCCCC.Xxiij. ([Erfurt], 1523), Br–Bv; henceforth *Das nit herren aber diener eyner yedenn Christlichen versamlung zugestelt werdenn.*

30 ". . . dan niemants kan verkeuffen das nit sein ist/ vnd also greydden die vnersettlichen gelt schlunden/ gott in seyn herligkeit/ vnd gütter/ die mit geldt nicht vergleycht sollen werden." *Widder den Si=//monieschen Tauff// vnd erkaufften ertich-ten// Chrissum vnd öl/ auch// worynn die recht/ // Christlich tauff// (allein von Chri=// sto aufgesetzt)// begriffen sei// ein genotti=//ge ser=//mon/ geprediget zu Eissnach,* ([Erfurt], 1523), Cr.

31 ". . . damit sy den dienst yres gottes/ das ist irs bauchs mit allem lust verbren-gen." *Kurtz vnd verstendig leer/ vber das wort. S.// Pauli/ zu den Römern/ der todt ist/ der ist von// sunden gerecht gemacht/ fast dienstlich der gemeynent wochen/ // so yn etlichen kirchen/ jn Francken/ vnd Döringen/ jerlich fur die// seelen gehalten.// Darynnen das fegfeur gar verleschet/ auch der// pfaffen vnd Münichen heyliger geytz// getziert/ vnd rechge=//schaffen abgemalet ist.* ([Erfurt, 1523]), Br.

32 Strauss attacks the escalating nature of this system of payments, involving both the parish priest and his hired *Beichtvatter*, in a passage in his pamphlet on the true nature of confession and penances in which the priests are described as merchants (*kaufleuthe*) and their conduct of the sacrament as a veritable trade (*ein gewisser handell*). *Ein new wunderbarlich beychtpuch=//lin in dem die warhafft gerecht beycht vnd// pueszfertyg//keit/ christenlychen gelert vnd angezeygt wirt/ vnd// kurtzlychenn all// tyranney ertichter menschlycher// beycht auff gehaben/ tzu seliger rewe/ frid vnnd// freud der armen gefangen gewissen.// D. Jacobus Straus Ecclesiastes tzw// Eyssenach in Düringen.* ([Erfurt], 1523), Cr.

33 "Wer daß nicht vesteen kan/ der hat weder sin/ nach witze/ das die beichte ein tzenichtig/ fleischlich vnd verfurlich wesen ist/ gebawet auff den abtgot den bauch. . . ." Ibid., Cv.

34 The term *Grempelmarkt* is also used by Karlstadt in his work on religious

little he has to spare on adorning idols, in giving alms to the mendicant friars, going on pilgrimages, and in celebrating feast days in his confraternity. This image of the cleric as "wolf, thief, and soul-murderer" permeates Strauss's works.[35]

Is this emphasis on money a deliberate attempt to strengthen Strauss's condemnation of these practices in the eyes of his audience? Here, the "common man"[36] is robbed directly by the plundering clergy through being forced to pay for unnecessary and occasionally idolatrous offices, and indirectly by the princes, whose duty it is to protect their "land and people," and who have been duped into spending the nation's wealth on relics:

> Just look, pious Christian, at the generous princes and feudal lords, how one of them shall squander two, three thousand gulden, yes much more, on honoring relics, but should he pardon the poor, his subjects, in their annual duty, then he could no longer be a king or prince. The poor man must pay and he and his wife and child shall suffer hunger and want.[37]

---

images: "Sye haben vermerckt/ was sie die schefflein/ yhn die bucher furtten/ yhr grempell marckt wurtd nichst tzunehmen." Andreas Bodenstein von Karlstadt, *Von abtuhung der Bylder*, Bv.

[35] "Wer ein wolff/ diep/ vnd selen mörder der versamlung Christliches volcks eintringt oder hanthabt/ der sehe vnd laß sein condition/ namen vnd titel/ im Euangelio vor sich selbs." *Das nit herren aber diener eyner yedenn Christlichen versamlung zugestelt werdenn*, Aiiijv. The image of the cleric as a wolf rather than a shepherd (Ezekiel 34:4; John 10:12) occurs frequently in Reformation propaganda, in both text and image. Luther used it in his 1522 work, *Against the Spiritual Estate of the Pope and the Bishops*, arguing that the unholy spiritual rulers are wolves and soul-murderers: "Aber geystlich hohe/ wo sie nicht heylig ist vnd Gottis wort treybt/ sind sie wolff vnd seel mörder...." *Widder den falsch// genannte[n] geistlichen// stand des Babst// vnd der bis=//choffen. // D. Martinus Luth.// Ecclesiasten zu// Wittemberg.//* ([Wittenberg, 1522]), Br. A broadsheet attributed to Hans Rudolph Manuel Deutsch, *The Monk and the Wolf as Devourers of the Widow's House*, depicts the rapacious clergy, in the guise of a wolf, preying on the vulnerable. This latter is reprinted in R. W. Scribner, *For the Sake of Simple Folk: Popular Propaganda for the German Reformation*, 2nd ed. (Oxford, 1994), p. 57.

[36] It should be noted, however, that Strauss does not often use this term and prefers the image of the "poor sheep." This is consistent with his portrayal of the clergy as wolves who attack their own flock in both a religious and a material sense.

[37] *Ein kurtz Christenlich vnterricht des// grossen jrrthumbs/ so im heiligthüm zů eren gehalten/ das dan// nach gemeinem gebrauch der abgötterey gantz gleich ist.// D.*

Not only is this harmful to the poor man's soul and to his pocket, he is being cheated by the same figures who are endangering his salvation by withholding the truth of the gospel. This does appear to be a direct appeal to a personal sense of injustice. Strauss is of course not especially innovative in this rhetoric; although his language can be particularly colorful in its derogatory emphasis on greed, matters of the flesh, and use of animal imagery, he is merely part of a long tradition of anticlerical criticism that took on a new aspect in the early Reformation and appears in much of the popular literature of the time, often used deliberately to appeal to the prejudices of the laity.[38] Furthermore, Strauss does not always restrict himself to condemning the practice at hand; having associated one of his targets with the financial difficulties of his audience, he is often reluctant to pass up the opportunity to make a general attack on all forms of spiritual "buying and selling."[39] In his pamphlet on the "Simonean baptism," for example, Strauss gives a list of duties for which the clergy expect to be paid (burial of the dead, consecration of marriages, and dispensing of sacraments), remarking that this exchange is deemed appropriate merely due to "long custom."[40]

Jacobus Strauß zu Eysenach// in Doringen Ecclesiastes. M.D.Xxiij ([Erfurt], 1523), Bjr. Similar sentiments are expressed in Johann Eberlin von Günzberg's *Mich wundert das// kein gelt ihm// land ist.// Ein schimpflich doch vnschedlich ge//=sprech dreyer Landtfarer/ vber yetz ge=//melten tyttel.// Lese das buchlin so wirdstu dich furo//hyn verwundern/ das ein pfennig ihm// landt bleiben ist* (Eilenberg, 1524).

[38] The adoption of medieval criticism of the clergy by those who called for the abolition of the first estate in its present form has been described as inserting "new notes and accents into old songs." Susan Karant-Nunn, "Clerical Anticlericalism in the Early German Reformation: An Oxymoron?" *Anticlericalism in Late Medieval and Early Modern Europe*, ed. Peter A. Dykema and Heiko A. Oberman (Leiden, 1994), pp. 521–34, 523. See also, among others, Scribner, *For the Sake of Simple Folk*; Henry Cohn, "Anti-clericalism and the German Peasants' War 1525," *Past & Present* 83 (1979), 3–31; Hans-Jürgen Goertz, *Pfaffenhaß und groß geschrei: die reformatorischen Bewegungen in Deutschland 1517–1529* (Munich, 1987); and the numerous relevant essays in Dykema and Oberman, *Anticlericalism*. Geoffrey Dipple has concluded that "given the strength and vitality of the late medieval antifraternal tradition, it is hardly surprising that Eberlin, and later other former Franciscans, adopted elements from it." Dipple, *Antifraternalism and Anticlericalism in the German Reformation: Johann Eberlin von Günzberg and the Campaign against the Friars* (Aldershot, 1996), p. 213.

[39] "Zü viel grausaz ist das wie in ettlichen kirchen kauff vnd verkauff stat geben wirt. . . ." *Widder den Simonieschen Tauff*, Cijv.

[40] Ibid., Cijr.

Given Strauss's position as an evangelical preacher, his primary goal would have been to end such practices, and so the benefits of accusing their exponents of greed and "false teaching" are obvious. However, he usually proceeds to make a direct link between this "simony" and the neglect of true charity. The victims of clerical exploitation consist not only of the common man, who is fooled into spending his money on something that cannot be bought; they are also "the poor, wretched people who cannot get their food for themselves."[41] Strauss only briefly mentions existing charities, and then merely to deplore their worthlessness in the face of the vast amounts of money poured into the service of relics.[42] He makes no acknowledgment of any possible charitable function of the confraternities and, although he admits that people do give alms as a form of penance, insists that this charity is not of the type recommended in the gospels but instead takes the form of excessive donations to "priests, monks, and nuns."[43] This motif of wasted money, siphoned away from the deserving poor, who were made in God's image, to finance pointless devotions, is not uncommon in the literature of the early Reformation, playing a particularly significant role in the writings of Ulrich Zwingli.[44]

---

[41] "Christus wil haben was übrigs ist den menschen von seiner narung/ sol geben werden armen durfftigen die yr narung von in selbß nit mugen haben." *Ein kurtz christenlich/ vntherricht// von dem besondern erdichten// pruderchafften denen/ von Hal/ im intal von doctor Jacob Straus// tzu gesant/ in dem du leichtlich// vernemen magst/ wie vnchriste[n]///lich in denen bruderschafften// wider got/ vnd den nechste[n]// geirt wirt.//* ([Erfurt, 1522]), Aijv; henceforth *Ein kurtz christenlich vntherricht.*

[42] "Es hilfft auch nichts das gesagt möcht werdenn/ wie neben der getzir vnd eer des hailtumbs viel schöner/ grosser almůsen verordnet seint/ den armen leuten zů vnterhaltüng vnd trost/ mag domit nit entschuldiget werden/ dan die selben almüsen allesam seint nit zů achten gegen dem grossen mißprauch bey dem hailthum/ vnd ob gleich wol etlich stet jr arment getrewlich vnterhielten/ so habet sy doch in der nachpurschafft wol vrsach der parmhertzigen hilff do der selb vberfluß des hailgthumbs hingehort." *Ein kurtz christenlich vntherricht*, Bjv.

[43] "Das ander theyl yres gnůg thůns nemen sye almusen geben/ aber nicht nach der ordnung die Christus ym euangelio antzeygt/ Aber pfaffen/ Munchen/ vnd nonnen/ mitt hauffen vnd vberflussig zůtragen vnd geben." *Kurtz vnd verstendig leer,* Br.

[44] On Zwingli and the poor as the "images of God," see Lee Palmer Wandel, *Always Among Us: Images of the Poor in Zwingli's Zurich* (Cambridge, 1990), particularly chap. 2, "The People's Preacher and the Living Images of God," pp. 36–76.

In his criticism of confraternities, Strauss exhorts those members who had formerly spent their money on decorating idols and arranging "singing, ringing, organ-playing, [and] piping" to use this money to help the poor.[45] He lists in a very striking manner the disparities between true and false brotherhood, allowing a sharp contrast to be drawn between the appropriate recipients of wealth and the uses to which it is put in the confraternities. Christ, Strauss argues, wishes that all surplus food should be given to the poor and needy who cannot feed themselves. The confraternities, on the other hand, "have no care for the poor," and instead endow unnecessary masses and hold lavish meals on the feasts of their patrons. It is not only the excluded poor who lose by this, but also the members themselves, as "many a poor artisan spends and consumes so much in one day, that he could support a wife and child on it for a week." Christ wants the naked to be clothed and the homeless to be housed, whereas the "dreadful brotherhoods" adorn their idols with gold and silver and buy houses to earn interest.[46] This is not simply a matter of the wealthy forsaking the poor; rather, the "poor artisan" shares the blame for this injustice. The poor themselves are not immune from accusations of ignoring the commandment of love.

This theme of misdirected wealth also surfaces in Strauss's treatment of purgatory, where he devotes a substantial section of the tract to the accompanying neglect of the poor. Although one is bound by God to use one's surplus wealth to assist one's "poor, needy, fellow brother," the latter is abandoned in favor of the dead and their requiem masses, vigils, and candles, the entire "foolish, invented service of souls."

---

45 *Ein kurtz christenlich vntherricht,* Aiijv.

46 "Christus wil haben was übrigs ist den menschen von seiner narung/ sol geben werden armen durfftigen die yr narung von in selbß nit mugen haben. Die pruderschafften haben/ deß armen kein acht/ aber daß vnnotdurfftigem erdichem gots dienst obgelegen werd. Christus wil das man sol den armen hungrigen speisen/ die pruderschaffen wellen gemeinlich an den tagen der patron vnd begegnussen ain vberflussigen pras halten. Also das meniger armen hantwercker auf ein tag so vil abwiert vnd vertzertt/ er mocht ein gantze wochen weib vnd kind da von vndterhalten. Christus wil daß man sol den nackenden bekleiden/ die ellenden pruderschafften wellen man sol die götzen vnd stangen mit golt vnd silber getzieren. Christus wil man sol den ellenden behausen/ die pruderschafften wellen heuser kauffen tzins tzu erreichen." *Ein kurtz christenlich vntherricht,* Aiijv, Aiijr.

O, how evident it is, that they who support the invented soul service with great, inestimable expense, are not moved to any compassion at all for the poverty and need of the living, and if they were to donate or present the thousandth part [of this money] to the local poor (*haus armen*), they would think that it would ruin them. It is ever found to be thus: that many, many [a person] must spend thirty or forty gulden on a chasuble or similar for the requiem mass, who would not lend or give one gulden or even less to his neighbor in need, even if he were to cry naked before him.[47]

Strauss continues by scolding those who withhold money from their friends and family during life, but who lavish the same on the clergy after their death. All of this, Strauss declares, is "against God and brotherly love, also natural fairness."[48]

Although this is largely the fault of the clergy, Strauss again extends his criticism to the "common man" himself. His most vehement expression of this is in his work on relics, where he gives a lengthy exposition of the economic consequences of this cult. The relic-lovers spend joyfully in their devotion, but again, echoing the purgatory pamphlet, if they "were to lend [their] brother neighbor a couple of gulden in his great need, they think that it would ruin them."[49] Strauss decries the "inestimable wealth" wasted in pilgrimage to Rome and Compostela and to various German shrines and asks, "How many thousand poor, needy people would be pleased and supported by this?"[50] In these pamphlets, Strauss makes a

---

[47] ". . . dem nerrischen erdichten selen dyenst." *Kurtz vnd verstendig leer,* Aiiijr.

[48] ". . . dz sye wydder vater nach mutter/ schwester nach brůder/ nach aller yrer freunde/ im leben nichtes achten/ aber nach irem tode/ dan erst thun sey den beuttel auff vnd helffen dan anfullen pfaffen/ vnnd Münich/ mit dem das sy wider got vnd bruderlich lieb auch der naturlichen billickeyt enttkegen/ an yren eltern vnd freunden ym leben ersparet haben." *Kurtz vnd verstendig leer,* Aiiijr, Aiiijv.

[49] "Es beweist sich an allen enden/ das die so dem heylosen heilgthum/ jren fleiß vnd auffmercken zů stellen/ dürffen auff ein tzeit ein grosse summa gelts daran wagen/ vnd mit freuden außgeben/ vnd solten sie jrem nechsten mitprůder in seinen grossen nöten einn par gulten leihen/ sie meinten es raichet jn zů verterbniß." *Ein kurtz Christenlich vnterricht,* Aiiijv.

[50] "Gedenckt doch ein iglicher was vnschatzlichenn gute verschwendt wirt sanct Jacobs grab haim zů suchen/ in Hispania/ Sant Peter vnd Paulus zů Rom/ in der hailthumbs fart geen Ach/ im vmbgang zů Nurnberg/ Bamberg/ Meidpurg/ zů sant Annenperg/ auch pey meinen lieben průdern/ vnd freynden zů Hall jm jntal/ so

direct connection between the "false" religious practices, which consume so much money, and a certain hard-heartedness in the face of poverty; he suggests that the especially pious are particularly insensitive to the needs of the poor, thereby (and this is his most serious accusation) preventing the exercise of brotherly love.

It is this latter consideration that ultimately determines Strauss's position on wealth and poverty. He continually introduces the concept of brotherliness or neighborliness, based on the New Testament commandment of love, in connection with this subject.[51] Although it might be going too far to speak of a "Straussian utopia," his frequent references to *naturlichen billickeyt* (natural fairness) indicate that society at present is "unnatural" in its injustice and requires drastic reform. Strauss did not propose any detailed model for such a society along the lines of the "Wolfaria" of Johann Eberlin von Günzburg, although there are some similarities with the latter, particularly regarding Eberlin's proposals for the remuneration of the clergy, and the services for the dead.[52] Nevertheless, we can glean some notion of this ideal from his approach to material considerations in these pamphlets.

It is perhaps most appropriate to describe Strauss's particular vision of society as a brotherhood, as it is in the pamphlet on confraternities, where the true brotherhood is contrasted with those of the confraternities, that he comes closest to a comprehensive explanation of the former.[53] The overall impression is of a society run on the basis of brotherly love; exploitation, both clerical and secular, must be abolished. Not only

---

gotis gepott solt gehalten werden/ wie vil tausent armer nötiger menschen wurden hie mit erfrewt vnd vnterhalten?" Ibid., Aiiijv.

[51] Matthew 22:39, "You shall love your neighbor as yourself," and John 15:12, "This is my commandment, that you love one another as I have loved you."

[52] Johann Eberlin von Günzberg, *New statute[n]/// die Psitacus gebracht hat// vß dem la[n]d Wolfaria wel=//che beträffendt reformie=//rung geystlichen stand.// Wan[n] man annäm diß re=//formatz/ //so geschweigt man=//che kloster katz/ //Die vornen äckt vnd hin//den kratz //Der. X. bu[n]dtgnosz.* ([Basel, 1521]), Aijv, Aiiijv. Also the eleventh "Bundgenoss," *Ein newe ord//nu[n]g welichs sta[n]dts das// Psitacus anzeigt hat// in Wolfaria beschri//ben.// Der .XI. bu[n]dt//gnosz,* [(Basel, 1521]).

[53] In his study of early Reformation anticlericalism, "'What a Tangled and Tenuous Mess the Clergy Is!' Clerical Anticlericalism in the Reformation Period," in Dykema and Oberman, *Anticlericalism,* pp. 499–519, Hans-Jürgen Goertz has identified a Straussian "fraternal [as opposed to monastic] ethic" in this pamphlet, which, he argues, "could not be equalled for decisiveness." Ibid., p. 506f.

will the poor sheep no longer be driven to market by the clergy, their income sacrificed to support the latter,[54] but a new culture of altruism and mutual assistance will emerge among the laity, where the needs of one's neighbor take precedence over one's own self-interest. In the confraternities pamphlet, there is a suggestion that Strauss believed that goods should be held in common: when describing the true brotherhood, he argues that nothing belongs to the individual (*eygens*); rather, all things are common (*gemein*), and each is entitled to share in all goods of his fellow brothers.[55] Is this community of goods a concrete, practical proposal on Strauss's part, or merely a rhetorical flourish? It is possible that it is simply a description of altruism, of the giving without hope of return mentioned in the later works on usury. The implication that all goods should be held in common is echoed in greater detail in Johann Lindenmaier's work of the following year on the correct distribution of wealth in a Christian society and the obligation to help one's neighbor, in which he argues that riches have been given to the prosperous so that they can accomplish their divinely ordered office (*ampt*) of assisting the poor, the neglect of whom is one of the vices inherent in wealth.[56] This assistance, he hopes, will soon become universal, thanks to the recently uncovered word of God. Similarly, it is probable that Strauss did in fact envisage a society of economic equality, based not on a forced or even centrally organized redistribution of goods but on a voluntary renunciation of material wealth by the faithful, comparable to that practiced in the apostolic community of the early church, the community of goods

---

[54] "Hie hebt sich vo[n] newe[n] an/ die grausam schinderey so d[er] taglöner absents/ reseruat/ pension/ gebe[n] soll/ so gehts dez schefleyn biß auffs marck." *Das nit herren aber diener eyner yedenn Christlichen versamlung zugestelt werdenn*, Bijr.

[55] *Ein kurtz christenlich vntherricht*, Aijr.

[56] Johannes Lindenmaier, *Ain kurtzer gründtlicher bericht// vnd vnderweisung/ auß der heyligen ge//schrifft/ Das der schöpffer aller ding// nit ansicht die person. Vnnd wie// ain mensch dem andern dienen// vnd helffen soll/ mit seym zeyt//lichen gütt/ von Gott jm// verlyhen/ auß zu spenden// vnd was schaden die// geyttigkeit bring/ // darumb nyemant// am zeitlichen// gütt han=//gen soll/ mit dem// hertzen &c.* ([Augsburg, 1524]). This pamphlet has been reprinted in Laube, *Flugschriften der frühen Reformationsbewegung*, pp. 1200–1209; see also Heinz Holeczek, "Johannes Lindenmaiers Schrift von der Gleichheit des Besitzes," *Archiv für Reformationsgeschichte* 66 (1975), 103–41.

mentioned above being described as "die gemeinschafft der heiligen" (the community of the saints).[57]

And it is in this context of brotherhood that Strauss's writings on usury must be understood. As mentioned in the introduction to this essay, he initially tackled this issue in fifty theses, printed in 1523, in which he denounced a practice lacking an obvious connection to church reform, but nevertheless contrary to God's teaching.[58] The lending of money at interest for the purpose of making a profit had its critics long before the Reformation, among them St. Thomas Aquinas, William of Ockham, and Bernardine of Siena, and such lending of money at interest by Christians to Christians had been classed as heresy by successive general councils of the Church during the Middle Ages.[59] As has been shown above, Strauss had already condemned the property speculation engaged in by the confraternities, and he was also to mention the harm caused to the common good by "rich merchants who practice usury" in his work on relics.[60] Usury, according to Strauss, is unacceptable not only because

---

[57] Acts 2:44f., "And all who believed were together and had all things in common; and they sold their possessions and goods and distributed them to all, as any had need." Lindenmaier, on the other hand, does hold out the possibility of an "external, temporal force" (*ain eusserlichen weltlichen gwalt*) that may come into play if the rich do not willingly give up their possessions. *Ain kurtzer gründtlicher bericht*, Aiijr.

[58] In all of the printed versions to which I have had access the articles number fifty-one; however, numbers 26 and 27 are, in fact, a single article, as follows: "xxvj. The written promises to pay usury actually read thus: xxvij. I promise and vow to pay [the] usury annually against God and his commandment, as someone despairing of God's help, I also do not want to be obedient to God." *Haubtstuck vnd artickel*, Aijr. That being said, articles 50 and 51 could also be said to constitute a single article.

[59] As non-Christians, Jews were exempt from this and, there being no Jewish prohibition on lending money at interest to Gentiles, Judaism became linked with usury in the popular imagination, leading to the stereotype of the greedy and unmerciful Jewish moneylender so prevalent in medieval and Renaissance literature. However, Strauss is not tempted to use this perception to condemn usury, usurers, or debtors through guilt by association. Strauss's usurers are Christians, and their sin is that they "burden [their] neighbor more grossly and also harshly than the godless Jews do to one another"; the Jews are in fact praised for following their law more faithfully than the Christians follow theirs. For a comprehensive treatment of the issue of usury and the Church in the Middle Ages, see John Noonan, *The Scholastic Analysis of Usury* (Cambridge, Mass., 1957).

[60] "Des gleichen sechstü and den reichen kauffleuten/ die vnersätlich vber all juden wuchern/ vnd mit falschem kauff vnd verkauff/ den gemain nutz gar zů reissen. . . ." *Ein kurtz Christenlich vnterricht*, Bjv.

of the Old Testament prohibition (Exodus 22 and Deuteronomy 23); it also contravenes the New Testament commandment of brotherly love.[61] It is necessary, he states, "that wealth that has come from usury must be recognized by Christians to be robbed, stolen and deserving of all dishonor," and there is no place in the Christian community for such a practice.[62] The term "usury" with all of its negative connotations had, over time, been modified in popular usage, so that by the sixteenth century it applied only to *excessive* interest, thus opening to many, including members of the clergy, a source of income that was apparently legitimate, if not strictly in accordance with canon law, and could be called by any one of a variety of euphemisms but most often simply "interest" (in German, *Zins*).[63] According to Strauss, however, all forms of interest are usurious, and it is as much a sin to pay usury as to demand it.[64] In his second, much longer, usury work, this type of profit-making is declared to be "against the nature of money,"[65] and Strauss advises that, if the original victims cannot be found to be recompensed, the temporal lords should use the money gained through usury to "comfort and support poor people" and "protect and regulate their kingdom and principality"; this is the closest he ever comes to a practical suggestion for the redistribution of wealth.[66] How might this brotherhood, with its basic criteria of selflessness, mutual assistance, and possible community of goods, have been received

---

[61] References to Mosaic Law and the Old Testament in the second usury work should not be taken as evidence that Strauss saw Mosaic Law as the basis for a Christian society. It is more probable that he merely used the idea of the Jubilee release to shore up his arguments against the practice of *Wiederkauf* ("repurchase"; i.e., borrowing against one's property, which one then "buys back." Critics of this practice saw the nomenclature as a deliberate euphemism used to disguise a form of usury).

[62] ". . . It můß von nöten der Christen gůter auß dem wůcher herfliessen/ geraubet/ gestolen/ vnd aller vneer gemeß erkant werden." *Haubtstuck vnd artickel*, Aijv.

[63] For the various forms of money-lending and interest charges common in this period, see Eric Kerridge, *Usury, Interest, and the Reformation* (Aldershot, 2002), and Benjamin Nelson, *The Idea of Usury: From Tribal Brotherhood to Universal Otherhood*, 2nd ed. (Chicago, 1969).

[64] Ibid., Aijr.

[65] ". . . yst hyrumb d[er] wucher wider die natur des geldes." *Das wucher zu nemen vnd geben*, B4v.

[66] Ibid., Giijv–Giiijr. Although Strauss does not go so far as to propose the establishment of a common chest, Rogge suggests that this recommendation was inspired by the Leisnig Common Chest Ordinance of 1523. Rogge, *Der Beitrag des Predigers Jakob Strauss zur frühen Reformationsgeschichte*, p. 84.

by Strauss's audience? If his employment of economic themes could be said to have a propagandistic purpose, how would this have worked? Is it too simplistic to say that Strauss was taking advantage of existing socioeconomic grievances to make his religious reforms more palatable? To be in a position to carry out these reforms in the first place, Strauss required more than the support of the poorer, disgruntled members of his congregation; he depended on those in power, particularly the prominent citizens of the towns in which he preached. Considering the difficulties involved in appealing to a broad audience while not offending certain groups (apart from the nonreformed clergy, who are not of course of any concern here), would it not have been safer to avoid the seemingly peripheral subject of money altogether? What was to be gained by identifying with the poor?

Most obviously, as with the abolition of clerical economic exploitation mentioned above, there is the consideration of the straightforward improvement of one's own position. A society based on the sharing of wealth between neighbors, according to one's need, would have offered the prospect of a degree of security, an alternative to the uncertainty of day-to-day survival experienced by a much larger section of society than the beggars and invalids, the openly destitute objects of charity.[67] Any popular resonance that may have been produced by the identification with the poor and oppressed present in Strauss's works would have been strengthened by the existing German discourse regarding social and economic injustice, evident in the *Bundschuh* groups of the early 1500s and in the iconic evangelical figure of the peasant Karsthans. The concept of brotherliness was a popular motif in the sermons and literature of the early Reformation. This sometimes occurred in a purely religious context, as in Sebastian Lötzer's *Salutary Admonition to the Inhabitants of*

---

[67] The financial insecurity of the common man in this period has been noted by, among others, Lee Palmer Wandel and Thomas A. Brady; Wandel, *Always Among Us*, p. 10f. According to Brady, "Europe's cities held no fixed class of 'the poor,' for the condition of potential poverty gripped a large part of the population and threatened a still larger part, depending on the variable economic conditions, such as harvests, prices, wages, and unemployment. As a result, in a broad sense the term 'the poor' was frequently and correctly used to designate the majority of the working population." Brady, "In Search of the Godly City: The Domestication of Religion in the German Urban Reformation," in *The German People and the Reformation*, ed. R. Po-chia Hsia (Ithaca, 1988) pp. 14–31, 17f.

Horb, in which the author condemns the unbrotherliness of the papacy and the clergy in oppressing their flock with false, invented teachings.[68] However, it was also commonly used when discussing economic matters, especially by the more radical elements of the Reformation. Strauss's universal brotherhood, with its repudiation of wealth, possible community of goods, and appeal to "natural fairness," finds an echo to varying degrees in the "Christian unions" of the Peasants' War, and in the various Anabaptist movements. Even his frequent employment of the term "brother" brings to mind the forms of address used by these groups.[69] His contempt for the *großen Hansen,* or "big shots" (another of Strauss's favored terms) is echoed by Thomas Müntzer, and he makes frequent references to exploitation and unjust servitude, often using the language of feudal hierarchy to denote injustice, referring to the usurers as *Wucherherren* (usury-lords) and *Zinsjunkern* (interest-squires) and to their victims as *Zinsknechten* (interest-servants).[70]

The denunciation of various forms of greed, gluttony, and excess constitutes another prevalent motif. In Strauss's 1523 pamphlet on the marriage of priests, he condemns weddings prompted by the "lust of the mortal flesh and blood for all the pleasures of the world" (these being occasions of "carousing, feasting, gluttony, dancing and leaping, and other work of the devil"), and in their place advises "moderation and

---

[68] Sebastian Lötzer, *Ain helisame Ermanu[n]//ge an die ynwoner zü horw das sy be//stendig beleyben an dem hailige[n] wort Gottes mit anzaigu[n]g// der göttlichen hailigen// geschrifft/ durch// Sebastian// lotzer vo[n]// Horw// Im Jar. M.D.Xxiij.// Herr wir wöllen Juchtzenvauff deyn hayl// vnd in deynem namen paner auffwerffe[n]// Psalmus am .19.* ([Augsburg, 1523]).

[69] On the vocabulary employed by the "radicals," see Hans-Joachim Diekmannshenke, *Die Schlagwörter der Radikalen der Reformationszeit (1520–1536)* (Frankfurt a.M., 1994).

[70] Conversely, when Strauss uses the word "servant" in relation to the position of the minister within the assembly, he indicates that it is laudatory and desirable to be a servant (although here he uses the term *Diener* rather than *Mann* or *Knecht*). Lindenmaier, on the other hand, uses *Knecht* in a positive sense, to describe the servant of God who fulfils his duty through serving the poor: "Darumb sollen die reychen/ die zeytliche gůter haben/ den armen schwachen an gůtern/ die aller besten gůter . . . mittaylen/ vnd sollen nitt faul in jrem ampt seyn/ vnnd auch iren aygnen nutz suchen/ mit den gůttern/ Sonder dem herren mit den gůtern dienen als trew knecht." Lindenmaier, *Ain kurtzer gründtlicher bericht,* Br.

shortage."[71] Similarly, on confraternity feast days, the members become so drunk that they "sing, dance, and leap."[72] Although it could be argued that this is a wholesale, hard-to-swallow criticism of Strauss's public and their behavior (a criticism evident in the caricatures of sixteenth-century artists, depicting drunken, coarse-featured peasants and artisans in assorted comic attitudes),[73] it is possible that this approach may have worked in Strauss's favor, from the point of view of winning over this same audience. Dissipation of this type was frowned upon, in principle at least. Who among Strauss's public would have been willing to admit to gluttony and loose behavior? The individual reader or listener would have recognized overindulgence as a sin, and it would not have been difficult to attribute this particular offense to any group better off than oneself, thus providing another opportunity to criticize one's oppressors who are yet again abusing their material good fortune. Such accusations of fleshly immoderation were regularly employed during this period as a stick with which to beat the clergy. In denouncing this behavior, Strauss could be seen to be identifying an evil in society (perpetrated not by the audience, but by its enemies) and proposing a remedy. The popularity of such a message could in fact have had a broader appeal than the simple admonition to share one's wealth with the poor, a positive reaction in this case stemming from envy rather than from need. Again, Strauss was not alone in this condemnation. There are noticeable similarities with the lay writer Haug Marschalck on this subject, particularly in a shared rejection of self-interest and a perceived common preoccupation with wealth.

---

[71] *Ain Sermon In// der deütlich angezeygt/ vnd geleert ist// die pfaffen Ee/ in Euangelischer leer// nit zů der freyhayt des flayschs/ vnnd// zü bekrefftig[e]n de[n] alten Adam/ wie et=//lich flayschlich Pfaffen das Eelich wesen mit aller pomp/ Hoffart vnnd// ander teüffels werck anheben gefun=//diert/ aber das Gotes werck vn[d] wort// allein angesehen mit forcht vnd Christ=//licher beschaydenhayt auch die wirt=//schafft vollenbracht damit die feind// des Ewangeliums vnns zů// schelten/ vnnd Gottes// wort zů lestere[n]/ nit// geursacht// werde[n].// 1.5.23.// D. Jac. Strauß zů Eyssenach eccle.* ([Ausburg], 1523), Av, Br.

[72] *Ein kurtz christenlich vntherricht,* Aijv.

[73] For example, the carousing, vomiting, and brawling figures in Bartel Beham's *Große Bauernkirchweih* (c. 1525), and Hans Sebald Beham's *Bauernfest* (1537) and *Bauerntanzfest oder die Zwölf Monate* (1546, 1547). Reprinted in Herbert Zschelletschky, *Die "drei gottlosen Maler" von Nürnberg. Sebald Beham, Barthel Beham und Georg Pencz. Historische Grundlagen und ikonologische Probleme ihrer Graphik zu Reformations und Bauernkriegszeit* (Leipzig, 1975), pp. 328f., 343ff.

Marschalck, in his *Mirror for the Blind*, denounces the material greed that he believes to be suffocating the world: "The world is entirely caught up in material lust . . . [and] many a man severely burdens and ruins his fellow men and Christian brothers, and in doing so he gains and piles up much wealth. . . ."[74]

Similarly, a society free from usury, a poison that contributed to the ruin of "land and people," would also have enjoyed a broad, popular appeal. Usury had been condemned by Luther in two separate pamphlets before the appearance of Strauss's *Hauptstuck vnd artickel* (the most significant divergence from Luther in the latter being the designation of the debtor as complicit in this "mortal sin") and also in the anonymous dialogue, *Here Comes a Peasant*.[75] In this latter pamphlet, the issue of *Wiederkauf*, or pledging of land, as security on a loan is described by the burgher who profits from it: when the payments are not made, he can evict the peasant from his land and the artisan from his house. This practice is defended by the priest, who calls it an "honest purchase"; the peasant of the title counters that the merchant risks his initial investment, whereas the usurer does not.[76] There are similarities with Strauss's approach to the subject, particularly his assertion that usury is "against the nature of money."

It could be argued that if lending at interest, rather than merely at excessive interest, were to be abolished altogether, this would only exacerbate the problems of the poor and desperate. "The poor" needed the usurers, even if they objected to the interest rates. Who would be willing to lend money without the prospect of profit? However, this apparent disregard for the needs of those forced to borrow money at interest can be resolved in the context of Strauss's reformed society. Here, such a consideration would not arise; a community of Christians, being true Christians who follow the commandment of brotherly love, would not hesitate to

---

[74] *Durch betrachtung vn[d]// Bekärung Der bößen gebreych in// schweren sünden/ Ist Gemacht Dy=//ser Spyegel Der Blinden.* ([Augsburg], 1522), Br.

[75] " . . . eyn schwarwichtig vnd offenbar tod sundt," *Haubtstuck vnd artickel*, Aijr. Martin Luther, *Eyn Sermon// von dem wucher // D.M.L.* (Leipzig, 1519), and his "long sermon" on the same subject, *Eyn Sermon von dem Wucher.// Doctoris Martini Luther// Augustiner zu Wittenbergk* (Wittenberg, 1520).

[76] *Hie kompt ein Beüerlein zu// einem reychen Burger von der gult/ den wucher// betreffen/ so kompt ein pfaff auch dar zu// vnd dar nach ine münch/ gar kurtz=//wey-lich zu lesen.* ([Speyer, 1522]).

lend to their neighbor in the manner recommended in Luke 6:35; in other words, to give freely. Although Strauss describes the problem as existing in all kingdoms, cities, and regions,[77] the condemnation of usury would have had particular resonance in Eisenach, where many among the populace owed *Wiederkäufliche Zins* to various ecclesiastical institutions.[78] Although clerical usurers are not the only culprits mentioned in Strauss's works, indicating that the usury issue was not merely a convenient means by which to create or increase resentment of the local clergy, the fact that the canons of the *Marienstift* and the other local religious communities were the principal collectors of interest in Eisenach would have provided an opportunity for some useful wealth-related anticlericalism.

Finally, the soteriological aspect should not be overlooked. In abolishing the possibility that one can be rewarded with an easier road to heaven for any good work, including that of giving to the poor, Luther in effect eliminated the strongest inducement for one Christian to give to another. How, then, does Strauss tackle this problem of persuading his audience of their obligation toward the poor? Although he vehemently denies that charity is a form of good work that can buy salvation, the refusal to obey the commandment of love entails for him the refusal of God's grace, without which man cannot be redeemed. God, he says, will have nothing to do with those who are "harsh and uncharitable" when faced with a neighbor in need.[79] Here, Strauss still allows for a connection between charity and salvation, but he appears to have come up with a negative interpretation of that relationship (that of the neglect of charity *preventing* salvation, rather than of the practice of charity *securing* eternal life) that does not contradict the evangelical rejection of works-righteousness. In 1520, in his "long" usury sermon, Luther stated that

---

[77] *Das wucher zu nemen vnd geben,* Eijr.

[78] On the significance of the usury question in Eisenach, see Rogge, *Der Beitrag des Predigers Jakob Strauss zur frühen Reformationsgeschichte,* pp. 39–41, and on the possessions and rights of the local monasteries and chapters, Joseph Kremer, *Beiträge zur geschichte der Klösterlichen Niederlassungen Eisenachs im Mittelalter,* Quellen und Abhandlungen zur Geschichte der Abtei und der Diözese Fulda (Fulda, 1905). The link between evangelical criticism of clerical landowners and the Peasants' War has been discussed by Henry Cohn, "Anti-clericalism," p. 10.

[79] "Dan so die rechtfertigkait/ vnd ledigung von sunden/ allain auß gotis parmhertzigkait herfeust/ die vns gar abgeschlagen/ so wir hert vnd vnmilte in der not vnsers nechsten gefunden werden/ so hat auch gott kainn tail an vnns. . . ." *Ein kurtz Christenlich vnterricht,* Bjr.

God would not ask each Christian upon death and on the Last Day, "How much money have you given to the church?" but would say instead, "I was hungry and you did not feed me."[80] In his study of lay pamphleteers in the 1520s, Paul A. Russell has noted the survival of the traditional link between charity and salvation, remarking that "a theology of the poor as the gateway to heaven was apparently so deeply rooted in medieval piety, that even these first Protestants could not so easily dispense with it."[81] Although this association is not so straightforward in Strauss, the apparent continuity would have struck a chord with his general audience. All of these elements combine to form a very persuasive argument for change, allowing Strauss to associate a reformed church with a fairer society and with the aspirations, financial and spiritual, of the laity. In any case, it could be said that the true brotherhood provides most of his audience with an attractive alternative, in that almost everyone could think of him- or herself as a beneficiary; few would have seen themselves as oppressors, instead viewing themselves as among the exploited.

On the other hand, is it possible that Strauss's arguments on economic matters may have provoked a negative reaction? The establishment of the true brotherhood is not merely a matter of abolishing the abuses of the spiritual *grempelmarkt* and of usury: the common man has a responsibility toward his neighbor. Strauss is not reluctant to criticize those, both rich and poor, whom he believes to be standing in the way of this brotherhood due to "self-interest" (*aigennutz*). How attractive would the commandment of brotherly love have been to the "common man"? Strauss declares in the second usury work that Christ has ordered that one should give to one's neighbor in need as far as one's means allow and should not expect the return of the loan itself, much less any interest.[82] To the artisan or peasant who risks his property as a pledge and pays a high rate of interest on borrowed money, the appeal of a society where each should lend to the other according to his need and expect no return

---

[80] *Eyn Sermon von dem Wucher*, biijr. This is Matthew 25:34f., a text used by Strauss in an identical manner in his condemnation of the confraternities, *Ein kurtz christenlich vntherricht*, Aiijv.

[81] Paul A. Russell, *Lay Theology in the Reformation—Popular Pamphleteers in Southwest Germany 1521–1525* (Cambridge, 1986), p. 214.

[82] "Christus gepoten hat/ gelt außzuliehen vnserm nechsten/ so wirs vermigen vnd nichtes dar gegen verhoffen/ wider hauptsum noch gesuch. Daurmb Christus den hellischen wucher handel gar außschlecht." *Das wucher zu nemen vnd geben*, Cr.

is obvious. However, even allowing for Strauss's modified version of the residual link between charity and salvation, the selflessness required by the commandment of love would not have been easy to achieve, and the level of "community spirit" in early modern society and the willingness of the same artisan to act in a similarly unselfish manner when asked should not be overestimated. This poses an important question: who would have gained or lost in a reformed society? In other words, who among Strauss's audience would have seen themselves as receivers, rather than givers?

Unusually for a writer so ready to engage with socioeconomic questions, Strauss rarely mentions the problem of begging. In his pamphlet on confraternities, he tells his readers to help the poor "without distinction," wherever there is "true need."[83] The phrase "true need" clearly excludes the "holy, pious hypocrites, the discalced and sabot-wearers" of the mendicant orders,[84] but it is unclear whether Strauss extends the definition of the undeserving, voluntary poor beyond the first estate. He never refers directly to the practice of begging as performed by the laity but could not have been unaware of the suspicion aroused by such figures—the various categories of liars, charlatans, and reprobates listed in the *Liber Vagatorum* and given voice in the form of Irides, Erasmus's able-bodied idler.[85] Indiscriminate charity to these people would surely not have been an attractive prospect in the eyes of "respectable" or "honorable" townspeople.

As has already been seen, Strauss at one point uses the term *haus armen* to describe the needy who lose out because of the channeling of

---

[83] "Aber nembtt euch vmb das heilig euangelium an vnd helfft von dem selben gelt den armen on vnderscheiden wo ir die war nodturfft erkennet. . . ." *Ein kurtz christenlich vntherricht*, Aiijv.

[84] ". . . heiligen fromenn gleissene . . . Barfusser vnd holtzschucher." *Ein new wunderbarlich beychtpuchlin*, Cr.

[85] Matthias Hütlin, *Liber vagatorum*, printed from 1523 in various editions as *Von der falschen betler bueberey. . . .* The 1529 edition held in the British Library, *Uon der falsche[n] bet//ler büeberey/ Mit einer Vorrede Martini Luther. Und hinden an ein Rotwelsch Vocabularius daraus man die wo[e]rter/// so yn diesem bu[e]chlin gebraucht/// verstehen kan* (Wittenberg [Nuremberg], 1529), has been translated as *The Book of Vagabonds and Beggars with a Vocabulary of Their Language and a Preface by Martin Luther*. Translated by J. C. Hotten, edited by D. B. Thomas (London, 1932); Erasmus, "Beggar talk (Πτωχολογία)," *Collected Works of Erasmus*, vol. 39, *Colloquies*, translated and edited by Craig Thompson (Toronto, 1997), pp. 262–570.

resources into the purchase of salvation. This literally translates as "house-poor"; however, its exact meaning is reasonably complex and deserves some discussion. In the language of sixteenth-century poor relief, it appears to have been used to designate the "deserving poor" mentioned earlier. It is employed in the Zurich Alms Statute of 1520 when discussing those to whom help should be given, including those who would prefer to work rather than be the recipients of public charity ("[die] sich vast gern wöltent erneren und ussbringen mit ir sorg, und arbeit, wo es in irem vermögen were") or who are too sick ("zo kranck und bresthafftig") to earn a living.[86] It has been defined by other historians as "the poor in their homes," or the "poor who had homes"; it is sometimes applied to the *verschämte Arme* ("shame-faced poor") who attempted to keep their poverty hidden from their neighbors.[87] In the Nuremburg Poor Ordinance of 1522, however, it is used to describe needy people who are forced to beg openly in the streets and outside the church to feed themselves and their families.[88] Its application was therefore somewhat flexible, but broadly speaking it can be interpreted as "local poor," signifying respectable members of the community who have reluctantly, through no fault of their own, become dependent on alms and for whose benefit the public welfare systems were established. "House-poor" was used by Luther in

---

[86] The text of the statute is reprinted in Wandel, *Always Among Us*, pp. 179–87. The quotations are taken from page 183.

[87] "Most of them [Lutheran ordinances] provided aid for nonresidents who were legitimate travelers, not vagabonds, and also for the poor in their homes (*Hausarme*), withholding the names from the public of those who were sensitive concerning their poverty." Harold J. Grimm, "Luther's Contributions to Sixteenth-Century Organization of Poor Relief," *Archiv für Reformationsgeschichte* 69 (1970), 222–34, 229; Brian Pullan, "Catholics, Protestants, and the Poor in Early Modern Europe," *Journal of Interdisciplinary History* 35, no. 3 (2005), 441–56, 445. Pullan uses *Hausarmen* as a synonym for *Haussitzenden*; Timothy Fehler has noted the use of the latter term in Emden, describing it as "the local term used to describe those 'shame-faced' local, or non-transient, poor who had housing of their own, yet were in need of additional support," Fehler, *Poor Relief and Protestantism*, p. 64.

[88] "Da es nun aber in der Stadt Nürnberg bisher gar viele bedürftige, hausarme und notleidende Menschen gegeben hat, die aus Not dazu gedrungen worden sind, zu ihrer und ihrer Verwandten Versorgung und Unterhalt öffentlich auf den Straßen und in den Kirchen zu betteln und um das Almosen zu bitten . . . daß die, welche in einem Glauben und in einer einzigen christlichen Gemeinschaft mit uns vereint . . . ja auf den Gassen und in den Häusern öffentlich verhungern . . . ," Sachsse and Tennstedt, *Geschichte der Armenfürsorge in Deutschland*, p. 67.

his preface to the 1523 edition of the *Liber Vagatorum* in conjunction with "needy neighbors," in contrast to the itinerant and possibly dangerous professional beggars, and it is possible that Strauss may have chosen this rather loaded term in order to make a similar distinction.[89] If so, his frequent employment of "neighbor" could be seen in this context as a qualification of the potentially more inclusive "brother." Furthermore, the voluntary poor could not be practitioners of brotherly love, as they shirk their duties towards their neighbors and are a burden on society. However, there is no real evidence that Strauss intended to use *Hausarmen* in this restrictive sense, and it must be remembered that the term appears here in a pamphlet dealing with the subject of purgatory, not in an official statute designed to regulate poor relief. In any case, Strauss's definition of the "many poor, sick, hungry, naked, and wretched people [who] are visible everywhere" (thus covering more than merely the "concealed poor") is sufficiently vague as to allow his readership to apply their own restrictions to the recipients of their charity.[90]

Beyond these unfortunates (who are the most obvious beneficiaries but perhaps not a particularly influential group and therefore, from a cynical point of view, not the most valuable target for persuasion), who else would have seen themselves as profiting from Strauss's brotherhood? Although it is clear that the "common man," and specifically the artisan, is also catered for under Strauss's description of the "poor, needy neighbor" and that the level at which one can be said to have wealth surplus to one's needs is left open to interpretation, it should not be assumed that all would willingly have classed themselves as such, despite the economic precariousness of sixteenth-century society. The extent to which notions of "honor" come into play must be considered, and it is questionable whether a majority of Strauss's audience would have been happy to be included in the same category as those on the margins of society. Despite a certain theoretical idealization of the poor in terms of their biblical closeness to God, which had earlier inspired the formation of the mendicant orders, the common designation of the deserving poor as "shamefaced" reflects the ignominy popularly associated with being forced to

---

89 "... wo man nit wil hauß armen vnd// nottrůftigen [*sic*] nachbawrn geben vnd helffen...." Hotten and Thomas, *The Book of Vagabonds*, pp. 62–64.

90 "... so vil armer/ krancker/ hungeriger/ nackender/ vnd elender leut/ an allen steten vnd enden vr augen seind...." *Kurtz vnd verstendig leer*, Aiiijr.

ask for assistance in order to support oneself and one's household.[91] On the whole, however, it remains plausible that readers of Strauss's works could have seen themselves as belonging to one of at least two types of "poor," both of whom qualify for the assistance that stems from brotherly love. There is the common man, who may be regarded as poor in comparison with his exploiters, and a second group consisting of otherwise respectable people who have fallen into difficulty (the common man *in extremis*). The brotherhood is a cooperative as well as a charitable society, in which one must be prepared to give freely, and not for spiritual gain, to the wretched and can expect the same from one's neighbor when beset by misfortune, even when this amounts to no more than a minor or temporary shortage. One would not have to be a member of the underclass to gain from this arrangement.

Even if the common man, rather than the long-term poor, were to be the principal beneficiary if this altruism, his prospects are not altogether attractive. Strauss's great Christian brotherhood is not a society of ease and plenty. The clergy are criticized for their excesses, but so too are the laity, who use religious feast days and weddings as opportunities for gluttony.[92] At times, Strauss recommends a severely ascetic ideal of daily life. The decree to lend freely to one's neighbor depends on the final purpose of that aid: he must not be helped to "play, feast, [or pursue] other knavery."[93] To avoid the possibility of financing sin, one should not provide any more to an individual than will meet his immediate need.

Furthermore, Strauss makes clear his disapproval not only of luxury but of money in general, in the 1523 usury articles going so far as to say that "the Lord Christ has called all wealth unjustifiable (*vnrechtfertig*)."[94]

---

[91] Brian Pullan, in his catalogue of the types of early-modern poor, points out that "shamefaced poor" was frequently used in a narrower sense than the more general *Hausarmen*; i.e., "those who had fallen from prosperity, could not maintain the style of living appropriate to their rank, and were threatened more with dishonor than with outright starvation. They were often the subject of the most systematic inquiries and the recipients of the greatest generosity, particularly those who had daughters in need of dowries." Pullan, *Catholics*, p. 445.

[92] *Ein kurtz christenlich vntherricht*, Aijv; *Ain Sermon In der deütlich angezeygt vnd geleert ist die pfaffen Ee*, Av.

[93] "zu spilen/ brassen/ vnd ander buberey." *Das wucher zu nemen vnd geben*, Biijr.

[94] *Haubtstuck vnd artickel* Aijv. This is probably a reference to Mark 10:23ff., "And Jesus looked around and said to his disciples, 'How hard it will be for those

His disdain for those who strive for material wealth is evident throughout these pamphlets: he denounces the "unholy, destructive preoccupation with the temporal,"[95] tells his public that they must "flee the ephemeral lust of the world,"[96] and repeatedly insists that they should trust God to provide for all their physical needs, as commanded in Matthew 6:26ff: "Look at the birds of the air; they neither sow nor reap not gather into barns, and yet your heavenly Father feeds them. . . . And why are you anxious about clothing? Consider the lilies of the field, how they grow; they neither toil nor spin; yet I tell you, even Solomon in all his glory was not arrayed like one of these. . . . Therefore do not be anxious, saying, 'What shall we eat?' or 'What shall we drink?' or 'What shall we wear?' For the Gentiles seek all these things; and your heavenly Father knows that you need them all."[97] Those "anxious and despairing men" who have the temerity to doubt God's promise to provide his children with food, drink, clothing, and support "are not Christians."[98] This accusation is echoed in Strauss's work on the Christian assembly, in which he criticizes the clergy whose principal concern is their own financial welfare, and whose assiduousness in ensuring that they, the servants of the church, should suffer no shortage is evidence of their lack of faith.[99]

---

who have riches to enter the kingdom of God!' And the disciples were amazed at his words. But Jesus said to them again, 'Children, how hard it is to enter the kingdom of God! It is easier for a camel to go through the eye of a needle than for a rich man to enter the kingdom of God.'" Alternatively, Laube suggests Matthew 13:22. Laube, *Flugschriften der frühen Reformationsbewegung,* p. 1074.

[95] ". . . die heylos zenichtig fursorg/ vmb das zeitlich." *Das wucher zu nemen vnd geben,* Aiij v.

[96] ". . . so wir fliehen die vorgenckliche lust der wellt." Ibid., Aiij r.

[97] Also Luke 11:9f., John 16:23f. These texts are cited frequently by Strauss, both directly and indirectly, e.g., *Ein kurtz Christenlich vnterricht,* Aiijv; *Haubtstuck vnd artickel,* Aijv; *Das wucher zu nemen vnd geben,* Aiijr–Aiijv.

[98] ". . . wir wolten dan Gottes vetterliche trew nit annemen/ oder vngenugsam achten/ dz weit mus sein von allem Christenlichem verstandt vnd wesen. Dan dieweil der mund der warheit vns furzeigt ein solchen haußhalter vber vnser narung/ der got selbert yst/ vnd nach vetterlicher eygenschafft vns speysen/ drencken/ bekleiden/ vnd vnderhalten wil/ wer kan dan hie zweiffeln vnd sorg tragen/ dann der Got nit erkennet/ vnnd sein hertz von Gott abgewendt yst/ so yst doch nichts Christlichs an yhm." *Das wucher zu nemen vnd geben,* Aiijv.

[99] "Die fursorg das die diener der kirchen kein abgang wurden haben/ kumbt von vnglauben/ vn vertzagtem hertzen zu gott." *Das nit herren aber diener eyner yedenn Christlichen versamlung zugestelt werdenn,* Bv.

The poor, who borrow money from the usurers, are therefore guilty along with the usurers themselves. Poverty does not give one a license to break God's commandment; apostasy cannot be justified by temporal need.[100] Strauss insists that the debtor's contract should be interpreted as follows: "I promise and vow to pay the usury annually against God and his commandment as someone despairing of God's help; I do not want to be content in poverty with God."[101] Ultimately, one must conquer the "old Adam," that is, one's own will and desire in all things. This exhortation to discard external things and instead rely on providence brings to mind the concept of *Gelassenheit*, or surrender to God, particularly as expressed by Karlstadt.[102]

Moreover, not only are the debtors themselves sinning, they are assisting their brothers, the usurers, in *their* sin. Brotherly love requires one to avoid harming one's neighbor's soul, as his salvation should be of more consequence than one's own physical welfare.[103] In obeying this commandment, one should be prepared for one's goods to be confiscated

---

[100] "Wie ist es denn so ein heylige Christliche glos? das angesehen zeitliche armut/ der Christen mensch von Christo/ one sunde/ moge abtrinnig werden?" *Das wucher zu nemen vnd geben*, Biijv.

[101] "xxvj. Die verschreybunge[n] wuecher zubetzale[n] lauten ynn der warheit also. xxvij. Ich versprich vnd gelob zu betzalen yerlich den wuecher/ widder Got vn[d] sein gepot/ als ein vertzagter an Gottes hilff/ ich wil auch/ ynn armuet mit Gott/ nyt verguet haben." *Haubtstuck vnd artickel*, Aiijr.

[102] "Solte es die frucht vnser erlosung bringen/ also yst auch not das wir yn ansehen des wort gottes vnserm aygen willen/ rechten/ vnd gefallen yn vns erstterben/ anderst werden wir kein euangelsiche frucht bringen." *Das wucher zu nemen vnd geben*, Fiijv–Fiiijr. Karlstadt, in his work on the meaning of *Gelassenheit*, makes the following points: "we must abandon all created things (*creaturen*), if we want to have God as [our] one protector and . . . ruler," and "Those who are poor should not worry about what they are to eat tomorrow, or how they are to feed themselves, neither should those with possessions comfort themselves with their money, if they were to be robbed of all their goods, they should say, God has given them, God has taken them." Andreas Bodenstein von Karlstadt, *Was gesagt ist/ Sich// gelassen/ vnd was das wort// gelassenhait bedeüt/ vnd wa es in hailiger ge=//schrifft begriffen. . . . Andres Bodenstain von Ca=//rolstat/ ain neüwer Lay* ([Augsburg, 1523]), Aijv, Biijr.

[103] "Dan hie nichtes anderst gelert/ wie vor augen/ als wore christliche bruder-liche liebe nach dem lebendygen glauben erfordert/ yn das verderben der selen des nechsten menschens yn keynen weg zu bewilligen/ oder eynige hulff vnd furderung zuthun. Dan eynem yeden frummen Christen/ auß Gottes gebot die selikeyt seynes nechsten hocher anlygen sol/ dan seyn aigen leiblich leben." *Das wucher zu nemen vnd geben*, Fiiijv.

against one's will, and should even be prepared to die.[104] No one, Strauss argues, would deny that a Christian should be prepared to die for the sake of God's word and brotherly love; how, then, could anyone refuse to suffer mere "temporal poverty and want"?[105] This admonition would appear to negate any advantage to the debtor resulting from such a policy, as, in practice, this allowing of one's goods to be seized could not have been any easier to bear than interest payments and such disobedience could entail further punishment.

This recommendation of economic, and possibly literal, martyrdom, along with the repeatedly voiced instruction to let God provide, indicates that Strauss is not concerned with the alleviation of economic oppression for its own sake, at least not in the short term. The acceptance of suffering does appear to be central to his thought, while on the other hand, there is an obvious advantage in holding out the possibility of change for the better and associating one's movement with this. In considering these pamphlets as an element in a campaign of persuasion, could Strauss's admonition to suffer injustice (combined with his version of *Gelassenheit*) be seen as an injunction not to question the social order?—that is, as a means of reassuring the wealthy and powerful while still giving hope to the poor? Is his Christian brotherhood a deliberately nebulous utopia that might never become a reality, in which the poor must come to terms with their poverty and indefinitely suffer with Christ? The method by which the new society is to be established may throw some light on the extent to which this may have been Strauss's intention. Who will be responsible for this process, and how soon will it be accomplished?

In the pamphlets written in 1522 and 1523, the inference is that each member of the brotherhood must take his own part in reform, both

---

104 "Hie mustu etwas thun/ das du nit vmbgehen magst/ vnnd must vill darumb erleyden/ das ist/ du must Gottes wort mitt festem glawben vnnd begyrden vnabtruniglichen erhaltenn/ vnnd must darneben deynn zeytlich narung eynem anndernn lassenn angreyffenn/ wiewol dir solichs peynnlichenn vnnd vnnlustig yst/ so sollt du doch als eynn gesunndt gelydt deynes leydenhafftigenn Haubts Christi/ leydlich vnnd gedultig dich beweysenn." *Das wucher zu nemen vnd geben*, Fiijv. "Ain yeder Christ sol hunger/ durst/ marter/ tod/ hell vnd alles übel ee erleiden/ dann er Christum vnd seines worts verlaugne." *Haubtstuck vnd artickel* Aijv.

105 "Oder ist der todt nit ein grossere nott dan zeitlich armut vnd abganck? wer wil aber sagen/ das zuuermeyden den leiblichen todt/ on schaden der selen/ das wort gottes vnd bruderlich lieb gelassen mog werden?" *Das wucher zu nemen vnd geben*, Biijv.

religious and social. If there is a widespread refusal to pay the confession penny, Strauss suggests, the practice will die out; similarly, all must refuse to spend money on chrism and oil for baptism and on other "invented" rituals, and instead give this surplus to the poor. The community as a whole is responsible for implementing reform, and there is no appeal to the secular authorities in these early pamphlets; rather, this is the common man acting for himself. This "active" form of reformation displays more urgency than Luther's preference for patience in outward matters while the whole congregation is prepared for change. Luther had outlined an alternative definition of "brotherly love" in his criticism of the radical direction taken by the Wittenberg movement during his time spent in hiding at the Wartburg in 1521 and 1522; that is, he insisted that one must not offend one's neighbor by precipitately abandoning the old forms of worship, as this neighbor may not yet be convinced of the need for such changes.[106] Strauss too is concerned with avoiding "offence" in the name of brotherly love, but offense in this interpretation indicates the preservation of one's neighbor's conscience and soul by a refusal to facilitate the "murderous trade in usury."[107] In his second usury pamphlet, Strauss denounces the "evangelical windbags" who "everywhere in corners express and preach love with the tongue and in sweet words: one should only preach faith and love, as though anything else could be preached in evangelical teaching," claiming that they bring shame upon Christ's

---

[106] In the Invocavit sermons, preached upon his return to Wittenberg, Luther argues that when all are not equally strong in faith, one must place above all else that course of action that is beneficial to one's brother: "Alhie lieben fraindt můß nicht ain yederman thon/ was er recht hat sonder sehen was seinem brůder nutzlich vnd fürderlich ist . . . aber alle ding seind nicht fürderlich wen[n] [w]ir seynd nit alle gleych starck im glauben." *Acht Ser=mon. D. M. Luthers vo[n]// im geprediget zů Wittemberg inn der// fasten/ Darinn kurtzlich begryffen/ // von den Messen/ Bildtnussen/ // bayderlay gestalt des Sa=//craments/ von denn// speysen vnd haim//lichen beycht//.&c.* ([Augsburg, 1523)], Br–Bv. Luther was to revisit this theme in his pamphlet, *Against the Heavenly Prophets. Widder die hyme=//lischen propheten/ // von den bilden// vnd Sacrament &c.* (Wittenberg, [1525]).

[107] "Und dz aller furnemlichst yn dez/ dz die sele beruret/ dan einleibung bruderlicher liebe/ erstliche vnd beschlußlich/ vor ergernis vnd schaden des gewissens/ vnsers nechsten/ vns enthalten. Darumb Christus ergernis zuuermeiden/ so hohen fleiß ankerett. Wo will dan der mörderisch wucher handel bleyben? In dem auffs wenigst zwo selen ermordet werden/ des/ der den wucher nimpt vnd der den wucher gibt." *Das wucher zu nemen vnd geben*, Biijr–Biijv.

name, and insists that "faith and love cannot be fulfilled in words and on the tongue; the divine word must come to fruition in faith through love."[108] The mocking cry, "faith, faith, love, love," is reminiscent of Karlstadt's "weak, weak, sick, sick, not too fast, slowly, slowly" from his 1524 attack on Luther's policy of caution and moderation.[109] This preference for active reform is akin to that of Zwingli, for whom, it has been argued, "the relation of faith to outward action is causal and immediate."[110]

However, there is in this same work a shift in emphasis away from the individual or congregation as the agent of reform. Although the refusal to pay usury could possibly be seen as rebellious, the mode of behavior recommended by Strauss is (as discussed above) that of the martyr, who may remonstrate with his oppressors but offer no active resistance.[111] By 1524, the secular authorities are clearly identified as those who should make any legal change. They must be asked, in a humble and submissive manner, to turn the usurers away from their "ungodly undertaking" and onto more Christian paths.[112] This emphasis on the role of the authori-

---

[108] "Folgt vnnd schleusst sych hye das wir vns al/ billich Christlichs namens/ beschemen sollen/ vnd besonderlichen die gemoleten euangelisten/ die auff der zungen vnd yn sussen wortten die lieb furtragen vnd predigen vberal yn winckeln/ man soll nur den glauben vnd die lieb predigen/ als ob sunst etwas yn euangelischer leer/ anders geprediget kund werden. Ja man must den selben gnadiunckern sagen/ glawb glaub/ lieb/ lieb/ vnd blos yn wynd schlahen/ da kan der glaub/ vnd die lieb in worten/ vnd auff der zungen nit volkomen sein/ es mus das gotliche wort yn glauben durch die lieb zu wercken komen/ das befynd sich dan wol bey den selben euangelischen schwetzern." Ibid., Br–Bv.

[109] "schrybet jr mir/ ir wolt bey euch gemach hernach ziechen . . . vnd thüt nichts anders/ denn dz die gantze welt itzt thüt/ welche schreyhet. Schwachen schwachen/ krancken krancken/ nit zu schnell/ gemach gemach. . . ." Andreas Bodenstein von Karlstadt, *Ob man gemach // faren/ vnd des ergernüssen // der schwachen verschonen // soll/ in sachen so // gottis wil=//len an=//gehn. // Andres Carolstadt* ([Basel], 1524), Aijr.

[110] Wandel, *Always Among Us*, p. 69: "Zwingli envisioned a true Christian as active, expressing his faith externally, through social and civic engagement. Piety is experienced; it cannot be known through words or study."

[111] This is a similar approach to that recommended by Luther to the inhabitants of Albertine Saxony when faced with the confiscation of Lutheran books. *Uon welltlich=//er vberkeytt/ //wie weytt man// yhr gehorsam// schudig sey* [(Wittenberg, 1523)], Diiijv–Er.

[112] ". . . dz dan der frumen christen die beschwerden vnd anlygen seiner gewissene der selben seiner zeytlichen oberkait/ aller christlicher bescheydenheit entdecke/ mit vntertheniger bitt/ dz sye den wucherherrn auff ander christliche wege weyse/

ties, however, could be simply an attempt at pragmatism following the events in Eisenach during 1524. Strauss was dependent on the city council, who had appointed him to his position as preacher and with whose consent he introduced religious change. He was also tolerated by Duke John of Saxony and could not afford to be socially radical. However, it is also clear that Strauss is trying to shame the authorities (particularly John and his brother, the Saxon Elector Frederick) into action; he says that although some "pious territorial princes" have recognized the harm of the *Zins*, for the moment their hands are tied (here being careful to blame the usurers rather than the princes). Nevertheless, he hopes that they will rectify this.[113] Conduct towards the poor is depicted as a duty or the fulfillment of social responsibilities, echoing his earlier criticism of those princes who spend money on relics and neglect the common good. Their protection of the *Wucherherren* is not only against God's commandment; it is contrary to their own interests and to those of their poor subjects. Although the emphasis is on the "poor, common man" as the principal victim of usury, his property and livelihood under threat from the extortionate payments demanded by the usurers, princes, lords, and governments are also in debt to these "money-grubbing usury-sacks" (*Geltsuchtygen Wuchersecken*), both clerical and lay; their treasuries are, he says, "pawned and pledged [to] the merchant, the nobleman, also sometimes [to] priests, and fat monks," to the general ruin of "land and people."[114] Strauss's use of the terms *Wucherherr* and *Zinsjunker* as noted above could be seen as inflammatory; however, this choice of language is not particularly revolutionary in itself, *Zinsjunker* having already been used by Luther.[115] Furthermore, the *Wucherherr* is presented as a usurper

---

vnd von eim sollichen vngothafften furnemen abwenden." *Das wucher zu nemen vnd geben,* Gv. This is closer to Luther's 1520 appeal to the nobility, in *To the Christian Nobility of the German Nation* (as note 12, above).

[113] "Vnd das will ich besunderlich geleert vnnd geradten haben/ vmb etlicher frummer Landsfursten willen/ die aus dem wort Gottes ytzundert/ Got hab lob/ den schaden des verdamlichen zinss erkennen/ vnd doch so ylends nit konnen abstellen . . . Wiewol die mittel/ so dem wort Gottes krefftlichenn geglawbt vnnd vertrawet wirt/ mogen yn kurtzer zeit sych geben das eyn yder frummer Christlicher Furst vnd Landßherr seyn landt vnd leut von der gleichen beschwerd erlosen vnd befreyen mag." *Das wucher zu nemen vnd geben,* Gijv.

[114] Ibid., Eijr.

[115] The term appears in Luther's "long sermon" on usury: "Drumb ist nit wunder/ das die zinß iunckern ßo schwind fur andern leuten reych werden," *Eyn Sermon*

of the powers of the temporal authorities; in a reversal of the natural order, the princes are in hock to their subjects and servants.[116] In this light, Strauss's proposals can be seen as socially conservative, or, from the perspective of the secular powers, restorative.

Strauss also hints that rebellion will be prevented if justice prevails, warning at one point that inequality will lead to unrest and criticism of the secular authorities. Self-interest, he maintains, is at the root of rebellion. The princes and lords must therefore conduct their business in a Christian manner, remembering that all are brothers, rather than deal with selfish people, as is presently the case.[117] Nevertheless, there is to be no violent action while waiting for this change of heart to take place. Usury will be uprooted through "faith and brotherly love."[118] Strauss recognizes, however, that for the moment "true Christians" who value God more than wealth are few in number.[119] Presumably, though, if the public were to refuse the option of borrowing money at interest, the usurer could not continue in his trade.

It could be argued that Strauss's usury works (particularly the second) are in fact, despite their notoriety, *less* radical than his other works from this period, which suggest a community taking matters into its own hands, in both the religious and the economic spheres. Despite the apparently provocative language, a fear of *Schwärmerei* or radicalism is allayed in the second usury work, although this could simply be due to a desire

---

von dem Wucher (Wittenberg, 1520), dr.

[116] "Vnd also haben die herren den tittel/ vnd yhre knecht vnd vnterthanen den nutze." *Das wucher zu nemen vnd geben,* Eijr.

[117] "Es ist auch fast not/ das alle Christenlichen Fursten vnd Herrn yhre sach mit Christo/ vnd nicht mit aigennutzigen lewten tractirn dan die auffrur/ die der aigennutz furwendet yst leichtlich fur zu komen. So man eynem yeden sein recht christenlich vnd gotlich last widerfaren/ auch die arme gemein rot/ wider Got vnnd die naturlich billigkait nit beschweret/ man muste gedencken yn christenlicher liebe das wir alle gebruder synd/ vnd darumben kainer auff den andern so verachtlich vnnd tyrannisch solte dryngen/ vnd yhm got lassen sein/ als ob yhm sein eben Christen mensch vnter den fussen gewachßen were." Ibid., Fijv.

[118] "Aber wir wollen den teuffel mit Gottes wort anlauffen. So muß er vns weichen/ vnd wirt der kauff ym glauben vnd bruderlicher lieb verschwinden." Ibid., Cijr.

[119] ". . . die warhafftygen kynder Gottes/ welchenn mehr an Gott/ vnnd seynem wortt gelegen yst/ dann an allen schetzenn vnnd reychtumben dieser wellt/ Der tzall leyder kleynn ist." Ibid., Dv.

to avoid alienating the most influential section of his audience. Strauss sought to persuade the authorities that they must not stand in the way of the establishment of the true brotherhood, not only in the interests of peace, stability, and justice but because this is their Christian duty, the neglect of which will endanger their souls.

It is clear from his writings that Strauss believed an overall reform of society was necessary, as there could be no true religious reformation without reforming the secular (or in this case, economic) sphere. The true brotherhood, whether as a result of individual or collective action on the part of the "common man" or, as implied in the second usury work, the influence of the authorities, will be established sooner rather than later, despite Strauss's pessimistic estimate as to the number of true Christians. In his insistence that the commandment of brotherly love should apply to the secular world and in feeling himself obliged to implement this, Strauss was demonstrating a radical departure from Luther's separation of two kingdoms, that of God and that of men. Luther had no plans for a Christian society, because of the scarcity of true Christians and because "it would make God's free grace into social legislation."[120] Strauss, on the other hand, could be seen as an optimist regarding both the possibility of an imminent conversion and the establishment of such a society. And it is this necessity for urgent, wide-ranging, even "total" reformation that accounts for the presence of these "material" subjects in Strauss's pamphlets. When brotherly love is ignored, the souls of the faithful are damned through the sins of usury and self-interest. Even assuming that most of Strauss's audience would have adopted those elements that suited them, while not taking this idealized brotherhood beyond the point where it began to cause them serious financial inconvenience, this cannot be seen as a mere ploy on Strauss's part to gain support for his religious reforms. This thorough reformation is not intended to be adopted or rejected as an ideal by the individual reader or listener, depending on

---

[120] Lindberg, *Beyond Charity*, p. 116. Lindberg argues that Luther regarded this type of wholesale reformation as "a confusion of social ethics and theology; in short, a reintroduction of the Christian legalism [he] opposed in the medieval Church (116)." Elsewhere, Lindberg has used the phrase "a this-worldly service to one's neighbor" to describe Luther's recommended approach to altruism. Lindberg, "Luther's Struggle with Social-ethical Issues," in *The Cambridge Companion to Martin Luther*, ed. Donald K. McKim (Cambridge, 2003), pp. 165–78, 174.

his or her economic standing; rather, it is a necessity toward which all must actively work.

In most of his pre-1525 writings, Strauss repeatedly refers to the monetary costs of theological errors and "human, invented teachings and practices." In this he is not unusual, and, like many evangelicals, he denounces the misuse of money that should otherwise be given to the indigent. However, in attempting to identify Strauss's "poor," a much broader picture emerges. This term could encompass anyone who might feel themselves financially exploited, and these discontented individuals are many and diverse: the laity, whose desire for salvation is manipu-lated by a clergy intent on swallowing their property; the particularly needy, whose alms are going to the same source; the town-dweller or peasant, who must risk his inheritance as a pledge and pay unjust inter-est on borrowed money; the country at large, whose rulers are siphoning their resources into relics and interest payments; and the rulers who are themselves at the mercy of the clergy and the usurers. Few, apart perhaps from the nobility, could be sure that they themselves would never be the "neighbor in need." In contrast to the growing trend for distinguishing between strictly defined categories of deserving and undeserving poor, it does appear that Strauss allows the responsibility for determining the object of this assistance to remain with the individual, specifying only the "false poor" of the nonreformed clergy as ineligible recipients.

Strauss's reflections on poverty appear here and there (often seem-ingly at random) within discussions of other matters, and his preoccupa-tion with the material, or rather with the rejection of the material, cannot by any means be said to form a coherent and complete philosophy on the subject. Given this, however, it is possible to isolate some basic principles, many of which are held in common with a variety of other figures, among them his contemporaries in the evangelical movement. Among those ele-ments that can be said to belong to the "mainstream" are his rejection of the traditional concept of charity as a good work that can be traded for a heavenly reward; the themes of self-interest and brotherly love also appear in the works of the major figures of the Reformation. Again, the anticlericalism that appears in Strauss's pamphlets is typical of the period, although his emphasis on the degree to which the clergy and the ceremonies and practices of the Church have impoverished the common man is unusually pronounced. In both his employment of vehemently anticlerical rhetoric and his insistence on brotherly love, Strauss holds out the prospect of a society where "natural fairness" is restored, and, presumably, unjust poverty is no longer. His rejection of wealth in general could be said to place him at the more radical end of the evangelical spectrum, his community of goods in particular bringing him into proximity with the Anabaptists. It must be noted, however, that, unlike the rebellious peasant movement, these works contain no suggestions that the reformed society may be established by violent means. On the other hand, his new society with its ascetic, almost subsistence-level economy could simply represent a return to the apostolic ideal, replacing the medieval fraternal mendicancy that in Strauss's eyes has become corrupted by greed and indolence. Strauss's approach and ideas are also reflected in the writings of minor and nonclerical pamphleteers, such as Lindenmaier and Marschalck. All of this indicates Strauss's links to the various currents present in the public conversation contained in the flurry of pamphlets in the 1520s, while also demonstrating his relative independence and underlining the *Wildwuchs* character of the early Reformation.

To what extent can the presence of such themes be attributed to their usefulness in gaining support for the Reformation? An awareness of their possible propaganda value is evident in their presentation. Along with the obvious material benefits, as outlined above, the traditional expectation that charity on earth would be rewarded in heaven is not wholly abandoned. Strauss rejects works-righteousness to the extent of denying any guarantee of salvation in return for charity, but it is made clear that selfishness entails alienation from God and therefore damnation. The arguments found in these pamphlets would, therefore, have been attractive to both receivers and givers, those (possibly interchangeable) groups who either saw themselves as benefactors of the destitute or who sought to lift themselves out of poverty, whether through charity, the redistribution of wealth from the undeserving to the deserving, or the abolition of the unjust practice of usury. This approach could have enabled Strauss to link his ecclesiastical reforms to the improvement of the station of the common man to some extent. However, an examination of the nature of his treatment of these issues reveals that their propagandistic value is not exploited to its full potential. The pamphlets contain a mixture of sympathy and admonition, Strauss never courting his audience unreservedly. The emphasis is on suffering rather than on comfort, on giving (and indeed sacrificing) rather than on receiving. Even the poor have responsibilities toward one another. No one should possess more than is necessary for his basic upkeep; there is to be no spare money to be squandered in fleshly pleasures. Despite the remnants of medieval soteriology and other apparent advantages, the adoption of Strauss's recommendations regarding wealth and poverty cannot be seen as an entirely attractive option.

Nonetheless, allowing for the possibility of selective interpretation (that is, the reader identifying himself as a victim, having no money to spare although not actually starving, yet with the potential to be generous should he find himself in a better financial position), their appeal cannot be ignored, and it must be asked whether the presence and frequency of socioeconomic references can be attributed to a deliberate strategy of persuasion. A preacher working for religious change would have been tempted to use all possible arguments and evidence to bolster his attack on the old, "false" rituals and beliefs. However, Strauss is concerned not only with those practices that play the double role of perpetuating false teaching while simultaneously emptying the pockets of the blindly faithful, but with a much more comprehensive type of reform. Although an effective means of gaining followers, the identification of injustice and of a unifying enemy, whether the nonreformed clergy or the "money-seeking" usurers, does not suffice for Strauss. He cannot separate the reform of the church from the reform of society; his overriding concern is obedience to the message of love found in the gospels, thereby ensuring the welfare of the soul. Thus, the creation of a society no longer fixated on material wealth, where brotherly love replaces self-interest, is both necessary and imminent. Using one's surplus wealth to help the poor rather than to fill the purses of the monks and the usurers or one's own belly is, for Strauss, an intrinsic part of the religious reformation; if God's law is to be followed, neighborly generosity must be universally practiced. This is indeed a form of propaganda, but one that goes beyond a purely opportunistic appeal to a worldly instinct for self-preservation; it is unlikely that Strauss would have been unaware of the advantages of the latter, but they would not have been his sole, or even his principal, concern.

Regarding Strauss's motives, it must be stressed that although Strauss despaired of the reluctance of his public to practice brotherly love, neither was "altruism" in and of itself his primary concern. Poverty and injustice were to be suffered until a deep-seated change occurred within each individual Christian. It could of course be argued that his proposals for the new brotherhood are deliberately ill-defined for fear of alienating the wealthy laity who may have stood to lose by such an arrangement, but in the early pamphlets at least there is no evidence of a reluctance to offend the powerful; the active role of the authorities in this process is emphasized only in his second usury work, a modification probably made on Luther's insistence. The most pernicious aspect of the unreformed society is not the suffering of the poor, but the selfishness of the common man. This is not to say that Strauss had no sympathy for the poor; the contrary is evident in his angry and heart-rending descriptions of the neglected and the miserable. However, the principal goal is not social justice for its own sake, but the elimination of self-interest, which is just as harmful as the ungodly practices.

It is tempting to speculate on what may have happened had Strauss retained the good will of his territorial lords and remained in Eisenach; to attempt to extrapolate from these pamphlets the way in which he might have influenced any program of poor relief eventually drawn up by the council and to assess this in the broader context of early modern social reforms. However, as has been mentioned, the single practical measure proposed by Strauss relating to the distribution of aid to the poor is that regarding the money made available from the confiscated profits of the usurers. It is plausible that the lack of such specific suggestions and even the absence of an evangelical Eisenach alms statute during his time there can be explained not by the unfortunate consequences of the Peasant's War for Strauss's reforming career, but by something more fundamental to the nature of his reform. Because of the individual character of Strauss's complete reformation, he would not have seen such measures as necessary. Poverty will be countered by the willingness to live according to the commandment of brotherly love, the latter stemming from a change of heart within the individual, and one cannot legislate for this.[121] Rather, it must be achieved through persuasion and conversion, and this is the purpose of his pamphlets and sermons. This concept could be seen as a reversal of that of Luther regarding the reform of church and that of society, for whom the people need to be persuaded (gradually) to give up their old religious practices; on the other hand, the secular authorities

---

[121] Quite apart from any issues regarding the necessity of obedience to the temporal authorities, this alone would explain the absence of any consideration of rebellion; just as brotherly love cannot be enforced from above, neither can it be enforced from below.

must legislate for poor relief, as a truly Christian society of voluntary love and charity will never exist. Individual reform and voluntary brotherly love are indispensable for Strauss because of his interpretation of the link between compassion and salvation.

Whatever Strauss's intentions regarding practical socioeconomic reforms and the desirability of "natural fairness" for reasons of compassion, the attention of his audience is always drawn back to the matter of salvation and "soul-murdering," and listeners are warned that a Christian society cannot coexist with self-interest. The people themselves will turn away from false practices and self-interest once they have understood the word of God; if they do not do this, they reject God and his grace and therefore jeopardize their own salvation. In the resounding condemnation with which he concludes his comparison of the one, true brotherhood and the existing culture of materialism as practiced in the confraternities, Strauss describes the dreadful consequences for those who selfishly ignore the New Testament instruction to help the poor—the motive at the center of his campaign of persuasion and at the same time the strongest argument he possesses:

> Go away, ye damned, into the eternal fire, as I have been hungry and you have not fed me etc. and that which you have not done for the littlest of mine, you also have not done for me. Ah God, what a great vice, and how entirely against God it is to lay gold and silver on stone and wood, and to abandon in poverty our fellow Christian, who is created according to God's image, and bought with [the] death and spilt blood of the son of God.[122]

---

[122] *Ein kurtz christenlich vntherricht*, Aiijv. The first sentence here is based on Matthew 25:40ff.

"The Double Variacioun of Wordly Blisse and Transmutacioun": Shakespeare's Return to Ovid in Troilus and Cressida

Bradley Greenburg
Northeastern Illinois University

> It is the lesser blot, modesty finds,
> Women to change their shapes than men their minds.[1]
> —William Shakespeare

THE TRADITION OF Cressida's faithlessness that Shakespeare inherits is a phenomenon of the Middle Ages that reaches Chaucer, pauses, then gains momentum once again through the sixteenth century.[2] In April of 1599, the Admiral's Men performed Thomas Dekker and Henry

---

The author would like to thank Jonathan Gil Harris, Heather James, and Lynn Enterline for their reading and suggestions regarding previous versions of this essay.

[1] *Two Gentlemen of Verona*, 5.4.106–7. Quotations from Shakespeare come from *The Norton Shakespeare*, ed. Stephen Greenblatt, Walter Cohen, Jean E. Howard, and Katharine Eisaman Maus (New York, 1997).

[2] See Gretchen Mieszkowski, *The Reputation of Criseyde: 1155-1500*, Transactions of the Connecticut Academy of Arts and Sciences, 3 (New Haven, 1971). This essay demonstrates Chaucer's sympathetic treatment of Cressida despite the tradition he inherited, a tradition that would renew itself in the versions that followed.

Chettle's *Troilus and Cressida*.[3] A fragment of this play survives, but otherwise little is known about it. We do not know, for instance, whether Cressida behaved treacherously, professing her love while going willingly and gladly to a people foreign to her to embrace immediately a new lover. Nor do we know the extent of Troilus's role as a member of the Trojan council of war, though we know from the fragment that there was such a council. Did he advocate Helen's return or stand fast by his brother Paris? We are also left to wonder about Troilus's reaction to the exchange of Antenor for Cressida, as well as how he behaved when his beloved had gone over to the other camp.[4] The surviving fragment does tell us that late in the action Cressida "with beggars" encounters Troilus. In this respect Dekker and Chettle follow Robert Henryson's *The Testament of Cresseid*, a version of the story published in 1532.[5] As David Bevington summarizes Henryson's narrative:

> Cresseid is deserted by a bored Diomed, lives reputedly for a time "in the courte as commune," returns to her father, dreams that she is to be punished by Venus and the other gods for her infidelity by contracting leprosy, awakens to find that she is indeed diseased, and is placed by her father (with her consent) in a "spittaill house," where she becomes a begging leper. In this pitiful plight she encounters Troilus, who, not recognizing her but somehow stirred by remembrances of his lost love, gives her alms. She dies, having sent her ruby ring to Troilus, who mournfully erects a monument in her memory.[6]

---

[3] For a list of sources as well as an account of versions of *Troilus and Cressida* in the latter part of the sixteenth century, see David Bevington's essay on sources in the introduction to his Arden Edition (Walton-on-Thames, 1998), pp. 375–97.

[4] See Geoffrey Bullough, "The Lost *Troilus and Cressida*," *Essays and Studies*, n.s. 17 (1964), 24–40; John S. P. Tatlock, "The Siege of Troy in Elizabethan Literature, Especially in Shakespeare and Heywood," *PMLA* 30 (1915), 673–770; W. W. Greg, ed., *Dramatic Documents from the Elizabethan Playhouses: Stage Plots; Actors' Parts; Prompt Books*, 2 vols. (Oxford, 1931); *Troilus and Cressida*, A New Variorum Edition, ed., Harold Hillebrand, supplemental ed. T. W. Baldwin (Philadelphia, 1953).

[5] *The Poems of Robert Henryson*, ed. Denton Fox (Oxford, 1981), pp. 111–31. Originally published in Thynne's edition of Chaucer in 1532, separately published in Edinburgh in 1593. See Bullough, ed., *Narrative and Dramatic Sources of Shakespeare*, 8 vols. (1957–75), 6:215–19.

[6] Bevington, pp. 392–93. Bevington quotes the 1593 edition of Henryson's poem.

Shakespeare's Cressida does not meet with such an abject fate. Nor would we expect him to follow such a plot drenched in neochivalry. However, the presence of Henryson in a play that precedes Shakespeare's by only a year or two and that is mounted by a rival group of players suggests that the type-casting of Cressida as a faithless wretch who comes to a bad end (while suffering Troilus plods faithfully forward) is alive and well.

This consistently derogatory characterization of a woman, raising a literary character to the status of an icon for feminine misbehavior, is an irresistible target for Shakespeare.[7] *Troilus and Cressida* critiques a strain of literary transmission that is virulently uncritical of the way it treats its characters as *already having* their character stamped upon them. This "notorious identity," in Linda Charnes's phrase, provokes a response that addresses the context in which such notoriety begins its literary-historical journey.[8] For a dramatist experienced in writing history plays, Shakespeare had developed a sophisticated method of taking historical figures with one reputation and either exploiting or altering it. Perhaps the rivalry gave him an opportunity to take stock *literary* figures and transform them. How, then, does *Troilus and Cressida* offer a transformation of Cressida, that stock figure for faithlessness?[9] It reconfigures the story of how Cressida got her reputation by attending to Troilus's actions (and calling them culpable) while also portraying Cressida's faithlessness as an Ovidian metamorphosis.

For Mihoko Suzuki, "Cressida as outsider is the only character who shares Shakespeare's perspective in offering an alternative mode of sense-making; but as woman, she is judged and categorized by the male warriors who control the language of love, politics, history, and literary tradition, and by the majority of male critics who have controlled the language of

---

[7] As detailed in Gayle Greene's "Shakespeare's Cressida: 'A Kind of Self,'" in *The Woman's Part: Feminist Criticism of Shakespeare*, ed. Carolyn Lenz, Gayle Greene, Carol Neely (Urbana, 1980), pp. 133–49.

[8] Linda Charnes, *Notorious Identity: Materializing the Subject in Shakespeare* (Cambridge, Mass., 1993).

[9] If we consider the rivalry between the Admiral's Men and Shakespeare's company, not to mention that between Shakespeare and Chapman, translator of Homer's *Iliad* (1598) and supposed "rival poet" of the Sonnets, then there is ample reason to suggest that *Troilus and Cressida* is an aggressive attempt to transform these grave literary figures into the conniving, duplicitous, overweening, and generally un-heroic characters that he makes them out to be.

literary criticism."[10] "As woman," Cressida suffers a fate far in excess of her actions as Shakespeare presents them, and it is the world of male ideology—in the play world as well as the literary-historical world—that has put her there. But what I want to explore here is this very "perspective" Suzuki alludes to rather casually, as though the drama were a place that just happens to offer a subtext in which Cressida might be seen to signify something other than the stigmatized object literary history came to characterize her as. The play works hard to offer a number of perspectives, which Suzuki rightly points out are typically those of critics who have weighed in on the side of, for example, Ulysses and "degree" (Tillyard) and of Troilus as the victim who holds fast to "truth."[11] The perspective in which Cressida is held to account by the system of male honor, by making her into its lamented, persecutory weakness, is forced open in the play through a careful rendering of the way in which we encounter a character who has come to signify one thing while demonstrating that she has done something quite different. The question is how Shakespeare's deployment of an array of source materials in the literary space of *Troilus and Cressida*, as moment of origin reinscribed in its reiteration, demonstrates Cressida becoming the signifier for "faithlessness" while at the same time offering a perspective that calls such a signifying system to account. This essay is an effort to demonstrate that the rehabilitation of Cressida in this play employs an Ovidian conceptual strategy that confronts its audience with a context that disrupts the literary historical progression of Cressida as a signifier for "faithlessness."

As pitiful as Cresseid's end is in Henryson's poem, we might say that at least she displays character development. Her transformation into a leper has all of the signs of an Ovidian metamorphosis: she dreams that she is to be punished by Venus and the other gods for her infidelity by contracting leprosy. Apparently, Henryson is not interested in having a Cresseid who changes form so radically that she cannot subsequently

---

[10] Mihoko Suzuki, "'Truth Tired with Iteration': Myth and Fiction in Shakespeare's *Troilus and Cressida*," *Philological Quarterly* 66, no. 2 (1987), 167.

[11] Suzuki, "'Truth Tired,'" p. 172, n 15. For Tillyard's use of Ulysses' "degree" speech, see *The Elizabethan World Picture* (London, 1943), chapters 2 and 7. In recent years, many critics have devastatingly criticized Tillyard for his thesis. See in particular Graham Holderness, *Shakespeare: The Histories* (New York, 1999); and Hugh Grady, *The Modernist Shakespeare: Critical Texts in a Material World* (Oxford, 1991).

encounter Troilus, yet he does alter her so that she is diseased or scarred beyond recognition. That Cresseid dies with neither recognition nor mercy, in what otherwise seems like the outline of a Christian allegory, shows the faithfulness of writers hewing to her image of abjection as a sinner who deserves her punishment. Troilus, here as elsewhere, soldiers on faithfully, fighting for his honor and in Spenserian fashion carrying his hurt with him like a wound that will not heal. The victimization conforms to the tradition of these characters as portrayed though literary history, excepting Chaucer's poem, where Criseyde is treated much more sympathetically. The metamorphosis that Henryson performs with his Cresseid, while Ovidian, since she takes on the quality her author thinks she deserves, is not what Shakespeare chooses to do in his version. He not only refuses to follow his sources and rival plays but deploys an Ovidian transformation in a more subtle and effectively dramatic manner.[12]

My title comes from John Lydgate's *Troy Book*, written between the years 1412 and 1420, another telling of the Troy story that narrates the failed relationship of Troilus and Cressida.[13] This is mostly a translation of Guido delle Colonne's *Historia destructionis Troiae* (written in Latin around 1287), in which Lydgate swerves from Guido's misogynist characterization of Cressida to follow the spirit of Chaucer's far more sympathetic reading of her.[14] But even as Lydgate repudiates the idea that women are fundamentally duplicitous, as Guido tries to show by Cressida's example, he nonetheless repeats at length the reasons that women

---

[12] See the important essay on Cressida and textuality by Carol Cook: "Unbodied Figures of Desire," *Theater Journal* 38 (1986), 34–52. See also Elizabeth Freund, "'Ariachne's Broken Woof': The Rhetoric of Citation in *Troilus and Cressida*," in *Shakespeare and the Question of Theory*, ed. Patricia Parker and Geoffrey Hartman, (New York, 1985), pp. 19–36; Norman Rabkin, "*Troilus and Cressida*: The Uses of the Double Plot," *Shakespeare Studies* 1 (1969), 265–82; and Janet Adelman, "'This Is and Is Not Cressid': The Characterization of Cressida," in *The (M)other Tongue*, ed. Shirley Nelson Garner, Claire Kahane, and Madelon Sprengnether (Ithaca, 1985), pp. 119–41.

[13] Henry Bergen, ed., *Early English Text Society* (London, 1906–35). Title taken from Book 3, lines 4227–28, where I read "wordly" for "worldly," following *Troy Book: Selections*, ed. Robert Edwards (Kalamazoo, 1998).

[14] Lydgate's "For levere she had chaunge and variaunce/Were founde in hir thanne lak of pité" repeats Chaucer's "Ne nevere mo ne lakked hire pite;/Tendreherted, slydynge of corage." *Troy Book: Selections*, Book 4, lines 2172–73; *Troilus and Crisyde* 5.824–25; Larry D. Benson, ed., *The Riverside Chaucer* (Boston, 1987).

might be so. He does this uncritically, failing to point out what Shake-speare insists upon: that the men who determine Cressida's fate, through their code of honor, bear the responsibility for her forced choice. It is also interesting to note the way that Lydgate expressly distances himself from a poetic method that has any relation to Ovid.[15] Lydgate accuses Ovid of using poetry to clothe falsehood with truth and thereby ensnare his read-ers into believing what is not true (this is opposed to the supposed first-hand account of Dares and Dictys, which stands in as "history"):

> Ovide also poetycally hath closyd
> Falshede with trouthe, that maketh men ennosed
> To whiche parte that thei schal hem holde;
> His mysty speche so hard is to unfolde
> That it entriketh rederis that it se.[16]

One wonders how, exactly, poetry that is so difficult can trick someone into taking it as truth. Lydgate has little interest in and tries hard to dis-tance himself from Ovid's metamorphic style. *Troilus and Cressida* is a play concerned with combating this element of the literary tradition that represses and effaces Ovid's style and subject matter.

Shakespeare's sources for *Troilus and Cressida* include Chaucer, the *Iliad* by way of Golding's translation with perhaps George Sandys's commentary, Caxton and Lydgate, and finally, Ovid. While all of these sources are more or less necessary for the cast of characters, their rela-tions, the setting, and the narrative of the war and its background, it is Ovid who is the greatest variable. That is to say, we can find details of the building of the walls of Troy and of Laomedon's cheating of Apollo and Poseidon in both Caxton and in Ovid's *Metamorphoses*, but there is a fundamental conceptual difference. Ovid's retelling of mythical stories has as its dynamic principle the metamorphosis of humans into things of nature: flowers, trees, water, stones, constellations, sounds, animals, and so on. The list is one that multiplies to populate the sensible world with creatures and things with a story behind them, an origin in desire or transgression or the escape from both. Whatever else about Ovid's

---

[15] A prime example of what Sidney discusses in his comparison between poetry and history in his *Defense of Poesy* (1595). In *Sir Philip Sidney: Selected Prose and Poetry*, ed. Robert Kimbrough (Madison, 1983).

[16] *Troy Book*, Prologue ll. 299–303.

poetry attracted Shakespeare, it is the drama of transformation that he uses to figure forth a change in character that results from a conflict in which power is dangerously unbalanced.[17]

For example, when the pedantic Holofernes in *Love's Labour's Lost* comments on Berowne's sonnet to Rosaline, he finds the "golden cadence of poesy" to be missing: "Ovidius Naso was the man. And why indeed 'Naso' but for smelling out the odoriferous flowers of fancy, the jerks of invention? *Imitari* is nothing. So doth the hound his master, the ape his keeper, the tired horse his rider" (4.2.115–18). Shakespeare's "jerks of invention" do not involve either a slavish copying of "golden cadence" or an imitation that relies, like Henryson's, upon an actual physical transformation. Cressida does not turn into an image of her sin, neither physically nor in the way in which she had been transformed in previous versions of the story, her name becoming a signifier for "faithless." Indeed, we come away from Shakespeare's play wondering whether Cressida has "sinned" at all, challenged to assign blame and victimhood to characters in unexpected ways. We are invited to reassign culpability through an opening of perspective that shuns the univocal commonplace rendering of a woman as fixed by her circumstance. The context in which Cressida is produced by the men who observe her in Act 5 not only calls into question her culpability but, more importantly, the mechanism of complicity by which such reification takes place.

This redistributing of complicities also brings us to another important facet of Ovid's work that Shakespeare follows, beginning with his use of Ovid's *Fasti* in writing *The Rape of Lucrece*.[18] In this poem, Shakespeare is concerned with what Jonathan Bate calls "the action of language, not a language of action," and this action consists primarily of the interior monologue and psychological shading of a female character whose

---

[17] Discussions of Ovid's importance to writers of the Elizabethan period, ranging from his place in the classroom to popular source of plot and interpreter of previously existing literary characters, include Raphael Lyne, *Ovid's Changing Worlds: English Metamorphoses, 1567–1632* (Oxford, 2001); Lynn Enterline, *The Rhetoric of the Body from Ovid to Shakespeare* (Cambridge, 2000); A. B. Taylor, ed., *Shakespeare's Ovid: The Metamorphoses in the Plays and Poems* (Cambridge, 2000); and Leonard Barkan, *The Gods Made Flesh: Metamorphosis and the Pursuit of Paganism* (New Haven, 1986).

[18] The phrase at the opening of the sentence is Harry Berger, Jr.'s, borrowed from the subtitle to his book *Making Trifles of Terrors: Redistributing Complicities in Shakespeare* (Stanford, 1997).

suffering results from a masculine code of honor.[19] Like Chaucer before him, Shakespeare attends closely to Cressida's material and psychological condition as the plots that surround her engineer her fate. Thus, when we come to the crucial scene in 5.2, in which Troilus sees Cressida with Diomed, Shakespeare presents a multidimensional tableau allowing us to view the various layers of auditing and spectating that reveal what Troilus calls "bifold authority." The suggestion of bifold authority, authority turned in on itself, forced to confront its unacknowledged assumptions, opens a new perspective. From this conceptual vantage point, the dramatization of the undoing of textual precedence that has ensconced a view of woman as faithless can take place. A woman like Cressida, says Shakespeare, is devalued for a supposedly individual reason or flaw, without taking into account the all-important context that has brought her to such an impasse. What is it that has been displaced or projected onto her? When Troilus warns not to "square the general sex by Cressid's rule" (5.2.132–33), he speaks to the audience from a place that can scarcely be taken in good faith, since he is implicated in bringing about his (and her) predicament. Nor is it possible, obviously, for Troilus to know that Cressida is to become an icon for faithlessness. As revisionist literary history, the play here and elsewhere goes out of its way to disrupt the proleptic knowledge it possesses about Cressida's fate. As Linda Charnes points out, though the characters of this play are "known," they continually seek to secure their own and others' identities.[20] In Cressida's case such a struggle for security results in not only the disruption of any future labeling of her as faithless, but in a careful consideration of the context within which such iconic fixations take place. Shakespeare's revision is Ovidian in its attaching to the frozen name of Cressida a beating, suffering, victimized heart, so that the contradictions of her situation disrupt literary tradition. It is as though Shakespeare were applying Heraclitus's famous dictum, "Character is fate,"[21] to this well worn story to illustrate just how inextricable these are and how difficult to separate. The differential move of this play is to insist that while character might not be enough to alter fate, the dramatic context can reveal the motivations that result in a woman such as Cressida or Lavinia becoming a "changing piece."

---

[19] Jonathan Bate, *Shakespeare and Ovid* (Oxford, 1993), p. 71.

[20] Charnes, *Notorious Identity*, pp. 70–71.

[21] Translating *ethos anthropoi daimon*.

A consideration of events leading to 5.2 will clarify this claim. Troilus and Cressida have been in the throes of desire from the outset. The play opens with Troilus wondering why he should do battle when an even greater battle rages inside him. The conflict between honor and love—or faith, in its more social configuration—begins here. These are the two registers in contention, and they are firmly gendered throughout the play: the men fight and make policy decisions based on honor and the promise of fame, where action and value depend entirely upon what others think. Troilus's "What's aught but as 'tis valued?" summarizes this line of thought.[22] The women in the play are concerned with family and love, and seem never to care for the reasons the men give for their chivalrous acts. They do not participate in the economy of honor, whose circulation is entirely masculine and based on making a name for oneself.[23] In this utterly masculine, martial world, names come to stand for abstract qualities affixed to the characters despite actions to the contrary. That a woman bears the worst of it is perhaps no surprise, since she is playing the weaker language game. Love and faith cannot compete with honor in a mythmaking world where value is based on use, on the extent to which something either can be directly exchanged or can enter the signifying chain as a commodity (daughters, desirable women, shiny suits of armor,

---

[22] Heather James writes: "Within the privileged tradition of the translation of empire, Shakespeare's contaminations of textual authorities collectively raise the question central to that most disruptive play, *Troilus and Cressida*: 'what's aught but as 'tis valued?' This question, posed by Troilus and seconded by Hector, the 'ethical Trojan,' assaults the values of central authority that Ulysses champions in his speech on degree. To compose plays that raise this question structurally rather than thematically both circumvents the censor and devastates the idea of transmissible value" (*Shakespeare's Troy: Drama, Politics, and the Translation of Empire*, [Cambridge, 1997], p. 33). Such "contaminations" are felt most acutely in the context of "honor" in the play, extending, I argue, to subvert the textual authority of Cressida's reputation of faithlessness as an internal quality. Instead of following this thematic conceit, the play overturns such an essentializing of Cressida on *precisely* structural grounds: Cressida's fate is an effect of causes stemming not from her *nature* but from the political *arts* of male Trojan policy.

[23] Suzuki points out that "from Cressida's perspective, the 'love plot' is yet another 'war plot'" (157). It is indeed, but again it is necessary to keep track of the way in which the play suggests all along that there is only one game, one discursive economy, one space in which a character can inhabit the signifying chain, and it is masculine. See Dympna Callahan, *Shakespeare without Women: Representing Gender and Race on the Renaissance Stage* (London, 2000).

symbolic favors). Love, on the other hand, in its individual, subjective state, is left vulnerable, forced to go begging.

Cressida is certainly aware of this difference and refers to it when she regrets having confessed her love to Troilus. As she says:

> If I confess much, you will play the tyrant.
> I love you now, but till now not so much
> But I might master it. In faith, I lie:
> My thoughts were like unbridled children, grown
> Too headstrong for their mother. See, we fools!
> Why have I blabbed? Who shall be true to us,
> When we are so unsecret to ourselves? (3.2.108–14)

In response, Troilus speaks abstractly about love and beauty, employing the language of chivalry to insist upon his truth and simplicity, setting himself up as a model for "true swains" to approve themselves. Shakespeare's Troilus postures in this most intimate of exchanges as a thoroughly literary character, available for citation as the paragon of truth and faith before a test or hazard—much less a relationship—has even appeared.[24] There is a fundamental difference here in the power relations between the lovers, which Cressida has all along been emphasizing while Troilus has remained content to fall back on the social construction of his place in the order of honorable men. Troilus has the support of the

---

[24] If, as Suzuki's title reminds us, truth—according to Troilus—is "tired with iteration," the play's weariness of such repetition rebounds directly onto the utterer. It is Troilus who has worn this mantle for too long, and his endless attempts to keep it fresh are no match for the stale circumstances in which he tries to do so in the action of the play. There are also moments in the play when Troilus's iteration is itself tiring, suggesting in its periphrastic verbosity a straining that indicates a speaker belaboring a subject about which he is claiming nonchalance. At the end of 3.2, for example, Troilus says: "Few words to fair faith. Troilus shall be such to Cressid as what envy can say worst shall be a mock for his truth, and what truth can speak truest not truer than Troilus" (3.2.92–94). As elsewhere, the play exhibits Troilus speaking his name and the signifiers that are meant to embroider it (here various forms of the word "truth") while, in the clause containing Cressida's name, the words pile up— envy, worst, mock—to signify something more negative. The dissonance set up here is again between behavior, or deeds, and stated intent. Troilus exhibits the confidence of one whose reputation in literary history is assured, while Cressida can only lament her fate in a situation that is not subject to her control. The iterary becomes the literary.

community; no matter what happens, he gains reward for his suffering, while Cressida is alone with her love, and once parted from its object she is isolated and ripe for scapegoating. This victimization does not arise from Cressida's inability to think for herself or to judge the situation correctly. At its manifest level, the play follows the preexisting narrative: Troilus iconically faithful, a suffering victim of lost love, while Cressida is faithless in accepting Diomed as her new man. Latently, though, the play does not support this as the whole story. Troilus has participated in bringing about the conditions for Cressida's exchange—Cressida does not go willingly, does not readily accept her new situation, and so on. The kind of faith the sources emphasize is sharply mitigated by circumstances, by the context in which this story unfolds.

The play is deeply concerned with how a code of masculine honor constructs itself as whole not through its inner consistency but by exclusion. The effort in the play to brand Cressida as faithless, flimsy as it is as a generalization of womankind, is the guarantee of Troilus's reputation, the literary destiny of his character. This surety, a kind of literary "faith," gathers its moral force by ensuring that such a signifying consistency is always underwritten by being paired with its opposite. The literary Troilus, in other words, needs Cressida far more than she needs him. The only way he has moved up in the world of fiction, from undistinguished younger brother to romantic icon, is by having a Cressida to distinguish himself from.

Troilus's role in Cressida's fate begins in 2.2, with his argument in favor of keeping Helen and continuing the war. He takes Paris's side against Hector and argues that honor is greater than love and reason. We may also see Cressida's view earlier when she describes the predicament of a woman in love:

> Women are angels, wooing;
> Things won are done. Joy's soul lies in the doing.
> That she beloved knows naught that knows not this:
> Men prize the thing ungained more than it is. . . .
> Therefore this maxim out of love I teach:
> Achievement is command; ungained, beseech. (1.2.264–71)

Her maxim here turns out to be more than apt, as Troilus repeats it upon learning that Cressida is to be ransomed: "How my achievements mock me!" (4.2.71). Troilus's double achievement, in successfully arguing for a continuation of the war that results in the loss of his beloved as well as in getting Cressida to admit her love for him, brings responsibility completely onto his shoulders. This he is perfectly willing to shrug off by appealing once again to the code of honor. Why does he not consider that his achievements mock Troilus *and* Cressida? What is his reaction to *her* plight? To accede to her role as a mistress that he can visit in the Greek camp.

Their leave-taking scene (4.5.12–139) follows her refusal to go, his insistence that there is nothing else to be done, and his assurance that he will visit her in her new surroundings. As they prepare to part, Cressida complains that she will be "A woeful Cressid 'mongst the merry Greeks" (4.5.55). This seemingly offhand remark, as René Girard points out,[25] inflames Troilus's jealousy and causes him to repeat over and over that she "be true." He warns her that compared to his true simplicity, the Greeks "play at subtle games" (4.5.88), and that she will be sorely tempted. She turns all his warnings aside, asking, "Do you think I will?" To which he replies:

> No, but something may be done that we will not,
> And sometimes we are devils to ourselves,
> When we will tempt the frailty of our powers,
> Presuming on their changeful potency. (4.5.93–97)

In this last face-to-face exchange that the lovers will have, Troilus issues a warning that turns in the last line to what he perhaps fears most—that Cressida might possess a "changeful potency." The drama at this moment calls upon its built-in referential potential. This ineffectual warning and observation about Cressida's future behavior cannot, as we know, change a plot whose end we know all too well. But it raises the possibility of a challenge to the textual authority that has stamped these characters indelibly.

Act 5, scene 2 does not follow any of the sources used elsewhere in the play. Shakespeare constructs this dramatic set-piece as the final interaction between the play's eponymous main characters. Before we look at the scene's complex and difficult language, I want to call attention to its overall dramatic structure. The scene takes place in the Greek camp,

---

[25] René Girard, "The Politics of Desire in *Troilus and Cressida*," in *Shakespeare and the Question of Theory*, pp. 195–96.

where Ulysses has accompanied Troilus to Calchas's tent, following Diomed, who has gone there to meet with Cressida. The configuration of the scene presents a multiperspectival deep space in which several scenes occur simultaneously at different levels. Cressida banters with Diomed; Troilus and Ulysses watch, hidden in the darkness just outside the torch-light; Ulysses also observes Troilus and his mounting agitation; and finally, Thersites looks on the entire scene unobserved. The focal point is Cressida, who has no one to comment to but herself. She cannot even appeal, as does Thersites, to the audience, as she is forced to inhabit her lonely role as one abandoned to her own resources. The speeches by Troilus and the comments upon them by Ulysses and Thersites are choric in nature, aimed at the audience as overhearing the emotional climax in which Troilus offers a corrective to textual "authority."

The Ovidian structure of this scene lies in its presentation of two contending possibilities: that of the faithless woman and that of the abandoned woman.[26] The first operates on the assumption that a woman such as Cressida has the means to put her will into action, in other words to choose whomever she prefers based solely on her desire. The second places the woman within a context that renders her an object of circulation, a pawn in a masculine game of honor, or, as Lavinia comes to be called in *Titus Andronicus*, a "changing piece" (1.1.306). The iterative stability of Cressida's place in literary history consists in ignoring, and therefore repressing, the narrative circumstances that reduce her character to a signifier for "faithless."[27] To present Cressida's plight in resisting textual authority at this crucial point, Shakespeare turns to Ovid. In Ovid's *Heroides* and *Metamorphoses*, Shakespeare found the means to counter the authoritative discourse of honor and power in which victims are blamed for their aggressors' conduct. Shakespeare's Ovidian move in this scene is to emphasize Cressida's metamorphosis as a shift from

---

[26] For a recent treatment of abandoned women in medieval literature that explores the "interrogat[ion of] literary genres and the nature of textual authority" (187) in the reiterations of classical material by Dante, Boccaccio, and Chaucer, see Suzanne C. Hagedorn, *Abandoned Women: Rewriting the Classics in Dante, Boccaccio, and Chaucer* (Ann Arbor, 2004).

[27] That Cressida's emblematic status might be taken as a displacement of Helen's as the *casus belli* is not something the play takes up. The idea of woman as cause of falls greater and lesser goes back, of course, all the way to the roots of the Western tradition.

victim to faithless icon in a manner that lingers over and preserves the contradiction inherent in her condition. In other words, like Arachne or Daphne, she becomes reified as a psychologically complex character whose casting as a type testifies to the power relations that have made her *what*, instead of *who*, she is. In response to the exigencies of her situation, Act 5 presents a Cressida whose *subjectivity* gives way to an *objectivity*. As Daphne is metamorphosed into a laurel to escape Apollo's predation, so is Cressida changed into the object that supports male faithfulness. Shakespeare has here borrowed this powerful trope from Ovid to mark the displacement that occurs in such power games, altering it to undermine a misogynistic strain of literary history.[28]

Here is Cressida's speech as she finally gives in to Diomed:

> Troilus, farewell. One eye yet looks on thee,
> But with my heart the other eye doth see.
> Ah, poor our sex! This fault in us I find:
> The error of our eye directs our mind.
> What error leads must err. O, then conclude:
> Minds swayed by eyes are full of turpitude. (5.2.107–12)

The logic of this admission does not quite make sense. What, exactly, is the "error"? Cressida's self-recrimination, that woman's fault lies in the eye, in an inability to resist surface attractions, is not a trait she has exhibited. On the contrary, in 1.2 it is Pandarus who copiously details Troilus's vir-

---

[28] Shakespeare seems particularly interested in the phenomenon of the fragility of female reputation in the constellation of plays he writes in the first years of the seventeenth century. The three "problem comedies" (*Troilus and Cressida*, *All's Well That Ends Well*, and *Measure for Measure*) articulate this same concern in very different contexts. When Helena wagers her life against her ability to cure the king in *All's Well*, the following exchange takes place:

> King: Upon thy certainty and confidence
> What dar'st thou venture?
> Helena: Tax of impudence,
> A strumpet's boldness, a divulged shame;
> Traduced by odious ballads, my maiden's name
> Seared otherwise. . . . (2.1.169–73)

tues, chief amongst these his outward beauty and manliness.[29] Cressida is having none of it and parries her uncle's shallow talk with insouciant wit. When he leaves she puts a finer point on it:

> Words, vows, gifts, tears, and love's full sacrifice
> He offers in another's enterprise;
> But more in Troilus thousandfold I see
> Than in the glass of Pandar's praise may be. . . . (1.2.260–63)

It would be difficult not to notice that it is Cressida who has "seen more deeply." Her eye seems never to have strayed or betrayed her before. If this is a rationalization for what is about to occur, Cressida's finding a convenient "fault" to blame her imminent defection to Diomed, then it betrays its cause. "What error leads must err" refers less to anything Cressida is or has done than it does to that error perpetrated by the Trojan men: they have sacrificed a woman for the sake of a man (Cressida for Antenor's freedom) and then blamed the woman for having any shred of desire. That Cressida is seen to get on with her life, no matter how reluctantly, serves as proof to Troilus of her faithlessness. But this has probitive value only to those who have ignored her character thus far. Cressida's plight indicts the Trojan War's impetus and the manner in which women are passed as objects of exchange rather than as agents of their own desires. Cressida's *eye* has not led her astray because she has found someone more physically attractive. The will that Shakespeare endows her with is that of survival, of prevailing in a situation she has no power to change.

Troilus responds to this with a lengthy speech that puts into play a number of complex ideas that run counter to his earlier actions and opinions. After Cressida and Diomed have exited, Ulysses asks the stricken Troilus, "Why stay we, then?" Troilus replies:

> To make a recordation to my soul
> Of every syllable that here was spoke.
> But if I tell how these two did co-act,
> Shall I not lie in publishing a truth? (5.2.115–19)

---

[29] The scene is filled with such details. For example: "Why, you know 'tis dimpled. I think his smiling becomes him better than any man in all Phrygia" (1.2.113–14). Cressida systematically eschews and makes fun of the importance of each of Pandarus's observations.

The key words that set Troilus's commentary on Cressida in motion—recordation, publishing—are textual, already beginning to inscribe her as exemplified in this scene rather than in those that have led up to it. Troilus turns on his recorder only when his part of the plot is safely out of the picture, and thus avoids becoming part of the production. But what creeps into Troilus's speech as it proceeds is an index of his own responsibility. He can scarcely avoid becoming a participant in the bifold authority that insists upon a code of honor while lamenting the faithlessness of those who are its victims. How can Troilus "lie in publishing a truth"? The readiest way to perpetrate such an oxymoronic-sounding act is by taking something out of its context: the event in question happened, but not in the way it is re-presented. *Troilus and Cressida* replays for its audience the primal literary scene in which Cressida's fate is set in motion. And it does so with the mechanisms that cast her role in literary history in full view.

From here Troilus begins his negation of Cressida's presence in an effort to preserve some hope that she has not deserted him. His first justification for doing so is not for himself:

> Let it not be believed, for womanhood.
> Think: we had mothers. Do not give advantage
> To stubborn critics, apt without a theme
> For depravation to square the general sex
> By Cressid's rule. Rather, think this not Cressid. (5.2.129–33)

Troilus's awareness of Cressida's textual fate casts him in the role of rewriting literary history at a point of its transmission disguised as inception. Just as Ovid rewrites Virgil, changing the emphasis from the establishment of empire to the expression of human, and especially female, suffering, so Shakespeare rewrites *The Iliad* by translating Ovid's physical changes into psychological and social ones.[30]

Troilus then delivers a long, rhetorically complex, and potentially radical speech concerning what we might call the interpolative force of a literary tradition that isolates and condemns Cressida as the sole perpetrator of faithlessness. One of the chief difficulties of the speech is that its manifest content is Troilus's attempt to manage his pain over what

---

[30] See James, *Shakespeare's Troy*, Introduction, pp. 1–6.

appears to be his beloved's change of affection from himself to Diomed. But his spasm of grief exceeds the purpose it seems to want to express, and here the playwright has carefully brought this set-piece to its climax. The latent content of this speech is its inability to avoid the fact that the Cressida who has been previously changed into an icon, by stubborn critics and writers alike, has a story to tell that is bound up inside her fixity.

Here is Troilus's speech:

> This, she? No, this is Diomed's Cressida.
> If beauty have a soul, this is not she.
> If souls guide vows, if vows be sanctimonies,
> If sanctimony be the gods' delight,
> If there be rule in unity itself,
> This is not she. O madness of discourse,
> That cause sets up with and against thyself!
> Bifold authority, where reason can revolt
> Without perdition, and loss assume all reason
> Without revolt! This is and is not Cressid.
> Within my soul there doth conduce a fight
> Of this strange nature, that a thing inseparate
> Divides more wider than the sky and earth,
> And yet the spacious breadth of this division
> Admits no orifex for a point as subtle
> As Ariachne's broken woof to enter.
> Instance, O instance, strong as Pluto's gates:
> Cressid is mine, tied with the bonds of heaven.
> Instance, O instance, strong as heaven itself:
> The bonds of heaven are slipped, dissolved, and loosed,
> And with another knot, five-finger-tied,
> The fractions of her faith, orts of her love,
> The fragments, scraps, the bits and greasy relics
> Of her o'ereaten faith, are bound to Diomed. (5.2.137–60)

Cressida is passed off to Diomed, completing her transformation into a changing piece, but not before something has happened to suggest a division. This cannot be the same Cressida, says Troilus, since she has here changed into someone capable of breaking a vow. That Troilus invokes the gods and their "delight" in sanctimonies is no accident, since he is here inhabiting that place in Ovidian discourse, about to be invoked in a dozen lines, in which the gods' rapaciousness leads women to become isolated and metamorphosed. Ovid's work is a menagerie of such instances of the human suffering wrought by the "gods' delight." Troilus is thus exposed in his own language as a participant in the situation he decries, and the division he seeks to effect here is an admission of that splitting technique in which one group of people, here the upholders of the patriarchal code of honor, abandons responsibility for the other group who must bear the burden of suffering. Shakespeare's conflation of the Arachne and Ariadne stories from Ovid offers a vivid conceptual image of the splitting of authority, of its bifold nature. In the former, the tableau of the gods' rapaciousness is sewn into Arachne's tapestry in her contest against Minerva, revealing the rape of women by the gods in various disguises.[31] The latter story appears in Ariadne's letter in Ovid's *Heroides*, where she laments her isolation on the island where Theseus has abandoned her. Both women use the thread to involve themselves in matters that they were powerless either to control or to extricate themselves from.

Of this scene, critics have either expressed a willingness to collaborate with Troilus's astonished defensiveness or have interrogated his language as holding within its splitting a duplicity that characterizes the *logos* itself. J. Hillis Miller, for example, suggests far-reaching philosophical issues implicit in the discursive slippage in Troilus's language.[32] And Elizabeth Freund usefully analyzes the play and its cast of characters as paradigmatic examples of a complex, contradictory rhetoric of citation. Yet even after such nuanced accounts of *Troilus and Cressida*, the tension between the play's own reputation as Shakespeare's "noblest failure" and as his "most daring experiment" remains.[33]

---

31 See Barkan, *The Gods Made Flesh*, pp. 1–8.

32 J. Hillis Miller, "Ariachne's Broken Woof," *Georgia Review* 31 (1977), 44–60.

33 Freund, "'Ariachne's Broken Woof,' p. 35. As she writes near the end of her essay, "[T]he basic dilemma of the Renaissance writer lay in the necessity to define the relationship between the epoch's reverential reinvestiture of classical texts, and the new privileging of the values of originality; and the relationship between the authority of an artist's writ and that of his unique and matchless forerunner text." A few lines later, she continues: "For the present I simply invoke my fable of Ariachne as Renaissance muse to gloss both the predicament of informing the fiction and the plight of its maker" (34, 35). While her concern for the "maker's" predicament is well taken, she never interrogates the relationship between text and drama. The question is how the playwright struggles to deploy *with a difference* plot and characters overdetermined by their literary precedents. This is an especially important point in

What I want to insist on is the taking up of the broken woof by the character who bears the most responsibility in bringing another woman into the space of transformation set forth in Ovid's *Metamorphoses*. Added to the broken threads of Ariadne (abandoned woman whose loyalty and ingenuity saved the "hero" Theseus) and Arachne (punished for her forwardness, aggressiveness in weaving skill, and representation of the fate of women at the hands of rapacious gods) is the reconsidered thread of Cressida: asserting her love in the context of a discursive economy of war that makes her vulnerable as a piece in a game that is not within her control and that leaves her with a token of loyalty (Troilus's sleeve), she embodies both women. Or, we might say, she *retextualizes* them. The difference implied in Shakespeare's conflation, and that tiny orifex he is trying to slip Cressida into in order to re-insert her properly into a revised literary history, is between a woman punished by a god and one abandoned by a man. If Troilus despairs in this scene over woman's faith, his language dredges up the latent material that both precedes and succeeds the drama's re-presentation of a literary historical event. It does so by suggesting a reinscription of the context in which a woman makes a place for herself in the patriarchal order: whether she iterates the truth of "the woman's part" (disadvantaged in love, powerless in a system of masculine construction) or willingly participates as the piece that saves a man whose use is in the game that exceeds her (Theseus, Antenor), she will bear the burden of that which is excluded in order to guarantee that the system remain whole and without contradiction. This is the same signifying practice that produced "the face that launched a thousand ships" and the deceived and deceiving "fair defect of Nature."[34]

---

regard to the reinscription of Cressida as much more than faithless, Troilus as much more (or less) than faithful. What we can say about this is that the tension between text, where a name like "Ariachne" preserves the enfolding of two stories into one, and drama, in which such enfolding can only be played as multi-perspectival astonishment, marks a difference in signifying registers. For a detailed study of potentialities in the text/performance difference, see Harry Berger, Jr., *Making Trifles of Terrors: Redistributing Complicities in Shakespeare* (Stanford, 1997). While this is a topic Berger terms "detextualization" and discusses throughout the book, see especially his chapter "Sneak's Noise; or, Rumor and Detextualization in *2 Henry IV*."

[34] The latter viewpoint is that of Adam, as John Milton offers the perspective of another character whose complicity is masked, or repressed, by shifting the burden of blame with careful emphasis on signification. As the editor's footnote to this passage (Book X, ll. 891–92) in *Paradise Lost* attests: "Differentiating between Milton's

Troilus's "bifold authority" dramatizes the way in which this play goes against the grain of the literary provenance of authorizing Cressida as an icon of faithlessness. The symptom of just what drives discourse to "madness" becomes available when we note that the cause that is advanced as the evidence against Cressida's behavior contradicts its own logic. The contradiction implies that the economy of honor hides within itself a dirty little secret: the excluded other bears the burden of grief, suffering, rape, and, despite context, is charged with faithlessness.

---

personal opinions and Adam's irrational diatribe in this passage is extremely difficult." *The Riverside Milton*, ed. Roy Flannagan (Boston, 1998), p. 651.

INDEX

Submission Guidelines

For current submission guidelines and calls for papers, please visit the *Studies in Medieval and Renaissance History* website at http://www.asu.edu/clas/clasjournals/smrh/submissionguidelines.htm.